DYLAN FOX

Artificial Intelligence And Serverless Machine Learning For Beginners

Copyright © 2024 by Dylan Fox

All rights reserved. No part of this publication may be reproduced, stored or transmitted in any form or by any means, electronic, mechanical, photocopying, recording, scanning, or otherwise without written permission from the publisher. It is illegal to copy this book, post it to a website, or distribute it by any other means without permission.

First edition

This book was professionally typeset on Reedsy.
Find out more at reedsy.com

Contents

What is Artificial Intelligence (AI)?	1
Getting Started with Machine Learning	17
Introduction to Serverless Computing	32
Why Serverless Machine Learning?	43
Exploring Serverless Platforms for Machine Learning	51
Setting Up Your Environment: Tools and Prerequisites	64
Building Your First Serverless Machine Learning Model	83
Training Machine Learning Models in a Serverless Environment	115
Deploying Machine Learning Models Using Serverless Functions	147
Monitoring and Scaling Serverless Machine Learning Models	194
Building a Serverless Machine Learning Pipeline	224
Case Studies: Real-World Serverless Machine Learning...	247
Security Considerations in Serverless Machine Learning	258
Advanced Topics: Edge Computing and Serverless AI	277
Serverless Machine Learning Best Practices	292
Conclusion: The Future of AI and Serverless Computing	313

What is Artificial Intelligence (AI)?

Introduction to Artificial Intelligence

Artificial Intelligence (AI) refers to the simulation of human intelligence in machines designed to think and act like humans. It encompasses a broad range of technologies and techniques that enable computers to perform tasks that typically require human cognition, such as understanding natural language, recognizing patterns, solving problems, and making decisions.

Historical Background

The concept of AI dates back to the mid-20th century. In 1950, British mathematician Alan Turing introduced the idea of a machine that could exhibit intelligent behavior indistinguishable from that of a human, proposing the famous Turing Test. In 1956, the term "Artificial Intelligence" was coined by John McCarthy during the Dartmouth Conference, which is considered the birthplace of AI as a field of study.

Types of Artificial Intelligence

AI can be categorized into two main types:

1. **Narrow AI (Weak AI):** This form of AI is designed to perform a specific task, such as voice recognition, image classification, or recommendation systems. Narrow AI systems operate under a limited set of constraints and cannot generalize beyond their programming.

2. **General AI (Strong AI):** General AI refers to systems that possess the

ability to understand, learn, and apply knowledge in a generalized way, much like a human being. Such AI can perform any intellectual task that a human can. While this remains a theoretical concept, research is ongoing to achieve this level of intelligence.

Core Areas of AI

AI encompasses several subfields, each focusing on different aspects of intelligence:

- **Machine Learning (ML):** ML is a subset of AI that involves the development of algorithms that allow computers to learn from data and improve over time without being explicitly programmed.
- **Natural Language Processing (NLP):** NLP enables machines to understand, interpret, and generate human language, facilitating interactions between computers and humans.
- **Computer Vision:** This field focuses on enabling machines to interpret and understand visual information from the world, such as images and videos.
- **Robotics:** AI in robotics involves creating intelligent machines capable of performing tasks in the physical world, often involving movement and manipulation.
- **Expert Systems:** These are AI programs that emulate the decision-making ability of a human expert, using knowledge and inference rules to solve complex problems.

Key Concepts in AI

- **Learning:** AI systems can learn from data, improving their performance over time. This learning can be supervised, unsupervised, or through reinforcement.
- **Reasoning:** AI involves the ability to draw conclusions appropriate to the situation at hand, using logical and probabilistic methods.
- **Perception:** AI systems can interpret sensory information to understand

the environment, such as recognizing speech or images.
- **Language Understanding:** AI can process and generate human language, enabling communication and comprehension.

Techniques and Algorithms

AI utilizes a variety of techniques and algorithms, including:

- **Neural Networks:** Inspired by the human brain, neural networks are computational models composed of interconnected nodes (neurons) that process data and learn patterns.
- **Deep Learning:** A subset of ML that uses multi-layered neural networks to model complex patterns in data.
- **Genetic Algorithms:** Optimization algorithms inspired by the process of natural selection, used to generate high-quality solutions to problems.
- **Fuzzy Logic:** A form of logic that deals with reasoning that is approximate rather than fixed and exact, useful in systems that handle uncertain or imprecise information.

Applications of AI

AI has a wide range of applications across various industries:

- **Healthcare:** AI aids in diagnostics, personalized medicine, drug discovery, and patient monitoring.
- **Finance:** AI is used for fraud detection, algorithmic trading, credit scoring, and risk management.
- **Transportation:** AI powers autonomous vehicles, traffic management systems, and route optimization.
- **Manufacturing:** AI enables predictive maintenance, quality control, and automation of production processes.
- **Customer Service:** AI-driven chatbots and virtual assistants enhance customer engagement and support.

Challenges and Considerations

While AI offers significant benefits, it also presents challenges:

- **Ethical Concerns:** Issues related to privacy, bias, accountability, and transparency need to be addressed.
- **Job Displacement:** Automation may lead to the displacement of certain jobs, necessitating workforce retraining.
- **Security Risks:** AI systems can be vulnerable to adversarial attacks or misuse.

Conclusion

Artificial Intelligence represents a transformative technology with the potential to revolutionize numerous aspects of society. Understanding what AI is and how it functions is crucial for leveraging its capabilities responsibly and effectively.

The Evolution of Machine Learning

Early Beginnings

Machine Learning (ML) is a subset of AI that focuses on the development of algorithms that enable computers to learn from and make decisions based on data. The roots of ML trace back to the 1950s, with pioneers like Arthur Samuel, who developed a self-learning checkers program. This program improved its performance by playing numerous games and learning from the outcomes, marking one of the first instances of a computer program exhibiting learning behavior.

Symbolic AI and the AI Winters

In the 1960s and 1970s, AI research predominantly focused on symbolic AI, which relied on explicit programming of rules and logic. However, this approach faced limitations due to the complexity and variability of real-world scenarios. The field experienced periods known as "AI Winters," characterized by reduced funding and interest due to unmet expectations.

The Rise of Statistical Methods

The 1980s and 1990s saw a shift towards statistical methods in ML.

Researchers began to focus on probabilistic models and algorithms capable of handling uncertainty and variability in data. Key developments included:

- **Decision Trees:** Algorithms that use a tree-like model of decisions and their possible consequences.
- **Support Vector Machines (SVMs):** Supervised learning models used for classification and regression tasks.
- **Ensemble Methods:** Techniques like boosting and bagging that combine multiple models to improve performance.

The Advent of Neural Networks

Neural networks, inspired by the human brain's structure, gained prominence with the development of the backpropagation algorithm in the 1980s. However, they faced challenges due to computational limitations and the vanishing gradient problem, which hindered training deep networks.

The Deep Learning Revolution

The 2000s and 2010s witnessed a resurgence of interest in neural networks, leading to the emergence of deep learning. Factors contributing to this revolution included:

- **Increased Computational Power:** The availability of powerful GPUs made it feasible to train deep neural networks.
- **Large Datasets:** The accumulation of vast amounts of data enabled models to learn complex patterns.
- **Algorithmic Innovations:** Techniques like rectified linear units (ReLU), dropout, and batch normalization improved training efficiency and model performance.

Deep learning models, such as convolutional neural networks (CNNs) and recurrent neural networks (RNNs), achieved significant breakthroughs in areas like image recognition, speech processing, and natural language understanding.

Emergence of Reinforcement Learning

Reinforcement Learning (RL), where agents learn to make decisions by interacting with an environment and receiving feedback, gained traction with notable successes:

- **AlphaGo:** Developed by DeepMind, AlphaGo defeated human champions in the game of Go, showcasing the potential of combining deep learning with RL.
- **Robotics:** RL has been applied to train robots for tasks like grasping objects, locomotion, and manipulation.

Current Trends and Developments

Today, ML continues to evolve rapidly, with trends including:

- **Transfer Learning:** Leveraging pre-trained models to solve new tasks with limited data.
- **Unsupervised and Self-Supervised Learning:** Techniques that enable models to learn from unlabeled data.
- **Federated Learning:** Training models across decentralized devices while preserving data privacy.
- **AutoML:** Automated processes for model selection and hyperparameter tuning, making ML more accessible.

Challenges and Future Directions

Despite advancements, ML faces challenges:

- **Data Quality:** Models are only as good as the data they are trained on, and biases in data can lead to biased outcomes.
- **Explainability:** Complex models, especially deep neural networks, often lack transparency, making it difficult to interpret their decisions.
- **Generalization:** Ensuring models perform well on unseen data and across different domains remains a critical goal.

The future of ML involves addressing these challenges, enhancing model robustness, and expanding applications across diverse fields.

Why AI and Machine Learning Matter Today (Approximately 1,000 Words)

Transformative Impact on Industries

AI and ML are revolutionizing industries by automating processes, enhancing decision-making, and creating new opportunities. Their importance today stems from their ability to handle complex tasks at scale and speed unattainable by humans alone.

Driving Innovation

AI and ML fuel innovation by enabling:

- **Data-Driven Insights:** Organizations can analyze vast datasets to uncover patterns, trends, and correlations, informing strategic decisions.
- **Automation:** Routine and repetitive tasks can be automated, increasing efficiency and freeing human resources for more creative endeavors.
- **Personalization:** Tailoring products and services to individual preferences enhances customer satisfaction and engagement.

Economic Growth

AI and ML contribute significantly to economic growth:

- **Productivity Gains:** Automation and optimization lead to increased productivity across sectors.
- **New Markets and Services:** AI technologies create new industries and job opportunities, such as AI development, data science, and specialized hardware manufacturing.
- **Competitive Advantage:** Early adopters of AI gain a competitive edge through innovation and efficiency.

Addressing Global Challenges

AI and ML play a crucial role in tackling pressing global issues:

- **Healthcare:** AI assists in disease diagnosis, drug discovery, and personalized medicine, improving healthcare outcomes.
- **Environmental Conservation:** AI helps monitor environmental changes, optimize resource usage, and develop sustainable practices.
- **Education:** Personalized learning platforms powered by AI enhance educational accessibility and effectiveness.

Enhancing Quality of Life

AI applications improve daily life:

- **Smart Assistants:** Voice-activated assistants like Siri and Alexa provide convenience and accessibility.
- **Transportation:** AI enhances safety and efficiency through autonomous vehicles and optimized traffic management.
- **Entertainment:** Personalized content recommendations enrich user experiences on platforms like Netflix and Spotify.

Advancements in Research

AI accelerates scientific discovery:

- **Data Analysis:** AI processes complex datasets in fields like genomics, astrophysics, and climate science.
- **Simulation and Modeling:** AI enables sophisticated simulations for research and development.

Challenges and Ethical Considerations

The proliferation of AI and ML raises important considerations:

- **Privacy:** The collection and analysis of personal data necessitate robust privacy protections.
- **Bias and Fairness:** Ensuring AI systems do not perpetuate or amplify societal biases is critical.
- **Employment Disruption:** Automation may displace certain jobs,

requiring workforce adaptation and reskilling.
- **Security:** Safeguarding AI systems against malicious use and cyber threats is essential.

Global Collaboration and Governance
Addressing these challenges requires:

- **Policy Development:** Governments and organizations must establish regulations that promote innovation while protecting public interests.
- **Ethical Frameworks:** Developing guidelines for responsible AI use ensures alignment with societal values.
- **International Cooperation:** Collaborative efforts can harmonize standards and facilitate the sharing of best practices.

Conclusion
AI and ML are integral to modern society, offering immense benefits while presenting challenges that must be managed thoughtfully. Their continued development and integration hold the promise of significant advancements in human well-being and global prosperity.

AI vs. Machine Learning: Key Differences (Approximately 1,000 Words)

Understanding the Relationship
Artificial Intelligence (AI) and Machine Learning (ML) are interconnected but distinct concepts. ML is a subset of AI, focusing on the development of systems that can learn from data. It's important to delineate their differences to appreciate their respective scopes and applications.

Scope and Objectives

- **Artificial Intelligence (AI):** AI encompasses a broad range of technologies and methodologies aimed at creating machines capable of performing tasks that typically require human intelligence. AI's objectives

include reasoning, understanding, problem-solving, perception, and language comprehension.
- **Machine Learning (ML):** ML specifically involves algorithms and statistical models that enable computers to perform tasks without explicit instructions, relying on patterns and inference. The primary goal of ML is to allow machines to learn from data and improve over time.

Techniques and Approaches

- **AI Techniques:**
- **Rule-Based Systems:** Utilizing predefined rules to make decisions.
- **Search and Optimization:** Algorithms like genetic algorithms and heuristic searches.
- **Knowledge Representation:** Symbolic representations of knowledge and reasoning.
- **ML Techniques:**
- **Supervised Learning:** Learning from labeled datasets.
- **Unsupervised Learning:** Identifying patterns in unlabeled data.
- **Reinforcement Learning:** Learning optimal actions through trial and error.
- **Deep Learning:** Neural networks with multiple layers extracting high-level features from data.

Data Dependency

- **AI Systems:** Some AI applications, like expert systems, rely on human knowledge encoded into rules and do not necessarily require large datasets.
- **ML Systems:** ML models require substantial amounts of data to learn effectively. Their performance is heavily dependent on data quality and quantity.

Flexibility and Adaptability

- **AI Systems:** Traditional AI systems may lack adaptability, as they operate based on predefined rules and logic.
- **ML Systems:** ML models are inherently adaptive, improving with more data and capable of adjusting to new information.

Explainability and Transparency

- **AI Systems:** Rule-based AI offers transparency, as the decision-making process is explicit and understandable.
- **ML Systems:** Complex ML models, especially deep learning networks, can be opaque ("black boxes"), making it challenging to interpret their internal workings.

Applications

- **AI Applications:**
- **Expert Systems:** Diagnosing medical conditions based on encoded knowledge.
- **Game Playing:** AI algorithms like Minimax for chess or Go.
- **Natural Language Processing:** Early chatbots using scripted responses.
- **ML Applications:**
- **Image and Speech Recognition:** Identifying objects in images or transcribing spoken words.
- **Recommendation Systems:** Suggesting products or content based on user behavior.
- **Predictive Analytics:** Forecasting trends or outcomes using historical data.

Integration

While ML is a component of AI, modern AI systems often integrate multiple methodologies, including ML, to achieve intelligent behavior. For example:

- **Autonomous Vehicles:** Combine ML for perception with AI planning

algorithms for navigation.
- **Voice Assistants:** Use ML for speech recognition and NLP for understanding and generating responses.

Misconceptions

- **AI Equals ML:** A common misconception is that AI and ML are the same. While ML is crucial for many AI advancements, AI encompasses a wider array of technologies.
- **All AI Uses ML:** Not all AI applications use ML. Some rely solely on predefined rules or logic.

Conclusion

Understanding the distinction between AI and ML clarifies their respective roles in technology. AI aims to create intelligent systems capable of complex tasks, while ML provides the tools for systems to learn from data. Recognizing their differences enables better application of each in solving real-world problems.

Real-World Applications of AI and ML (Approximately 1,000 Words)

Healthcare

- **Medical Imaging:** ML algorithms analyze medical images to detect diseases like cancer, enabling early diagnosis and treatment planning. For example, deep learning models have been developed to identify tumors in radiographs with high accuracy.
- **Predictive Analytics:** AI models predict patient outcomes, readmission risks, and potential complications, assisting healthcare providers in making informed decisions.
- **Drug Discovery:** AI accelerates drug development by predicting how different compounds interact with the body, significantly reducing research time and cost.

- **Personalized Medicine:** ML algorithms analyze genetic and molecular data to tailor treatments to individual patients, improving efficacy and reducing side effects.

Finance

- **Fraud Detection:** Banks use ML models to detect fraudulent activities by identifying unusual patterns in transaction data.
- **Algorithmic Trading:** AI-driven trading systems analyze market data to execute trades at optimal times, maximizing returns.
- **Credit Scoring:** ML enhances credit risk assessments by evaluating a broader range of data points, leading to more accurate lending decisions.
- **Customer Service:** AI-powered chatbots provide immediate assistance, handling routine inquiries and improving customer satisfaction.

Retail and E-commerce

- **Recommendation Engines:** E-commerce platforms use ML to suggest products based on user behavior and preferences, increasing engagement and sales.
- **Inventory Management:** AI predicts demand trends, optimizing stock levels and reducing holding costs.
- **Dynamic Pricing:** Retailers adjust prices in real-time based on factors like demand, competition, and customer profiles, maximizing revenue.
- **Visual Search:** Customers can search for products using images, enhancing user experience and conversion rates.

Transportation

- **Autonomous Vehicles:** Self-driving cars use AI for perception, decision-making, and control, aiming to improve safety and efficiency on roads.
- **Fleet Management:** ML optimizes routing and scheduling for logistics companies, reducing fuel consumption and delivery times.

- **Traffic Management:** AI analyzes traffic patterns to adjust signals and reduce congestion in urban areas.

Manufacturing

- **Predictive Maintenance:** AI systems monitor equipment performance to predict failures before they occur, minimizing downtime.
- **Quality Control:** ML models detect defects in products during the manufacturing process, ensuring high-quality output.
- **Robotics Automation:** AI-powered robots perform complex tasks with precision, increasing productivity and consistency.

Energy and Utilities

- **Smart Grids:** AI optimizes energy distribution, balancing supply and demand to improve efficiency and integrate renewable sources.
- **Consumption Forecasting:** Utilities use ML to predict energy usage patterns, aiding in resource planning.
- **Renewable Energy Management:** AI maximizes the output of renewable energy installations by predicting weather conditions and adjusting operations accordingly.

Agriculture

- **Precision Farming:** AI analyzes soil data, weather patterns, and crop health to optimize planting, irrigation, and harvesting.
- **Crop Monitoring:** Drones equipped with AI detect pest infestations or nutrient deficiencies, enabling timely interventions.
- **Supply Chain Optimization:** ML streamlines distribution from farm to market, reducing waste and improving profitability.

Education

- **Personalized Learning:** AI adapts educational content to individual student needs, pacing, and learning styles.
- **Administrative Automation:** AI assists with enrollment, scheduling, and resource allocation, improving operational efficiency.
- **Assessment and Feedback:** ML algorithms provide immediate feedback on assignments, helping students learn more effectively.

Entertainment and Media

- **Content Creation:** AI generates music, art, and writing, expanding creative possibilities.
- **Personalized Experiences:** Streaming services use ML to recommend movies, shows, or music tailored to user preferences.
- **Virtual Reality and Gaming:** AI enhances virtual environments by creating responsive and adaptive interactions.

Security and Surveillance

- **Facial Recognition:** AI identifies individuals for security purposes, access control, and law enforcement applications.
- **Anomaly Detection:** ML monitors network traffic to detect cybersecurity threats and prevent breaches.
- **Predictive Policing:** AI analyzes crime data to allocate resources effectively, though it raises ethical concerns regarding bias and privacy.

Environmental Conservation

- **Wildlife Protection:** AI analyzes data from sensors and cameras to monitor endangered species and detect poaching activities.
- **Climate Modeling:** ML improves the accuracy of climate predictions, aiding in environmental planning and policy-making.
- **Resource Management:** AI optimizes water and energy use, promoting sustainability and conservation.

Conclusion

AI and ML applications are transforming industries by enhancing efficiency, improving decision-making, and creating new opportunities. Their impact is felt in everyday life and holds the promise of addressing complex global challenges. As these technologies continue to advance, they will play an increasingly pivotal role in shaping the future.

Getting Started with Machine Learning

Machine learning is a transformative technology that enables computers to learn from data and improve their performance over time without being explicitly programmed. It's the backbone of many modern technologies, including recommendation systems, image recognition, and natural language processing. This section provides a comprehensive introduction to the fundamentals of machine learning, the different types of learning paradigms, key concepts, the machine learning pipeline, and the tools and frameworks commonly used in the field.

1. Machine Learning Fundamentals

Introduction to Machine Learning

Machine learning (ML) is a subset of artificial intelligence (AI) that focuses on the development of algorithms and statistical models that enable computers to perform tasks by learning from data, rather than following explicit instructions. The primary goal of machine learning is to create systems that can adapt and make accurate predictions or decisions based on historical data.

Key Characteristics of Machine Learning:
- **Data-Driven:** Relies heavily on data to learn and make predictions.
- **Pattern Recognition:** Identifies patterns and structures within data.
- **Adaptive Learning:** Improves performance over time with more data.
- **Generalization:** Applies learned knowledge to new, unseen data.

Why Machine Learning Matters

The exponential growth of data and advances in computational power have made machine learning an essential tool in various industries. It enables organizations to:

- **Automate Decision-Making:** Reduces the need for human intervention in routine tasks.
- **Enhance Customer Experience:** Personalizes services and recommendations.
- **Improve Operational Efficiency:** Optimizes processes and resource allocation.
- **Drive Innovation:** Facilitates new products and services through predictive analytics.

Fundamental Concepts in Machine Learning

1. **Data:** The foundational element of machine learning. Data can be structured (tables, spreadsheets) or unstructured (images, text, audio).
2. **Features:** Individual measurable properties or characteristics of the data used for analysis.
3. **Labels/Targets:** The output or result that the model aims to predict. In supervised learning, each data point has an associated label.
4. **Models:** Mathematical representations learned from data that can make predictions or decisions.
5. **Algorithms:** Procedures or formulas that the model uses to learn from data.
6. **Training:** The process where the model learns from the data.
7. **Testing/Validation:** Assessing the model's performance on unseen data to evaluate its generalization capabilities.

Types of Machine Learning Tasks

- **Classification:** Assigning input data into predefined categories (e.g.,

spam vs. not spam emails).
- **Regression:** Predicting continuous numeric values (e.g., forecasting sales).
- **Clustering:** Grouping similar data points together without predefined labels.
- **Dimensionality Reduction:** Reducing the number of features while retaining important information.
- **Anomaly Detection:** Identifying unusual data points that differ significantly from the majority.

Challenges in Machine Learning

- **Overfitting:** When a model learns the training data too well, including noise, and performs poorly on new data.
- **Underfitting:** When a model is too simple to capture the underlying patterns in the data.
- **Bias and Variance Trade-off:** Balancing the model's ability to generalize to new data while keeping errors low.
- **Data Quality:** Garbage in, garbage out; poor-quality data leads to poor model performance.
- **Computational Resources:** Training complex models requires significant processing power and memory.

2. Supervised, Unsupervised, and Reinforcement Learning

Machine learning encompasses various learning paradigms, each suited to different types of problems and data. The three primary paradigms are supervised learning, unsupervised learning, and reinforcement learning.

Supervised Learning

In supervised learning, the model is trained on a labeled dataset, which means each training example is paired with an output label. The goal is to learn a mapping from inputs to outputs and make accurate predictions on new, unseen data.

- **Key Characteristics:**
- **Labeled Data:** Requires a dataset where the correct output is known.
- **Objective:** Learn a function that maps input variables to output variables.
- **Applications:** Classification and regression tasks.
- **Common Algorithms:**
- **Linear Regression:** Predicts a continuous output based on linear relationships.
- **Logistic Regression:** Used for binary classification problems.
- **Decision Trees:** Models decisions and their possible consequences as a tree structure.
- **Support Vector Machines (SVM):** Finds the hyperplane that best separates classes.
- **k-Nearest Neighbors (k-NN):** Classifies based on the majority class among the k closest neighbors.
- **Neural Networks:** Computational models inspired by the human brain's network of neurons.
- **Use Cases:**
- **Email Spam Detection:** Classifying emails as spam or not spam.
- **Credit Scoring:** Predicting the likelihood of a borrower defaulting on a loan.
- **Image Recognition:** Identifying objects or faces in images.

Unsupervised Learning

Unsupervised learning deals with unlabeled data. The model tries to learn the underlying structure or distribution in the data to discover patterns or groupings without any guidance.

- **Key Characteristics:**
- **Unlabeled Data:** No output labels are provided.
- **Objective:** Find hidden structures or relationships in the data.
- **Applications:** Clustering, dimensionality reduction, anomaly detection.
- **Common Algorithms:**
- **K-Means Clustering:** Partitions data into k distinct clusters based on

feature similarity.
- **Hierarchical Clustering:** Builds a hierarchy of clusters either agglomeratively or divisively.
- **Principal Component Analysis (PCA):** Reduces the dimensionality of data while preserving variance.
- **Autoencoders:** Neural networks used for learning efficient codings of data.
- **Use Cases:**
- **Customer Segmentation:** Grouping customers based on purchasing behavior.
- **Anomaly Detection:** Identifying fraudulent transactions or network intrusions.
- **Market Basket Analysis:** Discovering associations between products.

Reinforcement Learning

Reinforcement learning (RL) involves an agent that learns to make decisions by performing actions in an environment to maximize cumulative rewards. It's inspired by behavioral psychology.

- **Key Characteristics:**
- **Trial and Error Learning:** The agent learns by interacting with the environment.
- **Feedback Loop:** Receives rewards or penalties based on actions taken.
- **Objective:** Develop a policy that dictates the best action to take in each state.
- **Common Algorithms:**
- **Q-Learning:** An off-policy RL algorithm that seeks to find the best action to take given the current state.
- **Deep Q-Networks (DQN):** Combines Q-learning with deep neural networks.
- **Policy Gradients:** Directly optimize the policy that the agent uses to decide actions.
- **Actor-Critic Methods:** Combines value function (critic) and policy

(actor) approaches.
- **Use Cases:**
- **Game Playing:** Training AI agents to play games like Go, chess, or video games.
- **Robotics:** Teaching robots to navigate and manipulate objects.
- **Resource Management:** Optimizing allocations in data centers or network traffic.

Comparison of Learning Paradigms

- **Supervised Learning:**
- **Pros:** Produces highly accurate models when labeled data is available.
- **Cons:** Requires large amounts of labeled data, which can be expensive and time-consuming to obtain.
- **Unsupervised Learning:**
- **Pros:** Useful when labeled data is scarce or unavailable; can discover hidden patterns.
- **Cons:** Results can be harder to interpret; no straightforward way to evaluate model performance.
- **Reinforcement Learning:**
- **Pros:** Learns optimal actions in complex environments; can handle sequential decision-making.
- **Cons:** Can be unstable and require a lot of data; challenging to design appropriate reward functions.

3. Key Concepts: Algorithms, Models, and Data

Understanding the interplay between algorithms, models, and data is crucial in machine learning.

Algorithms

An algorithm is a set of mathematical instructions that a machine learning model follows to learn from data. Different algorithms are suited to different types of data and problems.

- **Selection Criteria:**
- **Type of Problem:** Classification, regression, clustering, etc.
- **Size and Quality of Data:** Some algorithms perform better with large datasets.
- **Computational Resources:** Algorithms vary in computational complexity.
- **Interpretability:** Simpler algorithms are often more interpretable.
- **Common Machine Learning Algorithms:**
- **Linear Algorithms:** Linear regression, logistic regression.
- **Tree-Based Algorithms:** Decision trees, random forests, gradient boosting machines (XGBoost).
- **Support Vector Machines:** Effective in high-dimensional spaces.
- **Neural Networks:** Capable of modeling complex, non-linear relationships.

Models

A model is the output of a machine learning algorithm after it has been trained on data. It represents the learned patterns and can make predictions or decisions based on new input data.

- **Model Training:** The process where the algorithm adjusts the model's parameters to minimize errors on the training data.
- **Model Evaluation:** Assessing the model's performance using metrics such as accuracy, precision, recall, F1-score, mean squared error, etc.
- **Generalization:** The model's ability to perform well on new, unseen data.

Data

Data is the foundation upon which machine learning models are built. The quality and relevance of the data directly impact the model's performance.

- **Types of Data:**
- **Structured Data:** Organized in tables with rows and columns (e.g.,

spreadsheets, SQL databases).
- **Unstructured Data:** Lacks a predefined format (e.g., text, images, audio).
- **Semi-Structured Data:** Contains tags or markers to separate semantic elements (e.g., JSON, XML files).
- **Data Preprocessing:**
- **Cleaning:** Handling missing values, correcting errors, removing duplicates.
- **Normalization/Scaling:** Adjusting the range of features for better model performance.
- **Encoding Categorical Variables:** Converting categories into numerical values using one-hot encoding or label encoding.
- **Feature Selection/Extraction:** Identifying the most relevant features to improve model efficiency.

The Relationship Between Algorithms, Models, and Data

- **Data Feeds the Algorithm:** The algorithm learns patterns from the data during training.
- **Algorithm Produces the Model:** The algorithm's learning process results in a model that encapsulates the learned patterns.
- **Model Makes Predictions on Data:** The trained model can make predictions or decisions when provided with new data.

4. Understanding the Machine Learning Pipeline

The machine learning pipeline is a systematic process that guides the development of a machine learning project from conception to deployment.

Stages of the Machine Learning Pipeline

1. **Problem Definition:**

- **Identify the Objective:** Clearly define the problem you're trying to solve (e.g., predicting house prices).
- **Determine Success Criteria:** Establish metrics to evaluate the model's

performance.

1. **Data Collection:**

- **Gather Data:** Obtain data from various sources like databases, APIs, web scraping, or sensors.
- **Ensure Data Quality:** Verify that the data is accurate, relevant, and sufficient.

1. **Data Preprocessing:**

- **Data Cleaning:** Handle missing values, remove outliers, and correct inconsistencies.
- **Data Transformation:** Normalize or scale features, encode categorical variables.
- **Feature Engineering:** Create new features or modify existing ones to enhance model performance.

1. **Exploratory Data Analysis (EDA):**

- **Visualize Data:** Use plots and charts to understand data distributions and relationships.
- **Identify Patterns:** Detect correlations, trends, and anomalies.
- **Hypothesize:** Formulate hypotheses about the data that can guide model selection.

1. **Model Selection:**

- **Choose Algorithms:** Based on the problem type, data characteristics, and computational resources.
- **Consider Trade-offs:** Balance between model complexity, interpretability, and performance.

1. Model Training:

- **Split Data:** Divide data into training, validation, and test sets.
- **Train the Model:** Use the training set to adjust model parameters.
- **Hyperparameter Tuning:** Optimize model settings using techniques like grid search or randomized search.

1. Model Evaluation:

- **Performance Metrics:** Evaluate the model using appropriate metrics (e.g., accuracy for classification, RMSE for regression).
- **Validation:** Assess the model on the validation set to prevent overfitting.
- **Cross-Validation:** Use k-fold cross-validation for a more robust evaluation.

1. Model Deployment:

- **Integrate Model:** Deploy the model into a production environment where it can make real-time predictions.
- **API Development:** Expose the model through APIs for accessibility.
- **Scalability:** Ensure the model can handle the expected load.

1. Monitoring and Maintenance:

- **Performance Tracking:** Monitor the model's predictions over time.
- **Retraining:** Update the model with new data to maintain accuracy.
- **Feedback Loop:** Incorporate user feedback to improve the model.

Best Practices in the Machine Learning Pipeline

- **Reproducibility:** Document all steps and use version control for code and data.
- **Automation:** Use pipelines to automate repetitive tasks.

- **Collaboration:** Work closely with domain experts to ensure the model meets business needs.
- **Ethical Considerations:** Ensure data privacy and mitigate biases in the model.

5. Tools and Frameworks for Machine Learning

The machine learning ecosystem is rich with tools and frameworks that simplify the development process. These tools provide pre-built functions, algorithms, and utilities that allow practitioners to focus on solving problems rather than coding algorithms from scratch.

Popular Machine Learning Libraries and Frameworks

1. **Scikit-learn**

- **Language:** Python
- **Overview:** A widely-used library for classical machine learning algorithms.
- **Features:**
- Supports classification, regression, clustering, and dimensionality reduction.
- Easy-to-use API and excellent documentation.
- Integrates well with other Python libraries like NumPy and pandas.
- **Use Cases:** Suitable for beginners and for building models that require quick prototyping.

1. **TensorFlow**

- **Language:** Primarily Python (with APIs in other languages)
- **Overview:** An open-source platform developed by Google for building and deploying machine learning models, especially deep learning.
- **Features:**
- Supports computation on CPUs, GPUs, and TPUs.
- Provides high-level APIs like Keras for ease of use.

- TensorFlow Lite for mobile and embedded devices.
- **Use Cases:** Ideal for large-scale neural networks and deep learning research.

1. **PyTorch**

- **Language:** Python
- **Overview:** Developed by Facebook's AI Research lab, PyTorch is known for its dynamic computation graph and ease of use.
- **Features:**
- Dynamic computational graph allows for flexibility in building models.
- Strong community support and extensive documentation.
- Integration with Python debugging tools.
- **Use Cases:** Preferred in academic research and for projects that require rapid prototyping.

1. **Keras**

- **Language:** Python
- **Overview:** A high-level neural networks API capable of running on top of TensorFlow, Theano, or CNTK.
- **Features:**
- User-friendly, modular, and extensible.
- Simplifies the process of building deep learning models.
- Suitable for beginners in deep learning.
- **Use Cases:** Quick development of deep learning models without needing to manage the underlying complexities.

1. **XGBoost**

- **Language:** Supports Python, R, Java, and more
- **Overview:** An optimized gradient boosting framework designed to be highly efficient, flexible, and portable.

- **Features:**
- Handles missing values automatically.
- Parallel computation for faster training.
- Regularization to prevent overfitting.
- **Use Cases:** Excels in structured data for regression and classification tasks; commonly used in machine learning competitions.

1. **LightGBM**

- **Language:** Supports Python, R, C++, and more
- **Overview:** A gradient boosting framework that uses tree-based learning algorithms.
- **Features:**
- Faster training speed and higher efficiency.
- Lower memory usage compared to other gradient boosting tools.
- Capable of handling large-scale data.
- **Use Cases:** Ideal for large datasets and achieving high performance in competitions.

1. **Apache Spark MLlib**

- **Language:** Supports Java, Scala, Python, and R
- **Overview:** A scalable machine learning library built on top of Apache Spark.
- **Features:**
- Distributed computing capabilities.
- Integrates with big data tools and ecosystems.
- Supports a variety of algorithms for classification, regression, clustering, and more.
- **Use Cases:** Suitable for processing large datasets in distributed environments.

Integrated Development Environments (IDEs) and Tools

- **Jupyter Notebooks:**
- An open-source web application that allows you to create and share documents containing live code, equations, visualizations, and narrative text.
- Ideal for exploratory data analysis and sharing results.
- **Google Colaboratory (Colab):**
- A free cloud service that supports Jupyter notebooks with access to GPUs and TPUs.
- Allows for easy collaboration and sharing.
- **Anaconda Distribution:**
- A free, open-source distribution of Python and R for scientific computing.
- Comes with package and environment management tools like conda.

Cloud-Based Machine Learning Platforms

- **Amazon SageMaker:**
- A fully-managed service that provides tools for building, training, and deploying machine learning models at scale.
- **Google Cloud AI Platform:**
- Offers a suite of services including AutoML, AI Platform Notebooks, and AI Platform Training.
- **Microsoft Azure Machine Learning:**
- Provides an end-to-end platform for building, deploying, and managing machine learning models.

Version Control and Experiment Tracking

- **Git and GitHub/GitLab:**
- Essential for version control of code and collaboration among team members.
- **MLflow:**
- An open-source platform for managing the end-to-end machine learning lifecycle.

- **Weights & Biases:**
- A tool for tracking experiments, visualizing metrics, and collaborating on machine learning projects.

Choosing the Right Tool or Framework

- **Project Requirements:**
- Consider the complexity of the model, performance needs, and deployment environment.
- **Team Expertise:**
- Choose tools that align with the team's programming language proficiency and familiarity.
- **Community and Support:**
- Tools with active communities provide better support, more resources, and frequent updates.
- **Scalability:**
- For large-scale applications, consider tools that support distributed computing.

Conclusion

Getting started with machine learning involves understanding fundamental concepts, learning about different learning paradigms, familiarizing oneself with key concepts, grasping the machine learning pipeline, and knowing the tools and frameworks available. By building a strong foundation in these areas, you will be well-equipped to embark on machine learning projects and contribute to the field's exciting advancements.

Introduction to Serverless Computing

Serverless computing has emerged as a transformative technology in the cloud computing landscape. It abstracts the underlying infrastructure, allowing developers to focus solely on writing code without worrying about server management. This section delves into the fundamentals of serverless computing, its benefits, how it compares to traditional cloud models, the leading serverless platforms, and practical use cases.

What is Serverless Computing?
Definition and Concept

Serverless computing is a cloud computing execution model where the cloud provider dynamically manages the allocation and provisioning of servers. Despite the name, servers are still involved, but the term "serverless" signifies that developers and users do not need to manage or provision these servers themselves. Instead, they can write and deploy code in the form of functions, which are then executed in response to specific events or triggers.

Key Characteristics

- **Event-Driven Execution:** Functions are invoked in response to events such as HTTP requests, database updates, or message queue triggers.
- **Auto-Scaling:** The cloud provider automatically scales the number of function instances based on the volume of incoming events.
- **Pay-as-You-Go Pricing:** Users are billed only for the compute time they

consume, often measured in milliseconds, and not for idle resources.
- **Stateless Functions:** Each function invocation is independent, with no reliance on the state from previous executions.

How Serverless Computing Works

In a serverless architecture, developers write code (functions) and define the events that will trigger these functions. The cloud provider handles the deployment, scaling, and maintenance of the infrastructure required to run these functions. When an event occurs, the provider allocates resources to execute the function, and once execution is complete, the resources are freed.

Evolution and Background

Serverless computing gained prominence with the launch of AWS Lambda by Amazon Web Services in 2014. It represented a shift from traditional server-based computing to a model where the underlying infrastructure is entirely abstracted away. This evolution aligns with the broader trend in cloud computing toward increased abstraction and managed services, enabling faster development cycles and more efficient resource utilization.

Benefits of Serverless Architecture

Serverless architecture offers several advantages that can significantly impact the way applications are developed and deployed.

1. Cost Efficiency

- **Pay-Per-Use Model:** Billing is based on actual compute time and resource usage, eliminating costs associated with idle server time.
- **Reduced Operational Costs:** No need to invest in or maintain physical servers, leading to savings on hardware, power, and cooling.

2. Scalability

- **Automatic Scaling:** Functions scale up or down automatically in response to the volume of incoming events.
- **No Capacity Planning:** Developers don't need to predict traffic loads or provision resources in advance.

3. Simplified Development

- **Focus on Code:** Developers can concentrate on writing business logic without worrying about server configuration or management.
- **Rapid Deployment:** Functions can be deployed quickly, accelerating the development lifecycle.

4. Reduced Operational Overhead

- **Managed Infrastructure:** The cloud provider handles server maintenance, updates, and security patches.
- **High Availability:** Built-in redundancy and fault tolerance ensure that functions are highly available.

5. Improved Time-to-Market

- **Faster Iterations:** Simplified deployment and management enable quicker iterations and updates.
- **Microservices-Friendly:** Encourages a microservices architecture, where applications are composed of small, independent services.

6. Environmental Impact

- **Efficient Resource Utilization:** Dynamic scaling and resource allocation lead to more efficient energy use, reducing the environmental footprint.

7. Security Enhancements

- **Isolation:** Functions run in isolated environments, enhancing security.
- **Provider Security Measures:** Cloud providers implement robust security protocols and compliance certifications.

Comparing Serverless with Traditional Cloud Models

Understanding the differences between serverless computing and traditional cloud models is crucial for making informed architectural decisions.

Traditional Cloud Models

1. **Infrastructure as a Service (IaaS):**

- **Definition:** Provides virtualized computing resources over the internet.
- **Characteristics:**
- Users manage operating systems, storage, and deployed applications.
- Requires handling of server provisioning, scaling, and maintenance.

1. **Platform as a Service (PaaS):**

- **Definition:** Offers hardware and software tools over the internet.
- **Characteristics:**
- Users focus on application development, while the provider manages the underlying infrastructure.
- Limited control over the environment compared to IaaS.

Serverless Computing

- **Execution Model:** Functions-as-a-Service (FaaS), where code is executed in response to events.
- **Management:** The cloud provider fully manages the infrastructure, scaling, and execution environment.
- **Billing:** Based on compute time and resources used during function execution.

Comparison

1. **Resource Management:**

- **Traditional Models:** Users are responsible for provisioning and managing servers, including scaling and load balancing.
- **Serverless:** No server management; scaling is automatic and handled by the provider.

1. **Cost Structure:**

- **Traditional Models:** Often involves fixed costs for allocated resources, regardless of utilization.
- **Serverless:** Pay only for actual usage, leading to potential cost savings.

1. **Scalability:**

- **Traditional Models:** Requires manual scaling or predefined auto-scaling configurations.
- **Serverless:** Automatically scales in response to demand without user intervention.

1. **Deployment Complexity:**

- **Traditional Models:** Deployment can be complex, involving setting up servers, configuring environments, and managing dependencies.
- **Serverless:** Simplified deployment of individual functions, focusing on code and event triggers.

1. **Use Cases:**

- **Traditional Models:** Suitable for applications requiring long-running processes, persistent connections, or custom server configurations.
- **Serverless:** Ideal for event-driven applications, microservices, and workloads with variable or unpredictable traffic.

Considerations

- **Cold Starts:** Serverless functions may experience latency during initial invocation, known as a "cold start."
- **Execution Time Limits:** Functions may have maximum execution time constraints.
- **Vendor Lock-In:** Potential dependency on specific cloud provider services and architectures.

Popular Serverless Platforms

Several major cloud providers offer serverless computing platforms, each with unique features and integrations.

1. AWS Lambda

- **Overview:**
- Launched by Amazon Web Services (AWS) in 2014.
- Supports multiple programming languages, including Node.js, Python, Java, C#, Go, and Ruby.
- **Key Features:**
- **Event Sources:** Integrates with AWS services like S3, DynamoDB, Kinesis, and API Gateway.
- **Function Versioning and Aliases:** Manage different versions of functions for deployment and testing.
- **Environment Variables:** Customize function behavior without changing code.
- **Monitoring:** Integrated with AWS CloudWatch for logging and monitoring.

2. Google Cloud Functions

- **Overview:**
- Google's serverless execution environment for building and connecting cloud services.
- Supports languages like Node.js, Python, Go, Java, .NET, Ruby, and PHP.
- **Key Features:**

- **Event-Driven Functions:** Responds to events from Google Cloud services such as Pub/Sub, Cloud Storage, and Firebase.
- **HTTP Functions:** Expose functions as HTTP endpoints.
- **Automatic Scaling:** Scales based on the number of incoming requests.
- **Debugging and Monitoring:** Integrated with Stackdriver for logging and performance insights.

3. Azure Functions

- **Overview:**
- Microsoft's serverless solution, part of the Azure cloud platform.
- Supports languages including C#, JavaScript, F#, Java, Python, and PowerShell.
- **Key Features:**
- **Triggers and Bindings:** Respond to events and seamlessly integrate with other Azure services.
- **Flexible Hosting Options:** Consumption Plan (serverless) or App Service Plan (dedicated resources).
- **Development Tools:** Visual Studio integration and local development with Azure Functions Core Tools.
- **Security and Identity:** Integration with Azure Active Directory and other identity providers.

Comparison of Platforms

- **Language Support:**
- **AWS Lambda:** Wide language support; custom runtimes allowed.
- **Google Cloud Functions:** Expanding language support; may lag behind AWS in custom runtime flexibility.
- **Azure Functions:** Strong support for .NET languages; broadening support for other languages.
- **Integration with Cloud Services:**
- Each platform offers tight integration with its respective cloud services,

enabling seamless event-driven architectures.
- **Pricing Models:**
- All platforms use a pay-per-use model, but pricing structures and free tier offerings may vary.
- **Deployment and Tooling:**
- **AWS Lambda:** Uses AWS CLI, SDKs, and third-party frameworks like Serverless Framework and AWS SAM.
- **Google Cloud Functions:** Deployment via gcloud CLI; supports Cloud Functions Framework for local development.
- **Azure Functions:** Provides Azure CLI, Azure Portal, and integration with Visual Studio tools.

Serverless Use Cases

Serverless computing is versatile and can be applied to various scenarios, particularly where scalability and cost-efficiency are paramount.

1. Web Applications

- **API Backends:**
- Use serverless functions to handle HTTP requests, process data, and interact with databases.
- Example: A RESTful API built with AWS Lambda and API Gateway.
- **Static Websites with Dynamic Functionality:**
- Host static content on services like Amazon S3 or Azure Blob Storage, with serverless functions handling form submissions or user interactions.

2. Data Processing and ETL Tasks

- **Real-Time Data Processing:**
- Process streaming data from sources like IoT devices or user interactions.
- Example: Use Google Cloud Functions to process Pub/Sub messages.
- **Batch Processing:**
- Perform data transformations, aggregations, or migrations triggered by events.

- Example: AWS Lambda functions triggered by S3 file uploads to process and store data.

3. Image and Video Manipulation

- **On-the-Fly Processing:**
- Generate thumbnails, transcode videos, or apply filters when new media files are uploaded.
- Example: Automatically resizing images uploaded to a storage bucket.

4. Chatbots and Virtual Assistants

- **Natural Language Processing:**
- Use serverless functions to process messages, integrate with AI services, and respond to users.
- Example: An Azure Function that handles bot messages and connects to Language Understanding Intelligent Service (LUIS).

5. IoT Backends

- **Event Handling:**
- Manage data from IoT devices, triggering functions based on sensor data or device events.
- Example: Processing temperature sensor data and triggering alerts when thresholds are exceeded.

6. Scheduled Tasks and Cron Jobs

- **Automated Workflows:**
- Execute functions on a schedule for tasks like data backups, report generation, or system maintenance.
- Example: A nightly AWS Lambda function that aggregates daily user activity.

7. Machine Learning Inference

- **Model Serving:**
- Deploy machine learning models for inference, scaling based on request volume.
- Example: Using serverless functions to classify images or analyze text in real-time.

8. Backend for Mobile Applications

- **Microservices Architecture:**
- Implement backend services for mobile apps, handling authentication, data storage, and notifications.
- Example: Google Cloud Functions handling Firebase events for a mobile app.

9. Rapid Prototyping and Development

- **Proof of Concepts:**
- Quickly develop and deploy prototypes without investing in infrastructure.
- Ideal for startups and small teams.

10. Event-Driven Workflows

- **Automation and Integration:**
- Orchestrate workflows that react to events across different services.
- Example: An Azure Function that triggers when a new item is added to a queue, processes it, and updates a database.

Conclusion

Serverless computing represents a significant shift in how applications are developed and deployed. By abstracting server management, it allows developers to focus on delivering value through code. The benefits of cost efficiency, scalability, and simplified development make serverless architectures an attractive option for a wide range of applications. Understanding the fundamentals, benefits, platform options, and practical use cases equips developers and organizations to leverage serverless computing effectively in their projects.

Why Serverless Machine Learning?

Serverless computing has revolutionized the way applications are developed and deployed by abstracting away server management and allowing developers to focus solely on writing code. When applied to machine learning (ML), serverless architectures offer significant advantages that address common challenges in ML deployment and scalability. This section explores the benefits of using serverless computing in machine learning, including scalability, cost-effectiveness, simplified infrastructure management, and key use cases where serverless ML shines.

Advantages of Serverless in Machine Learning

Integrating serverless computing with machine learning brings together the strengths of both technologies, resulting in several compelling advantages.

1. Cost Efficiency

- **Pay-Per-Use Model:** Serverless platforms charge based on actual usage, meaning you pay only for the compute resources consumed during function execution. This is particularly beneficial for ML workloads with variable or unpredictable traffic patterns.
- **Reduced Idle Costs:** Traditional ML deployments often involve provisioning servers that may sit idle when demand is low, incurring unnecessary costs. Serverless eliminates this waste by scaling down to zero when not in use.

2. Automatic Scaling

- **Dynamic Scaling:** Serverless functions automatically scale up or down in response to the volume of incoming requests or events. This is crucial for ML applications that may experience sudden spikes in usage, such as during peak business hours or promotional events.
- **Handling Variable Workloads:** ML tasks like model inference can have unpredictable workloads. Serverless computing ensures that the necessary resources are available when needed without manual intervention.

3. Simplified Infrastructure Management

- **No Server Management:** Developers can focus on writing and improving ML models without worrying about provisioning, configuring, or maintaining servers.
- **Managed Dependencies:** Serverless platforms often handle dependencies and runtime environments, simplifying deployment processes.

4. Faster Development and Deployment

- **Rapid Iterations:** Serverless architectures enable quick deployment of ML models and updates, facilitating rapid experimentation and continuous improvement.
- **Microservices Architecture:** ML functions can be developed and deployed independently as microservices, improving modularity and maintainability.

5. Integration with Event-Driven Architectures

- **Real-Time Processing:** Serverless functions can be triggered by events such as data uploads, database changes, or messages in a queue, enabling real-time data processing and model inference.

- **Seamless Integration:** Easy integration with other cloud services (storage, databases, messaging) allows for building complex ML workflows efficiently.

6. Enhanced Security and Compliance

- **Isolated Execution Environments:** Serverless functions run in isolated environments, reducing the attack surface.
- **Managed Security:** Cloud providers handle security patches and updates, ensuring that the underlying infrastructure is secure.

Scalability and Cost-Effectiveness

Scalability and cost are critical considerations in deploying machine learning applications. Serverless computing addresses these concerns effectively.

Scalability in Machine Learning

- **Model Inference at Scale:** ML applications often require scaling inference workloads to handle varying numbers of requests. Serverless architectures automatically adjust to meet demand without overprovisioning.
- **Global Availability:** Serverless platforms offer multi-region deployments, allowing ML applications to serve users with low latency worldwide.

Cost-Effectiveness

- **Optimized Resource Utilization:** By executing code only in response to events and scaling resources dynamically, serverless computing ensures that you're not paying for idle time.
- **Budget-Friendly for Sporadic Workloads:** For applications with intermittent usage patterns, serverless can significantly reduce costs compared to running dedicated servers continuously.

- **Fine-Grained Billing:** Many serverless platforms bill in increments as small as 100 milliseconds, providing granular control over costs.

Comparison with Traditional Models

- **Upfront Costs:** Traditional deployments may require significant upfront investment in infrastructure, whereas serverless eliminates these initial costs.
- **Operational Expenses:** The operational overhead of managing servers, including staff time and maintenance, is reduced or eliminated in a serverless model.

Cost Management Strategies

- **Monitoring and Optimization:** Utilize cloud provider tools to monitor function execution times and invocations, optimizing code to reduce costs.
- **Resource Limits:** Set appropriate memory and timeout settings for serverless functions to control resource consumption.

Simplified Infrastructure Management

Managing infrastructure for machine learning applications can be complex, involving provisioning servers, configuring environments, and ensuring scalability and reliability. Serverless computing simplifies this process significantly.

Eliminating Server Management

- **Abstracted Infrastructure:** Developers do not need to manage servers, operating systems, or runtime environments, allowing them to focus on developing ML models and logic.
- **Automated Maintenance:** The cloud provider handles updates, patches, and maintenance of the infrastructure.

Simplifying Deployment

- **Function Deployment:** Deploying ML code as serverless functions simplifies the process. Code can be packaged and uploaded directly to the serverless platform.
- **Continuous Integration/Continuous Deployment (CI/CD):** Integrate serverless functions into CI/CD pipelines for automated testing and deployment.

Environment Consistency

- **Standardized Environments:** Serverless platforms provide consistent runtime environments, reducing issues caused by discrepancies between development and production environments.
- **Dependency Management:** Serverless functions can include necessary dependencies, ensuring that all required libraries and packages are available during execution.

Scaling without Complexity

- **Automatic Scaling:** Developers do not need to configure auto-scaling groups or load balancers; the serverless platform handles scaling seamlessly.
- **No Capacity Planning:** Eliminates the need to predict traffic patterns and provision resources accordingly.

Operational Efficiency

- **Reduced DevOps Load:** Less time spent on infrastructure management translates to more time for model development and optimization.
- **Monitoring and Logging:** Serverless platforms offer integrated monitoring and logging tools, simplifying the tracking of function performance and troubleshooting.

Key Use Cases for Serverless Machine Learning

Serverless computing is particularly well-suited for certain machine learning scenarios. Here are some key use cases where serverless ML provides significant benefits.

1. Real-Time Data Processing and Inference

- **Event-Driven Inference:** Trigger ML models in response to events, such as data uploads or API calls, providing immediate predictions.
- **Use Case Example:** An e-commerce site uses serverless functions to provide real-time product recommendations when a user views an item.

2. Batch Processing and ETL Pipelines

- **Data Transformation:** Use serverless functions to process and transform large datasets in response to scheduled events or data triggers.
- **Use Case Example:** A marketing analytics company processes daily logs uploaded to cloud storage, transforming them for analysis.

3. Image and Video Analysis

- **On-Demand Processing:** Analyze images or videos as they are uploaded, using ML models for tasks like object detection, facial recognition, or content moderation.
- **Use Case Example:** A social media platform automatically moderates user-uploaded images for inappropriate content using serverless ML functions.

4. Natural Language Processing (NLP) Tasks

- **Text Analysis:** Perform sentiment analysis, language translation, or entity recognition on text data as it is received.
- **Use Case Example:** A customer service chatbot uses serverless functions to process user messages and generate responses using NLP models.

5. Internet of Things (IoT) Applications

- **Sensor Data Processing:** Process and analyze data from IoT devices in real-time to make predictions or trigger alerts.
- **Use Case Example:** An environmental monitoring system analyzes sensor data for anomalies, triggering alerts when thresholds are exceeded.

6. Serverless Model Serving

- **Model Deployment:** Deploy ML models as serverless functions to handle inference requests without managing servers.
- **Use Case Example:** A finance application uses serverless functions to evaluate credit risk scores in response to loan applications.

7. A/B Testing and Model Experimentation

- **Rapid Deployment of Models:** Easily deploy multiple versions of models as serverless functions for testing and comparison.
- **Use Case Example:** A recommendation engine deploys different models to different user segments to determine which performs best.

8. Chatbots and Voice Assistants

- **Conversational Interfaces:** Use serverless functions to process user inputs and generate responses using ML models.
- **Use Case Example:** A virtual assistant processes voice commands using serverless functions that transcribe and interpret speech.

9. Personalized Content and Recommendations

- **User Behavior Analysis:** Analyze user interactions to provide personalized content, leveraging serverless functions for scalability.
- **Use Case Example:** A news aggregator uses serverless ML functions to

recommend articles based on reading history.

10. Fraud Detection and Security

- **Anomaly Detection:** Monitor transactions or activities in real-time to detect and respond to fraudulent behavior.
- **Use Case Example:** A payment processing system uses serverless functions to analyze transactions for signs of fraud.

Conclusion

Serverless computing offers compelling advantages for machine learning applications, addressing common challenges related to scalability, cost, and infrastructure management. By leveraging serverless architectures, organizations can deploy ML models more efficiently, respond quickly to changing demands, and focus on delivering value through data-driven insights. The integration of serverless computing and machine learning paves the way for innovative solutions that are both agile and cost-effective, making it an attractive approach for modern application development.

Exploring Serverless Platforms for Machine Learning

Serverless computing has transformed the way developers build and deploy applications by abstracting away the underlying infrastructure management. This paradigm shift is particularly impactful in the field of machine learning (ML), where scalability, cost-efficiency, and rapid deployment are crucial. This section explores how major cloud providers—AWS, Google Cloud, and Microsoft Azure—offer serverless platforms tailored for machine learning workloads. We will delve into the features, benefits, and considerations of using AWS Lambda, Google Cloud Functions, and Azure Functions for ML, and compare these platforms to help you choose the best fit for your ML projects.

AWS Lambda for Machine Learning

Introduction to AWS Lambda

AWS Lambda is Amazon Web Services' (AWS) serverless computing service that lets you run code without provisioning or managing servers. Lambda executes your code only when needed and scales automatically, from a few requests per day to thousands per second. It supports various programming languages, including Python, which is widely used in the machine learning community.

Using AWS Lambda for Machine Learning

AWS Lambda can be effectively utilized for machine learning tasks, particularly for model inference. Here's how you can leverage Lambda for ML:

1. Deploying ML Models for Inference

- **Model Packaging:** Package your trained ML model along with the necessary code and dependencies into a deployment package or container image.
- **Function Creation:** Create a Lambda function, specifying the runtime environment (e.g., Python 3.8) and uploading your deployment package.
- **Memory and Timeout Configuration:** Configure the function's memory allocation (up to 10 GB) and timeout settings (maximum of 15 minutes) to suit your model's resource requirements.
- **Integration with AWS Services:** Use AWS API Gateway to expose your Lambda function as a RESTful API for real-time predictions. Alternatively, trigger the function via events from services like S3 or DynamoDB.

2. Preprocessing and Data Transformation

- **Event-Driven Data Processing:** Use Lambda functions to preprocess input data before feeding it to your ML model. For example, when a new file is uploaded to S3, a Lambda function can be triggered to transform the data.
- **Streaming Data Processing:** Integrate Lambda with AWS Kinesis Data Streams or AWS IoT Core to process streaming data in real-time.

3. Batch Processing

While Lambda is optimized for short-lived tasks, you can use it for batch processing small datasets. For larger datasets, consider AWS Step Functions to orchestrate multiple Lambda invocations or AWS Batch for handling large-scale batch jobs.

4. Orchestrating ML Workflows

- **AWS Step Functions:** Coordinate multiple Lambda functions to build complex ML workflows, such as data preprocessing, model inference, and post-processing steps.
- **Error Handling and Retries:** Step Functions provide built-in error handling, making your ML pipelines more robust.

Advantages of Using AWS Lambda for ML

- **Scalability:** Automatic scaling ensures your ML inference can handle varying loads without manual intervention.
- **Cost-Effectiveness:** Pay-per-use pricing reduces costs, especially for workloads with intermittent traffic.
- **Integration with AWS Ecosystem:** Seamless integration with AWS services like S3, DynamoDB, and API Gateway simplifies building end-to-end ML solutions.
- **Managed Infrastructure:** AWS handles server maintenance, security patches, and scaling.

Considerations and Limitations

- **Execution Time Limit:** Lambda functions have a maximum execution time of 15 minutes, which may not be suitable for long-running tasks like model training.
- **Resource Constraints:** Maximum memory allocation is 10 GB, and temporary storage is limited to 512 MB (/tmp directory).
- **Cold Starts:** Initial invocation latency can impact performance for latency-sensitive applications.
- **Deployment Package Size:** The uncompressed deployment package size limit is 250 MB (including layers), which can be a constraint for large ML models and dependencies.

Optimizing ML Models for AWS Lambda

- **Model Compression:** Use techniques like quantization or pruning to reduce model size.
- **Dependency Management:** Include only necessary libraries and use AWS Lambda Layers to manage dependencies efficiently.
- **Container Image Support:** AWS Lambda supports container images up to 10 GB, allowing you to include larger models and custom runtimes.

Example Use Case: Real-Time Image Classification

A company wants to provide real-time image classification through an API. They can:

1. **Train the Model:** Use AWS SageMaker to train an image classification model.
2. **Package the Model:** Export the trained model and package it with the inference code.
3. **Deploy on Lambda:** Create a Lambda function to load the model and handle inference requests.
4. **Expose via API Gateway:** Set up AWS API Gateway to expose the Lambda function as an API endpoint.
5. **Optimize Performance:** Utilize AWS Lambda's provisioned concurrency to reduce cold start latency.

Google Cloud Functions and ML Integration
Introduction to Google Cloud Functions

Google Cloud Functions is a serverless execution environment that lets you run code in response to events without managing servers. It supports multiple programming languages, including Python, Node.js, Go, Java, and more. Cloud Functions are integrated with other Google Cloud services, making it suitable for building scalable ML applications.

Integrating ML with Google Cloud Functions
1. Deploying ML Models for Inference

- **Model Hosting:** Host your trained ML models on Google Cloud Storage

or include them in your function's deployment package.
- **Function Creation:** Write a Cloud Function that loads the model and processes inference requests.
- **HTTP Triggers:** Use HTTP functions to handle web requests, enabling real-time inference via RESTful APIs.

2. Preprocessing and Data Transformation

- **Event-Driven Processing:** Trigger functions in response to events from services like Cloud Storage (file uploads) or Cloud Pub/Sub (message queues).
- **Data Preparation:** Use functions to preprocess data before it's input into ML models, such as data cleaning or feature extraction.

3. Integrating with AI Platform and AutoML

- **AI Platform Prediction:** Instead of deploying models on Cloud Functions, you can call the AI Platform Prediction service from within a function to handle inference.
- **AutoML Integration:** Leverage AutoML models by invoking them via REST APIs from your Cloud Functions.

Advantages of Using Google Cloud Functions for ML

- **Scalability:** Automatic scaling to handle fluctuating workloads.
- **Cost Savings:** Pay only for the compute resources used during function execution.
- **Integration with Google Cloud Services:** Seamless interaction with services like Cloud Storage, BigQuery, and AI Platform.
- **Ease of Development:** Quick deployment and updates facilitate rapid iteration.

Considerations and Limitations

- **Execution Time Limit:** Cloud Functions have a maximum execution time of 9 minutes.
- **Memory Allocation:** Functions can be allocated up to 8 GB of memory.
- **Cold Starts:** Similar to AWS Lambda, initial invocations may experience latency due to cold starts.
- **Dependency Management:** Deployment package size limit is 500 MB when uncompressed, which may limit large models.

Optimizing ML Models for Google Cloud Functions

- **Model Size Reduction:** Compress models to fit within deployment package limits.
- **Dependency Management:** Use requirements.txt (for Python) to manage dependencies and exclude unnecessary packages.
- **Environment Variables:** Use environment variables to configure functions without changing code.

Example Use Case: Sentiment Analysis on Streaming Data

A company wants to analyze customer feedback in real-time:

1. **Data Ingestion:** Customer feedback messages are published to a Cloud Pub/Sub topic.
2. **Trigger Function:** A Cloud Function is triggered for each new message.
3. **Perform Inference:** The function uses a pre-trained sentiment analysis model to analyze the message.
4. **Store Results:** Analysis results are stored in BigQuery for further reporting.
5. **Scalable Processing:** The serverless architecture scales automatically with the volume of incoming messages.

Azure Functions and Machine Learning
Introduction to Azure Functions

Azure Functions is Microsoft's serverless computing solution that enables you to run code on-demand without managing infrastructure. It supports multiple programming languages, including C#, JavaScript, Python, Java, and PowerShell. Azure Functions integrates seamlessly with Azure's suite of cloud services, making it suitable for building ML applications.

Leveraging Azure Functions for Machine Learning
1. Deploying ML Models for Inference

- **Function App Creation:** Create an Azure Function App to host your functions.
- **Model Inclusion:** Package your trained ML model with the function code or store it in Azure Blob Storage for retrieval during execution.
- **HTTP Triggers:** Use HTTP-triggered functions to handle API requests for real-time inference.

2. Preprocessing and Data Transformation

- **Event-Driven Triggers:** Azure Functions can be triggered by events from Azure Blob Storage, Event Hubs, or Service Bus.
- **Data Processing Pipelines:** Use functions to preprocess data before feeding it into ML models or storing it in databases.

3. Integration with Azure Machine Learning Services

- **Azure ML Integration:** Invoke Azure Machine Learning models hosted as web services directly from Azure Functions.
- **Batch Scoring:** Use functions to submit batch scoring jobs to Azure ML for processing large datasets.

Advantages of Using Azure Functions for ML

- **Scalability:** Automatic scaling based on demand.
- **Cost Efficiency:** Consumption-based pricing model reduces costs for variable workloads.

- **Integration with Azure Ecosystem:** Easy access to services like Azure Blob Storage, Cosmos DB, and Azure Machine Learning.
- **Flexible Hosting Options:** Choose between Consumption Plan (serverless) and Premium Plan (dedicated resources with advanced features).

Considerations and Limitations

- **Execution Time Limit:** On the Consumption Plan, functions have a default timeout of 5 minutes, extendable to 10 minutes. Premium Plan offers unlimited execution time.
- **Memory Allocation:** Functions can be allocated up to 14 GB of memory on the Premium Plan.
- **Cold Starts:** Functions on the Consumption Plan may experience cold start delays. Premium Plan offers pre-warmed instances to mitigate this.
- **Deployment Complexity:** May require more configuration compared to AWS Lambda or Google Cloud Functions.

Optimizing ML Models for Azure Functions

- **Model Storage:** Store large models in Azure Blob Storage and load them during function execution to avoid deployment size limits.
- **Dependency Management:** Use requirements.txt (Python) or project files (C#) to manage dependencies efficiently.
- **Premium Plan Benefits:** Consider the Premium Plan for advanced features like increased memory, longer execution times, and reduced cold starts.

Example Use Case: Fraud Detection in Financial Transactions

A financial institution wants to detect fraudulent transactions in real-time:

1. **Event Trigger:** Transactions are sent to an Azure Event Hub.
2. **Function Invocation:** An Azure Function is triggered for each transaction event.

3. **Model Inference:** The function loads a fraud detection model and evaluates the transaction.
4. **Alerting Mechanism:** If fraud is suspected, the function triggers an alert or blocks the transaction.
5. **Scalability and Performance:** Azure Functions scale automatically to handle high transaction volumes.

Comparing Serverless Providers for ML Workloads

Choosing the right serverless platform for your machine learning workloads depends on various factors, including the specific requirements of your application, the ecosystem of services you plan to use, and cost considerations. Here's a comparison of AWS Lambda, Google Cloud Functions, and Azure Functions for ML workloads.

1. Supported Languages and Environments

- **AWS Lambda:**
- Supports Python, Node.js, Java, C#, Go, Ruby, and custom runtimes via container images.
- Provides up to 10 GB of memory and 15 minutes of execution time.
- **Google Cloud Functions:**
- Supports Python, Node.js, Go, Java, .NET, Ruby, PHP.
- Offers up to 8 GB of memory and 9 minutes of execution time.
- **Azure Functions:**
- Supports C#, JavaScript, Python, Java, PowerShell, TypeScript.
- On Premium Plan, provides up to 14 GB of memory and unlimited execution time.

2. Integration with Cloud Services

- **AWS Lambda:**
- Tight integration with AWS services like S3, DynamoDB, Kinesis, SageMaker.
- Extensive ecosystem makes it suitable for complex ML workflows within

AWS.
- **Google Cloud Functions:**
- Seamless integration with Google Cloud services like Cloud Storage, Pub/Sub, BigQuery, AI Platform.
- Ideal if you're leveraging Google's ML and data analytics services.
- **Azure Functions:**
- Strong integration with Azure services like Blob Storage, Event Hubs, Cosmos DB, Azure Machine Learning.
- Best suited for organizations invested in the Azure ecosystem.

3. Scalability and Performance

- **Automatic Scaling:**
- All platforms offer automatic scaling based on demand.
- **Cold Start Latency:**
- AWS Lambda and Google Cloud Functions may experience higher cold start times compared to Azure Functions on the Premium Plan.
- Provisioned Concurrency (AWS) and pre-warmed instances (Azure) can mitigate cold starts but may incur additional costs.

4. Pricing Models

- **AWS Lambda:**
- Charges based on the number of requests and compute time (GB-seconds).
- Includes a free tier offering 1 million free requests and 400,000 GB-seconds of compute time per month.
- **Google Cloud Functions:**
- Charges based on invocations, compute time, and memory allocation.
- Provides a free tier with 2 million invocations per month.
- **Azure Functions:**
- Consumption Plan charges based on executions and resource consumption.

- Offers a free grant of 1 million requests and 400,000 GB-seconds of compute time per month.
- Premium Plan has different pricing and includes reserved resources.

5. Deployment and Management Tools

- **AWS Lambda:**
- Deployment via AWS CLI, AWS SDKs, AWS SAM (Serverless Application Model), and third-party frameworks like Serverless Framework.
- Supports container images for functions up to 10 GB.
- **Google Cloud Functions:**
- Deployment using gcloud CLI, Cloud Console, or Cloud Functions Framework.
- Emphasis on simplicity and ease of use.
- **Azure Functions:**
- Deployment via Azure CLI, Azure Portal, Visual Studio, and Azure Functions Core Tools.
- Supports containerized deployments with Azure Container Registry.

6. Advanced Features

- **AWS Lambda:**
- Provisioned Concurrency for reduced cold starts.
- Lambda Layers for code and dependency sharing.
- **Google Cloud Functions:**
- EventArc for advanced event routing.
- Cloud Functions 2nd Gen (in preview) offers longer execution times and improved performance.
- **Azure Functions:**
- Durable Functions for stateful workflows.
- Premium Plan for advanced features like virtual network connectivity and unlimited execution time.

7. Community and Support

- **AWS Lambda:**
- Large community and extensive documentation.
- Wide range of tutorials, forums, and third-party tools.
- **Google Cloud Functions:**
- Growing community with strong support for data analytics and ML.
- **Azure Functions:**
- Supported by Microsoft's developer ecosystem.
- Strong integration with enterprise tools and services.

8. Security and Compliance

- All platforms provide robust security measures, including encryption, identity and access management, and compliance certifications.
- Consider the specific compliance requirements of your industry when choosing a provider.

Choosing the Right Platform

- **AWS Lambda:** Ideal if you're heavily invested in AWS services or require features like extended execution time and larger memory allocation.
- **Google Cloud Functions:** Suitable if your ML workloads leverage Google's data analytics and AI services.
- **Azure Functions:** Best for organizations using Microsoft's technology stack and needing features like unlimited execution time on the Premium Plan.

Consider Multi-Cloud Strategies

- In some cases, you may benefit from using multiple cloud providers to leverage specific strengths.
- Be mindful of the complexity and potential overhead associated with

multi-cloud deployments.

Conclusion

Serverless platforms offer a powerful and flexible way to deploy machine learning workloads, providing scalability, cost-efficiency, and simplified management. AWS Lambda, Google Cloud Functions, and Azure Functions each have their strengths and are integrated deeply with their respective cloud ecosystems. By understanding the capabilities and limitations of each platform, you can choose the one that best aligns with your project's requirements and organizational strategy.

When exploring serverless platforms for machine learning, consider factors such as execution time limits, memory constraints, integration with other cloud services, pricing models, and developer tooling. Optimizing your ML models and functions to work within these platforms' constraints will help you build efficient and scalable applications.

Embracing serverless architectures in machine learning allows you to focus on developing models and delivering value, rather than managing infrastructure. As serverless technology continues to evolve, it will play an increasingly significant role in the deployment and scaling of machine learning solutions.

Setting Up Your Environment: Tools and Prerequisites

Embarking on a journey into artificial intelligence (AI) and serverless machine learning requires a robust and well-configured environment. This setup ensures that you have all the necessary tools and services at your disposal to develop, test, and deploy machine learning models efficiently. This section provides a comprehensive guide to setting up your environment, covering the creation of accounts on major cloud platforms, an introduction to essential cloud services, and the installation of key libraries and tools required for machine learning.

1. Setting Up an AWS Account for Machine Learning

Introduction to AWS

Amazon Web Services (AWS) is a comprehensive cloud computing platform offering a wide array of services that cater to various computing needs, including machine learning. AWS provides scalable computing power, storage options, and a suite of tools that make it easier to build, train, and deploy machine learning models.

Step-by-Step Guide to Creating an AWS Account

Step 1: Visit the AWS Website

- Navigate to the AWS homepage at https://aws.amazon.com/.
- Click on the "Create an AWS Account" button.

Step 2: Enter Account Details

- **Email Address:** Provide a valid email address that will be associated with your AWS account.
- **Password:** Choose a strong password.
- **AWS Account Name:** Enter a name for your account (e.g., "MyMachine LearningAccount").

Step 3: Choose Account Type

- Select "Personal" or "Professional" depending on your use case.

Step 4: Provide Contact Information

- Enter your full name, phone number, and address.
- Agree to the AWS Customer Agreement.

Step 5: Payment Information

- Enter your credit or debit card information.
- AWS requires a payment method for identity verification and to charge for any services that exceed the free tier limits.
- Note: AWS offers a free tier that provides limited access to many services for 12 months.

Step 6: Identity Verification

- AWS may perform an identity verification via a phone call or SMS.
- Enter the provided PIN to complete verification.

Step 7: Select a Support Plan

- Choose the "Basic" support plan, which is free and suitable for most users starting out.

Step 8: Confirmation

- Once all steps are completed, you will receive a confirmation email.
- Your AWS account is now set up.

Securing Your AWS Account
Enable Multi-Factor Authentication (MFA):

- Log in to the AWS Management Console.
- Click on your account name in the top-right corner and select "My Security Credentials."
- Under "Multi-Factor Authentication (MFA)," click "Activate MFA."
- Choose a virtual MFA device (e.g., Google Authenticator).
- Scan the QR code and enter the authentication codes to enable MFA.

Create IAM Users and Roles:

- Avoid using the root account for everyday tasks.
- Go to the AWS IAM (Identity and Access Management) console.
- Create a new user with administrative privileges.
- Assign permissions using IAM roles and policies.
- Use this IAM user for regular AWS activities.

Understanding AWS Free Tier

AWS offers a free tier that allows new users to explore AWS services without incurring charges. Key components relevant to machine learning include:

- **Amazon EC2:** 750 hours per month of t2.micro instances.
- **Amazon S3:** 5 GB of standard storage.
- **AWS Lambda:** 1 million free requests per month and 3.2 million seconds of compute time.

- **Amazon SageMaker:** 250 hours per month of t2.medium notebook usage.

Key AWS Services for Machine Learning
Amazon SageMaker:

- A fully-managed service that provides tools to build, train, and deploy machine learning models.
- Supports popular frameworks like TensorFlow, PyTorch, and Scikit-learn.

Amazon EC2 (Elastic Compute Cloud):

- Provides resizable compute capacity in the cloud.
- Useful for running custom machine learning environments or training models on GPU instances.

Amazon S3 (Simple Storage Service):

- Scalable storage solution for storing large datasets.
- Provides high durability and availability.

AWS Lambda:

- Serverless compute service that runs code in response to events.
- Ideal for deploying machine learning models for inference.

AWS IAM (Identity and Access Management):

- Manages access to AWS services and resources securely.
- Essential for setting up roles and permissions for your machine learning applications.

2. Introduction to S3, EC2, and Lambda for Serverless

Amazon S3 (Simple Storage Service)
Overview:

- Amazon S3 is an object storage service offering industry-leading scalability, data availability, security, and performance.
- It allows you to store and retrieve any amount of data from anywhere on the web.

Key Features:

- **Scalability:** Automatically scales to meet your storage needs.
- **Durability:** Designed for 99.999999999% durability.
- **Security:** Supports encryption and access control features.

Uses in Machine Learning:

- **Data Storage:** Store large datasets required for training machine learning models.
- **Data Lake:** Central repository for storing structured and unstructured data at any scale.
- **Model Storage:** Save trained models for deployment or sharing.

Amazon EC2 (Elastic Compute Cloud)
Overview:

- Amazon EC2 provides scalable computing capacity in the AWS cloud.
- Allows you to launch virtual servers (instances) with various configurations.

Key Features:

- **Variety of Instance Types:** Choose instances optimized for compute,

SETTING UP YOUR ENVIRONMENT: TOOLS AND PREREQUISITES

memory, storage, or GPU acceleration.
- **Scalability:** Scale up or down based on demand.
- **Flexibility:** Full control over the configuration of your instances.

Uses in Machine Learning:

- **Model Training:** Utilize GPU instances (e.g., P3, G4) for accelerated training of deep learning models.
- **Custom Environments:** Set up custom machine learning environments with specific libraries and configurations.
- **Distributed Training:** Run large-scale training jobs across multiple instances.

AWS Lambda
Overview:

- AWS Lambda is a serverless compute service that runs your code in response to events and automatically manages the underlying compute resources.
- Supports multiple programming languages including Python, Node.js, Java, and more.

Key Features:

- **Event-Driven Execution:** Trigger functions in response to events from other AWS services.
- **Automatic Scaling:** Scales automatically based on the number of incoming requests.
- **Pay-Per-Use Pricing:** Pay only for the compute time you consume.

Uses in Machine Learning:

- **Model Inference:** Deploy machine learning models for inference

without managing servers.
- **Data Processing:** Perform real-time data processing and transformations.
- **Microservices Architecture:** Build scalable and modular machine learning applications.

Integrating S3, EC2, and Lambda in ML Workflows
Data Ingestion and Storage:

- **S3 Buckets:** Store raw data files in S3 buckets.
- **Lambda Triggers:** Configure Lambda functions to trigger when new data is uploaded to S3 for preprocessing.

Model Training:

- **EC2 Instances:** Use EC2 instances with appropriate compute resources to train models.
- **Accessing Data:** EC2 instances can access training data stored in S3.

Model Deployment:

- **Lambda Functions:** Deploy trained models as Lambda functions for serverless inference.
- **API Gateway:** Use AWS API Gateway to expose Lambda functions as RESTful APIs.

Automating ML Pipelines:

- **AWS Step Functions:** Orchestrate complex workflows by coordinating Lambda functions and other AWS services.
- **EventBridge:** Set up scheduled events to automate periodic tasks like model retraining.

Security and Access Control:

- **IAM Roles and Policies:** Assign roles to EC2 instances and Lambda functions to control access to S3 buckets and other resources.
- **Encryption:** Use server-side encryption for data at rest in S3 and SSL/TLS for data in transit.

3. Google Cloud Setup for Serverless ML
Introduction to Google Cloud Platform (GCP)

Google Cloud Platform offers a suite of cloud computing services that run on the same infrastructure that Google uses internally for its end-user products. GCP provides powerful tools and services for machine learning, including serverless computing options.

Creating a Google Cloud Account
Step 1: Visit the GCP Website

- Navigate to https://cloud.google.com/.
- Click on "Get started for free."

Step 2: Sign In or Create a Google Account

- Use your existing Google account or create a new one.

Step 3: Accept Terms and Conditions

- Review and accept the Google Cloud Terms of Service.

Step 4: Set Up Your Payment Profile

- Provide your country and account type (business or individual).
- Enter your name, address, and contact information.

Step 5: Add a Payment Method

- Input your credit or debit card information.
- Note: GCP offers a $300 free trial credit valid for 90 days.

Step 6: Start the Free Trial

- Confirm the details and start your free trial.

Understanding GCP Free Tier

- **$300 Credit:** Use towards any GCP services.
- **Always Free Usage Limits:** Access to certain resources with usage limits, such as:
- **Cloud Functions:** 2 million invocations per month.
- **Compute Engine:** 1 f1-micro instance per month.
- **Cloud Storage:** 5 GB of regional storage.

Setting Up a GCP Project for Machine Learning
Step 1: Create a New Project

- In the GCP Console, click on the project dropdown and select "New Project."
- Enter a project name (e.g., "ServerlessMLProject") and click "Create."

Step 2: Enable Billing

- Ensure billing is enabled for your project to use paid services.

Step 3: Enable APIs and Services

- Go to "APIs & Services" and enable the APIs required for your project, such as:
- **Cloud Functions API**
- **Cloud Storage API**

SETTING UP YOUR ENVIRONMENT: TOOLS AND PREREQUISITES

- AI Platform API

GCP Services for Machine Learning
Cloud Functions

- Serverless execution environment for building and connecting cloud services.
- Supports multiple languages like Python, Node.js, Go, and more.

AI Platform

- Managed service for training and deploying machine learning models.
- Supports custom training with popular frameworks.

Compute Engine

- Scalable, high-performance virtual machines (VMs).
- Ideal for custom environments or when you need more control over the infrastructure.

Cloud Storage

- Unified object storage solution for developers and enterprises.
- Stores data for machine learning, such as datasets and trained models.

Setting Up Cloud Functions for ML
Step 1: Install the Cloud SDK

- Download and install the Google Cloud SDK from https://cloud.google.com/sdk/docs/install.
- Initialize the SDK by running gcloud init and following the prompts.

Step 2: Write Your Function

- Create a Python script (e.g., main.py) containing your function code.
- Define an entry point function that Cloud Functions will invoke.

Step 3: Specify Dependencies

- Create a requirements.txt file listing the Python libraries your function depends on.

Step 4: Deploy the Function

- Use the gcloud command-line tool to deploy your function:

```css
Copy code
gcloud functions deploy my_ml_function \
    --runtime python39 \
    --trigger-http \
    --memory 2048MB \
    --timeout 540s
```

Step 5: Test the Function

- Invoke the function via HTTP request to ensure it works correctly.

Security and Access Control in GCP

- **IAM Roles:** Assign roles to control access to resources.
- **Service Accounts:** Use service accounts for authentication between services.
- **VPC Service Controls:** Define security perimeters around resources.

4. Installing Key Libraries and Tools (Python, NumPy, Pandas, etc.)
Importance of Python in Machine Learning

SETTING UP YOUR ENVIRONMENT: TOOLS AND PREREQUISITES

Python is the most widely used programming language in machine learning due to its simplicity and the vast ecosystem of libraries and frameworks available. It supports procedural, object-oriented, and functional programming paradigms, making it versatile for various tasks.

Setting Up Python Environment
Option 1: Anaconda Distribution

- Anaconda is a free and open-source distribution of Python and R for scientific computing.
- It includes Python, Conda package manager, and over 1,500 packages.

Installation Steps:

- Download Anaconda from https://www.anaconda.com/products/individual.
- Choose the Python 3.x version for your operating system.
- Run the installer and follow the on-screen instructions.

Option 2: Python.org Installation

- Download the latest Python 3.x version from https://www.python.org/downloads/.
- Install Python by running the installer and selecting "Add Python to PATH" during installation.

Setting Up Virtual Environments

- **Why Use Virtual Environments?**
- Isolate project dependencies.
- Avoid conflicts between packages.
- **Creating a Virtual Environment:**
- Using venv module:

```
Copy code
python -m venv myenv
```

- Activate the environment:
- On Windows:

```
Copy code
myenv\Scripts\activate
```

- On macOS/Linux:

```bash
Copy code
source myenv/bin/activate
```

Installing Key Python Libraries
1. NumPy

- **Description:** Fundamental package for numerical computing with Python.
- **Installation:**

```
Copy code
pip install numpy
```

2. Pandas

- **Description:** Library providing high-performance, easy-to-use data structures and data analysis tools.
- **Installation:**

```
Copy code
pip install pandas
```

3. Matplotlib

- **Description:** Plotting library for creating static, animated, and interactive visualizations.
- **Installation:**

```
Copy code
pip install matplotlib
```

4. Scikit-learn

- **Description:** Machine learning library providing simple and efficient tools for predictive data analysis.
- **Installation:**

```
Copy code
pip install scikit-learn
```

5. TensorFlow

- **Description:** Open-source platform for machine learning developed by Google.
- **Installation:**

```
Copy code
pip install tensorflow
```

6. PyTorch

- **Description:** Open-source machine learning library developed by Facebook's AI Research lab.
- **Installation:**

```
Copy code
pip install torch torchvision
```

7. Jupyter Notebook

- **Description:** Web-based interactive computing platform for creating notebooks that contain live code, equations, visualizations, and narrative text.
- **Installation:**

```
Copy code
pip install notebook
```

Integrated Development Environments (IDEs)
1. Jupyter Notebook

- **Usage:** Ideal for interactive data analysis and visualization.
- **Launching Jupyter Notebook:**

SETTING UP YOUR ENVIRONMENT: TOOLS AND PREREQUISITES

```
Copy code
jupyter notebook
```

2. Visual Studio Code (VS Code)

- **Description:** Lightweight but powerful source code editor with built-in support for Python.
- **Extensions:**
- **Python Extension:** Provides IntelliSense, linting, debugging, and more.
- **Download:** https://code.visualstudio.com/

3. PyCharm

- **Description:** Feature-rich Python IDE with support for web development and data science.
- **Versions:**
- **Community Edition:** Free and open-source.
- **Professional Edition:** Paid version with additional features.
- **Download:** https://www.jetbrains.com/pycharm/

Configuring Your IDE

- **Interpreter Selection:** Ensure your IDE is using the Python interpreter from your virtual environment.
- **Linting and Formatting:**
- **Flake8 or Pylint:** For code linting.
- **Black or Autopep8:** For code formatting.
- **Extensions and Plugins:**
- Install extensions that enhance productivity, such as Git integration and code snippets.

Version Control with Git

- **Installation:**
- Download Git from https://git-scm.com/downloads.
- **Basic Commands:**
- **Initialize Repository:**

```csharp
Copy code
git init
```

- **Clone Repository:**

```bash
Copy code
git clone <repository_url>
```

- **Commit Changes:**

```sql
Copy code
git add .
git commit -m "Commit message"
```

- **Push to Remote:**

```css
Copy code
```

```
git push origin main
```

Using GitHub

- **Create a GitHub Account:** Sign up at https://github.com/.
- **Create a Repository:** Host your code and collaborate with others.
- **Integrate with IDE:** Use extensions to integrate GitHub with your IDE for seamless version control.

Setting Up Environment Variables

- **Why Use Environment Variables?**
- Securely store sensitive information like API keys and database credentials.
- **Setting Variables:**
- On Windows:
- Use the System Properties dialog to add variables.
- On macOS/Linux:
- Edit the .bash_profile or .bashrc file.

Best Practices for Managing Dependencies

- **Requirements File:**
- Generate a requirements.txt file listing all your project's dependencies.

```
Copy code
pip freeze > requirements.txt
```

- Install dependencies from the requirements file:

```
Copy code
pip install -r requirements.txt
```

- **Dependency Management Tools:**
- **Pipenv:** Combines pip and virtualenv for better dependency management.
- **Poetry:** Manages dependencies and packaging in a single tool.

Conclusion

Setting up your environment is a critical first step in your machine learning journey. By creating accounts on AWS and Google Cloud, you gain access to powerful cloud services that facilitate serverless computing and scalable machine learning solutions. Understanding key services like S3, EC2, and Lambda on AWS, and Cloud Functions and AI Platform on GCP, allows you to leverage these platforms effectively.

Installing essential libraries and tools such as Python, NumPy, Pandas, and machine learning frameworks like TensorFlow and PyTorch equips you with the necessary software to develop and experiment with machine learning models. Utilizing virtual environments, IDEs, and version control systems enhances your productivity and ensures that your projects are organized and maintainable.

With your environment set up, you are now prepared to delve deeper into machine learning, explore serverless architectures, and build applications that harness the power of AI. Remember to follow best practices for security, dependency management, and code organization as you progress in your learning and development.

Building Your First Serverless Machine Learning Model

Building your first serverless machine learning (ML) model involves several critical steps, from data collection and preprocessing to deploying, testing, and monitoring your model. This comprehensive guide will walk you through each stage, providing detailed instructions and best practices to help you successfully implement your ML model using serverless architectures, specifically leveraging AWS Lambda.

1. Data Collection and Preprocessing

Introduction

Data is the cornerstone of any machine learning project. The quality, quantity, and relevance of your data directly influence the performance and accuracy of your ML models. In a serverless environment, efficient data handling becomes even more crucial due to the ephemeral nature of serverless functions and the need for optimized resource utilization.

Steps for Data Collection

1. **Identify Data Sources:**

   - **Internal Databases:** Use organizational data from relational databases (e.g., MySQL, PostgreSQL) or NoSQL databases (e.g., DynamoDB).
   - **External APIs:** Integrate data from third-party services via RESTful

APIs.
- **Public Datasets:** Leverage publicly available datasets from repositories like Kaggle, UCI Machine Learning Repository, or AWS Public Datasets.
- **IoT Devices:** Collect real-time data from sensors and devices if applicable.

1. **Automate Data Ingestion:**

- **AWS S3 Triggers:** Use AWS S3 to store incoming data and configure triggers to invoke Lambda functions upon new data uploads.
- **AWS Kinesis:** Stream real-time data into Kinesis Data Streams, which can then trigger Lambda functions for processing.
- **Scheduled Events:** Utilize AWS EventBridge (formerly CloudWatch Events) to schedule data collection tasks.

Data Preprocessing Techniques

Preprocessing transforms raw data into a format suitable for ML models. It involves cleaning, normalizing, and structuring data to enhance model performance.

1. **Data Cleaning:**

- **Handling Missing Values:** Impute missing data using techniques like mean/median imputation or advanced methods like K-Nearest Neighbors (KNN).
- **Removing Duplicates:** Eliminate duplicate records to prevent bias.
- **Outlier Detection:** Identify and handle outliers that may skew model training.

1. **Data Transformation:**

- **Normalization and Scaling:** Scale numerical features to a standard range (e.g., 0-1) using Min-Max scaling or Z-score normalization to

BUILDING YOUR FIRST SERVERLESS MACHINE LEARNING MODEL

ensure uniformity.
- **Encoding Categorical Variables:**
- **One-Hot Encoding:** Convert categorical variables into binary vectors.
- **Label Encoding:** Assign unique numerical labels to categorical data.
- **Feature Engineering:** Create new features from existing data to provide additional insights (e.g., extracting date components from timestamps).

1. **Data Splitting:**

- **Training Set:** Used to train the ML model.
- **Validation Set:** Used to tune hyperparameters and prevent overfitting.
- **Test Set:** Used to evaluate the final model's performance on unseen data.

Tools and Libraries for Preprocessing

- **Pandas:** Essential for data manipulation and analysis.

```python
Copy code
import pandas as pd
df = pd.read_csv('data.csv')
```

- **NumPy:** Fundamental for numerical computations.

```python
Copy code
import numpy as np
data = np.array([1, 2, 3, 4, 5])
```

- **Scikit-learn:** Provides utilities for preprocessing tasks like scaling and encoding.

```python
Copy code
from sklearn.preprocessing import StandardScaler, OneHotEncoder
scaler = StandardScaler()
scaled_data = scaler.fit_transform(data)
encoder = OneHotEncoder()
encoded_data = encoder.fit_transform(categorical_data)
```

Best Practices for Data Preprocessing in Serverless Environments

1. **Optimize Data Size:**

- Minimize the size of data being processed to reduce execution time and costs. Use efficient data formats like Parquet or Avro instead of CSV when possible.

1. **Parallel Processing:**

- Leverage AWS Lambda's ability to handle multiple concurrent executions to preprocess large datasets in parallel, speeding up the overall process.

1. **Stateless Processing:**

- Ensure that each Lambda function execution is stateless to facilitate scalability and reliability. Use external storage (e.g., S3) to store intermediate results if necessary.

1. **Error Handling:**

- Implement robust error handling and logging to capture preprocessing issues. Use AWS CloudWatch Logs for monitoring and debugging.

Example Workflow: Data Collection and Preprocessing with AWS

Lambda

1. **Data Upload:**

- A new dataset is uploaded to an S3 bucket.

1. **Trigger Lambda Function:**

- S3 triggers a Lambda function upon the upload event.

1. **Lambda Execution:**

- The Lambda function retrieves the data from S3.
- Performs data cleaning, transformation, and feature engineering using Pandas and Scikit-learn.
- Saves the preprocessed data back to another S3 bucket for model training.

1. **Logging and Monitoring:**

- Logs are sent to CloudWatch for monitoring the preprocessing steps and handling any errors.

Conclusion

Effective data collection and preprocessing are fundamental to building high-performing machine learning models. In a serverless environment, leveraging AWS Lambda for these tasks ensures scalability, cost-efficiency, and seamless integration with other AWS services. By following best practices and utilizing appropriate tools, you can streamline your data workflows and set a solid foundation for your machine learning endeavors.

2. Choosing the Right Machine Learning Model
Introduction

Selecting the appropriate machine learning model is pivotal to the success of your project. The choice depends on various factors, including the nature of your data, the problem you're trying to solve, and the resources available. This section explores the considerations and steps involved in choosing the right ML model, along with an overview of different model types and their applications.

Understanding the Problem

Before selecting a model, clearly define the problem you aim to solve. Machine learning tasks can be broadly categorized into:

1. **Supervised Learning:**

- **Classification:** Predicting categorical labels (e.g., spam vs. not spam).
- **Regression:** Predicting continuous values (e.g., house prices).

1. **Unsupervised Learning:**

- **Clustering:** Grouping similar data points (e.g., customer segmentation).
- **Dimensionality Reduction:** Reducing the number of features while retaining essential information (e.g., PCA).

1. **Reinforcement Learning:**

- **Sequential Decision Making:** Learning policies to maximize cumulative rewards (e.g., game playing, robotics).

Factors to Consider When Choosing a Model

1. **Nature of the Data:**

- **Structured vs. Unstructured:** Structured data (e.g., tabular data) may be suited for models like decision trees or linear regression, while unstructured data (e.g., images, text) may require deep learning models like CNNs or RNNs.
- **Size of the Dataset:** Large datasets may benefit from complex models

like deep neural networks, whereas smaller datasets might be better suited for simpler models to prevent overfitting.

1. **Complexity of the Problem:**

- **Simple Relationships:** Linear models (e.g., linear regression) are effective for problems with linear relationships between features and targets.
- **Non-Linear Relationships:** Non-linear models (e.g., decision trees, neural networks) can capture complex patterns.

1. **Interpretability:**

- **Transparent Models:** Models like linear regression and decision trees are easier to interpret, which is important in applications requiring explainability (e.g., healthcare, finance).
- **Black-Box Models:** Deep learning models offer high accuracy but lack interpretability, making them suitable for tasks where performance is prioritized over explainability.

1. **Computational Resources:**

- **Training Time:** Complex models like deep neural networks require significant computational power and time to train.
- **Inference Time:** Models deployed in real-time applications need to provide quick predictions, influencing the choice of model architecture.

1. **Scalability:**

- **Large-Scale Applications:** Models that can scale efficiently with data volume and complexity are essential for enterprise-level applications.

Overview of Common Machine Learning Models

1. **Linear Regression:**

- **Type:** Supervised learning (regression).
- **Use Cases:** Predicting continuous variables like sales, prices.
- **Pros:** Simple, interpretable, fast.
- **Cons:** Assumes linear relationships, may underperform on complex data.

1. **Logistic Regression:**

- **Type:** Supervised learning (classification).
- **Use Cases:** Binary classification tasks like spam detection.
- **Pros:** Simple, interpretable, efficient.
- **Cons:** Limited to linear decision boundaries.

1. **Decision Trees:**

- **Type:** Supervised learning (classification and regression).
- **Use Cases:** Customer segmentation, risk assessment.
- **Pros:** Easy to interpret, handles both numerical and categorical data.
- **Cons:** Prone to overfitting, can be unstable with small data variations.

1. **Random Forests:**

- **Type:** Supervised learning (ensemble method).
- **Use Cases:** Fraud detection, feature importance analysis.
- **Pros:** Reduces overfitting, handles large datasets well.
- **Cons:** Less interpretable than single decision trees, higher computational cost.

1. **Support Vector Machines (SVM):**

- **Type:** Supervised learning (classification and regression).
- **Use Cases:** Image classification, text categorization.

- **Pros:** Effective in high-dimensional spaces, robust to overfitting.
- **Cons:** Memory-intensive, challenging to tune for large datasets.

1. **k-Nearest Neighbors (k-NN):**

- **Type:** Supervised learning (classification and regression).
- **Use Cases:** Recommendation systems, anomaly detection.
- **Pros:** Simple, no training phase.
- **Cons:** Computationally expensive during inference, sensitive to irrelevant features.

1. **Neural Networks:**

- **Type:** Supervised learning (deep learning).
- **Use Cases:** Image recognition, natural language processing, speech recognition.
- **Pros:** Highly flexible, capable of modeling complex patterns.
- **Cons:** Requires large datasets, computationally intensive, less interpretable.

1. **Convolutional Neural Networks (CNNs):**

- **Type:** Supervised learning (deep learning).
- **Use Cases:** Image and video analysis.
- **Pros:** Excellent at capturing spatial hierarchies in data.
- **Cons:** Requires significant computational resources, complex to design and train.

1. **Recurrent Neural Networks (RNNs):**

- **Type:** Supervised learning (deep learning).
- **Use Cases:** Sequence prediction, language modeling.
- **Pros:** Effective for sequential data, captures temporal dependencies.

- **Cons:** Prone to vanishing/exploding gradients, computationally intensive.

1. **Gradient Boosting Machines (e.g., XGBoost, LightGBM):**

- **Type:** Supervised learning (ensemble method).
- **Use Cases:** Structured data tasks like ranking, classification, and regression.
- **Pros:** High performance, handles missing data, feature importance.
- **Cons:** Requires careful tuning, can be prone to overfitting.

Model Selection Process

1. **Define Evaluation Metrics:**

- **Classification:** Accuracy, precision, recall, F1-score, ROC-AUC.
- **Regression:** Mean Absolute Error (MAE), Mean Squared Error (MSE), Root Mean Squared Error (RMSE), R-squared.

1. **Baseline Model:**

- Start with a simple model to establish a performance baseline.
- Example: Use logistic regression for a classification task.

1. **Experiment with Different Models:**

- Train multiple models and compare their performance based on chosen metrics.
- Use cross-validation to ensure robustness.

1. **Hyperparameter Tuning:**

- Optimize model parameters to enhance performance.

- Techniques: Grid search, random search, Bayesian optimization.

1. **Model Evaluation:**

- Assess models on validation and test sets.
- Check for overfitting or underfitting by comparing training and validation performance.

1. **Final Model Selection:**

- Choose the model that best balances accuracy, interpretability, and computational efficiency based on your specific requirements.

Considerations for Serverless Deployment

1. **Model Size:**

- Serverless functions like AWS Lambda have size limitations (e.g., 250 MB uncompressed for Lambda). Choose models that fit within these constraints or use model compression techniques.

1. **Inference Latency:**

- Serverless functions can experience cold starts, leading to increased latency. Optimize model loading times and consider provisioned concurrency if low latency is critical.

1. **Statelessness:**

- Ensure that the model does not rely on persistent state between function invocations. Use external storage (e.g., S3, DynamoDB) for any necessary state persistence.

1. **Scalability:**

- Serverless architectures automatically handle scaling, but ensure your model can handle multiple concurrent invocations without conflicts or resource contention.

Example: Selecting a Model for Real-Time Sentiment Analysis

1. **Problem Definition:**

- **Task:** Classify social media posts as positive, negative, or neutral.
- **Type:** Supervised learning (classification).

1. **Data Characteristics:**

- **Data Type:** Text data.
- **Dataset Size:** Large (millions of posts).
- **Feature Representation:** Bag-of-words, TF-IDF, or word embeddings.

1. **Model Options:**

- **Logistic Regression:** Simple, interpretable, fast inference.
- **Support Vector Machines (SVM):** High accuracy, suitable for high-dimensional data.
- **Deep Learning Models (e.g., LSTM, BERT):** State-of-the-art performance, especially for capturing context.

1. **Evaluation Metrics:**

- **F1-Score:** Balances precision and recall.
- **ROC-AUC:** Measures overall classification performance.

1. **Model Selection:**

- Start with logistic regression for baseline performance.
- Experiment with SVM for improved accuracy.
- Explore deep learning models like BERT for potentially higher performance, keeping in mind increased computational requirements.

1. **Final Decision:**

- Choose a BERT-based model for its superior understanding of context, optimizing it for deployment in a serverless environment by using model distillation or quantization to reduce size and latency.

Conclusion

Choosing the right machine learning model involves a thorough understanding of your problem, data, and the trade-offs associated with different models. In a serverless environment, considerations like model size, inference latency, and statelessness become paramount. By following a systematic model selection process and leveraging the strengths of serverless architectures, you can deploy efficient and scalable ML models tailored to your specific use cases.

3. Deploying Machine Learning Models with AWS Lambda
Introduction

Deploying machine learning models in a serverless environment like AWS Lambda offers numerous advantages, including automatic scaling, cost-efficiency, and simplified infrastructure management. AWS Lambda allows you to run your ML models as functions that can be triggered by various events, making it ideal for real-time inference and event-driven architectures. This section provides a step-by-step guide to deploying your first ML model using AWS Lambda, covering model packaging, function creation, integration with AWS services, and optimization strategies.

Step 1: Preparing Your Machine Learning Model

Before deploying, ensure that your ML model is trained, tested, and saved in a format suitable for inference.

1. **Train Your Model:**

- Use your preferred ML framework (e.g., Scikit-learn, TensorFlow, PyTorch) to train your model on your preprocessed dataset.
- Example with Scikit-learn:

```python
Copy code
from sklearn.ensemble import RandomForestClassifier
import joblib

# Train model
model = RandomForestClassifier(n_estimators=100)
model.fit(X_train, y_train)

# Save model
joblib.dump(model, 'model.joblib')
```

1. **Save the Model:**

- Save your trained model using serialization libraries like joblib for Scikit-learn, pickle for Python objects, or model-specific saving functions for TensorFlow and PyTorch.

1. **Optimize the Model:**

- **Compression:** Compress the model to reduce size (e.g., using gzip).
- **Quantization:** Convert model weights to lower precision to decrease size and increase inference speed.

Step 2: Setting Up AWS Lambda Function

1. **Create a Lambda Function:**

BUILDING YOUR FIRST SERVERLESS MACHINE LEARNING MODEL

- Navigate to the AWS Lambda console.
- Click "Create function."
- **Function Name:** Choose a descriptive name (e.g., MLModelInference).
- **Runtime:** Select the appropriate runtime (e.g., Python 3.8).
- **Permissions:** Create or choose an existing execution role with necessary permissions (e.g., access to S3).

1. **Configure the Function:**

- **Memory Allocation:** Allocate sufficient memory based on your model's requirements. AWS Lambda allows up to 10 GB.
- **Timeout Setting:** Set an appropriate timeout limit. The maximum is 15 minutes, but inference tasks typically require much less.

1. **Upload the Model and Code:**

- **Deployment Package:** Create a deployment package that includes your model, inference code, and all dependencies.
- **Using ZIP:**
- Structure your project directory:

```
Copy code
MLModelInference/
  model.joblib
  inference.py
  requirements.txt
```

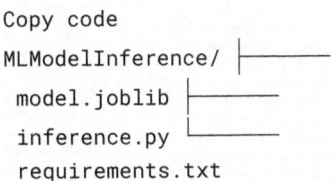

- Install dependencies locally:

```
Copy code
pip install -r requirements.txt -t .
```

- Zip the contents:

```python
Copy code
zip -r MLModelInference.zip .
```

- **Using AWS Lambda Layers:** If your dependencies are large or shared across multiple functions, consider using Lambda Layers to include them separately.

1. **Inference Code Example (inference.py):**

```python
Copy code
import json
import joblib
import boto3

# Load the model
s3 = boto3.client('s3')
s3.download_file('your-bucket-name', 'model.joblib', '/tmp/model.joblib')
model = joblib.load('/tmp/model.joblib')

def lambda_handler(event, context):
    # Parse input data
    data = json.loads(event['body'])
    features = data['features']
```

```
# Make prediction
prediction = model.predict([features])
result = prediction[0]

# Return response
return {
    'statusCode': 200,
    'body': json.dumps({'prediction': result})
}
```

1. **Deploy the Function:**

- Upload the ZIP file via the Lambda console or use the AWS CLI:

```css
Copy code
aws lambda update-function-code --function-name MLModelInference
--zip-file fileb://MLModelInference.zip
```

Step 3: Integrating with AWS API Gateway

To expose your Lambda function as a RESTful API for real-time predictions, integrate it with AWS API Gateway.

1. **Create an API:**

- Navigate to the API Gateway console.
- Click "Create API" and choose "REST API."

1. **Configure API Resources and Methods:**

- **Resource:** Create a new resource (e.g., /predict).
- **Method:** Add a POST method to the /predict resource.

- **Integration:** Select "Lambda Function" and choose your MLModelInference function.
- **Permissions:** Allow API Gateway to invoke your Lambda function.

1. **Deploy the API:**

- Click "Actions" and select "Deploy API."
- Choose or create a new stage (e.g., prod).
- Note the API endpoint URL for making inference requests.

Step 4: Testing the Deployment

1. **Send a Test Request:**

- Use tools like Postman, cURL, or your application to send a POST request to the API endpoint.
- **Example cURL Command:**

```bash
Copy code
curl -X POST
https://your-api-id.execute-api.region.amazonaws.com/prod/predict \
-H "Content-Type: application/json" \
-d '{"features": [feature1, feature2, feature3, ...]}'
```

- **Expected Response:**

```json
Copy code
{
  "prediction": "class_label"
```

BUILDING YOUR FIRST SERVERLESS MACHINE LEARNING MODEL

}

1. **Verify Function Execution:**

- Check AWS Lambda logs in CloudWatch to ensure the function executed correctly and returned the expected output.

Step 5: Monitoring and Logging
Effective monitoring and logging are essential to maintain and troubleshoot your serverless ML model.

1. **AWS CloudWatch Logs:**

- Lambda automatically sends logs to CloudWatch. Navigate to the CloudWatch console and find logs under /aws/lambda/MLModelInference.
- **Log Insights:** Use CloudWatch Logs Insights to query and analyze logs for performance metrics and error tracking.

1. **AWS CloudWatch Metrics:**

- Monitor key metrics like invocation count, error rates, duration, and throttles.
- Set up CloudWatch Alarms to notify you of unusual behaviors or performance issues.

1. **Performance Optimization:**

- **Provisioned Concurrency:** Reduce cold start latency by pre-warming a specified number of Lambda instances.
- **Function Memory Allocation:** Adjust memory settings to optimize execution time and cost. Higher memory allocations also provide more

CPU power.

1. **Security Monitoring:**

- Use AWS Identity and Access Management (IAM) to ensure that your Lambda function has the least privileges necessary.
- Enable encryption for data at rest (S3) and in transit (HTTPS).

Step 6: Scaling and Optimization

1. **Auto-Scaling:**

- AWS Lambda automatically scales to handle incoming requests, ensuring that your ML model can handle high traffic without manual intervention.

1. **Cost Optimization:**

- **Monitor Usage:** Regularly review CloudWatch metrics to understand usage patterns and optimize resource allocation.
- **Optimize Code:** Ensure that your inference code is efficient to minimize execution time and costs.
- **Use Lambda Layers:** Share common dependencies across multiple functions to reduce duplication and manage dependencies efficiently.

1. **Versioning and Aliases:**

- **Version Control:** Publish versions of your Lambda function to manage updates and rollbacks.
- **Aliases:** Use aliases (e.g., dev, prod) to point to specific versions, facilitating staged deployments and testing.

Example: Deploying a Sentiment Analysis Model

BUILDING YOUR FIRST SERVERLESS MACHINE LEARNING MODEL

1. **Train and Save the Model:**

```python
Copy code
from sklearn.feature_extraction.text import TfidfVectorizer
from sklearn.linear_model import LogisticRegression
import joblib

# Sample training data
X_train = ["I love this product!", "This is the worst experience.", ...]
y_train = [1, 0, ...]  # 1 for positive, 0 for negative

# Vectorize text data
vectorizer = TfidfVectorizer()
X_train_vec = vectorizer.fit_transform(X_train)

# Train model
model = LogisticRegression()
model.fit(X_train_vec, y_train)

# Save model and vectorizer
joblib.dump(model, 'sentiment_model.joblib')
joblib.dump(vectorizer, 'vectorizer.joblib')
```

1. **Modify Inference Code to Include Vectorizer:**

```python
Copy code
import json
import joblib
import boto3

s3 = boto3.client('s3')
```

```python
s3.download_file('your-bucket', 'sentiment_model.joblib',
'/tmp/sentiment_model.joblib')
s3.download_file('your-bucket', 'vectorizer.joblib',
'/tmp/vectorizer.joblib')
model = joblib.load('/tmp/sentiment_model.joblib')
vectorizer = joblib.load('/tmp/vectorizer.joblib')

def lambda_handler(event, context):
    data = json.loads(event['body'])
    text = data['text']
    features = vectorizer.transform([text])
    prediction = model.predict(features)
    result = 'Positive' if prediction[0] == 1 else 'Negative'
    return {
        'statusCode': 200,
        'body': json.dumps({'sentiment': result})
    }
```

1. **Deploy and Test:**

- Upload the updated deployment package.
- Invoke the API with sample text to receive sentiment predictions.

```bash
Copy code
curl -X POST
https://your-api-id.execute-api.region.amazonaws.com/prod/predict \
-H "Content-Type: application/json" \
-d '{"text": "I am extremely happy with this service!"}'
```

- **Response:**

```json
Copy code
{
  "sentiment": "Positive"
}
```

Conclusion

Deploying machine learning models with AWS Lambda offers a scalable, cost-effective, and efficient way to serve real-time predictions. By following the outlined steps—from preparing your model and setting up the Lambda function to integrating with API Gateway and implementing robust monitoring—you can create a reliable serverless ML deployment. Optimizing for performance and cost, along with adhering to best practices, ensures that your deployed model remains effective and maintainable as your application grows.

4. Testing and Monitoring Your Serverless Model

Introduction

Once your machine learning model is deployed in a serverless environment like AWS Lambda, ensuring its reliability, performance, and accuracy is paramount. Testing and monitoring are essential practices that help you maintain the quality of your model, identify and troubleshoot issues, and optimize performance over time. This section covers strategies and tools for effectively testing and monitoring your serverless ML model.

Testing Your Serverless Machine Learning Model

Effective testing ensures that your ML model performs as expected and can handle various input scenarios gracefully.

1. Unit Testing:

- **Purpose:** Validate individual components of your Lambda function, such as data preprocessing, feature extraction, and prediction logic.
- **Tools:**
- **PyTest:** A powerful testing framework for Python.
- **Mocking Libraries:** Use unittest.mock to simulate AWS services (e.g.,

S3 interactions).

- **Example:**

```python
Copy code
import pytest
from unittest.mock import patch, MagicMock
from inference import lambda_handler

@patch('inference.joblib.load')
@patch('inference.boto3.client')
def test_lambda_handler(mock_boto3_client, mock_joblib_load):
    # Mock S3 download
    mock_s3 = MagicMock()
    mock_boto3_client.return_value = mock_s3

    # Mock model and vectorizer
    mock_model = MagicMock()
    mock_vectorizer = MagicMock()
    mock_joblib_load.side_effect = [mock_model, mock_vectorizer]
    mock_model.predict.return_value = [1]

    # Define event
    event = {
        'body': '{"text": "I love this product!"}'
    }

    # Call lambda_handler
    response = lambda_handler(event, None)

    # Assertions
    assert response['statusCode'] == 200
    assert json.loads(response['body'])['sentiment'] == 'Positive'
```

2. Integration Testing:

- **Purpose:** Ensure that all components of your serverless architecture (e.g., Lambda function, S3, API Gateway) work together seamlessly.

BUILDING YOUR FIRST SERVERLESS MACHINE LEARNING MODEL

- **Approach:**
- Deploy the function in a test environment.
- Send test requests through the API Gateway.
- Verify end-to-end functionality and data flow.
- **Tools:**
- **Postman:** For sending HTTP requests and validating responses.
- **AWS SAM (Serverless Application Model):** For local testing and deployment simulation.

3. Load Testing:

- **Purpose:** Assess how your Lambda function performs under high traffic conditions and identify potential bottlenecks.
- **Tools:**
- **AWS Lambda Power Tuning:** An open-source tool to optimize Lambda memory settings based on performance and cost.
- **Apache JMeter:** For simulating concurrent requests and measuring response times.
- **Artillery:** A modern, powerful, and easy-to-use load testing toolkit.
- **Example with Artillery:**

```yaml
Copy code
config:
  target:
  'https://your-api-id.execute-api.region.amazonaws.com/prod/predict'
  phases:
    - duration: 60
      arrivalRate: 100
scenarios:
  - flow:
      - post:
          url: "/predict"
          json:
```

```
      text: "This is a test sentence for sentiment analysis."
```

- Run the test:

```bash
Copy code
artillery run load_test.yml
```

4. A/B Testing:

- **Purpose:** Compare the performance of different versions of your ML model to determine which one delivers better results.
- **Approach:**
- Deploy multiple versions of your Lambda function.
- Route a percentage of traffic to each version using API Gateway or AWS Lambda aliases.
- Analyze performance metrics and user feedback to select the optimal model.

5. Functional Testing:

- **Purpose:** Verify that your Lambda function handles different input scenarios correctly, including edge cases and invalid data.
- **Approach:**
- Create test cases for various input types and values.
- Ensure the function returns appropriate responses and error messages.
- **Example: Handling Invalid Inputs**

BUILDING YOUR FIRST SERVERLESS MACHINE LEARNING MODEL

```python
Copy code
def test_lambda_handler_invalid_input():
    event = {
        'body': '{"text": ""}'  # Empty text
    }
    response = lambda_handler(event, None)
    assert response['statusCode'] == 400
    assert 'error' in json.loads(response['body'])
```

Monitoring Your Serverless Machine Learning Model

Continuous monitoring ensures that your ML model maintains its performance and reliability over time. It helps in detecting anomalies, performance degradation, and operational issues promptly.

1. AWS CloudWatch Monitoring:

- **CloudWatch Logs:**
- Automatically collects logs generated by your Lambda function.
- Use structured logging to make it easier to parse and analyze logs.
- Example:

```python
Copy code
import logging

logger = logging.getLogger()
logger.setLevel(logging.INFO)

def lambda_handler(event, context):
    logger.info("Received event: %s", event)
    # Inference logic
```

- **CloudWatch Metrics:**
- **Invocation Count:** Number of times your function is invoked.

- **Duration:** Time taken by your function to execute.
- **Error Count:** Number of failed executions.
- **Throttles:** Number of requests that were throttled due to concurrency limits.
- **Setting Up Alarms:**
- Create CloudWatch Alarms to notify you when certain thresholds are breached, such as high error rates or increased latency.

2. AWS X-Ray for Tracing:

- **Purpose:** Provides end-to-end tracing of requests as they travel through your Lambda function and other AWS services.
- **Benefits:**
- Visualize service maps to identify performance bottlenecks.
- Analyze latency distributions and pinpoint slow components.
- **Setup:**
- Enable X-Ray tracing in your Lambda function settings.
- Instrument your code to include X-Ray annotations and metadata.

3. Application Performance Monitoring (APM) Tools:

- **Third-Party Tools:**
- **Datadog:** Offers comprehensive monitoring, tracing, and logging capabilities for serverless applications.
- **New Relic:** Provides real-time monitoring and insights into Lambda function performance.
- **Lumigo:** Specialized in serverless monitoring with deep insights into function invocations and dependencies.
- **Benefits:**
- Enhanced visibility into function performance and dependencies.
- Advanced analytics and anomaly detection.
- Simplified troubleshooting with intuitive dashboards.

4. Model Performance Monitoring:

- **Concept Drift Detection:**
- Monitor changes in data distribution that may affect model accuracy.
- Use statistical tests or ML-based methods to detect drift.
- **Accuracy and Prediction Tracking:**
- Track the accuracy of your model over time using validation datasets or feedback loops.
- Implement automated alerts when performance drops below a predefined threshold.
- **Tools:**
- **Amazon SageMaker Model Monitor:** Continuously monitors ML models deployed on SageMaker for data and model quality.
- **Custom Dashboards:** Build custom dashboards using CloudWatch or third-party APM tools to visualize model metrics.

5. Logging Best Practices:

- **Structured Logging:**
- Use JSON format for logs to facilitate parsing and analysis.
- Example:

```python
Copy code
logger.info(json.dumps({
    "event": "inference",
    "input": "I love this product!",
    "prediction": "Positive",
    "response_time": 150  # in milliseconds
}))
```

- **Sensitive Data Handling:**
- Avoid logging sensitive information such as personally identifiable

information (PII) or confidential data.
- Implement data masking or redaction where necessary.
- **Centralized Logging:**
- Aggregate logs from all Lambda functions into a centralized location for easier access and analysis.

6. **Security Monitoring:**

- **AWS Security Services:**
- **AWS CloudTrail:** Logs API calls and user activities within your AWS account.
- **AWS Config:** Tracks resource configurations and compliance.
- **Amazon GuardDuty:** Provides intelligent threat detection and continuous security monitoring.
- **Best Practices:**
- Implement the principle of least privilege for IAM roles and permissions.
- Regularly review and audit access logs to detect unauthorized activities.
- Enable encryption for data at rest and in transit to protect sensitive information.

Example: Monitoring and Alerting for Inference Latency

1. **Define Latency Threshold:**

- Set a maximum acceptable inference latency (e.g., 200 milliseconds).

1. **Create a CloudWatch Alarm:**

- Monitor the Duration metric of your Lambda function.
- Configure the alarm to trigger if the average duration exceeds 200 milliseconds over a 5-minute period.

1. **Set Up Notifications:**

- Use Amazon SNS to send notifications via email or SMS when the alarm is triggered.

1. **Analyze and Respond:**

- Investigate the cause of increased latency by reviewing CloudWatch Logs and X-Ray traces.
- Optimize your function code or allocate more memory to reduce execution time.

Automated Model Retraining and Deployment

To maintain model accuracy and performance, implement automated workflows that trigger model retraining and redeployment based on monitoring insights.

1. **Trigger Conditions:**

- Detect concept drift or significant drops in model performance.
- Schedule periodic retraining (e.g., daily, weekly) to incorporate new data.

1. **Orchestrate with AWS Step Functions:**

- Create state machines to automate the retraining process using Step Functions.
- Steps may include data ingestion, model training, evaluation, and deployment.

1. **CI/CD Integration:**

- Use AWS CodePipeline and CodeBuild to automate the deployment of updated models.
- Implement version control to manage different model iterations.

Conclusion

Testing and monitoring are critical components of deploying machine learning models in a serverless environment. By implementing comprehensive testing strategies and leveraging AWS's robust monitoring tools, you can ensure that your ML models remain reliable, accurate, and performant. Continuous monitoring allows you to detect and address issues proactively, while effective testing ensures that your models behave as expected under various conditions. Adopting these practices not only enhances the quality of your machine learning applications but also builds confidence in their deployment within production environments.

Training Machine Learning Models in a Serverless Environment

Training machine learning (ML) models traditionally involves provisioning and managing dedicated infrastructure, which can be time-consuming, costly, and inflexible. Serverless computing revolutionizes this process by abstracting away the underlying infrastructure, allowing data scientists and developers to focus solely on building and optimizing their models. This section explores how to leverage serverless platforms, specifically AWS SageMaker and Google Cloud ML Engine, for training ML models. It also outlines best practices to ensure efficient, scalable, and cost-effective model training in a serverless environment.

1. Using AWS SageMaker for Model Training

Introduction to AWS SageMaker

Amazon SageMaker is a fully managed service provided by Amazon Web Services (AWS) that simplifies the process of building, training, and deploying machine learning models at scale. SageMaker offers a suite of integrated tools and capabilities that streamline the ML workflow, from data preparation and model training to deployment and monitoring. It is designed to cater to both beginners and experienced ML practitioners by providing pre-built algorithms, support for popular ML frameworks, and automated machine learning (AutoML) features.

Key Features of AWS SageMaker

- **Built-In Algorithms:** Optimized algorithms for various ML tasks, including linear regression, classification, and deep learning.
- **Jupyter Notebooks:** Integrated notebooks for interactive data exploration and preprocessing.
- **Automatic Model Tuning:** Hyperparameter optimization to enhance model performance.
- **Managed Training Infrastructure:** Automatic provisioning and scaling of compute resources.
- **Model Deployment:** One-click deployment of trained models to production environments.
- **Integration with AWS Ecosystem:** Seamless integration with AWS services like S3, Lambda, and IAM for data storage, serverless computing, and security.

Setting Up SageMaker

1. **Create an AWS Account:**

- If you haven't already, create an AWS account and sign in to the AWS Management Console.

1. **Access SageMaker:**

- Navigate to the SageMaker service from the AWS Management Console.

1. **Configure IAM Roles:**

- SageMaker requires specific IAM roles to access AWS resources securely.
- Create an IAM role with the necessary permissions for SageMaker to access S3 buckets, CloudWatch logs, and other services.
- Assign this role when creating SageMaker notebooks or training jobs.

1. **Set Up S3 Buckets:**

- Create an S3 bucket to store your training data and model artifacts.
- Ensure proper access permissions are set for the SageMaker IAM role to read from and write to the bucket.

Training a Model on SageMaker

Training a machine learning model on SageMaker involves several steps, from preparing your data to executing the training job and evaluating the model's performance.

Step 1: Data Preparation

1. **Upload Data to S3:**

- Store your training and validation datasets in an S3 bucket.
- Example:

```bash
Copy code
aws s3 cp training_data.
csv s3://your-sagemaker-bucket/data/
aws s3 cp validation_data.
csv s3://your-sagemaker-bucket/data/
```

1. **Launch a SageMaker Notebook Instance:**

- In the SageMaker console, create a new notebook instance.
- Attach the previously created IAM role to the notebook.
- Once the instance is ready, open Jupyter Notebook to begin data exploration and preprocessing.

Step 2: Exploratory Data Analysis (EDA)

1. **Load Data:**

```python
Copy code
import pandas as pd

training_data = pd.
read_csv('s3://your-sagemaker
-bucket/data/training_data.csv')
validation_data = pd.
read_csv('s3://your-sagemaker
-bucket/data/validation_data.csv')
```

1. **Analyze Data:**

- Perform statistical analysis, visualize distributions, and identify patterns or anomalies.
- Example:

```python
Copy code
training_data.describe()
training_data.hist(figsize=(10, 8))
```

Step 3: Data Preprocessing

1. **Handle Missing Values:**

```python
Copy code
training_data.fillna
(training_data.mean(), inplace=True)
```

```
validation_data.
fillna(validation_data.
mean(), inplace=True)
```

1. **Feature Engineering:**

- Create new features or transform existing ones to improve model performance.
- Example:

```python
Copy code
training_data['feature_ratio'] =
 training_data['feature1']
/ training_data['feature2']
validation_data['feature_ratio'] =
 validation_data['feature1']
/ validation_data['feature2']
```

1. **Encoding Categorical Variables:**

```python
Copy code
training_data = pd.
get_dummies(training_data,
columns=['categorical_feature'])
validation_data = pd.
get_dummies
(validation_data,
 columns=['categorical_feature'])
```

Step 4: Model Selection and Training

1. **Choose a Built-In Algorithm:**

- SageMaker offers several built-in algorithms. For example, to use XGBoost:

```python
Copy code
from sagemaker import get_execution_role
import sagemaker

role = get_execution_role()
sagemaker_session = sagemaker.Session()

xgboost_container = sagemaker.image_uris.retrieve("xgboost", sagemaker_session.boto_region_name, "1.0-1")
```

1. **Configure the Training Job:**

```python
Copy code
from sagemaker.estimator import Estimator

xgb = Estimator(
    image_uri=xgboost_container,
    role=role,
    instance_count=1,
    instance_type='ml.m5.large',
    volume_size=5,
    max_run=3600,
    sagemaker_session=sagemaker_session
)
```

```
xgb.set_hyperparameters(
    objective='binary:logistic',
    num_round=100
)
```

1. **Specify Input Data Channels:**

```
python
Copy code
from sagemaker.inputs import TrainingInput

train_input = TrainingInput
(s3_data='s3://your-sagemaker
-bucket/data/training_
data.csv', content_type='csv')
validation_input = TrainingInput
(s3_data='s3://your-sagemaker
-bucket/data/validation_data.csv',
 content_type='csv')

data_channels = {'train': train_input, 'validation':
validation_input}
```

1. **Launch the Training Job:**

```
python
Copy code
xgb.fit(inputs=data_channels)
```

Step 5: Hyperparameter Tuning

1. **Define Hyperparameter Ranges:**

```python
Copy code
from sagemaker.tuner import
HyperparameterTuner, ContinuousParameter,
CategoricalParameter

hyperparameter_ranges = {
    'eta': ContinuousParameter(0.1, 0.5),
    'max_depth':
CategoricalParameter([3, 5, 7]),
    'min_child_weight':
 ContinuousParameter(1, 10)
}
```

1. **Set Objective Metric:**

```python
Copy code
objective_metric_name = 'validation:auc'
objective_type = 'Maximize'
metric_definitions =
[{'Name': 'validation:auc',
  'Regex': 'validation-auc=(\\S+)'}]
```

1. **Configure the Tuner:**

```python
Copy code
tuner = HyperparameterTuner(
    estimator=xgb,
    objective_metric_name=
```

```
    objective_metric_name,
        hyperparameter_ranges=
    hyperparameter_ranges,
        metric_definitions=
    metric_definitions,
        max_jobs=20,
        max_parallel_jobs=5
    )
```

1. **Start Hyperparameter Tuning:**

```
python
Copy code
tuner.fit(inputs=data_channels)
```

Step 6: Model Evaluation

1. **Deploy the Best Model:**

```
python
Copy code
predictor = tuner.deploy(
    initial_instance_count=1,
    instance_type='ml.m5.large'
)
```

1. **Evaluate Model Performance:**

- Send sample predictions and compare them against validation data.
- Example:

```python
Copy code
import numpy as np

sample_data = validation_data.
iloc[:10, :-1].values
predictions = predictor.
predict(sample_data)
print(predictions)
```

1. **Cleanup:**

- Delete the deployed endpoint to avoid incurring additional costs.

```python
Copy code
sagemaker_session.delete_
endpoint(predictor.endpoint_name)
```

Advantages of Using AWS SageMaker for ML

- **End-to-End Managed Service:** Handles infrastructure, allowing you to focus on model development.
- **Scalability:** Easily scale training jobs by selecting appropriate instance types.
- **Integration:** Seamless integration with other AWS services like S3, Lambda, and IAM.
- **Flexibility:** Support for multiple ML frameworks and custom algorithms.
- **AutoML Capabilities:** SageMaker Autopilot automates the ML pipeline, from data preprocessing to model tuning.

TRAINING MACHINE LEARNING MODELS IN A SERVERLESS ENVIRONMENT

Considerations and Limitations

- **Cost:** While SageMaker offers powerful features, costs can accumulate with large-scale training and high resource usage. It's essential to monitor usage and optimize resource allocation.
- **Learning Curve:** Familiarity with AWS services and SageMaker's interface is necessary to fully leverage its capabilities.
- **Vendor Lock-In:** Using proprietary services may make it challenging to migrate to other platforms in the future.

Example Use Case: Image Classification with SageMaker

1. **Data Preparation:**

- Store labeled images in an S3 bucket, organized by class labels.

1. **Launch a Jupyter Notebook Instance:**

- Use the notebook to explore and preprocess image data.

1. **Select a Pre-Built Algorithm:**

- Use SageMaker's built-in image classification algorithm, which leverages transfer learning with ResNet.

1. **Configure and Launch the Training Job:**

- Specify hyperparameters such as image size, batch size, and number of epochs.

1. **Deploy the Trained Model:**

- Create an endpoint for real-time image classification.

1. **Integrate with Applications:**

- Use the endpoint to classify images uploaded via an application interface.

Conclusion

AWS SageMaker provides a robust and scalable environment for training machine learning models in a serverless context. Its comprehensive suite of tools and seamless integration with other AWS services make it an ideal choice for organizations looking to streamline their ML workflows. By leveraging SageMaker's capabilities, data scientists can efficiently build, train, and deploy models without the overhead of managing infrastructure, thereby accelerating the path from experimentation to production.

2. Training and Tuning Models with Google Cloud ML Engine

Introduction to Google Cloud AI Platform (ML Engine)

Google Cloud AI Platform, formerly known as Google Cloud ML Engine, is a managed service that enables developers and data scientists to build, train, and deploy machine learning models at scale. AI Platform integrates seamlessly with other Google Cloud services, providing a robust ecosystem for data storage, processing, and model deployment. It supports popular ML frameworks such as TensorFlow, PyTorch, and Scikit-learn, offering flexibility and scalability for diverse ML workloads.

Key Features of Google Cloud AI Platform

- **Managed Training:** Automatically handles infrastructure provisioning, scaling, and management for training jobs.
- **Hyperparameter Tuning:** Facilitates automated hyperparameter optimization to enhance model performance.
- **Distributed Training:** Supports distributed training across multiple GPUs or TPUs for large-scale models.
- **Model Deployment:** Simplified deployment of trained models to scalable serving infrastructure.
- **Integration with BigQuery and Dataflow:** Streamlines data ingestion and preprocessing workflows.

- **Version Control:** Manage multiple versions of models for experimentation and deployment.

Setting Up Google Cloud AI Platform

1. **Create a Google Cloud Account:**

- If you don't have one, [create a Google Cloud account](#) and sign in to the Google Cloud Console.

1. **Create a New Project:**

- In the Google Cloud Console, click on the project dropdown and select "New Project."
- Provide a project name (e.g., "ServerlessMLProject") and click "Create."

1. **Enable Billing:**

- Ensure that billing is enabled for your project to access all AI Platform features.

1. **Enable Required APIs:**

- Navigate to "APIs & Services" and enable the following APIs:
- **AI Platform API**
- **Cloud Storage API**
- **Compute Engine API**

1. **Set Up Authentication:**

- Install the Google Cloud SDK and initialize it:

```bash
Copy code
gcloud init
```

- Authenticate with your Google account:

```bash
Copy code
gcloud auth login
```

1. **Set Default Project and Region:**

```bash
Copy code
gcloud config set project your-project-id
gcloud config set compute/region us-central1
```

Training a Model with Google Cloud AI Platform

Training a machine learning model on AI Platform involves preparing your code and data, submitting a training job, and monitoring its progress.

Step 1: Data Preparation

1. **Upload Data to Cloud Storage:**

- Create a Cloud Storage bucket to store your training and validation data.

```bash
Copy code
```

```
gsutil mb gs://your-bucket-name/
```

- Upload your datasets:

```bash
Copy code
gsutil cp training_data.
csv gs://your-bucket-name/data/
gsutil cp validation_data.
csv gs://your-bucket-name/data/
```

Step 2: Develop Your Training Code

1. **Structure Your Project Directory:**

```arduino
Copy code
my_ml_project/
  trainer/
    __init__.py
    task.py
    utils.py
  setup.py
  requirements.txt
  training.yaml
```

1. **Define Training Logic (trainer/task.py):**

```python
Copy code
import argparse
import joblib
import pandas as pd
from sklearn.ensemble import RandomForestClassifier
from sklearn.metrics import accuracy_score

def train_model(train_data,
  validation_data, model_output):
    # Load training data
    train_df = pd.read_csv(train_data)
    X_train = train_df.drop('label', axis=1)
    y_train = train_df['label']

    # Load validation data
    val_df = pd.read_csv(validation_data)
    X_val = val_df.drop('label', axis=1)
    y_val = val_df['label']

    # Initialize and train the model
    model = RandomForestClassifier
(n_estimators=100, random_state=42)
    model.fit(X_train, y_train)

    # Evaluate the model
    predictions = model.predict(X_val)
    accuracy = accuracy_score(y_val, predictions)
    print(f'Validation Accuracy: {accuracy}')

    # Save the trained model
    joblib.dump(model, model_output)

if __name__ == '__main__':
    parser = argparse.ArgumentParser()
    parser.add_argument
('--train-data', type=str, required=True)
    parser.add_argument
('--validation-data', type=str, required=True)
    parser.add_argument
```

```
('--model-output', type=str, required=True)
    args = parser.parse_args()

    train_model(args.train_data,
args.validation_data, args.model_output)
```

1. **Define Dependencies (requirements.txt):**

```
Copy code
pandas
scikit-learn
joblib
```

1. **Setup Script (setup.py):**

```python
Copy code
from setuptools import setup, find_packages

setup(
    name='trainer',
    version='0.1',
    packages=find_packages(),
    install_requires=[
        'pandas',
        'scikit-learn',
        'joblib'
    ],
    include_package_data=True,
    description='My ML training project'
)
```

Step 3: Configure the Training Job

1. **Create a Training Configuration File (training.yaml):**

```yaml
Copy code
trainingInput:
  scaleTier: BASIC
  packageUris:
    - gs://your-bucket-name/packages/trainer-0.1.tar.gz
  pythonModule: trainer.task
  args:
    - --train-data
    - gs://your-bucket-name/data/training_data.csv
    - --validation-data
    - gs://your-bucket-name/data/validation_data.csv
    - --model-output
    - gs://your-bucket-name/models/model.joblib
  region: us-central1
```

1. **Package and Upload Your Code:**

```bash
Copy code
cd my_ml_project/
python setup.py sdist
gsutil cp dist/trainer-0.1.tar.gz gs://your-bucket-name/packages/
```

Step 4: Submit the Training Job

1. **Submit the Job Using gcloud:**

```bash
Copy code
gcloud ai-platform jobs submit training my_ml_job_$(date +%Y%m%d_%H%M%S) \
    --config training.yaml \
    --region us-central1 \
    -- \
    --train-data gs://your-bucket-name/data/training_data.csv \
    --validation-data gs://your-bucket-name/data/validation_data.csv \
    --model-output gs://your-bucket-name/models/model.joblib
```

1. **Monitor the Training Job:**

- Navigate to the AI Platform Jobs page in the Google Cloud Console.
- View logs and status updates in real-time.
- Use Cloud Logging for detailed insights.

Step 5: Hyperparameter Tuning

1. **Define Hyperparameter Tuning Configuration (tuning.yaml):**

```yaml
Copy code
trainingInput:
  scaleTier: BASIC
  packageUris:
    - gs://your-bucket-name/packages/trainer-0.1.tar.gz
  pythonModule: trainer.task
  args:
    - --train-data
```

```
    - gs://your-bucket-name/data/training_data.csv
    - --validation-data
    - gs://your-bucket-name/data/validation_data.csv
    - --model-output
    - gs://your-bucket-name/models/model.joblib
hyperparameters:
  goal: MAXIMIZE
  objectiveMetricName: validation_accuracy
  hyperparameterMetricTag: validation_accuracy
  maxTrials: 10
  maxParallelTrials: 2
  params:
    - parameterName: n_estimators
      type: INTEGER
      minValue: 50
      maxValue: 200
    - parameterName: max_depth
      type: INTEGER
      minValue: 3
      maxValue: 15
    - parameterName: min_samples_split
      type: INTEGER
      minValue: 2
      maxValue: 10
  region: us-central1
```

1. **Submit the Hyperparameter Tuning Job:**

```bash
Copy code
gcloud ai-platform jobs submit training my_ml_tuning_job_$(date +%Y%m%d_%H%M%S) \
    --config tuning.yaml \
    --region us-central1 \
    -- \
    --train-data gs://your-bucket-name/data/training_data.csv \
```

```
    --validation-data gs://your-
bucket-name/data/validation_data.csv \
    --model-output gs:
//your-bucket-name/models/model.joblib
```

1. **Review Tuning Results:**

- Access the AI Platform Hyperparameter Tuning page to review the performance of different hyperparameter combinations.
- Select the best-performing model based on validation accuracy or your chosen metric.

Step 6: Model Deployment

1. **Deploy the Trained Model to AI Platform Prediction:**

```bash
Copy code
gcloud ai-platform models create my_ml_model --regions us-central1

gcloud ai-platform versions create v1 \
    --model my_ml_model \
    --origin gs://your-bucket-name/models/ \
    --runtime-version 2.1 \
    --python-version 3.7 \
    --framework SCIKIT_LEARN \
    --machine-type n1-standard-4
```

1. **Make Predictions Using the Deployed Model:**

```python
Copy code
from google.cloud import aiplatform

client = aiplatform.gapic.PredictionServiceClient()

endpoint = client.endpoint_path(
    project='your-project-id',
    location='us-central1',
    endpoint='your-endpoint-id'
)

instances = [{"feature1": value1,
"feature2": value2, ...}]
parameters = {}

response = client.predict(
    endpoint=endpoint,
    instances=instances,
    parameters=parameters
)

print("Predictions:", response.predictions)
```

Advantages of Using Google Cloud AI Platform for ML

- **Managed Infrastructure:** Automates the provisioning and scaling of resources for training and serving models.
- **Flexibility:** Supports multiple ML frameworks and custom training scripts.
- **Integration:** Seamless integration with other GCP services like BigQuery, Dataflow, and Cloud Storage.
- **Hyperparameter Tuning:** Efficiently optimizes model performance through automated hyperparameter searches.
- **Distributed Training:** Enables training on multiple GPUs or TPUs for large-scale models.

Considerations and Limitations

- **Cost Management:** Like AWS SageMaker, costs can escalate with extensive training jobs and resource usage. Monitor and optimize usage to manage expenses.
- **Learning Curve:** Familiarity with GCP services and AI Platform's specific configurations is necessary to maximize its benefits.
- **Vendor Lock-In:** Relying on GCP-specific services may complicate migrations to other cloud providers.

Example Use Case: Text Classification with AI Platform

1. **Data Preparation:**

- Store labeled text data in a Cloud Storage bucket.

1. **Develop Training Code:**

- Use TensorFlow or Scikit-learn to build a text classification model.
- Include preprocessing steps like tokenization and vectorization.

1. **Submit a Training Job:**

- Package the training code and dependencies.
- Launch a training job with AI Platform, specifying the compute resources and training parameters.

1. **Hyperparameter Tuning:**

- Configure a hyperparameter tuning job to optimize parameters like learning rate, batch size, and number of layers.

1. **Deploy the Model:**

- Deploy the trained model to AI Platform Prediction.
- Integrate the prediction endpoint with your application to classify incoming text data in real-time.

Conclusion

Google Cloud AI Platform offers a robust and scalable environment for training and deploying machine learning models in a serverless fashion. Its integration with a wide array of Google Cloud services and support for multiple ML frameworks make it a versatile choice for diverse ML projects. By leveraging AI Platform's managed services, data scientists can accelerate the model development lifecycle, from data preprocessing and training to hyperparameter tuning and deployment, all while maintaining flexibility and control over their ML workflows.

3. Serverless Model Training Best Practices

Training machine learning models in a serverless environment offers numerous benefits, including scalability, cost-efficiency, and simplified infrastructure management. However, to fully harness these advantages and mitigate potential challenges, it is essential to follow best practices tailored to serverless ML workflows. This section outlines key best practices for training ML models in a serverless context, focusing on optimization, automation, security, and performance.

1. Optimize Resource Utilization

Efficient use of computational resources is crucial to minimize costs and ensure timely model training.

- **Select Appropriate Instance Types:**
- Choose serverless platforms that offer a variety of instance types optimized for different workloads (e.g., CPU vs. GPU).
- For example, AWS SageMaker provides instance types like ml.p3 for GPU-accelerated training.
- **Right-Size Your Resources:**
- Allocate just enough memory and compute power required for your training jobs to avoid over-provisioning.

TRAINING MACHINE LEARNING MODELS IN A SERVERLESS ENVIRONMENT

- Monitor resource usage and adjust configurations based on performance metrics.
- **Leverage Spot Instances (If Available):**
- Use spot or preemptible instances to reduce costs, especially for non-critical or time-flexible training tasks.
- Be aware of the potential for interruptions and design your workflows to handle instance terminations gracefully.

2. Automate ML Pipelines

Automation enhances efficiency, reduces manual errors, and accelerates the ML lifecycle.

- **Use Managed Pipelines:**
- Utilize services like AWS SageMaker Pipelines or Google Cloud AI Platform Pipelines to orchestrate complex ML workflows.
- Define pipeline steps for data ingestion, preprocessing, training, evaluation, and deployment.
- **Implement CI/CD for ML:**
- Integrate continuous integration and continuous deployment (CI/CD) practices to automate testing and deployment of models.
- Tools like AWS CodePipeline, Google Cloud Build, and Jenkins can facilitate automated workflows.
- **Scheduled Retraining:**
- Automate periodic retraining of models to incorporate new data and maintain model accuracy.
- Use scheduling services like AWS EventBridge or Google Cloud Scheduler to trigger retraining jobs.

3. Monitor and Log Training Jobs

Continuous monitoring and logging are essential for maintaining model performance and diagnosing issues.

- **Centralized Logging:**

- Aggregate logs from all training jobs into a centralized logging service (e.g., AWS CloudWatch, Google Cloud Logging).
- Use structured logging formats (e.g., JSON) to simplify log parsing and analysis.
- **Performance Metrics:**
- Track key metrics such as training time, resource utilization, model accuracy, and loss.
- Implement dashboards using tools like AWS CloudWatch Dashboards or Google Data Studio to visualize metrics.
- **Alerting and Notifications:**
- Set up alerts for abnormal training behaviors, such as unexpected increases in training time or drops in model performance.
- Use notification services like AWS SNS or Google Cloud Pub/Sub to receive real-time alerts.

4. Ensure Security and Compliance

Protecting data and maintaining compliance with regulations are paramount in ML workflows.

- **Data Encryption:**
- Encrypt data at rest using services like AWS KMS or Google Cloud KMS.
- Ensure data in transit is secured using TLS/SSL protocols.
- **Access Control:**
- Implement the principle of least privilege by assigning minimal IAM roles and permissions required for training jobs.
- Regularly audit and review IAM policies to prevent unauthorized access.
- **Secure Storage:**
- Store sensitive data in secure storage services like AWS S3 with proper access controls or Google Cloud Storage with appropriate bucket policies.
- **Compliance Certifications:**
- Ensure that your serverless ML workflows comply with industry-specific regulations (e.g., GDPR, HIPAA) by leveraging compliant cloud services.

TRAINING MACHINE LEARNING MODELS IN A SERVERLESS ENVIRONMENT

5. Manage Costs Effectively

Cost management is critical to maintaining budget constraints while scaling ML workloads.

- **Monitor Usage:**
- Continuously monitor resource usage and costs using cloud provider dashboards (e.g., AWS Cost Explorer, Google Cloud Billing).
- Identify and address cost drivers, such as underutilized resources or inefficient training jobs.
- **Implement Budget Alerts:**
- Set budget limits and receive notifications when spending approaches or exceeds predefined thresholds.
- Use tools like AWS Budgets or Google Cloud Budgets for automated cost tracking.
- **Optimize Training Jobs:**
- Reduce training times by optimizing code and leveraging efficient algorithms.
- Utilize early stopping techniques to halt training once performance criteria are met.
- **Use Reserved Resources:**
- For predictable workloads, consider reserved instances or committed use contracts to benefit from discounted pricing.

6. Ensure Scalability and Reliability

Building scalable and reliable ML training workflows ensures that your models can grow and adapt to changing demands.

- **Design for Scalability:**
- Architect your ML pipelines to handle increasing data volumes and complexity.
- Utilize scalable storage solutions and distributed training techniques where necessary.
- **Implement Fault Tolerance:**

- Design training jobs to recover gracefully from failures by implementing retry mechanisms and checkpoints.
- Use services like AWS Step Functions or Google Cloud Workflows to manage retries and error handling.
- **High Availability:**
- Deploy training jobs across multiple regions or availability zones to enhance resilience.
- Use multi-zone or multi-region storage solutions to prevent data loss and ensure continuity.

7. Maintain Reproducibility and Version Control

Reproducibility ensures that ML experiments can be reliably repeated, while version control facilitates tracking changes and collaboration.

- **Version Control for Code and Models:**
- Use Git repositories (e.g., GitHub, GitLab) to manage training scripts and configuration files.
- Store trained model artifacts with versioning enabled in storage services like AWS S3 or Google Cloud Storage.
- **Experiment Tracking:**
- Implement experiment tracking tools like MLflow, Weights & Biases, or TensorBoard to log experiments, parameters, and results.
- Maintain a centralized repository of experiment logs for analysis and comparison.
- **Environment Consistency:**
- Use containerization (e.g., Docker) to encapsulate training environments, ensuring consistency across development, testing, and production stages.
- Leverage environment management tools like Conda or virtualenv to manage dependencies.

8. Handle Data Efficiently

Efficient data handling is essential to reduce bottlenecks and ensure smooth training workflows.

- **Data Storage Optimization:**
  - Use optimized data formats like Parquet or TFRecord to enhance read and write performance.
  - Partition large datasets to improve parallel processing and reduce data retrieval times.
- **Data Streaming:**
  - Implement data streaming techniques for real-time data ingestion and preprocessing.
  - Use services like AWS Kinesis or Google Cloud Pub/Sub to handle streaming data effectively.
- **Data Caching:**
  - Cache frequently accessed data in-memory using services like AWS ElastiCache or Google Cloud Memorystore to speed up data retrieval during training.

9. Model Versioning

Managing multiple versions of ML models is crucial for experimentation, deployment, and rollback purposes.

- **Version Control Systems:**
  - Use systems like Git to manage different versions of training scripts and model configurations.
- **Model Registry:**
  - Implement a model registry (e.g., SageMaker Model Registry, MLflow Model Registry) to catalog and manage different model versions systematically.
- **Deployment Strategies:**
  - Use blue-green deployments or canary releases to deploy new model versions gradually, minimizing the impact of potential issues.

10. Experiment Tracking

Keeping track of experiments, including hyperparameters, metrics, and artifacts, is vital for informed decision-making and model improvement.

- **Tools for Experiment Tracking:**
- **MLflow:** An open-source platform for managing the ML lifecycle, including experimentation, reproducibility, and deployment.
- **Weights & Biases:** Provides experiment tracking, model optimization, and collaboration features.
- **TensorBoard:** Offers visualization tools for TensorFlow models, tracking metrics, and visualizing model architectures.
- **Implementing Experiment Tracking:**
- Integrate tracking tools into your training scripts to log hyperparameters, metrics, and artifacts automatically.
- Example with MLflow:

```python
Copy code
import mlflow
import mlflow.sklearn

def train_model():
    with mlflow.start_run():
        model = RandomForestClassifier(n_estimators=100, random_state=42)
        model.fit(X_train, y_train)
        predictions = model.predict(X_val)
        accuracy = accuracy_score(y_val, predictions)

        mlflow.log_param("n_estimators", 100)
        mlflow.log_metric("accuracy", accuracy)
        mlflow.sklearn.log_model(model, "model")
```

Best Practices Summary

- **Resource Optimization:** Continuously monitor and adjust resource allocations to balance performance and cost.
- **Pipeline Automation:** Automate repetitive tasks to enhance efficiency and reduce human error.

- **Robust Monitoring:** Implement comprehensive monitoring and alerting to maintain model performance and operational health.
- **Security First:** Prioritize data security and compliance to protect sensitive information and adhere to regulations.
- **Cost Awareness:** Regularly review and optimize costs to ensure budget adherence without compromising performance.
- **Scalability Planning:** Design ML workflows to scale seamlessly with growing data and user demands.
- **Reproducibility and Versioning:** Maintain consistent and trackable workflows to facilitate collaboration and reliable model performance.
- **Efficient Data Management:** Optimize data storage and processing to support fast and effective training.
- **Model Governance:** Implement strict governance practices to manage model versions, deployments, and lifecycle effectively.

Conclusion

Training machine learning models in a serverless environment requires a strategic approach to leverage the inherent benefits of serverless computing while addressing its unique challenges. By following best practices focused on optimization, automation, security, and scalability, you can build efficient and robust ML workflows that maximize performance and minimize costs. Embracing these practices ensures that your serverless ML models are not only powerful and accurate but also maintainable and scalable as your projects evolve.

Conclusion

Training machine learning models in a serverless environment opens up new possibilities for scalability, cost-efficiency, and streamlined workflows. Platforms like AWS SageMaker and Google Cloud AI Platform provide robust, managed services that handle the heavy lifting of infrastructure management, allowing you to focus on what truly matters—developing and optimizing your models. By adhering to serverless ML best practices, you can ensure that your training processes are efficient, secure, and scalable, setting the foundation for successful ML deployments.

Whether you choose AWS SageMaker for its comprehensive integration with the AWS ecosystem or Google Cloud AI Platform for its flexibility and powerful ML tools, the key is to leverage the strengths of these platforms to meet your specific ML needs. As serverless technologies continue to evolve, they will undoubtedly play an increasingly pivotal role in the machine learning landscape, enabling faster innovation and more accessible ML solutions for organizations of all sizes.

Deploying Machine Learning Models Using Serverless Functions

Deploying machine learning (ML) models using serverless functions offers a streamlined, scalable, and cost-effective approach to serving predictions in real-time. Serverless architectures abstract away the complexities of server management, allowing developers and data scientists to focus solely on model development and inference logic. This comprehensive guide delves into the process of deploying ML models using serverless functions, with a particular focus on AWS Lambda and API Gateway. We will cover creating serverless functions to deploy models, integrating them with API Gateway for real-time predictions, building a RESTful API for ML model inference, and managing serverless deployments effectively.

1. Creating Serverless Functions to Deploy Models

Serverless functions, such as AWS Lambda, enable you to run your ML models without managing servers. This section outlines the steps to create and deploy serverless functions for ML model inference.

1.1. Overview of Serverless Functions for ML Deployment

- **Advantages:**
- **Scalability:** Automatically scales with the number of incoming requests.
- **Cost-Efficiency:** Pay only for the compute time consumed during

function execution.
- **Simplified Management:** No need to provision or manage servers.
- **Quick Deployment:** Rapidly deploy updates and new models.
- **Use Cases:**
  - Real-time predictions (e.g., image classification, sentiment analysis).
  - Batch processing and data transformations.
  - Integrating ML models into microservices architectures.

1.2. Setting Up AWS Lambda for ML Deployment

AWS Lambda is a popular serverless compute service that can be leveraged to deploy ML models. Below are the detailed steps to create and deploy a Lambda function for model inference.

Step 1: Prepare Your ML Model

1. **Train and Save the Model:**

- Train your ML model using your preferred framework (e.g., Scikit-learn, TensorFlow, PyTorch).
- Save the trained model to a file using serialization libraries like joblib or pickle.

```python
Copy code
# Example with Scikit-learn
from sklearn.ensemble import RandomForestClassifier
import joblib

# Train the model
model = RandomForestClassifier(n_estimators=100, random_state=42)
model.fit(X_train, y_train)

# Save the model
joblib.dump(model, 'model.joblib')
```

1. **Optimize the Model:**

- **Compression:** Reduce the model size using techniques like quantization or pruning.
- **Dependency Minimization:** Include only essential libraries to minimize the deployment package size.

Step 2: Create an S3 Bucket for Model Storage

1. **Navigate to Amazon S3:**

- Log in to the AWS Management Console.
- Go to the S3 service.

1. **Create a New Bucket:**

- Click "Create bucket."
- Enter a unique bucket name (e.g., my-ml-models).
- Choose the desired region.
- Configure any additional settings as needed (e.g., versioning, encryption).

1. **Upload the Model:**

- Upload your serialized model file (model.joblib) to the S3 bucket.

Step 3: Create an IAM Role for Lambda

1. **Navigate to IAM:**

- Go to the IAM (Identity and Access Management) service in the AWS Console.

1. **Create a New Role:**

- Click "Roles" > "Create role."
- Select "Lambda" as the use case.
- Click "Next: Permissions."

1. **Attach Policies:**

- **AWSLambdaBasicExecutionRole:** Grants permissions for CloudWatch Logs.
- **AmazonS3ReadOnlyAccess:** Allows the Lambda function to read the model from S3.
- Alternatively, create a custom policy with least privilege.

1. **Name and Create the Role:**

- Name the role (e.g., LambdaS3AccessRole).
- Complete the creation process.

Step 4: Develop the Lambda Function Code

1. **Set Up Your Development Environment:**

- Install the AWS CLI and AWS SAM (Serverless Application Model) if you plan to use infrastructure as code.

1. **Function Code Example (lambda_function.py):**

```python
Copy code
import json
import joblib
import boto3
import os
```

DEPLOYING MACHINE LEARNING MODELS USING SERVERLESS FUNCTIONS

```python
s3 = boto3.client('s3')

# Environment variables for bucket and model file
MODEL_BUCKET = os.environ['MODEL_BUCKET']
MODEL_KEY = os.environ['MODEL_KEY']

# Load the model once when the Lambda function initializes
def load_model():
    local_path = '/tmp/model.joblib'
    s3.download_file
(MODEL_BUCKET, MODEL_KEY, local_path)
    model = joblib.load(local_path)
    return model

# Initialize the model
model = load_model()

def lambda_handler(event, context):
    try:
        # Parse input data
        body = json.loads(event['body'])
        features = body['features']
# Expecting a list of feature values

        # Make prediction
        prediction = model.predict([features])
        result = prediction[0]

        # Prepare response
        response = {
            'statusCode': 200,
            'body': json.dumps
({'prediction': result})
        }
    except Exception as e:
        # Handle errors
        response = {
            'statusCode': 500,
            'body': json.dumps
```

```
({'error': str(e)})
      }

    return response
```

1. **Package Dependencies:**

- Create a deployment package that includes your function code and any dependencies.

```bash
Copy code
mkdir package
cd package
pip install joblib -t .
pip install scikit-learn -t .
pip install numpy -t .
cp ../lambda_function.py .
zip -r ../function.zip .
```

- Alternatively, use Lambda Layers to manage dependencies separately.

Step 5: Deploy the Lambda Function

1. **Navigate to AWS Lambda:**

- In the AWS Management Console, go to the Lambda service.

1. **Create a New Function:**

- Click "Create function."
- **Name:** MLModelInferenceFunction

- **Runtime:** Python 3.8 (or your preferred runtime)
- **Permissions:** Choose "Use an existing role" and select LambdaS3AccessRole.

1. **Upload the Deployment Package:**

- Under "Function code," select "Upload from" > ".zip file."
- Upload the function.zip file created earlier.

1. **Configure Environment Variables:**

- **MODEL_BUCKET:** my-ml-models
- **MODEL_KEY:** model.joblib

1. **Adjust Memory and Timeout Settings:**

- **Memory:** Allocate sufficient memory based on model requirements (e.g., 512 MB to 3 GB).
- **Timeout:** Set an appropriate timeout (e.g., 30 seconds for inference).

1. **Save the Function:**

- Click "Save" to finalize the Lambda function creation.

1.3. Alternative: Deploying with AWS SAM (Serverless Application Model)

AWS SAM allows you to define serverless applications using YAML templates, enabling infrastructure as code and simplified deployments.

Step 1: Install AWS SAM

- Follow the AWS SAM installation guide.

Step 2: Define the SAM Template (template.yaml)

```yaml
Copy code
AWSTemplateFormatVersion: '2010-09-09'
Transform: AWS::Serverless-2016-10-31
Description: Serverless ML Model Inference

Resources:
  MLModelInferenceFunction:
    Type: AWS::Serverless::Function
    Properties:
      Handler: lambda_function.lambda_handler
      Runtime: python3.8
      Role: arn:aws:iam::123456789012:role/LambdaS3AccessRole
      CodeUri: ./function.zip
      MemorySize: 1024
      Timeout: 30
      Environment:
        Variables:
          MODEL_BUCKET: my-ml-models
          MODEL_KEY: model.joblib
      Policies:
        - S3ReadPolicy:
            BucketName: my-ml-models
```

Step 3: Build and Deploy with SAM

```bash
Copy code
# Package the application
sam package --template-file template.yaml --output-template-file packaged.yaml --s3-bucket your-deployment-bucket

# Deploy the application
sam deploy --template-
```

DEPLOYING MACHINE LEARNING MODELS USING SERVERLESS FUNCTIONS

```
file packaged.yaml
--stack-name MLModelInferenceStack
--capabilities CAPABILITY_IAM
```

2. API Gateway Integration for Real-Time Predictions

Integrating AWS Lambda with API Gateway enables you to expose your ML model as a RESTful API, allowing applications to make real-time predictions via HTTP requests. This section details the steps to set up API Gateway and integrate it with your Lambda function.

2.1. Overview of API Gateway

Amazon API Gateway is a fully managed service that makes it easy to create, publish, maintain, monitor, and secure APIs at any scale. It acts as a "front door" for applications to access data, business logic, or functionality from your backend services, such as Lambda functions.

- **Key Features:**
- **Scalability:** Handles thousands of concurrent API calls.
- **Security:** Offers authentication and authorization via IAM, Cognito, and Lambda authorizers.
- **Monitoring:** Integrates with CloudWatch for logging and metrics.
- **Transformation:** Supports request/response transformations and data mapping.

2.2. Setting Up API Gateway
Step 1: Create a New API

1. **Navigate to API Gateway:**

- In the AWS Management Console, go to the API Gateway service.

1. **Create a New REST API:**

- Click "Create API."

- Select "REST API" and choose "Build."

1. **Configure API Settings:**

- **API Name:** MLModelAPI
- **Description:** API for ML Model Inference
- **Endpoint Type:** Regional (default) or Edge-Optimized based on your needs.
- Click "Create API."

Step 2: Define API Resources and Methods

1. **Create a Resource:**

- Under your API, click "Actions" > "Create Resource."
- **Resource Name:** predict
- **Resource Path:** /predict
- Click "Create Resource."

1. **Create a POST Method:**

- Select the /predict resource.
- Click "Actions" > "Create Method" > select "POST" from the dropdown and click the checkmark.

1. **Configure the Integration Request:**

- **Integration Type:** Lambda Function
- **Lambda Region:** Select the region where your Lambda function resides (e.g., us-east-1).
- **Lambda Function:** Enter MLModelInferenceFunction
- **Use Default Timeout:** Checked
- Click "Save."

- **Grant API Gateway Permission to Invoke Lambda:** Click "OK."

1. **Configure Method Request and Response (Optional):**

- **Request Validation:** Validate input payloads if necessary.
- **Response Models:** Define models for different response types (e.g., success, error).

Step 3: Deploy the API

1. **Create a Deployment Stage:**

- Click "Actions" > "Deploy API."
- **Deployment Stage:** prod (or create a new stage, e.g., dev, staging)
- **Stage Description:** Production stage
- **Deployment Description:** Initial deployment
- Click "Deploy."

1. **Note the Invoke URL:**

- After deployment, you will receive an Invoke URL (e.g., https://your-api-id.execute-api.region.amazonaws.com/prod/predict).

2.3. Securing the API

Securing your API is crucial to prevent unauthorized access and ensure data integrity.

1. **Enable Authentication and Authorization**

- **API Keys:** Require API keys for accessing the API.
- **IAM Roles:** Use IAM roles and policies to control access.
- **Cognito User Pools:** Integrate with Amazon Cognito for user authentication.
- **Lambda Authorizers:** Implement custom authorization logic using

Lambda functions.

2. Enable HTTPS

- **Endpoint Security:** API Gateway automatically provisions HTTPS endpoints, ensuring that all data is encrypted in transit.

3. Rate Limiting and Throttling

- **Prevent Abuse:** Configure usage plans and set limits on the number of requests per second or per day.
- **Burst Limits:** Define burst capacity to handle sudden spikes in traffic.

4. Input Validation and Transformation

- **Model Validation:** Validate incoming data to ensure it meets the required format and constraints.
- **Transformation Templates:** Use VTL (Velocity Template Language) to transform request and response payloads.

2.4. Testing the API Integration

1. **Using Postman or cURL:**

- **Sample Request:**

```bash
Copy code
curl -X POST
https://your-api-id.execute-api.region.amazonaws.com/prod/predict \
-H "Content-Type: application/json" \
-d '{"features":
```

DEPLOYING MACHINE LEARNING MODELS USING SERVERLESS FUNCTIONS

```
[value1, value2, value3, ...]}'
```

- **Expected Response:**

```json
Copy code
{
  "prediction": "class_label"
}
```

1. **Verify Lambda Execution:**

- Check CloudWatch Logs for your Lambda function to ensure it received and processed the request correctly.

1. **Handle Errors:**

- **Invalid Inputs:** Ensure the API gracefully handles invalid or malformed requests.
- **Internal Errors:** Return meaningful error messages without exposing sensitive information.

2.5. Enhancing API Performance

- **Caching:**
- Enable API Gateway caching to store responses for identical requests, reducing Lambda invocations and improving response times.
- **Provisioned Concurrency:**
- Use AWS Lambda's provisioned concurrency to reduce cold start latencies, especially for latency-sensitive applications.
- **Optimize Payload Size:**

- Minimize the size of request and response payloads to enhance transmission speeds and reduce processing time.

3. Building a RESTful API for ML Model Inference

Creating a RESTful API provides a standardized way for applications to interact with your ML model, facilitating integration and scalability. This section outlines the principles of RESTful APIs, designs the API endpoints, and provides implementation details using AWS services.

3.1. Understanding RESTful APIs

- **REST (Representational State Transfer):**
- An architectural style for designing networked applications.
- Emphasizes stateless communication, resource-based URLs, and standard HTTP methods.
- **Key Principles:**
- **Statelessness:** Each request contains all the information needed to process it.
- **Client-Server Architecture:** Separation of concerns between client and server.
- **Uniform Interface:** Standardized methods and response formats.
- **Scalability:** Supports horizontal scaling through stateless interactions.

3.2. Designing the API Endpoints

- **Endpoint Structure:**
- **Base URL:** https://your-api-id.execute-api.region.amazonaws.com/prod
- **Resources:** Represent entities or services (e.g., /predict).
- **Common HTTP Methods:**
- **POST:** Create or process resources (e.g., submit data for prediction).
- **GET:** Retrieve resources (e.g., check API status).
- **Response Formats:**
- **JSON:** Standard format for sending structured data over APIs.

DEPLOYING MACHINE LEARNING MODELS USING SERVERLESS FUNCTIONS

- **Example Endpoint:**
- **POST /predict:** Accepts input features and returns the ML model's prediction.

3.3. Implementing the RESTful API with AWS Services
Step 1: Define the API Structure

1. **Identify Resources:**

- For ML inference, the primary resource is the prediction endpoint.

1. **Define HTTP Methods:**

- **POST /predict:** Submit data for prediction.

Step 2: Develop the Lambda Function for Inference

1. **Refine the Lambda Function Code:**

- Ensure the function can handle different types of input data and return structured responses.

```python
Copy code
import json
import joblib
import boto3
import os

s3 = boto3.client('s3')

MODEL_BUCKET = os.environ['MODEL_BUCKET']
MODEL_KEY = os.environ['MODEL_KEY']
```

```python
def load_model():
    local_path = '/tmp/model.joblib'
    s3.download_file(MODEL_BUCKET, MODEL_KEY, local_path)
    model = joblib.load(local_path)
    return model

model = load_model()

def lambda_handler(event, context):
    try:
        body = json.loads(event['body'])
        features = body['features']

        # Validate input
        if not isinstance(features, list):
            raise ValueError("Features should be a list of numerical values.")

        prediction = model.predict([features])
        result = prediction[0]

        response = {
            'statusCode': 200,
            'body': json.dumps({'prediction': result})
        }
    except Exception as e:
        response = {
            'statusCode': 400,
            'body': json.dumps({'error': str(e)})
        }

    return response
```

1. **Handle Input Validation:**

- Ensure the input data is in the expected format and handle exceptions gracefully.

Step 3: Enhance API Gateway with Swagger/OpenAPI (Optional)

1. **Define API Specifications:**

- Use Swagger/OpenAPI to define your API endpoints, request/response schemas, and authentication methods.

1. **Import API Definition:**

- In API Gateway, import the Swagger/OpenAPI definition to automate the API setup.

Step 4: Implement Additional API Features

1. **Request Validation:**

- Define JSON schema validators to ensure incoming requests meet the required structure.
- Example: Validate that the features field is present and is an array of numbers.

1. **Response Transformation:**

- Modify the response payload to include additional information or reformat data as needed.

1. **Throttling and Quotas:**

- Implement rate limits to protect your backend services from being overwhelmed by excessive requests.

1. **Caching:**

- Cache frequent prediction results to reduce latency and Lambda invocations.

1. **Security Enhancements:**

- **CORS (Cross-Origin Resource Sharing):** Configure CORS settings to allow or restrict API access from different domains.
- **API Keys and Usage Plans:** Restrict access to authorized users and monitor usage.

3.4. Example: Building a Sentiment Analysis RESTful API

Let's walk through an example of deploying a sentiment analysis ML model as a RESTful API using AWS Lambda and API Gateway.

Step 1: Train and Save the Sentiment Analysis Model

1. **Train the Model:**

```python
Copy code
from sklearn.feature_extraction.text import TfidfVectorizer
from sklearn.linear_model import LogisticRegression
import joblib
import pandas as pd

# Sample training data
data = pd.DataFrame({
    'text': ["I love this product!",
 "This is the worst experience.", ...],
    'label': [1, 0, ...]
 # 1 for positive, 0 for negative
})
```

DEPLOYING MACHINE LEARNING MODELS USING SERVERLESS FUNCTIONS

```
# Vectorize text data
vectorizer = TfidfVectorizer
(max_features=1000)
X = vectorizer.
fit_transform(data['text'])
y = data['label']

# Train the model
model = LogisticRegression()
model.fit(X, y)

# Save the model and vectorizer
joblib.dump(model, 'sentiment_model.joblib')
joblib.dump(vectorizer, 'vectorizer.joblib')
```

1. **Upload Models to S3:**

- Upload sentiment_model.joblib and vectorizer.joblib to your S3 bucket (my-ml-models).

Step 2: Create and Configure the Lambda Function

1. **Function Code (lambda_function.py):**

```python
Copy code
import json
import joblib
import boto3
import os

s3 = boto3.client('s3')

MODEL_BUCKET = os.environ['MODEL_BUCKET']
```

```python
MODEL_KEY = os.environ['MODEL_KEY']
VECTORIZER_KEY = os.environ['VECTORIZER_KEY']

def load_artifacts():
    # Download and load the model
    model_path = '/tmp/sentiment_model.joblib'
    vectorizer_path = '/tmp/vectorizer.joblib'
    s3.download_file(MODEL_BUCKET,
 MODEL_KEY, model_path)
    s3.download_file(MODEL_BUCKET,
VECTORIZER_KEY, vectorizer_path)
    model = joblib.load(model_path)
    vectorizer = joblib.load(vectorizer_path)
    return model, vectorizer

# Load model and vectorizer at initialization
model, vectorizer = load_artifacts()

def lambda_handler(event, context):
    try:
        body = json.loads(event['body'])
        text = body['text']

        if not isinstance(text, str)
 or not text.strip():
            raise ValueError
("Input 'text' must be a non-empty string.")

        # Preprocess input
        X = vectorizer.transform([text])

        # Make prediction
        prediction = model.predict(X)[0]
        sentiment = 'Positive'
 if prediction == 1 else 'Negative'

        # Return response
        response = {
            'statusCode': 200,
            'body': json.dumps
```

```
({'sentiment': sentiment})
        }
    except Exception as e:
        response = {
            'statusCode': 400,
            'body': json.dumps
({'error': str(e)})
        }
    return response
```

1. **Package the Function and Dependencies:**

```bash
Copy code
mkdir package
cd package
pip install joblib scikit-learn pandas -t .
cp ../lambda_function.py .
zip -r ../sentiment_api.zip .
```

1. **Create the Lambda Function:**

- Follow the steps in **1.2.2** to create a new Lambda function named SentimentAnalysisFunction.
- Upload sentiment_api.zip.
- Set environment variables:
- **MODEL_BUCKET:** my-ml-models
- **MODEL_KEY:** sentiment_model.joblib
- **VECTORIZER_KEY:** vectorizer.joblib
- Allocate sufficient memory (e.g., 1024 MB) and set an appropriate timeout (e.g., 30 seconds).

Step 3: Integrate Lambda with API Gateway

1. **Create a New REST API:**

- As described in **2.2.1**, create an API named SentimentAPI.

1. **Create a /sentiment Resource and POST Method:**

- **Resource Name:** sentiment
- **Method:** POST
- **Integration Type:** Lambda Function (SentimentAnalysisFunction)

1. **Deploy the API:**

- Deploy to the prod stage.
- Obtain the Invoke URL, e.g., https://your-api-id.execute-api.region.amazonaws.com/prod/sentiment

Step 4: Test the Sentiment Analysis API

1. **Send a Test Request:**

```bash
Copy code
curl -X POST https://your-api-id.execute-api.region.amazonaws.com/prod/sentiment \
-H "Content-Type: application/json" \
-d '{"text": "I am extremely happy with the service!"}'
```

1. **Expected Response:**

```json
Copy code
{
  "sentiment": "Positive"
}
```

1. **Error Handling:**

- Test with invalid inputs to ensure error responses are handled correctly.

```bash
Copy code
curl -X POST https://your-api-id.execute-api.region.amazonaws.com/prod/sentiment \
-H "Content-Type: application/json" \
-d '{"text": ""}'
```

1. **Response:**

```json
Copy code
{
  "error": "Input 'text' must be a non-empty string."
}
```

3.5. Securing the RESTful API

Security is paramount to protect your ML models and data from unauthorized access and malicious attacks.

1. Implement Authentication and Authorization

- **AWS IAM Authorization:**
- Restrict API access using IAM roles and policies.
- Require signed requests using AWS Signature Version 4.
- **Amazon Cognito:**
- Integrate with Amazon Cognito User Pools for user authentication.
- Use JWT tokens to authorize API requests.
- **Lambda Authorizers:**
- Create custom Lambda functions to handle complex authorization logic.
- Validate tokens or API keys before allowing access to the API.

2. Enable CORS (Cross-Origin Resource Sharing)

- **Purpose:** Allow or restrict API access from different domains.
- **Configuration:**
- In API Gateway, enable CORS for the /predict resource.
- Specify allowed origins, headers, and methods.

3. Enable API Throttling and Quotas

- **Usage Plans:**
- Define usage plans that set limits on the number of requests per second and per day.
- Associate API keys with usage plans to enforce rate limits.

4. Implement Data Encryption

- **At Rest:**
- Ensure that data stored in S3 is encrypted using server-side encryption (SSE-S3 or SSE-KMS).
- **In Transit:**
- Use HTTPS endpoints to encrypt data as it travels between clients and

the API.

4. Managing Serverless Deployments

Effective management of serverless deployments ensures that your ML models remain reliable, scalable, and maintainable. This section discusses strategies and tools for managing serverless deployments, including version control, CI/CD pipelines, monitoring, and updating deployed models.

4.1. Version Control and Deployment Strategies

Managing different versions of your Lambda functions and APIs is essential for maintaining stability and enabling smooth updates.

1. Lambda Function Versioning

- **Publish Versions:**
- AWS Lambda allows you to publish immutable versions of your functions.
- Each version has a unique ARN (Amazon Resource Name).
- **Aliases:**
- Use aliases (e.g., dev, prod) to point to specific versions.
- Facilitate blue-green deployments by routing a portion of traffic to new versions.
- **Benefits:**
- Easy rollback to previous versions in case of issues.
- Isolate environments for testing and production.

2. API Gateway Stages and Versions

- **Stages:**
- Define stages (e.g., dev, test, prod) for your API.
- Each stage can have different configurations and deployments.
- **Deployment Management:**
- Deploy new API configurations to specific stages without affecting others.
- Use stage variables to manage environment-specific settings.
- **Documentation:**
- Automatically generate and publish API documentation for each stage.

4.2. Implementing CI/CD Pipelines for Serverless Deployments

Continuous Integration and Continuous Deployment (CI/CD) pipelines automate the process of building, testing, and deploying serverless applications, ensuring consistency and reducing manual errors.

1. Using AWS CodePipeline and CodeBuild

- **AWS CodePipeline:**
- Automates the build, test, and deploy phases of your application.
- Integrates with source repositories (e.g., GitHub, AWS CodeCommit).
- **AWS CodeBuild:**
- Compiles source code, runs tests, and produces artifacts for deployment.
- **Setup Steps:**

1. **Create a CodeCommit Repository:**

- Store your Lambda function code and API definitions.

1. **Define a Build Project in CodeBuild:**

- Specify the build commands (e.g., packaging code, installing dependencies).

1. **Create a CodePipeline:**

- Define the source, build, and deploy stages.
- Connect CodeCommit, CodeBuild, and AWS SAM or CloudFormation for deployments.

2. Integrating with GitHub and Third-Party CI/CD Tools

- **GitHub Actions:**
- Use GitHub Actions to define workflows that automate deployment tasks.
- Example Workflow (.github/workflows/deploy.yml):

DEPLOYING MACHINE LEARNING MODELS USING SERVERLESS FUNCTIONS

```yaml
Copy code
name: Deploy Lambda and API Gateway

on:
  push:
    branches:
      - main

jobs:
  build-and-deploy:
    runs-on: ubuntu-latest

    steps:
      - name: Checkout Code
        uses: actions/checkout@v2

      - name: Set up Python
        uses: actions/setup-python@v2
        with:
          python-version: '3.8'

      - name: Install Dependencies
        run: |
          python -m pip install --upgrade pip
          pip install -r requirements.txt -t .

      - name: Package Lambda Function
        run: |
          zip -r function.zip .

      - name: Deploy to AWS Lambda
        uses: appleboy/lambda-action@master
        with:
          access_key_id: ${{ secrets.AWS_ACCESS_KEY_ID }}
          secret_access_key: ${{ secrets.AWS_SECRET_ACCESS_KEY }}
```

```
        region: us-east-1
        function_name:
MLModelInferenceFunction
        zip_file: function.zip
```

- **Terraform or AWS CloudFormation:**
- Use Infrastructure as Code (IaC) tools to define and manage your serverless resources declaratively.
- Example Terraform Configuration:

```hcl
Copy code
provider "aws" {
  region = "us-east-1"
}

resource "aws_s3_bucket" "ml_models" {
  bucket = "my-ml-models"
}

resource "aws_lambda_function" "ml_inference" {
  function_name = "MLModelInferenceFunction"
  handler       = "lambda_function.lambda_handler"
  runtime       = "python3.8"
  role          = aws_iam_role.lambda_exec.arn
  s3_bucket     = aws_s3_bucket.ml_models.bucket
  s3_key        = "model-deployment/function.zip"
  environment {
    variables = {
      MODEL_BUCKET = aws_s3_bucket.ml_models.bucket
      MODEL_KEY    = "model.joblib"
    }
  }
  memory_size = 1024
  timeout     = 30
```

DEPLOYING MACHINE LEARNING MODELS USING SERVERLESS FUNCTIONS

```
}

resource "aws_api_gateway_rest_api" "ml_api" {
  name        = "MLModelAPI"
  description = "API for ML Model Inference"
}

resource "aws_api_gateway_resource" "predict" {
  rest_api_id = aws_api_gateway_rest_api.ml_api.id
  parent_id   = aws_api_gateway_rest_api.ml_api.root_resource_id
  path_part   = "predict"
}

resource "aws_api_gateway_method" "post_predict" {
  rest_api_id   = aws_api_gateway_rest_api.ml_api.id
  resource_id   = aws_api_gateway_resource.predict.id
  http_method   = "POST"
  authorization = "NONE"
}

resource "aws_api_gateway_integration" "lambda_integration" {
  rest_api_id = aws_api_gateway_rest_api.ml_api.id
  resource_id = aws_api_gateway_resource.predict.id
  http_method = aws_api_gateway_method.post_predict.http_method

  integration_http_method = "POST"
  type                    = "AWS_PROXY"
  uri                     = aws_lambda_function.ml_inference.invoke_arn
}

resource "aws_lambda_permission" "api_gateway" {
  statement_id  = "AllowAPIGatewayInvoke"
  action        = "lambda:InvokeFunction"
  function_name = aws_lambda_function.ml_inference.function_name
  principal     = "apigateway.amazonaws.com"
  source_arn    =
```

```
    "${aws_api_gateway_rest_api.ml_api.execution_arn}/*/*"
}

resource "aws_api_gateway_deployment" "api_deployment" {
  depends_on = [
    aws_api_gateway_integration.lambda_integration
  ]

  rest_api_id = aws_api_gateway_rest_api.ml_api.id
  stage_name  = "prod"
}
```

3. Automate Deployment with AWS SAM

- **Using AWS SAM CLI:**
- Define serverless applications using template.yaml.
- Automate packaging and deployment with SAM commands.
- **Example SAM Template (template.yaml):**

```yaml
Copy code
AWSTemplateFormatVersion: '2010-09-09'
Transform: AWS::Serverless-2016-10-31
Description: Serverless ML Model Inference

Resources:
  MLModelInferenceFunction:
    Type: AWS::Serverless::Function
    Properties:
      Handler: lambda_function.lambda_handler
      Runtime: python3.8
      CodeUri: ./function.zip
      MemorySize: 1024
      Timeout: 30
      Environment:
        Variables:
          MODEL_BUCKET: my-ml-models
```

DEPLOYING MACHINE LEARNING MODELS USING SERVERLESS FUNCTIONS

```yaml
          MODEL_KEY: model.joblib
      Policies:
        - S3ReadPolicy:
            BucketName: my-ml-models

  MLModelAPI:
    Type: AWS::Serverless::Api
    Properties:
      StageName: prod
      DefinitionBody:
        swagger: "2.0"
        info:
          title: "MLModelAPI"
          version: "1.0"
        paths:
          /predict:
            post:
              consumes:
                - application/json
              produces:
                - application/json
              responses:
                "200":
                  description: "Successful prediction"
              x-amazon-apigateway-integration:
                uri: !Sub arn:aws:apigateway:${AWS::Region}:lambda:path/2015-03-31/functions/${MLModelInferenceFunction.Arn}/invocations
                httpMethod: POST
                type: aws_proxy
```

- **Deploy with SAM:**

```bash
Copy code
sam build
sam package --output-template-file packaged.
yaml --s3-bucket your-deployment-bucket
sam deploy --template-file packaged.yaml --stack-name
MLModelInferenceStack
  --capabilities CAPABILITY_IAM
```

3.6. API Documentation and Client SDKs

Providing clear documentation and client SDKs enhances the usability and adoption of your ML inference API.

- **Swagger/OpenAPI Documentation:**
- Define your API using the OpenAPI specification.
- Use tools like Swagger UI to visualize and interact with your API.
- **AWS API Gateway Console:**
- Automatically generates API documentation based on your API definitions.
- Customize descriptions, models, and examples for each endpoint.
- **Client SDK Generation:**
- Generate SDKs for various programming languages (e.g., JavaScript, Python) using API Gateway.
- Facilitate easy integration of the API into client applications.

3.7. Error Handling and Response Management

Implement robust error handling to provide meaningful feedback to API consumers and maintain API reliability.

- **Standardized Error Responses:**
- Use consistent error formats, including error codes and messages.

```json
Copy code
{
  "error": "Invalid input:
'features' must be a list of numbers."
}
```

- **HTTP Status Codes:**
- **200 OK:** Successful prediction.
- **400 Bad Request:** Invalid input data.
- **500 Internal Server Error:** Server-side issues.
- **Logging Errors:**
- Log detailed error information in CloudWatch for troubleshooting.
- Avoid exposing sensitive error details in API responses.
- **Retries and Idempotency:**
- Design your API and Lambda functions to handle retries gracefully.
- Ensure idempotent operations to prevent duplicate processing.

4. Managing Serverless Deployments

Managing serverless deployments involves overseeing the lifecycle of your serverless applications, ensuring they are robust, maintainable, and scalable. This section discusses strategies and best practices for managing serverless deployments, including version control, continuous integration and deployment (CI/CD), monitoring, and updating deployed models.

4.1. Version Control and Deployment Strategies

Effective version control and deployment strategies ensure smooth updates and maintain the stability of your ML inference API.

1. Lambda Function Versioning

- **Publishing Versions:**
- AWS Lambda allows you to publish immutable versions of your functions.
- Each version has a unique ARN and cannot be changed once published.

```bash
Copy code
aws lambda publish-version --function-name MLModelInferenceFunction
```

- **Using Aliases:**
- Aliases act as pointers to specific versions, enabling blue-green deployments and traffic shifting.
- **Create an Alias:**

```bash
Copy code
aws lambda create-alias --function-name MLModelInferenceFunction --name prod --function-version 1
```

- **Update an Alias:**

```bash
Copy code
aws lambda update-alias --function-name MLModelInferenceFunction --name prod --function-version 2
```

- **Benefits:**
- **Rollback:** Quickly revert to a previous version if issues arise.
- **Environment Separation:** Use different aliases for development, staging, and production.

DEPLOYING MACHINE LEARNING MODELS USING SERVERLESS FUNCTIONS

2. API Gateway Stages and Deployment

- **Stages:**
- Represent different environments (e.g., dev, test, prod).
- **Deployment Process:**
- Deploy API configurations to specific stages without affecting others.
- **Stage Variables:**
- Manage environment-specific settings using stage variables (e.g., API endpoints, database connections).
- **Example:**
- Route /prod/predict to the production Lambda function and /dev/predict to the development version.

3. Blue-Green Deployments

- **Strategy:**
- Deploy a new version of your Lambda function alongside the existing one.
- Gradually shift traffic to the new version while monitoring performance.
- Fully switch to the new version once confirmed stable.
- **Implementation with Aliases:**
- Use aliases to manage traffic shifting between versions.

```bash
Copy code
aws lambda update-alias
--function-name MLModelInferenceFunction
--name prod --function-version 3 --routing-config
'{"AdditionalVersionWeights": {"4": 0.1}}'
```

- This routes 90% of the traffic to version 3 and 10% to version 4.

4. Canary Releases

- **Definition:**
- Deploy updates to a small subset of users before rolling out to the entire user base.
- **Benefits:**
- Mitigate risks by exposing updates to a limited audience.
- Monitor real-world performance before full deployment.
- **Implementation:**
- Similar to blue-green deployments, use aliases and routing configurations to control traffic distribution.

4.2. Implementing CI/CD Pipelines for Serverless Deployments

Automating the build, test, and deployment processes through CI/CD pipelines enhances efficiency, consistency, and reliability.

1. Using AWS CodePipeline and CodeBuild

- **AWS CodePipeline:**
- Orchestrates the CI/CD process, integrating various AWS services.
- **AWS CodeBuild:**
- Compiles code, runs tests, and packages artifacts for deployment.
- **Setup Steps:**

1. **Source Stage:**

- Connect to your source repository (e.g., GitHub, CodeCommit).

1. **Build Stage:**

- Use CodeBuild to install dependencies, run tests, and create deployment packages.

1. **Deploy Stage:**

DEPLOYING MACHINE LEARNING MODELS USING SERVERLESS FUNCTIONS

- Use AWS SAM or CloudFormation to deploy the Lambda function and API Gateway configurations.
- **Example Pipeline:**

```yaml
Copy code
version: 0.2

phases:
  install:
    commands:
      - pip install -r requirements.txt -t .
  build:
    commands:
      - zip -r function.zip .
  post_build:
    commands:
      - aws lambda update-function-code --function-name
        MLModelInferenceFunction --zip-file fileb://function.zip
artifacts:
  files:
    - function.zip
```

2. Integrating with GitHub Actions

- **GitHub Actions:**
- Define workflows in your repository to automate CI/CD tasks.
- **Example Workflow (.github/workflows/deploy.yml):**

```yaml
Copy code
name: Deploy Serverless ML Model

on:
  push:
```

```yaml
    branches:
      - main

jobs:
  build-deploy:
    runs-on: ubuntu-latest

    steps:
      - name: Checkout Code
        uses: actions/checkout@v2

      - name: Set up Python
        uses: actions/setup-python@v2
        with:
          python-version: '3.8'

      - name: Install Dependencies
        run: |
          pip install -r requirements.txt -t .

      - name: Package Lambda Function
        run: |
          zip -r function.zip .

      - name: Deploy to AWS Lambda
        uses: appleboy/lambda-action@master
        with:
          access_key_id: ${{ secrets.AWS_ACCESS_KEY_ID }}
          secret_access_key: ${{ secrets.AWS_SECRET_ACCESS_KEY }}
          region: us-east-1
          function_name: MLModelInferenceFunction
          zip_file: function.zip

      - name: Update API Gateway
        run: |
          aws apigateway create-deployment --rest-api-id your-api-id --stage-name prod
```

- **Benefits:**
- **Automation:** Reduces manual intervention and errors.
- **Consistency:** Ensures uniform deployment across environments.
- **Speed:** Accelerates the development lifecycle by enabling rapid iterations.

3. Infrastructure as Code (IaC) with Terraform or AWS CloudFormation

- **Terraform:**
- An open-source IaC tool that enables you to define and provision infrastructure using a declarative configuration language.
- **AWS CloudFormation:**
- AWS-native IaC service for modeling and setting up AWS resources.
- **Example Terraform Configuration:**

```hcl
Copy code
provider "aws" {
  region = "us-east-1"
}

resource "aws_lambda_function" "ml_inference" {
  function_name = "MLModelInferenceFunction"
  handler       = "lambda_function.lambda_handler"
  runtime       = "python3.8"
  role          = aws_iam_role.lambda_exec.arn
  s3_bucket     = aws_s3_bucket.ml_models.bucket
  s3_key        = "model-deployment/function.zip"
  environment {
    variables = {
      MODEL_BUCKET = aws_s3_bucket.ml_models.bucket
      MODEL_KEY    = "model.joblib"
    }
  }
  memory_size = 1024
```

```
  timeout     = 30
}

resource "aws_api_gateway_rest_api" "ml_api" {
  name        = "MLModelAPI"
  description = "API for ML Model Inference"
}

resource "aws_api_gateway_resource" "predict" {
  rest_api_id = aws_api_gateway_rest_api.ml_api.id
  parent_id   = aws_api_gateway_rest_api.ml_api.root_resource_id
  path_part   = "predict"
}

resource "aws_api_gateway_method" "post_predict" {
  rest_api_id   = aws_api_gateway_rest_api.ml_api.id
  resource_id   = aws_api_gateway_resource.predict.id
  http_method   = "POST"
  authorization = "NONE"
}

resource "aws_api_gateway_integration" "lambda_integration" {
  rest_api_id             = aws_api_gateway_rest_api.ml_api.id
  resource_id             = aws_api_gateway_resource.predict.id
  http_method             = aws_api_gateway_method.post_predict.http_method
  integration_http_method = "POST"
  type                    = "AWS_PROXY"
  uri                     = aws_lambda_function.ml_inference.invoke_arn
}

resource "aws_lambda_permission" "api_gateway" {
  statement_id  = "AllowAPIGatewayInvoke"
  action        = "lambda:InvokeFunction"
  function_name = aws_lambda_function.ml_inference.function_name
  principal     = "apigateway.amazonaws.com"
  source_arn    = "${aws_api_gateway_rest_api.ml_api.execution_arn}/*/*"
```

```
}

resource "aws_api_gateway_deployment" "api_deployment" {
  depends_on = [
    aws_api_gateway_integration.lambda_integration
  ]

  rest_api_id = aws_api_gateway_rest_api.ml_api.id
  stage_name  = "prod"
}
```

- **Benefits:**
- **Repeatability:** Easily recreate environments across different stages.
- **Version Control:** Manage infrastructure changes alongside application code.
- **Collaboration:** Enable team collaboration on infrastructure configurations.

4.3. Monitoring and Logging

Monitoring and logging are essential for maintaining the health, performance, and reliability of your serverless ML deployments.

1. AWS CloudWatch Monitoring

- **CloudWatch Logs:**
- Automatically captures logs from Lambda functions.
- Use structured logging for easier parsing and analysis.

```python
Copy code
import logging

logger = logging.getLogger()
```

```
logger.setLevel(logging.INFO)

def lambda_handler(event, context):
    logger.info("Received event: %s", event)
    # Inference logic
```

- **CloudWatch Metrics:**
- **Invocation Count:** Number of times the function is invoked.
- **Duration:** Time taken for each function execution.
- **Error Count:** Number of errors during execution.
- **Throttles:** Number of requests throttled due to concurrency limits.
- **CloudWatch Alarms:**
- Set alarms based on metric thresholds (e.g., high error rates, increased latency).
- Notify via Amazon SNS (Simple Notification Service) when alarms are triggered.

2. AWS X-Ray for Tracing

- **Purpose:** Provides end-to-end tracing of requests through your serverless architecture.
- **Benefits:**
- Visualize the flow of requests through API Gateway, Lambda, and other AWS services.
- Identify performance bottlenecks and latency issues.
- **Setup:**
- Enable X-Ray tracing in both API Gateway and Lambda function configurations.
- Use the X-Ray SDK in your Lambda function code for detailed tracing.

```python
Copy code
from aws_xray_sdk.core import xray_recorder
from aws_xray_sdk.core import patch_all

patch_all()

def lambda_handler(event, context):
    # Traced code
    pass
```

3. Third-Party Monitoring Tools

- **Datadog, New Relic, Lumigo:**
- Provide advanced monitoring, alerting, and visualization capabilities.
- Offer deep insights into serverless function performance and dependencies.
- **Benefits:**
- Enhanced visibility with user-friendly dashboards.
- Anomaly detection and proactive issue resolution.
- Integration with multiple cloud services for comprehensive monitoring.

4. Implementing Model Performance Monitoring

- **Concept Drift Detection:**
- Monitor changes in input data distributions that may affect model accuracy.
- Use statistical tests or ML-based methods to detect drift.
- **Accuracy Tracking:**
- Continuously evaluate model predictions against ground truth or user feedback.
- Implement metrics like precision, recall, F1-score, and ROC-AUC.
- **Tools:**
- **Amazon SageMaker Model Monitor:** Monitors data and model quality

over time.
- **Custom Dashboards:** Build dashboards using CloudWatch or third-party tools to visualize performance metrics.

5. Logging Best Practices

- **Structured Logging:**
- Use JSON or other structured formats to make logs machine-readable.
- Facilitate easier searching and filtering in CloudWatch Logs.

```python
Copy code
logger.info(json.dumps({
    "event": "inference",
    "input": "I love this product!",
    "prediction": "Positive",
    "response_time_ms": 150
}))
```

- **Sensitive Data Handling:**
- Avoid logging PII or confidential information.
- Implement data masking or anonymization techniques if necessary.
- **Centralized Logging:**
- Aggregate logs from multiple Lambda functions into centralized dashboards for holistic monitoring.

4.4. Updating and Redeploying Models

Keeping your ML models updated is essential for maintaining performance and accuracy. Serverless architectures simplify the process of updating and redeploying models.

1. Preparing the Updated Model

1. **Retrain the Model:**

- Incorporate new data and retrain your ML model using the latest datasets.
- Perform hyperparameter tuning to optimize performance.

1. **Save and Upload the Updated Model:**

- Serialize the updated model and upload it to the designated S3 bucket.

```python
Copy code
joblib.dump(updated_model, 'model.joblib')
s3.upload_file('model.joblib',
'my-ml-models', 'model.joblib')
```

2. Updating the Lambda Function

1. **Automate Deployment:**

- Use CI/CD pipelines to automate the packaging and deployment of updated Lambda functions.

1. **Deploy New Versions:**

- Publish a new version of the Lambda function after updating the code and model.
- Update the API Gateway integration to point to the new version via aliases.

1. **Example Using AWS SAM:**

- **Update lambda_function.py:**
- Modify the inference logic or include additional preprocessing steps if needed.
- **Repackage and Deploy:**

```bash
Copy code
zip -r function.zip .
sam deploy --template-file packaged.yaml --stack-name MLModelInferenceStack --capabilities CAPABILITY_IAM
```

3. Rolling Back to Previous Versions

1. **Identify the Faulty Deployment:**

- Use CloudWatch Logs and monitoring tools to detect issues introduced in the new version.

1. **Revert the Alias to the Previous Version:**

```bash
Copy code
aws lambda update-alias --function-name MLModelInferenceFunction --name prod --function-version 2
```

1. **Verify Stability:**

- Ensure that reverting to the previous version resolves the issues and restores normal functionality.

4. Blue-Green Deployments for Zero Downtime

1. **Deploy the New Version:**

- Create a new version of the Lambda function with the updated model.

1. **Shift Traffic Gradually:**

- Use aliases to gradually shift traffic from the old version to the new one.
- Monitor performance and error rates during the transition.

1. **Finalize Deployment:**

- Once the new version is verified, route 100% of the traffic to it.
- Retain the old version for rollback purposes if needed.

Conclusion

Deploying machine learning models using serverless functions like AWS Lambda and integrating them with API Gateway provides a powerful and efficient way to serve real-time predictions. This architecture leverages the scalability, cost-efficiency, and simplified management inherent in serverless platforms, enabling rapid deployment and seamless integration with various applications.

By following the detailed steps outlined in this guide—from creating and deploying serverless functions, integrating with API Gateway, building a robust RESTful API, to managing deployments through version control and CI/CD pipelines—you can establish a reliable and scalable infrastructure for your ML models. Additionally, implementing comprehensive monitoring and logging ensures that your deployed models maintain high performance and reliability over time.

Embracing serverless deployments for machine learning not only accelerates the development and deployment process but also allows organizations to focus on refining their models and delivering value-driven AI solutions without the overhead of managing complex infrastructure. As serverless technologies continue to evolve, they will undoubtedly play a pivotal role in the democratization and scalability of machine learning applications across diverse industries.

Monitoring and Scaling Serverless Machine Learning Models

Deploying machine learning (ML) models using serverless architectures, such as AWS Lambda or Google Cloud Functions, offers significant advantages in terms of scalability, cost-efficiency, and simplified infrastructure management. However, to fully leverage these benefits, it is crucial to implement robust monitoring and scaling strategies. Effective monitoring ensures that your ML models maintain high performance and accuracy, while intelligent scaling strategies handle varying traffic loads and optimize costs. This section delves into monitoring ML model performance in a serverless environment, strategies for auto-scaling and managing traffic spikes, cost management practices for serverless ML projects, and best practices for debugging and troubleshooting common issues.

1. Monitoring ML Model Performance in a Serverless Environment

Monitoring the performance of ML models deployed in a serverless environment is essential to ensure that they deliver accurate and timely predictions. Effective monitoring allows you to detect anomalies, track model drift, and maintain the overall health of your ML applications.

1.1. Importance of Monitoring ML Models

MONITORING AND SCALING SERVERLESS MACHINE LEARNING MODELS

- **Performance Tracking:** Continuously assess the accuracy, latency, and throughput of your ML models to ensure they meet the desired performance metrics.
- **Anomaly Detection:** Identify unusual patterns or behaviors that may indicate issues such as data drift, model degradation, or infrastructure problems.
- **Resource Optimization:** Monitor resource utilization to optimize memory, CPU, and other compute resources, thereby reducing costs and improving efficiency.
- **User Experience:** Ensure that the end-users receive consistent and reliable predictions, enhancing the overall user experience.

1.2. Key Performance Indicators (KPIs)

- **Accuracy Metrics:**
- **Precision, Recall, F1-Score:** For classification models to evaluate the correctness of predictions.
- **Mean Absolute Error (MAE), Mean Squared Error (MSE), Root Mean Squared Error (RMSE):** For regression models to measure prediction errors.
- **Area Under the Curve (AUC):** To assess the performance of binary classifiers.
- **Latency Metrics:**
- **Invocation Duration:** Time taken for the serverless function to process a request and return a prediction.
- **Cold Start Time:** Latency introduced when a serverless function is invoked after being idle.
- **Throughput Metrics:**
- **Request Rate:** Number of prediction requests handled per second or minute.
- **Concurrent Executions:** Number of serverless function instances running simultaneously.
- **Operational Metrics:**

- **Error Rates:** Percentage of failed predictions or exceptions thrown during inference.
- **Throttling Counts:** Number of requests denied due to exceeding concurrency limits.

1.3. Tools and Services for Monitoring

- **AWS CloudWatch:**
- **CloudWatch Logs:** Capture detailed logs from Lambda functions, including input data, prediction results, and error messages.
- **CloudWatch Metrics:** Track invocation counts, durations, error rates, and other performance metrics.
- **CloudWatch Alarms:** Set thresholds for specific metrics to trigger notifications or automated responses when anomalies are detected.
- **AWS X-Ray:**
- **Distributed Tracing:** Visualize the flow of requests through your serverless architecture, identifying bottlenecks and latency sources.
- **Service Maps:** Understand dependencies between services and how they interact during prediction requests.
- **Third-Party Monitoring Tools:**
- **Datadog, New Relic, Lumigo:** Provide advanced monitoring, alerting, and visualization capabilities tailored for serverless applications.
- **Benefits:** Enhanced dashboards, real-time alerting, anomaly detection, and integration with various cloud services.
- **ML-Specific Monitoring Tools:**
- **Prometheus and Grafana:** For custom metric collection and visualization, particularly useful in complex ML pipelines.
- **Weights & Biases, MLflow:** Offer experiment tracking and model performance monitoring, integrating seamlessly with serverless deployments.

1.4. Model Drift Detection

- **Definition:** Model drift occurs when the statistical properties of the input data change over time, leading to a decline in model performance.
- **Types of Drift:**
- **Data Drift:** Changes in the input data distribution.
- **Concept Drift:** Changes in the relationship between input data and the target variable.
- **Detection Techniques:**
- **Statistical Tests:** Use tests like the Kolmogorov-Smirnov test to compare current data distributions with historical data.
- **Monitoring Prediction Quality:** Continuously evaluate model predictions against ground truth labels (if available) to detect performance degradation.
- **Automated Alerts:** Set up alerts to notify stakeholders when drift is detected, prompting retraining or model updates.
- **Tools for Drift Detection:**
- **Amazon SageMaker Model Monitor:** Automatically monitors deployed models for data and model quality, detecting drift and anomalies.
- **Custom Implementations:** Utilize logging and metric collection to build bespoke drift detection pipelines using tools like TensorFlow Data Validation.

1.5. Logging Best Practices

- **Structured Logging:**
- **Format:** Use JSON or other structured formats to facilitate easy parsing and analysis.
- **Consistent Schemas:** Maintain uniform log structures across different serverless functions for consistency.

```
python
Copy code
```

```python
import json
import logging

logger = logging.getLogger()
logger.setLevel(logging.INFO)

def lambda_handler(event, context):
    try:
        features = event['features']
        prediction = model.predict([features])[0]
        log_entry = {
            "event": "inference",
            "features": features,
            "prediction": prediction,
            "status": "success"
        }
        logger.info(json.dumps(log_entry))
        return {
            'statusCode': 200,
            'body': json.dumps({'prediction': prediction})
        }
    except Exception as e:
        log_entry = {
            "event": "inference",
            "error": str(e),
            "status": "failure"
        }
        logger.error(json.dumps(log_entry))
        return {
            'statusCode': 500,
            'body': json.dumps({'error': 'Internal Server Error'})
        }
```

- **Sensitive Data Handling:**
- **Avoid Logging PII:** Do not log personally identifiable information or sensitive data to prevent security breaches.
- **Data Masking:** If necessary, mask or anonymize sensitive data before

logging.

- **Centralized Logging:**
- **Aggregation:** Consolidate logs from all serverless functions into a centralized logging system like AWS CloudWatch Logs or a third-party service.
- **Retention Policies:** Define log retention periods based on compliance requirements and storage considerations.
- **Correlation IDs:**
- **Purpose:** Track and correlate requests across different services and components.
- **Implementation:** Generate unique identifiers for each request and include them in logs to trace the entire request lifecycle.

1.6. Example Workflow: Monitoring ML Model Performance with AWS CloudWatch

1. **Lambda Function Configuration:**

- Ensure that your Lambda function is configured to send logs to CloudWatch.
- Attach the necessary IAM permissions to allow logging.

1. **Define Custom Metrics:**

- Within your Lambda function code, emit custom metrics such as prediction accuracy or confidence scores.

```python
Copy code
import boto3
import json
import logging
```

```python
logger = logging.getLogger()
logger.setLevel(logging.INFO)

cloudwatch = boto3.client('cloudwatch')

def lambda_handler(event, context):
    try:
        features = event['features']
        prediction = model.predict([features])[0]
        confidence = model.predict_proba([features])[0].max()

        # Log prediction
        log_entry = {
            "event": "inference",
            "features": features,
            "prediction": prediction,
            "confidence": confidence,
            "status": "success"
        }
        logger.info(json.dumps(log_entry))

        # Emit custom metric
        cloudwatch.put_metric_data(
            Namespace='ServerlessML',
            MetricData=[
                {
                    'MetricName': 'PredictionConfidence',
                    'Dimensions': [
                        {
                            'Name': 'Model',
                            'Value': 'RandomForest'
                        },
                    ],
                    'Value': confidence,
                    'Unit': 'None'
                },
            ]
        )
```

```
        return {
            'statusCode': 200,
            'body': json.dumps({'prediction': prediction,
            'confidence': confidence})
        }
    except Exception as e:
        log_entry = {
            "event": "inference",
            "error": str(e),
            "status": "failure"
        }
        logger.error(json.dumps(log_entry))
        return {
            'statusCode': 500,
            'body': json.dumps
({'error': 'Internal Server Error'})
        }
```

1. **Create CloudWatch Alarms:**

- Set up alarms based on custom metrics and standard metrics.
- Example: Trigger an alarm if the average PredictionConfidence drops below a certain threshold over a specified period.

1. **Visualize Metrics:**

- Use CloudWatch Dashboards to create visual representations of your metrics.
- Example Dashboard Widgets:
- Line charts for prediction accuracy over time.
- Bar graphs for error rates across different time intervals.
- Heatmaps for latency distributions.

1. **Automate Responses:**

- Configure CloudWatch Alarms to notify teams via SNS or trigger automated remediation actions (e.g., retraining models, scaling resources).

2. Auto-Scaling and Handling Traffic Spikes

One of the standout features of serverless architectures is their inherent ability to scale automatically in response to varying workloads. This section explores how serverless platforms handle scaling, strategies for managing traffic spikes, and best practices to ensure optimal performance and cost-efficiency.

2.1. How Serverless Handles Scaling

- **Automatic Scaling:**
- Serverless platforms dynamically allocate resources based on the number of incoming requests.
- Each request can trigger a separate instance of the serverless function, allowing for high concurrency without manual intervention.
- **Stateless Execution:**
- Serverless functions are stateless, meaning each invocation is independent. This design facilitates horizontal scaling as functions do not rely on shared state.
- **Concurrency Limits:**
- Platforms impose default concurrency limits to prevent resource exhaustion.
- Example: AWS Lambda has a default concurrency limit of 1,000 concurrent executions per region, which can be increased upon request.

2.2. Configuring Auto-Scaling Parameters

- **AWS Lambda:**
- **Reserved Concurrency:**
- Allocate a fixed number of concurrent executions to ensure availability and prevent functions from using excessive resources.
- Example:

MONITORING AND SCALING SERVERLESS MACHINE LEARNING MODELS

```bash
Copy code
aws lambda put-function-concurrency --function-name MLModelInferenceFunction --reserved-concurrent-executions 500
```

- **Provisioned Concurrency:**
- Pre-warm a specified number of function instances to reduce cold start latency, ensuring consistent performance.
- Example:

```bash
Copy code
aws lambda put-provisioned-concurrency-config
--function-name MLModelInferenceFunction
--qualifier $LATEST
--provisioned-concurrent-executions 100
```

- **Google Cloud Functions:**
- **Max Instances:**
- Set the maximum number of function instances to control scaling.
- Example:

```bash
Copy code
gcloud functions deploy MLModelInferenceFunction
  --max-instances 500
```

- **Min Instances:**

- Define a minimum number of instances to keep warm, reducing cold start occurrences.
- Example:

```bash
Copy code
gcloud functions deploy MLModelInferenceFunction --min-instances 10
```

- **Azure Functions:**
- **Premium Plan:**
- Offers enhanced scaling features, including the ability to set minimum and maximum instances.
- **Configuration:**
- Set the minimum and maximum number of instances based on anticipated traffic.

2.3. Strategies to Handle Sudden Traffic Spikes

- **Implementing Rate Limiting:**
- Control the number of incoming requests to prevent overloading serverless functions.
- Use API Gateway throttling settings to limit requests per second (RPS) and burst rates.
- **Circuit Breaker Pattern:**
- Prevent cascading failures by temporarily halting requests to a failing service until it recovers.
- Implement logic within your API Gateway or Lambda functions to detect failures and stop sending traffic.
- **Queueing Requests:**
- Use message queues (e.g., AWS SQS, Google Cloud Pub/Sub) to buffer incoming requests during peak traffic periods.

MONITORING AND SCALING SERVERLESS MACHINE LEARNING MODELS

- Lambda functions can process queued messages at a controlled rate, smoothing out traffic spikes.
- **Load Balancing:**
- Distribute incoming traffic evenly across multiple instances or regions to avoid concentration of load.
- Utilize services like AWS Global Accelerator or Route 53 for global load balancing.
- **Graceful Degradation:**
- Design your application to maintain core functionalities even under high load, sacrificing non-essential features if necessary.
- **Scaling Policies:**
- Define scaling policies that adjust resource allocation based on real-time traffic patterns and performance metrics.

2.4. Best Practices for Auto-Scaling in Serverless ML Deployments

- **Predictive Scaling:**
- Analyze historical traffic patterns to anticipate and prepare for future traffic surges.
- Use machine learning-based forecasting tools to predict scaling needs.
- **Optimize Function Performance:**
- Reduce execution time by optimizing code and minimizing dependencies, allowing more concurrent executions within resource limits.
- **Monitor Concurrency Usage:**
- Keep track of your serverless functions' concurrency limits and adjust them based on usage patterns and business requirements.
- **Implement Fallback Mechanisms:**
- Provide alternative responses or redirect traffic to secondary models or services during extreme load conditions.
- **Leverage Multi-Region Deployments:**
- Distribute serverless functions across multiple regions to balance load and reduce latency.
- **Use Caching Strategically:**

- Implement caching layers (e.g., AWS CloudFront, API Gateway caching) to serve frequent requests without invoking serverless functions.
- **Test Scaling Behavior:**
- Conduct load testing and simulate traffic spikes to understand how your serverless ML models behave under stress and identify potential bottlenecks.

2.5. Example Workflow: Handling Traffic Spikes with AWS Lambda and API Gateway

1. **Configure API Gateway Throttling:**

- Set a maximum of 200 RPS with a burst capacity of 500 requests.

```bash
Copy code
aws apigateway update-stage
--rest-api-id your-api-id
--stage-name prod --patch-operations
op=replace,path=/throttle/rateLimit,value=200
op=replace,path=/throttle/burstLimit,value=500
```

1. **Set Up AWS SQS Queue:**

- Create an SQS queue named PredictionQueue to buffer incoming requests.

```bash
Copy code
aws sqs create-queue --queue-name PredictionQueue
```

MONITORING AND SCALING SERVERLESS MACHINE LEARNING MODELS

1. **Modify Lambda Function to Poll SQS:**

- Adjust the Lambda function to be triggered by messages in the PredictionQueue instead of direct API requests.

1. **Implement Lambda Function Logic:**

- Process messages from the queue, perform predictions, and send responses back to clients or another service.

1. **Integrate with API Gateway:**

- When a client makes a prediction request, enqueue the request data to PredictionQueue and immediately return an acknowledgment.

```python
Copy code
import json
import boto3

sqs = boto3.client('sqs')
QUEUE_URL = 'https://sqs.region.amazonaws.com/123456789012/PredictionQueue'

def lambda_handler(event, context):
    try:
        body = json.loads(event['body'])
        features = body['features']

        # Send message to SQS
        sqs.send_message(
            QueueUrl=QUEUE_URL,
            MessageBody=json.dumps({'features': features})
        )
```

```
        return {
            'statusCode': 202,
            'body': json.dumps({'message':
 'Request received and is being processed.'})
        }
    except Exception as e:
        return {
            'statusCode': 400,
            'body': json.dumps({'error': str(e)})
        }
```

1. **Benefits:**

- **Smooth Handling of Spikes:** The SQS queue buffers excess requests, preventing Lambda functions from being overwhelmed.
- **Asynchronous Processing:** Clients receive immediate acknowledgments while predictions are processed in the background.
- **Scalability:** Lambda functions scale automatically based on the number of messages in the queue.

3. Managing Serverless Costs for ML Projects

While serverless architectures offer cost-efficiency by charging only for actual usage, managing costs effectively remains essential, especially for ML projects that may involve resource-intensive computations. This section explores the cost components associated with serverless ML deployments, strategies to optimize costs, monitoring and budgeting techniques, and best practices to ensure cost-effective operations.

3.1. Cost Components in Serverless ML Deployments

- **Compute Costs:**
- **Invocation Charges:** Fees based on the number of function invocations.
- **Duration Charges:** Costs calculated based on the time a function runs, measured in milliseconds.

- **Provisioned Concurrency:** Additional costs for pre-warming function instances to reduce latency.
- **Storage Costs:**
- **Model Storage:** Costs for storing serialized models in services like AWS S3 or Google Cloud Storage.
- **Data Storage:** Expenses for storing training and inference data.
- **Data Transfer Costs:**
- **Inbound Data:** Typically free, but costs may apply for large data transfers.
- **Outbound Data:** Charges for data transferred out of cloud services.
- **API Gateway Costs:**
- **Request Charges:** Fees based on the number of API calls.
- **Data Transfer:** Costs associated with data sent through API Gateway.
- **Additional Services:**
- **Monitoring Tools:** Costs for services like AWS CloudWatch or third-party monitoring tools.
- **Security Services:** Expenses for implementing security measures like AWS WAF or encryption services.

3.2. Strategies to Optimize Serverless Costs

- **Right-Size Function Resources:**
- Allocate only the necessary memory and CPU resources based on the function's requirements. Over-provisioning leads to unnecessary costs.

```bash
Copy code
# Example: Adjusting memory allocation for AWS Lambda
aws lambda update-function-configuration --function-name MLModelInferenceFunction --memory-size 512
```

- **Optimize Function Code:**

- **Reduce Execution Time:** Streamline your code to minimize processing time, thereby reducing duration-based charges.
- **Efficient Algorithms:** Use optimized ML algorithms and libraries that require fewer computational resources.
- **Use Reserved or Provisioned Concurrency Wisely:**
- Reserve concurrency only for critical functions that require low latency, balancing cost with performance needs.
- **Implement Caching:**
- Cache frequent predictions or intermediate results to reduce the number of function invocations.
- Use services like AWS CloudFront or API Gateway caching to serve cached responses.
- **Leverage Spot Instances (Where Applicable):**
- While not directly applicable to serverless functions, consider using spot instances for related workloads like data preprocessing or batch training to reduce costs.
- **Monitor and Optimize Data Transfer:**
- Minimize unnecessary data transfers by processing data within the same region or using compression techniques.
- **Automate Cost Optimization:**
- Use tools like AWS Trusted Advisor or Google Cloud's Recommender to receive automated suggestions for cost savings.
- **Delete Unused Resources:**
- Regularly audit and remove unused or underutilized resources such as obsolete Lambda functions, S3 buckets, or API Gateway endpoints.

3.3. Monitoring and Budgeting Techniques

- **Set Up Cost Alerts:**
- Configure budget alerts to receive notifications when your spending approaches or exceeds predefined thresholds.
- **AWS Budgets:**

MONITORING AND SCALING SERVERLESS MACHINE LEARNING MODELS

```bash
bash
Copy code
aws budgets create-budget
--account-id 123456789012
--budget file://budget.json
```

- **Example budget.json:**

```json
json
Copy code
{
  "Budget": {
    "BudgetName": "MLProjectBudget",
    "BudgetLimit": {
      "Amount": "1000",
      "Unit": "USD"
    },
    "TimeUnit": "MONTHLY",
    "BudgetType": "COST",
    "NotificationTriggers": ["ACTUAL"],
    "NotificationThreshold": 80,
    "NotificationComparisonOperator": "GREATER_THAN",
    "NotificationType": "FORECASTED"
  },
  "NotificationsWithSubscribers": [
    {
      "Notification": {
        "NotificationType": "FORECASTED",
        "ComparisonOperator": "GREATER_THAN",
        "Threshold": 80
      },
      "Subscribers": [
        {
          "SubscriptionType": "EMAIL",
```

```
            "Address": "your-email@example.com"
        }
    ]
  }
]
}
```

- **Use Cost Explorer:**
- Analyze your spending patterns over time to identify cost drivers and areas for optimization.
- Create custom reports to visualize costs associated with specific services or projects.
- **Implement Tagging:**
- Tag resources with identifiers (e.g., project name, environment) to allocate and track costs accurately.

```bash
Copy code
# Example: Tagging an AWS Lambda function
aws lambda tag-resource
--resource
arn:aws:lambda:region:account-id:function:MLModelInferenceFunction
--tags Project=ServerlessML Environment=Production
```

- **Analyze Cost Allocation Reports:**
- Generate detailed cost allocation reports to understand expenses at a granular level.
- Utilize these insights to make informed decisions on resource allocation and optimization.

3.4. Cost-Aware Model Optimization

MONITORING AND SCALING SERVERLESS MACHINE LEARNING MODELS

- **Simplify Models:**
- Use simpler models that require fewer computational resources without significantly compromising accuracy.
- **Model Pruning and Quantization:**
- Reduce model size through techniques like pruning (removing unnecessary neurons) and quantization (using lower precision weights).
- **Batch Inference:**
- Process multiple inference requests in a single function invocation to amortize execution costs.
- **Asynchronous Processing:**
- Offload intensive computations to background processes, allowing the main serverless function to handle lightweight tasks.
- **Use Managed ML Services:**
- Leverage managed services like AWS SageMaker or Google AI Platform, which offer optimized infrastructure and cost management features for ML workloads.

3.5. Example Workflow: Cost Optimization for a Serverless Sentiment Analysis API

1. **Monitor Usage Patterns:**

- Use CloudWatch to track invocation counts, durations, and error rates of the SentimentAnalysisFunction.

1. **Identify Cost Drivers:**

- Determine if high execution durations or excessive invocations are contributing to increased costs.

1. **Optimize Function Memory Allocation:**

- Analyze the relationship between allocated memory and execution time.

- Adjust memory settings to find the optimal balance between performance and cost.

```bash
Copy code
aws lambda update-function-configuration --function-name SentimentAnalysisFunction --memory-size 512
```

1. **Implement API Caching:**

- Enable caching on the /sentiment resource in API Gateway to serve frequent predictions without invoking Lambda.

1. **Use Environment Variables for Configurations:**

- Store configuration parameters like model bucket names and thresholds in environment variables to avoid hardcoding and enable easier updates.

1. **Set Up Budget Alerts:**

- Define a monthly budget of $200 for the sentiment analysis API.
- Configure CloudWatch to send notifications when spending reaches 80% of the budget.

1. **Analyze Cost Reports:**

- Use Cost Explorer to visualize spending trends and identify opportunities for further optimization.

1. **Automate Deployment Pipelines:**

- Integrate CI/CD pipelines to automate deployments, ensuring that cost optimizations are consistently applied across deployments.

4. Debugging and Troubleshooting Common Issues

Deploying ML models in a serverless environment introduces unique challenges that require specialized debugging and troubleshooting approaches. This section addresses common issues encountered in serverless ML deployments and provides strategies to effectively diagnose and resolve them.

4.1. Common Issues in Serverless ML Deployments

- **Cold Start Latency:**
- **Description:** Delays that occur when a serverless function is invoked after a period of inactivity, as the platform initializes the function environment.
- **Impact:** Increased response times, affecting user experience.
- **Timeout Errors:**
- **Description:** Functions exceeding their maximum execution time limit.
- **Impact:** Incomplete predictions and failed requests.
- **Resource Exhaustion:**
- **Description:** Functions running out of memory or CPU, leading to crashes or slow performance.
- **Impact:** Reduced prediction accuracy and increased error rates.
- **Data Serialization Issues:**
- **Description:** Errors in loading or processing serialized models, often due to version mismatches or corrupted files.
- **Impact:** Function failures and inconsistent predictions.
- **Incorrect Environment Configurations:**
- **Description:** Mismatched environment variables, dependencies, or runtime settings.
- **Impact:** Function misbehavior or inability to execute correctly.
- **Security Misconfigurations:**
- **Description:** Improper IAM roles, over-permissioned access, or exposed sensitive data.

- **Impact:** Potential security breaches and unauthorized access.
- **Scaling Limits:**
- **Description:** Hitting concurrency or rate limits, leading to throttled requests.
- **Impact:** Denied service availability during high traffic periods.

4.2. Debugging Tools and Techniques

- **AWS CloudWatch Logs:**
- **Usage:** Access detailed logs generated by Lambda functions to trace execution flow and identify errors.
- **Best Practices:** Implement structured logging and use log filters to quickly locate relevant log entries.
- **AWS X-Ray:**
- **Usage:** Perform distributed tracing to visualize the path of requests through your serverless architecture.
- **Benefits:** Identify performance bottlenecks, latency sources, and service dependencies.
- **Third-Party APM Tools:**
- **Examples:** Datadog, New Relic, Lumigo.
- **Features:** Advanced monitoring, real-time alerts, anomaly detection, and in-depth performance analytics.
- **Local Testing and Emulation:**
- **AWS SAM (Serverless Application Model):**
- Use SAM CLI to emulate Lambda functions locally, allowing for faster development and debugging.

```bash
Copy code
sam local invoke
MLModelInferenceFunction -e event.json
```

MONITORING AND SCALING SERVERLESS MACHINE LEARNING MODELS

- **Docker Containers:**
- Package Lambda functions with Docker to replicate the serverless environment locally for comprehensive testing.
- **Error Monitoring and Alerting:**
- **CloudWatch Alarms:** Set up alarms for critical metrics like error rates and latency.
- **SNS Notifications:** Receive alerts via email or SMS when alarms are triggered.
- **Version Control and Rollbacks:**
- **Lambda Versions:** Use published versions and aliases to revert to stable versions in case of deployment issues.
- **API Gateway Stages:** Maintain separate stages for development and production to isolate changes and facilitate rollbacks.

4.3. Best Practices for Troubleshooting

- **Implement Comprehensive Logging:**
- Log essential information, including input data, intermediate processing steps, and output predictions.
- Avoid logging sensitive or personally identifiable information (PII).
- **Use Environment Variables for Configurations:**
- Manage configurations and secrets through environment variables to prevent hardcoding and facilitate easier updates.
- **Monitor Function Metrics:**
- Regularly review metrics such as invocation counts, durations, error rates, and throttles to detect anomalies early.
- **Isolate Issues:**
- Use step-by-step debugging to isolate the source of errors, whether in data preprocessing, model inference, or external service interactions.
- **Automate Testing:**
- Implement automated unit, integration, and load tests to identify issues before deploying to production.
- **Maintain Clear Documentation:**

- Document your serverless ML architecture, deployment processes, and troubleshooting steps to facilitate easier issue resolution.
- **Leverage Blue-Green Deployments:**
- Deploy new function versions alongside existing ones, allowing you to test and validate before fully switching over.
- **Collaborate Across Teams:**
- Foster communication between data scientists, developers, and operations teams to ensure a holistic approach to troubleshooting and optimization.

4.4. Example Scenario: Debugging High Error Rates in a Serverless Sentiment Analysis API

1. **Identify the Problem:**

- Users report an increase in failed prediction requests.

1. **Check CloudWatch Logs:**

- Navigate to CloudWatch Logs for the SentimentAnalysisFunction.
- Look for error messages or stack traces that indicate the source of failures.

1. **Analyze Error Logs:**

- **Error Example:** ValueError: Input 'text' must be a non-empty string.
- **Cause:** Clients are sending empty strings or invalid data formats.

1. **Implement Input Validation:**

- Update the Lambda function to include robust input validation and return meaningful error messages.

MONITORING AND SCALING SERVERLESS MACHINE LEARNING MODELS

```python
Copy code
def lambda_handler(event, context):
    try:
        body = json.loads(event['body'])
        text = body.get('text', '')

        if not isinstance(text, str) or not text.strip():
            raise ValueError("Input 'text' must be a non-empty string.")

        # Proceed with prediction
        ...
    except ValueError as ve:
        logger.error(json.dumps({"error": str(ve)}))
        return {
            'statusCode': 400,
            'body': json.dumps({'error': str(ve)})
        }
    except Exception as e:
        logger.error(json.dumps({"error": str(e)}))
        return {
            'statusCode': 500,
            'body': json.dumps({'error': 'Internal Server Error'})
        }
```

1. **Deploy the Updated Function:**

- Update the Lambda function with the new code via the AWS Console, SAM, or CI/CD pipeline.

1. **Test the Fix:**

- Send test requests with both valid and invalid inputs to ensure that error handling works as expected.

1. **Monitor Post-Fix Performance:**

- Observe CloudWatch metrics to confirm a reduction in error rates.
- Verify that users are receiving appropriate error messages for invalid requests.

1. **Educate API Consumers:**

- Update API documentation to clearly specify input requirements, helping users avoid sending invalid data.

4.5. Example Workflow: Debugging Cold Start Latency in AWS Lambda

1. **Identify the Issue:**

- Users experience inconsistent response times, especially after periods of inactivity.

1. **Analyze Metrics:**

- Use CloudWatch Metrics to observe invocation durations.
- Notice spikes in latency correlated with cold starts.

1. **Enable Provisioned Concurrency:**

- Allocate a number of pre-warmed function instances to reduce cold start occurrences.

```bash
Copy code
aws lambda put-provisioned-concurrency-config --function-name SentimentAnalysisFunction --qualifier $LATEST
```

```
--provisioned-concurrent-executions 50
```

1. **Monitor Impact:**

- Track changes in invocation durations after enabling provisioned concurrency.
- Verify a reduction in cold start latency and improved response times.

1. **Optimize Function Initialization:**

- **Lazy Loading:** Delay loading of heavy resources until they are needed within the function.
- **Minimize Dependencies:** Reduce the size and number of dependencies to speed up function initialization.

```python
Copy code
import json
import joblib
import boto3
import os

def lambda_handler(event, context):
    try:
        # Lazy load model only when needed
        if 'model' not in globals():
            s3 = boto3.client('s3')
            model_path = '/tmp/model.joblib'
            s3.download_file(os.environ['MODEL_BUCKET'],
            os.environ['MODEL_KEY'], model_path)
            global model
            model = joblib.load(model_path)

        # Proceed with prediction
```

...

1. **Implement Warm-Up Strategies:**

- Schedule periodic invocations to keep function instances warm, reducing the likelihood of cold starts.
- Use AWS EventBridge to trigger dummy requests at regular intervals.

```bash
Copy code
aws events put-rule --name "KeepLambdaWarm" --schedule-expression "rate(5 minutes)"
aws events put-targets --rule "KeepLambdaWarm" --targets "Id"="1","Arn"="arn:aws:lambda:region:account-id:function:SentimentAnalysisFunction"
```

1. **Evaluate Results:**

- Observe improvements in response times and overall user experience.
- Balance the costs associated with provisioned concurrency against the performance gains.

Conclusion

Monitoring and scaling are pivotal aspects of maintaining robust and efficient serverless ML deployments. By implementing comprehensive monitoring strategies, leveraging advanced tools and services, and adopting best practices for scaling and cost management, you can ensure that your ML models perform optimally under varying workloads and maintain high levels of accuracy and reliability. Additionally, proactive debugging and troubleshooting techniques enable you to swiftly address and resolve issues, minimizing downtime and enhancing user satisfaction.

Building a Serverless Machine Learning Pipeline

Creating a serverless machine learning (ML) pipeline leverages the scalability, cost-efficiency, and flexibility of serverless architectures to automate the end-to-end ML workflow. From data ingestion and preprocessing to model training, deployment, and monitoring, a serverless pipeline ensures that each stage operates seamlessly without the need for managing underlying infrastructure. This section explores the key components of building a serverless ML pipeline, including automating data ingestion and preprocessing, implementing Continuous Integration and Deployment (CI/CD) for ML models, utilizing AWS Step Functions for orchestration, and optimizing the pipeline for performance and cost.

1. Automating Data Ingestion and Preprocessing

Automating data ingestion and preprocessing is the foundational step in any ML pipeline. It ensures that data is consistently and efficiently collected, cleaned, transformed, and made ready for model training and inference.

1.1. Data Ingestion

Data Sources:
- **Batch Data:** Periodically updated datasets stored in repositories like Amazon S3.
- **Streaming Data:** Real-time data streams from sources like IoT devices,

social media feeds, or application logs.

AWS Services for Data Ingestion:

- **Amazon S3:** Object storage service for batch data ingestion.
- **Amazon Kinesis Data Streams:** Managed service for real-time data streaming.
- **AWS IoT Core:** Platform to connect IoT devices and ingest data.
- **Amazon API Gateway:** Facilitates data ingestion from web and mobile applications.

Automated Ingestion with AWS Lambda: Lambda functions can be triggered by events such as new objects in S3 buckets or messages in Kinesis streams to automate data ingestion processes.

Example: S3 Event Triggered Lambda Function

1. **Set Up S3 Bucket and Event Notification:**

- Create an S3 bucket (e.g., ml-data-bucket).
- Configure event notifications to trigger a Lambda function upon object creation.

1. **Lambda Function to Ingest Data:**

```python
Copy code
import json
import boto3
import gzip
import pandas as pd
from io import BytesIO

def lambda_handler(event, context):
```

```python
    s3 = boto3.client('s3')

    # Extract bucket name and object key from the event
    bucket = event['Records'][0]['s3']['bucket']['name']
    key = event['Records'][0]['s3']['object']['key']

    # Get the object from S3
    response = s3.get_object(Bucket=bucket, Key=key)
    compressed_data = response['Body'].read()

    # Decompress the data (assuming gzip)
    with gzip.GzipFile(fileobj=BytesIO(compressed_data)) as f:
        data = f.read()

    # Convert bytes to pandas DataFrame (assuming CSV format)
    df = pd.read_csv(BytesIO(data))

    # Perform preprocessing (e.g., handling missing values)
    df.fillna(method='ffill', inplace=True)

    # Save the preprocessed data to another S3 bucket
    preprocessed_bucket = 'ml-preprocessed-data'
    preprocessed_key = f'preprocessed/{key}'

    # Convert DataFrame back to CSV bytes
    csv_buffer = BytesIO()
    df.to_csv(csv_buffer, index=False)

    # Upload the preprocessed data
    s3.put_object(Bucket=preprocessed_bucket, Key=preprocessed_key, Body=csv_buffer.getvalue())

    return {
        'statusCode': 200,
        'body': json.dumps('Data ingestion and preprocessing
```

```
completed successfully.')
    }
```

1. **Explanation:**

- **Trigger:** The function is triggered when a new object is uploaded to ml-data-bucket.
- **Process:** It retrieves the object, decompresses it, loads it into a pandas DataFrame, performs preprocessing (e.g., filling missing values), and saves the cleaned data to ml-preprocessed-data bucket.

1.2. Data Preprocessing

Data preprocessing involves cleaning and transforming raw data into a suitable format for ML models. Automation ensures consistency and efficiency, especially when dealing with large or continuously streaming datasets.

Common Preprocessing Steps:

- **Data Cleaning:** Handling missing values, removing duplicates, correcting inconsistencies.
- **Feature Engineering:** Creating new features, encoding categorical variables, normalizing or scaling numerical features.
- **Data Transformation:** Aggregating data, filtering irrelevant information, splitting datasets into training and validation sets.

Automated Preprocessing with AWS Glue: AWS Glue is a fully managed extract, transform, and load (ETL) service that makes it easy to prepare and load data for analytics. It can be integrated with serverless pipelines to perform complex preprocessing tasks.

Example: AWS Glue ETL Job for Data Transformation

1. **Set Up AWS Glue Crawler:**

- Crawl the ml-preprocessed-data S3 bucket to catalog the data schema.

1. **Create an AWS Glue ETL Job:**

```python
Copy code
import sys
from awsglue.transforms import *
from awsglue.utils import getResolvedOptions
from pyspark.context import SparkContext
from awsglue.context import GlueContext
from awsglue.job import Job

args = getResolvedOptions
(sys.argv, ['JOB_NAME'])
sc = SparkContext()
glueContext = GlueContext(sc)
spark = glueContext.spark_session
job = Job(glueContext)
job.init(args['JOB_NAME'], args)

# Load data from catalog
datasource0 = glueContext.
create_dynamic_frame.
from_catalog(database =
"ml_database", table_name =
"preprocessed_data",
transformation_ctx = "datasource0")

# Apply transformations
(e.g., feature engineering)
applymapping1 = ApplyMapping.apply
(frame = datasource0, mappings =
 [("feature1", "double",
"feature1_scaled", "double"),
("feature2", "string",
"feature2_encoded", "string")
], transformation_ctx = "applymapping1")
```

```
# Write transformed data back to S3
datasink2 = glueContext.
write_dynamic_frame.from_
options(frame = applymapping1, connection_type
= "s3", connection_options =
 {"path": "s3://ml-transformed-data/"},
 format = "csv",
transformation_ctx = "datasink2")

job.commit()
```

1. **Explanation:**

- **Load Data:** Reads preprocessed data from the ml_database.preprocessed_data table.
- **Transform:** Applies feature scaling and encoding transformations.
- **Write Data:** Saves the transformed data to ml-transformed-data S3 bucket.

2. Continuous Integration and Deployment (CI/CD) for ML Models

Implementing CI/CD pipelines for ML models ensures that model updates, code changes, and infrastructure modifications are tested, validated, and deployed automatically. This leads to faster iterations, higher quality, and reduced manual errors.

2.1. Importance of CI/CD in ML Pipelines

- **Automated Testing:** Ensures that new code and models meet quality standards before deployment.
- **Consistent Deployments:** Reduces discrepancies between development, staging, and production environments.
- **Rapid Iterations:** Accelerates the cycle of experimentation and deployment, enabling quicker improvements.
- **Version Control:** Maintains a history of changes, facilitating rollback

and auditing.

2.2. Components of an ML CI/CD Pipeline

1. **Source Control:**

- **Repositories:** Host code, model artifacts, and configuration files.
- **Tools:** GitHub, GitLab, AWS CodeCommit.

1. **Build and Test:**

- **Build Process:** Compile code, install dependencies, and package artifacts.
- **Testing:** Run unit tests, integration tests, and model validation.

1. **Deployment:**

- **Infrastructure as Code (IaC):** Define and provision infrastructure using tools like AWS CloudFormation or Terraform.
- **Model Deployment:** Update deployed models with new versions or configurations.

1. **Monitoring and Feedback:**

- **Performance Monitoring:** Track model performance metrics post-deployment.
- **Automated Alerts:** Notify teams of issues or anomalies.

2.3. Implementing CI/CD with AWS CodePipeline and CodeBuild
Step 1: Set Up Source Repository

- **Example:** Use AWS CodeCommit to host your ML project repository.

Step 2: Define Build Project with AWS CodeBuild

- **Buildspec File (buildspec.yml):**

```yaml
Copy code
version: 0.2

phases:
  install:
    commands:
    - pip install -r requirements.txt -t .
  build:
    commands:
      - zip -r function.zip .
  post_build:
    commands:
    - aws s3 cp function.zip s3://ml-deployment-bucket/function.zip
artifacts:
  files:
    - function.zip
```

Step 3: Create AWS CodePipeline

- **Pipeline Stages:**

1. **Source Stage:** Connect to CodeCommit repository.
2. **Build Stage:** Use CodeBuild to package Lambda function.
3. **Deploy Stage:** Deploy the packaged Lambda function using AWS CloudFormation or AWS SAM.

Step 4: Define Deployment with AWS SAM

- **SAM Template (template.yaml):**

```yaml
Copy code
AWSTemplateFormatVersion: '2010-09-09'
Transform: AWS::Serverless-2016-10-31
Description: CI/CD for Serverless ML Model

Resources:
  MLModelInferenceFunction:
    Type: AWS::Serverless::Function
    Properties:
      Handler: lambda_function.lambda_handler
      Runtime: python3.8
      CodeUri: s3://ml-deployment-bucket/function.zip
      MemorySize: 1024
      Timeout: 30
      Environment:
        Variables:
          MODEL_BUCKET: my-ml-models
          MODEL_KEY: model.joblib
      Policies:
        - S3ReadPolicy:
            BucketName: my-ml-models

  MLModelAPIGateway:
    Type: AWS::Serverless::Api
    Properties:
      StageName: prod
      DefinitionBody:
        swagger: "2.0"
        info:
          title: "MLModelAPI"
          version: "1.0"
        paths:
          /predict:
            post:
              consumes:
                - application/json
```

BUILDING A SERVERLESS MACHINE LEARNING PIPELINE

```
              produces:
                - application/json
              responses:
                "200":
description: "Successful prediction"
x-amazon-apigateway-integration:
uri: !Sub arn:aws:
apigateway:${AWS::Region}:
lambda:path/2015-03-31/functions/$
{MLModelInferenceFunction.Arn}/invocations
              httpMethod: POST
              type: aws_proxy
```

Step 5: Automate Deployment with CodePipeline

- **Outcome:** Upon code commit, CodePipeline triggers CodeBuild to package the Lambda function and deploys it using the SAM template, ensuring that the latest model and code are live.

2.4. Example Workflow: CI/CD Pipeline for Serverless Sentiment Analysis Model

1. **CodeCommit Repository Structure:**

```arduino
Copy code
sentiment-analysis/     ├──
  lambda_function.py    ├──
  requirements.txt      ├──
  buildspec.yml         └──
  template.yaml
```

1. **Commit and Push Changes:**

- Developers push updates to lambda_function.py or dependencies in requirements.txt.

1. **CodePipeline Triggers:**

- **Source Stage:** Detects new commits in CodeCommit.
- **Build Stage:** CodeBuild packages the Lambda function, runs tests, and uploads function.zip to S3.
- **Deploy Stage:** SAM deploys the updated Lambda function and API Gateway configurations.

1. **Automated Testing:**

- Integrate unit tests within the buildspec.yml to validate function logic before deployment.

```yaml
Copy code
phases:
  install:
    commands:
      - pip install -r requirements.txt -t .
  build:
    commands:
      - pytest tests/
      - zip -r function.zip .
```

1. **Deployment Confirmation:**

- Upon successful build and tests, the pipeline deploys the updated model to the production environment, ensuring minimal downtime and consistent performance.

3. Using AWS Step Functions for Serverless Pipelines

AWS Step Functions is a serverless orchestration service that allows you to coordinate multiple AWS services into unified workflows. It is particularly useful for building complex ML pipelines that require sequential and parallel processing, error handling, and retries.

3.1. Introduction to AWS Step Functions
Key Features:

- **State Machines:** Define workflows using states and transitions.
- **Built-In Error Handling:** Retry mechanisms and catch blocks to handle failures gracefully.
- **Parallel Execution:** Run multiple tasks concurrently.
- **Integration with AWS Services:** Seamlessly connect with Lambda, SageMaker, S3, DynamoDB, and more.

3.2. Designing an ML Pipeline with Step Functions
Typical ML Pipeline Stages:

1. **Data Ingestion:** Collect raw data from various sources.
2. **Data Preprocessing:** Clean and transform data into a suitable format.
3. **Model Training:** Train the ML model on the preprocessed data.
4. **Model Evaluation:** Assess the model's performance using validation metrics.
5. **Model Deployment:** Deploy the trained model to a production environment.
6. **Monitoring:** Continuously monitor model performance and data quality.

Example ML Pipeline Workflow:

1. **Start:** Initiate the pipeline.
2. **Data Ingestion Task:** Trigger a Lambda function to collect data.
3. **Data Preprocessing Task:** Invoke a Lambda function or AWS Glue job

for preprocessing.
4. **Model Training Task:** Use SageMaker to train the model.
5. **Model Evaluation Task:** Assess model performance metrics.
6. **Decision Task:** Decide whether to deploy the model based on evaluation.
7. **Model Deployment Task:** Deploy the model if it meets performance criteria.
8. **End:** Complete the pipeline.

3.3. Implementing the ML Pipeline with Step Functions
Step 1: Define the State Machine

- **Example State Machine Definition (ml_pipeline.asl.json):**

```json
Copy code
{
  "Comment": "A serverless ML pipeline",
  "StartAt": "DataIngestion",
  "States": {
    "DataIngestion": {
      "Type": "Task",
"Resource": "arn:aws:lambda:us-east-1:123456789012:function:DataIngestionFunction",
"Next": "DataPreprocessing"
    },
    "DataPreprocessing": {
      "Type": "Task",
      "Resource": "arn:aws:lambda:us-east-1:123456789012:function:DataPreprocessingFunction",
      "Next": "ModelTraining"
    },
"ModelTraining": {
"Type": "Task",
```

BUILDING A SERVERLESS MACHINE LEARNING PIPELINE

```
"Resource": "arn:aws:states:::sagemaker:createTrainingJob.sync",
      "Parameters": {
"TrainingJobName": "SentimentAnalysisTrainingJob",
"AlgorithmSpecification": {
"TrainingImage": "123456789012.dkr.ecr.us-east-1.amazonaws.com/xgboost:latest",
"TrainingInputMode": "File"
        },
"RoleArn": "arn:aws:iam::123456789012:role/SageMakerRole",
"InputDataConfig": [
          {
"ChannelName": "train",
"DataSource": {
"S3DataSource": {
"S3DataType": "S3Prefix",
"S3Uri": "s3://ml-transformed-data/train/",
"S3DataDistributionType": "FullyReplicated"
            }
          },
"ContentType": "text/csv",
"CompressionType": "None"
        }
      ],
"OutputDataConfig": {
"S3OutputPath": "s3://ml-model-artifacts/"
        },
"ResourceConfig": {
"InstanceType": "ml.m5.large",
"InstanceCount": 1,
"VolumeSizeInGB": 10
        },
"StoppingCondition": {
"MaxRuntimeInSeconds": 3600
        }
      },
```

```
    "Next": "ModelEvaluation"
 },
"ModelEvaluation": {
"Type": "Task",
"Resource": "arn:aws:
lambda:us-east-1:123456789012:function:
ModelEvaluationFunction",
      "Next": "Decision"
 },
    "Decision": {
"Type": "Choice",
"Choices": [
        {
"Variable": "$.evaluationResult.accuracy",
"NumericGreaterThan": 0.8,
"Next": "ModelDeployment"
        }
    ],
    "Default": "EndState"
   },
"ModelDeployment": {
"Type": "Task",
"Resource": "arn:aws:lambda:
us-east-1:123456789012:function:
ModelDeploymentFunction",
      "End": true
   },
    "EndState": {
      "Type": "Pass",
      "End": true
    }
  }
}
```

Explanation:

- **DataIngestion:** Triggers data ingestion Lambda function.
- **DataPreprocessing:** Triggers data preprocessing Lambda function.
- **ModelTraining:** Initiates a synchronous SageMaker training job.

- **ModelEvaluation:** Invokes a Lambda function to evaluate model performance.
- **Decision:** Checks if the model's accuracy exceeds 80%.
- **ModelDeployment:** Deploys the model if it meets the criteria.
- **EndState:** Ends the workflow if the model doesn't meet performance standards.

Step 2: Deploy the State Machine

- **Using AWS CLI:**

```bash
Copy code
aws stepfunctions create-state-machine --name MLModelPipeline --definition file://ml_pipeline.asl.json --role-arn arn:aws:iam::123456789012:role/StepFunctionsExecutionRole
```

Step 3: Trigger the Pipeline

- **Manual Trigger:**

```bash
Copy code
aws stepfunctions start-execution --state-machine-arn arn:aws:states:us-east-1:123456789012:stateMachine:MLModelPipeline --input '{}'
```

- **Automated Trigger:**
- Schedule the pipeline using Amazon EventBridge (formerly CloudWatch

Events) to run at specified intervals or in response to specific events.

Step 4: Monitor and Manage the Pipeline

- Use the AWS Step Functions console to visualize the workflow execution, monitor progress, and handle errors.
- Integrate CloudWatch Logs and AWS X-Ray for detailed monitoring and tracing.

3.4. Benefits of Using AWS Step Functions

- **Orchestration:** Coordinates multiple AWS services into cohesive workflows.
- **Error Handling:** Built-in retry mechanisms and error-catching capabilities.
- **State Management:** Maintains the state of each step, enabling complex logic and conditional transitions.
- **Scalability:** Automatically scales with the pipeline's demands without manual intervention.

4. Optimizing Your Machine Learning Pipeline

Optimization ensures that your serverless ML pipeline operates efficiently, cost-effectively, and maintains high performance. This involves fine-tuning various components of the pipeline, from data processing to model deployment and monitoring.

4.1. Performance Optimization

- **Efficient Data Processing:**
- **Parallel Processing:** Utilize parallel Lambda invocations or AWS Glue's parallel processing capabilities to handle large datasets.
- **Data Partitioning:** Split data into smaller partitions to enable concurrent processing and reduce latency.
- **Model Optimization:**

- **Model Compression:** Apply techniques like pruning, quantization, or knowledge distillation to reduce model size and inference time.
- **Lightweight Models:** Use simpler models that require fewer computational resources without significantly sacrificing accuracy.
- **Lambda Function Optimization:**
- **Minimize Cold Starts:** Use provisioned concurrency for frequently invoked functions to reduce latency.
- **Optimize Code:** Refactor code to execute faster, remove unnecessary dependencies, and leverage efficient algorithms.
- **SageMaker Optimization:**
- **Instance Selection:** Choose appropriate instance types based on the model's computational requirements.
- **Distributed Training:** Leverage distributed training across multiple instances to accelerate model training.

4.2. Cost Optimization

- **Resource Allocation:**
- **Right-Size Lambda Functions:** Allocate only the necessary memory and CPU resources to avoid over-provisioning.
- **Use Spot Instances:** For training jobs, consider using SageMaker's managed spot training to reduce costs.
- **Efficient Data Storage:**
- **Lifecycle Policies:** Implement S3 lifecycle policies to transition or delete unused data, reducing storage costs.
- **Data Compression:** Store data in compressed formats to minimize storage usage and reduce data transfer costs.
- **API Gateway Optimization:**
- **Caching:** Enable caching for frequently accessed endpoints to reduce Lambda invocations and lower costs.
- **Throttle Settings:** Set appropriate throttling limits to prevent excessive requests that can drive up costs.
- **Monitor and Adjust Usage:**

- Regularly review CloudWatch Metrics and Cost Explorer reports to identify and address cost drivers.
- Implement budget alerts to stay informed about spending and take corrective actions when necessary.

4.3. Security and Compliance Optimization

- **Secure Data Handling:**
- **Encryption:** Ensure all data at rest and in transit is encrypted using AWS Key Management Service (KMS).
- **Access Controls:** Implement strict IAM policies to enforce the principle of least privilege.
- **Compliance:**
- **Audit Trails:** Use AWS CloudTrail to monitor and log API calls for compliance auditing.
- **Data Privacy:** Adhere to data protection regulations like GDPR or HIPAA by implementing necessary data handling and storage practices.

4.4. Automating Pipeline Optimization

- **Automated Scaling:**
- Utilize AWS Lambda's auto-scaling capabilities and Step Functions' dynamic task management to adjust resources based on workload demands automatically.
- **Continuous Monitoring and Feedback:**
- Integrate monitoring tools like Amazon CloudWatch and third-party services to continuously assess pipeline performance and trigger automated remediation actions when issues are detected.

4.5. Example: Optimizing a Serverless Sentiment Analysis Pipeline

1. **Identify Bottlenecks:**

BUILDING A SERVERLESS MACHINE LEARNING PIPELINE

- Use CloudWatch Logs and X-Ray to pinpoint stages with high latency or resource utilization.

1. **Optimize Lambda Functions:**

- Refactor the sentiment analysis Lambda function to reduce execution time by optimizing the inference code and removing unnecessary computations.

```python
Copy code
import json
import joblib
import boto3
import os
from functools import lru_cache

s3 = boto3.client('s3')
MODEL_BUCKET = os.environ['MODEL_BUCKET']
MODEL_KEY = os.environ['MODEL_KEY']

@lru_cache(maxsize=1)
def load_model():
    local_path = '/tmp/model.joblib'
    s3.download_file(MODEL_BUCKET,
MODEL_KEY, local_path)
    model = joblib.load(local_path)
    return model

model = load_model()

def lambda_handler(event, context):
    try:
        body = json.loads(event['body'])
        text = body['text']

        if not isinstance(text, str)
```

```python
    or not text.strip():
        raise ValueError
("Input 'text' must be a non-empty string.")

        # Preprocess text (e.g., tokenization)
        processed_text = preprocess_text(text)

        # Make prediction
        prediction = model.predict([processed_text])[0]
        confidence = model.predict_proba([processed_text])[0].max()

        return {
            'statusCode': 200,
            'body': json.dumps({'prediction': prediction,
             'confidence': confidence})
        }
    except Exception as e:
        return {
            'statusCode': 400,
            'body': json.dumps({'error': str(e)})
        }

def preprocess_text(text):
    # Implement efficient preprocessing steps
    return text.lower().strip()
```

1. **Enable Provisioned Concurrency:**

- Allocate provisioned concurrency to the Lambda function to reduce cold starts.

```bash
Copy code
aws lambda put-provisioned-
concurrency-config
--function-name SentimentAnalysisFunction
--qualifier $LATEST
--provisioned-concurrent-executions 50
```

1. **Implement API Gateway Caching:**

- Enable caching for the /sentiment endpoint to serve frequent predictions from the cache.

1. **Configuration Steps:**

- Navigate to the API Gateway console.
- Select your API and resource (/sentiment).
- Enable caching and set an appropriate TTL (Time to Live) value based on prediction request patterns.

1. **Monitor and Adjust:**

- Continuously monitor CloudWatch Metrics to observe changes in latency, error rates, and cost.
- Adjust memory allocations, concurrency settings, and caching configurations as needed to maintain optimal performance and cost-efficiency.

Conclusion

Building a serverless machine learning pipeline harnesses the power of serverless architectures to deliver scalable, efficient, and cost-effective ML solutions. By automating data ingestion and preprocessing, implementing robust CI/CD pipelines, orchestrating workflows with AWS Step Functions, and optimizing for performance and cost, organizations can streamline their ML operations and accelerate the deployment of intelligent applications.

Embracing serverless ML pipelines not only simplifies infrastructure management but also enhances the agility and responsiveness of ML workflows, enabling teams to focus on innovation and model improvement. As serverless technologies continue to evolve, integrating them into ML pipelines will become increasingly essential for organizations aiming to maintain a competitive edge in the rapidly advancing field of artificial intelligence.

By following the best practices and leveraging the comprehensive suite of AWS services outlined in this guide, you can construct a resilient and high-performing serverless ML pipeline tailored to your specific needs and objectives.

Case Studies: Real-World Serverless Machine Learning Applications

Serverless architectures have revolutionized the way organizations deploy and manage machine learning (ML) applications. By abstracting away the complexities of infrastructure management, serverless platforms enable rapid development, scalability, and cost-efficiency. This section explores real-world case studies across various domains, showcasing how businesses have leveraged serverless ML to drive innovation and achieve their goals. We will delve into predictive analytics, image recognition and processing, natural language processing (NLP), and chatbot development within serverless environments.

1. Predictive Analytics with Serverless ML

Case Study Overview: Retail Demand Forecasting

Company: *ShopSmart Retailers*

Objective:

ShopSmart Retailers aimed to enhance inventory management and optimize supply chains by accurately forecasting product demand across multiple stores and regions.

Challenges:

- **Scalability:** Handling vast amounts of sales data generated daily from numerous outlets.

- **Real-Time Processing:** Providing timely predictions to adjust inventory levels dynamically.
- **Cost Management:** Minimizing operational costs associated with infrastructure provisioning and maintenance.

Implementation:
Architecture Components:

- **Data Ingestion:** Utilized Amazon S3 for storing historical sales data and Amazon Kinesis Data Streams for real-time sales transactions.
- **Data Processing:** AWS Lambda functions processed incoming data, performing aggregation and feature engineering.
- **Model Training:** Leveraged Amazon SageMaker to train predictive models using historical data.
- **Model Deployment:** Deployed trained models as serverless endpoints with SageMaker Hosting Services.
- **Visualization:** Integrated Amazon QuickSight for dashboarding and visualizing demand forecasts.

Workflow Steps:

1. **Data Collection:** Sales data from POS systems was continuously streamed to Amazon Kinesis and archived in Amazon S3.
2. **Preprocessing:** AWS Lambda functions triggered by new data arrivals performed cleaning, normalization, and feature extraction.
3. **Model Training:** Scheduled SageMaker training jobs periodically retrained models with the latest data to capture evolving sales trends.
4. **Inference:** Deployed models generated daily demand forecasts, which were stored back in Amazon S3 and visualized via QuickSight dashboards.
5. **Alerting:** Set up CloudWatch Alarms to notify inventory managers of significant forecast deviations.

Benefits:

- **Scalability:** Automatically handled data spikes during peak sales periods without manual intervention.
- **Cost-Efficiency:** Paid only for compute resources used during data processing and model training, reducing overall costs.
- **Agility:** Enabled rapid iterations and model updates, allowing ShopSmart to adapt to changing market conditions swiftly.
- **Real-Time Insights:** Provided inventory managers with timely forecasts, minimizing stockouts and overstock situations.

Tools and Services Used:

- Amazon S3
- Amazon Kinesis Data Streams
- AWS Lambda
- Amazon SageMaker
- Amazon QuickSight
- Amazon CloudWatch

Results:

- **Accuracy Improvement:** Enhanced demand forecasting accuracy by 15%, leading to better inventory optimization.
- **Cost Reduction:** Achieved a 20% reduction in infrastructure costs by leveraging serverless services.
- **Operational Efficiency:** Streamlined data processing workflows, reducing manual overhead and accelerating decision-making processes.

2. Image Recognition and Processing on Serverless Platforms

Case Study Overview: Automated Quality Inspection in Manufacturing

Company: *PrecisionParts Manufacturing*

Objective:

To implement an automated quality inspection system that leverages image recognition to detect defects in manufactured parts, ensuring high product quality and reducing manual inspection costs.

Challenges:

- **High Volume of Images:** Processing thousands of images daily from production lines.
- **Low Latency Requirements:** Providing immediate feedback to halt production lines in case of defects.
- **Scalability:** Scaling processing capabilities dynamically based on production volume.

Implementation:

Architecture Components:

- **Image Ingestion:** Connected cameras on production lines streamed images to Amazon S3 in real-time.
- **Processing Pipeline:** AWS Lambda functions triggered by S3 uploads performed image preprocessing and defect detection.
- **Machine Learning Model:** Utilized Amazon SageMaker to develop and train a convolutional neural network (CNN) for image classification.
- **Notification System:** Integrated Amazon SNS to send alerts to operators upon defect detection.
- **Data Storage:** Stored processed results and metadata in Amazon DynamoDB for further analysis.

Workflow Steps:

1. **Image Capture:** High-resolution images of manufactured parts were captured and uploaded to a designated S3 bucket.
2. **Triggering Processing:** Each new image upload triggered an AWS Lambda function via S3 event notifications.

3. **Preprocessing:** The Lambda function resized images, normalized pixel values, and prepared them for model inference.
4. **Inference:** The preprocessed images were passed to the SageMaker-hosted CNN model to classify as 'Defective' or 'Non-Defective.'
5. **Alerting:** If a defect was detected, Amazon SNS sent immediate notifications to production supervisors.
6. **Data Logging:** Results were logged in DynamoDB for historical analysis and continuous improvement of the model.

Benefits:

- **Real-Time Detection:** Enabled immediate identification of defective parts, reducing waste and preventing faulty products from reaching customers.
- **Scalability:** Serverless architecture seamlessly scaled during high production periods without performance degradation.
- **Cost Savings:** Eliminated the need for extensive on-premises infrastructure, lowering capital expenditures.
- **Improved Quality Control:** Enhanced consistency and reliability in defect detection compared to manual inspections.

Tools and Services Used:

- **Amazon S3**
- **AWS Lambda**
- **Amazon SageMaker**
- **Amazon SNS**
- **Amazon DynamoDB**
- **Amazon CloudWatch**

Results:

- **Defect Detection Rate:** Increased defect detection rate by 25%, signifi-

cantly enhancing product quality.
- **Operational Efficiency:** Reduced manual inspection labor by 40%, allowing reallocating resources to other critical areas.
- **Cost Efficiency:** Lowered inspection costs by 30% through automation and reduced waste.

3. Serverless Natural Language Processing (NLP)

Case Study Overview: Sentiment Analysis for Customer Feedback

Company: *FeedbackPro Solutions*

Objective:

To develop a sentiment analysis system that automatically processes and analyzes customer feedback from various channels, providing actionable insights to improve products and services.

Challenges:

- **Diverse Data Sources:** Aggregating feedback from emails, social media, surveys, and chat logs.
- **Language Variability:** Handling multiple languages and dialects in customer feedback.
- **Scalability:** Managing fluctuating volumes of feedback data, especially during product launches or campaigns.

Implementation:

Architecture Components:

- **Data Collection:** Integrated Amazon API Gateway with AWS Lambda to collect feedback from web forms and APIs. Utilized Amazon Kinesis Firehose for streaming social media data.
- **Data Storage:** Stored raw feedback data in Amazon S3 and indexed metadata in Amazon Elasticsearch Service for quick retrieval.
- **Preprocessing:** AWS Lambda functions performed text cleaning, language detection, and tokenization.
- **Sentiment Analysis Model:** Employed Amazon Comprehend for out-

of-the-box sentiment analysis and fine-tuned custom models using SageMaker for domain-specific accuracy.
- **Visualization and Reporting:** Used Amazon QuickSight to create dashboards displaying sentiment trends and key insights.
- **Alerting:** Configured Amazon CloudWatch Alarms to notify teams of significant negative sentiment spikes.

Workflow Steps:

1. **Data Ingestion:** Customer feedback was collected through various channels and centralized in Amazon S3 and Elasticsearch.
2. **Preprocessing:** Lambda functions cleaned and prepared the text data, ensuring consistency and readiness for analysis.
3. **Sentiment Analysis:** Processed texts were analyzed using Amazon Comprehend and custom SageMaker models to determine sentiment polarity and intensity.
4. **Data Aggregation:** Analyzed results were aggregated and stored in DynamoDB for historical tracking.
5. **Visualization:** QuickSight dashboards provided real-time insights into customer sentiment across different products and regions.
6. **Proactive Actions:** CloudWatch Alarms triggered notifications when negative sentiment exceeded predefined thresholds, enabling prompt remedial actions.

Benefits:

- **Automated Insights:** Streamlined the analysis of large volumes of unstructured text data, providing timely and actionable insights.
- **Multi-Language Support:** Handled feedback in multiple languages, broadening the scope of analysis.
- **Scalability:** Serverless components seamlessly scaled to handle varying loads, ensuring consistent performance.
- **Cost Efficiency:** Reduced costs by leveraging managed services like

Amazon Comprehend and serverless compute for processing.

Tools and Services Used:

- **Amazon API Gateway**
- **AWS Lambda**
- **Amazon Kinesis Firehose**
- **Amazon S3**
- **Amazon Elasticsearch Service**
- **Amazon Comprehend**
- **Amazon SageMaker**
- **Amazon QuickSight**
- **Amazon CloudWatch**

Results:

- **Enhanced Customer Understanding:** Gained deeper insights into customer sentiments, enabling targeted improvements in products and services.
- **Operational Agility:** Responded swiftly to negative feedback, improving customer satisfaction and retention.
- **Cost Savings:** Minimized infrastructure and operational costs by utilizing serverless and managed NLP services.

4. Building Chatbots with Serverless AI

Case Study Overview: Customer Support Chatbot for E-Commerce
Company: *ShopEase Online Store*
Objective:
To develop an intelligent chatbot that provides real-time customer support, handling inquiries related to orders, product information, and troubleshooting without human intervention.
Challenges:

- **24/7 Availability:** Ensuring the chatbot is available round-the-clock to assist customers across different time zones.
- **Natural Language Understanding:** Accurately interpreting and responding to diverse customer queries.
- **Integration with Backend Systems:** Seamlessly connecting the chatbot with order management, inventory systems, and user databases.
- **Scalability:** Managing high volumes of simultaneous interactions during peak shopping seasons.

Implementation:
Architecture Components:

- **Chat Interface:** Deployed on the company website and mobile app using Amazon Lex for natural language understanding.
- **Backend Integration:** Utilized AWS Lambda functions to interact with internal systems like order tracking, inventory databases, and customer profiles.
- **Data Storage:** Stored conversation logs and user data in Amazon DynamoDB for personalized interactions and continuous improvement.
- **Analytics and Monitoring:** Implemented Amazon CloudWatch and AWS X-Ray to monitor chatbot performance and user interactions.
- **Security:** Ensured secure data handling with AWS IAM roles and encryption mechanisms.

Workflow Steps:

1. **User Interaction:** Customers interacted with the chatbot via the website or mobile app, submitting queries in natural language.
2. **Intent Recognition:** Amazon Lex processed the input to determine the user's intent (e.g., track order, inquire about product details).
3. **Backend Processing:** Based on the identified intent, Lambda functions fetched relevant information from DynamoDB or other services.
4. **Response Generation:** The chatbot formulated appropriate responses

and provided them to the user through Lex.
5. **Continuous Learning:** Collected conversation data was analyzed to refine intents and improve the chatbot's understanding and responses over time.
6. **Monitoring:** CloudWatch monitored chatbot metrics like response times, error rates, and user satisfaction scores, enabling proactive optimizations.

Benefits:

- **24/7 Customer Support:** Provided instant assistance to customers at any time, enhancing user experience and satisfaction.
- **Scalability:** Handled thousands of simultaneous interactions during high-traffic periods without performance degradation.
- **Cost Efficiency:** Reduced the need for a large customer support team, lowering operational costs.
- **Improved Accuracy:** Leveraged machine learning to continuously improve intent recognition and response relevance.
- **Personalization:** Used customer data to offer personalized responses, fostering stronger customer relationships.

Tools and Services Used:

- **Amazon Lex**
- **AWS Lambda**
- **Amazon DynamoDB**
- **Amazon CloudWatch**
- **AWS X-Ray**
- **AWS IAM**

Results:

- **Enhanced Customer Engagement:** Increased customer engagement

by 35% through interactive and responsive support.
- **Operational Cost Savings:** Reduced customer support costs by 50% by automating common inquiries and support tasks.
- **High Availability:** Maintained consistent performance and availability, even during peak shopping events like Black Friday.
- **Continuous Improvement:** Leveraged conversation analytics to iteratively enhance chatbot capabilities, achieving higher accuracy and user satisfaction over time.

Conclusion

The adoption of serverless architectures for machine learning applications has enabled organizations across diverse industries to innovate rapidly, scale effortlessly, and manage costs effectively. Through the case studies presented—ranging from predictive analytics in retail and automated quality inspection in manufacturing to sentiment analysis in customer feedback and intelligent chatbots in e-commerce—it is evident that serverless ML solutions offer robust, flexible, and scalable frameworks to address complex business challenges.

By leveraging managed services such as AWS Lambda, Amazon SageMaker, Amazon Comprehend, and Amazon Lex, companies can focus on developing sophisticated ML models and delivering value-driven insights without the burden of managing underlying infrastructure. The seamless integration of serverless components not only accelerates deployment cycles but also ensures that ML applications remain resilient and adaptable to evolving business needs.

As serverless technologies continue to advance, their integration into ML pipelines will become increasingly pivotal in driving efficiency, fostering innovation, and maintaining competitive advantage in a data-driven world. Organizations aiming to harness the full potential of machine learning are encouraged to explore and implement serverless strategies, tailoring them to their specific requirements and objectives for sustained success.

Security Considerations in Serverless Machine Learning

Deploying machine learning (ML) applications using serverless architectures offers numerous benefits, including scalability, cost-efficiency, and reduced operational overhead. However, security remains a paramount concern, as the abstraction of infrastructure does not eliminate the need for robust security measures. This section delves into the key security considerations for serverless ML applications, focusing on securing serverless functions, ensuring data privacy and compliance, managing access and permissions, and protecting sensitive data within serverless workflows.

1. Securing Serverless Functions

Serverless functions, such as AWS Lambda, are the backbone of serverless ML applications. Securing these functions is critical to prevent unauthorized access, data breaches, and other security threats.

1.1. Secure Coding Practices

- **Input Validation:** Ensure all inputs are validated to prevent injection attacks and malformed data from affecting the function's behavior.

SECURITY CONSIDERATIONS IN SERVERLESS MACHINE LEARNING

```python
Copy code
import json

def lambda_handler(event, context):
    try:
        data = json.loads(event['body'])
        features = data.get('features')
        if not isinstance(features, list):
            raise ValueError("Features must be a list.")
        # Proceed with processing
    except Exception as e:
        return {
            'statusCode': 400,
            'body': json.dumps({'error': str(e)})
        }
```

- **Error Handling:** Avoid exposing sensitive information in error messages. Log detailed errors internally but provide generic messages to users.

```python
Copy code
import json
import logging

logger = logging.getLogger()
logger.setLevel(logging.INFO)

def lambda_handler(event, context):
    try:
        # Processing logic
        pass
    except ValueError as ve:
        logger.error(f"ValueError: {ve}")
        return {
```

```python
            'statusCode': 400,
            'body': json.dumps({'error': 'Invalid input
            provided.'})
        }
    except Exception as e:
        logger.error(f"Unexpected error: {e}")
        return {
            'statusCode': 500,
            'body': json.dumps({'error': 'Internal server error.'})
        }
```

1.2. Runtime and Dependency Security

- **Update Runtimes:** Use the latest supported runtime versions to benefit from security patches and improvements.
- **Manage Dependencies:** Regularly update third-party libraries to patch known vulnerabilities. Use tools like AWS Lambda Layers to manage dependencies separately.
- **Minimal Privileges:** Only include necessary dependencies to reduce the attack surface.

1.3. Function Configuration

- **Environment Variables:** Encrypt sensitive environment variables using AWS Key Management Service (KMS).

```bash
Copy code
aws lambda update-function-configuration --function-name MyFunction \
    --environment "Variables={MODEL_BUCKET=encrypted-bucket-name}" \
    --kms-key-arn arn:aws:kms:region:account-id:key/key-id
```

SECURITY CONSIDERATIONS IN SERVERLESS MACHINE LEARNING

- **Timeout and Memory Settings:** Configure appropriate timeout and memory allocations to mitigate denial-of-service (DoS) attacks and resource exhaustion.

1.4. Network Security

- **VPC Integration:** Place Lambda functions inside a Virtual Private Cloud (VPC) to control network access and integrate with other secure resources.
- **Private Subnets:** Use private subnets without direct internet access to enhance security.
- **Security Groups:** Define strict security group rules to allow only necessary inbound and outbound traffic.

1.5. Monitoring and Logging

- **Enable Detailed Logging:** Use AWS CloudWatch Logs to monitor function execution and detect anomalies.
- **AWS CloudTrail:** Track API calls and changes to Lambda functions for auditing and forensic analysis.

1.6. Example: Securing an AWS Lambda Function for ML Inference

1. **Create a Secure IAM Role:**
2. Assign least privilege permissions required for the function to operate.

```json
Copy code
{
  "Version": "2012-10-17",
  "Statement": [
    {
```

```json
      "Effect": "Allow",
      "Action": [
        "s3:GetObject",
        "s3:PutObject"
      ],
      "Resource": [
        "arn:aws:s3:::ml-models-bucket/*",
        "arn:aws:s3:::ml-inference-results/*"
      ]
    },
    {
      "Effect": "Allow",
      "Action": [
        "logs:CreateLogGroup",
        "logs:CreateLogStream",
        "logs:PutLogEvents"
      ],
      "Resource": "arn:aws:logs:*:*:*"
    }
  ]
}
```

1. **Configure Environment Variables with Encryption:**
2. Use AWS KMS to encrypt sensitive variables.
3. **Deploy the Function within a VPC:**
4. Assign the function to a secure VPC with appropriate security groups.

2. Data Privacy and Compliance in ML Projects

Ensuring data privacy and adhering to compliance regulations is essential in serverless ML projects, especially when handling sensitive or regulated data.

2.1. Understanding Data Privacy Regulations

- **GDPR (General Data Protection Regulation):** Protects personal data of individuals in the EU.
- **HIPAA (Health Insurance Portability and Accountability Act):**

Governs the handling of protected health information (PHI) in the US.
- **CCPA (California Consumer Privacy Act):** Provides data privacy rights to California residents.

2.2. Data Encryption

- **At Rest:** Encrypt data stored in S3, DynamoDB, or other storage services using AWS KMS.

```bash
Copy code
aws s3api put-bucket-encryption --bucket ml-data-bucket
--server-side-encryption-configuration '{
  "Rules": [{
    "ApplyServerSideEncryptionByDefault": {
      "SSEAlgorithm": "AES256"
    }
  }]
}'
```

- **In Transit:** Use TLS/SSL protocols to encrypt data as it moves between services.

2.3. Data Minimization and Anonymization

- **Minimize Data Collection:** Only collect data necessary for the ML tasks to reduce exposure.
- **Anonymization Techniques:** Apply techniques like tokenization, hashing, or masking to anonymize personal or sensitive data.

2.4. Compliance Auditing and Reporting

- **AWS Artifact:** Access compliance reports and manage licenses.

- **AWS Config:** Monitor and evaluate the configuration of AWS resources to ensure compliance.
- **Audit Trails:** Use AWS CloudTrail to maintain detailed logs of data access and modifications.

2.5. Example: Ensuring GDPR Compliance in a Serverless ML Pipeline

1. **Data Collection:**
2. Implement consent mechanisms and ensure explicit permission before collecting personal data.
3. **Data Storage:**
4. Encrypt personal data in S3 using AWS KMS.
5. Implement access controls to restrict data access to authorized roles only.
6. **Data Processing:**
7. Use AWS Lambda to process data with environment variables encrypted.
8. Ensure that processed data does not contain identifiable information unless necessary.
9. **Data Deletion:**
10. Implement data lifecycle policies to delete or archive data as per GDPR requirements.
11. **Audit and Reporting:**
12. Regularly review AWS CloudTrail logs to ensure compliance.
13. Use AWS Config to monitor resource configurations and compliance statuses.

3. Managing Access and Permissions

Proper access control is fundamental to securing serverless ML applications. This involves managing who has access to what resources and ensuring that permissions are tightly controlled.

3.1. Principle of Least Privilege

- **Grant Minimal Permissions:** Assign only the permissions necessary

SECURITY CONSIDERATIONS IN SERVERLESS MACHINE LEARNING

for users and services to perform their tasks.

```json
Copy code
{
   "Version": "2012-10-17",
   "Statement": [
     {
       "Effect": "Allow",
       "Action": "lambda:InvokeFunction",
       "Resource":
       "arn:aws:lambda:region:account-id:function:MLModelInferenceFunction"
     }
   ]
}
```

3.2. IAM Roles and Policies

- **Service Roles:** Assign roles to AWS services (e.g., Lambda functions) to grant necessary permissions without embedding credentials.
- **User Roles:** Create roles for users with permissions scoped to their job functions.
- **Managed Policies vs. Inline Policies:**
- **Managed Policies:** Reusable and easier to manage across multiple entities.
- **Inline Policies:** Attach directly to a single user or service, suitable for specific permissions.

3.3. Fine-Grained Permissions

- **Resource-Level Permissions:** Control access to specific resources like S3 buckets, DynamoDB tables, or SageMaker endpoints.

```json
Copy code
{
  "Version": "2012-10-17",
  "Statement": [
    {
      "Effect": "Allow",
      "Action": [
        "s3:GetObject",
        "s3:PutObject"
      ],
      "Resource": "arn:aws:s3:::ml-data-bucket/*"
    }
  ]
}
```

- **Conditional Access:** Use condition keys to grant permissions based on context, such as IP addresses or MFA authentication.

```json
Copy code
{
  "Version": "2012-10-17",
  "Statement": [
    {
      "Effect": "Allow",
      "Action": "s3:ListBucket",
      "Resource": "arn:aws:s3:::ml-data-bucket",
      "Condition": {
        "IpAddress": {"aws:SourceIp": "203.0.113.0/24"}
      }
    }
  ]
}
```

3.4. Temporary Credentials with AWS STS

SECURITY CONSIDERATIONS IN SERVERLESS MACHINE LEARNING

- **AWS Security Token Service (STS):** Issue temporary, limited-privilege credentials for users or services that need temporary access.

```bash
Copy code
aws sts assume-role --role-arn
arn:aws:iam::account-id:role/RoleName --role-session-name
SessionName
```

3.5. Example: Implementing Least Privilege for a SageMaker Training Job

1. **Create an IAM Role for SageMaker:**

```json
Copy code
{
  "Version": "2012-10-17",
  "Statement": [
    {
      "Effect": "Allow",
      "Action": [
        "s3:GetObject",
        "s3:PutObject"
      ],
      "Resource": [
        "arn:aws:s3:::ml-training-data/*",
        "arn:aws:s3:::ml-model-artifacts/*"
      ]
    },
    {
      "Effect": "Allow",
      "Action": [
        "logs:CreateLogGroup",
        "logs:CreateLogStream",
```

```
            "logs:PutLogEvents"
        ],
        "Resource": "*"
    }
  ]
}
```

1. **Attach the Role to SageMaker Training Job:**

```
python
Copy code
import boto3

sagemaker = boto3.client('sagemaker')

response = sagemaker.create_training_job(
    TrainingJobName='SentimentAnalysisTraining',
    AlgorithmSpecification={
        'TrainingImage':
        '123456789012.dkr.ecr.region.amazonaws.com/xgboost:latest',
        'TrainingInputMode': 'File'
    },
    RoleArn='arn:aws:iam::account-id:role/SageMakerRole',
    InputDataConfig=[...],
    OutputDataConfig={
        'S3OutputPath': 's3://ml-model-artifacts/'
    },
    ResourceConfig={
        'InstanceType': 'ml.m5.large',
        'InstanceCount': 1,
        'VolumeSizeInGB': 10
    },
    StoppingCondition={
        'MaxRuntimeInSeconds': 3600
    }
)
```

SECURITY CONSIDERATIONS IN SERVERLESS MACHINE LEARNING

3.6. Multi-Factor Authentication (MFA)

- **MFA Enforcement:** Require MFA for privileged operations to add an extra layer of security.

```json
Copy code
{
  "Version": "2012-10-17",
  "Statement": [
    {
      "Effect": "Deny",
      "Action": [
        "s3:DeleteObject"
      ],
      "Resource": "arn:aws:s3:::ml-data-bucket/*",
      "Condition": {
        "Bool": {"aws:MultiFactorAuthPresent": "false"}
      }
    }
  ]
}
```

4. Protecting Sensitive Data in Serverless Workflows

Handling sensitive data securely within serverless ML workflows is critical to prevent data breaches and maintain trust. This involves implementing robust encryption, access controls, and data handling practices throughout the data lifecycle.

4.1. Data Encryption

- **Encryption at Rest:**
- **Amazon S3:** Enable server-side encryption (SSE) using AES-256 or AWS KMS-managed keys.

```bash
Copy code
aws s3api put-bucket-encryption --bucket ml-data-bucket
--server-side-encryption-configuration '{
  "Rules": [{
    "ApplyServerSideEncryptionByDefault": {
      "SSEAlgorithm": "AES256"
    }
  }]
}'
```

- **Amazon DynamoDB:** Enable encryption at rest using AWS KMS.
- **Encryption in Transit:**
- **TLS/SSL:** Ensure all data transfers use secure protocols like HTTPS and SSL/TLS.
- **API Gateway:** Enforces HTTPS endpoints by default.
- **Lambda Functions:** Use HTTPS when accessing external APIs or services.

4.2. Data Access Controls

- **IAM Policies:** Restrict data access to only those functions or users that require it, adhering to the principle of least privilege.
- **S3 Bucket Policies:** Define bucket policies to control access based on roles, IP addresses, or other conditions.

```json
Copy code
{
  "Version": "2012-10-17",
  "Statement": [
    {
```

```
    "Sid": "AllowLambdaAccess",
    "Effect": "Allow",
    "Principal": {
      "AWS": "arn:aws:iam::account-id:role/LambdaExecutionRole"
    },
    "Action": [
      "s3:GetObject",
      "s3:PutObject"
    ],
    "Resource": "arn:aws:s3:::ml-data-bucket/*"
  }
 ]
}
```

- **VPC Endpoints:** Use VPC endpoints to secure data traffic between serverless functions and AWS services, preventing data from traversing the public internet.

4.3. Data Masking and Tokenization

- **Data Masking:** Anonymize or obfuscate sensitive data fields to prevent exposure during processing.

```
python
Copy code
def mask_pii(data):
    return {
        "name": "****",
        "email": "****@example.com",
        "phone": "****-****"
    }
```

- **Tokenization:** Replace sensitive data with non-sensitive equivalents (tokens) that can be mapped back to the original data securely.

4.4. Secure Data Transfer Between Services

- **AWS Secrets Manager:** Store and retrieve sensitive information like API keys, database credentials, and encryption keys securely.

```python
Copy code
import boto3
from botocore.exceptions import ClientError

def get_secret():
    secret_name = "my_secret"
    region_name = "us-east-1"

    client = boto3.client(service_name='secretsmanager',
    region_name=region_name)

    try:
        get_secret_value_response =
        client.get_secret_value(SecretId=secret_name)
    except ClientError as e:
        raise e
    else:
        return get_secret_value_response['SecretString']
```

- **Secure APIs:** Use mutual TLS authentication or API keys to secure interactions between serverless functions and external services.

4.5. Example: Protecting Sensitive Data in a Serverless ML Inference Pipeline

1. **Data Storage with Encryption:**

SECURITY CONSIDERATIONS IN SERVERLESS MACHINE LEARNING

- Store raw and preprocessed data in S3 buckets with SSE-KMS encryption.
- Enable DynamoDB encryption for storing model predictions and user data.

1. **Access Control with IAM Roles:**

- Assign least privilege roles to Lambda functions, granting only necessary S3 and DynamoDB permissions.

1. **Data Masking in Lambda Functions:**

```python
Copy code
import json
import boto3
import os
import joblib

s3 = boto3.client('s3')
dynamodb = boto3.resource('dynamodb')

MODEL_BUCKET = os.environ['MODEL_BUCKET']
MODEL_KEY = os.environ['MODEL_KEY']
TABLE_NAME = os.environ['TABLE_NAME']

def load_model():
    local_path = '/tmp/model.joblib'
    s3.download_file(MODEL_BUCKET, MODEL_KEY, local_path)
    model = joblib.load(local_path)
    return model

model = load_model()
table = dynamodb.Table(TABLE_NAME)

def lambda_handler(event, context):
```

```python
    try:
        body = json.loads(event['body'])
        features = body['features']
        pii_data = body.get('pii', {})
        
        # Mask PII
        masked_pii = mask_pii(pii_data)
        
        # Make prediction
        prediction = model.predict([features])[0]
        confidence = model.predict_proba([features])[0].max()
        
        # Store result with masked PII
        table.put_item(
            Item={
                'request_id': body.get('request_id'),
                'prediction': prediction,
                'confidence': confidence,
                'pii': masked_pii
            }
        )
        
        return {
            'statusCode': 200,
            'body': json.dumps({'prediction': prediction,
            'confidence': confidence})
        }
    except Exception as e:
        return {
            'statusCode': 400,
            'body': json.dumps({'error': str(e)})
        }

def mask_pii(pii_data):
    return {
        "name": "****",
        "email": "****@example.com",
        "phone": "****-****"
    }
```

1. **Use Secrets Manager for Sensitive Configurations:**

- Store API keys and database credentials in Secrets Manager and retrieve them securely within Lambda functions.

1. **Implement VPC Endpoints:**

- Configure Lambda functions to access S3 and DynamoDB via VPC endpoints, ensuring data does not traverse the public internet.

Conclusion

Securing serverless machine learning applications is a multifaceted endeavor that requires careful consideration of various aspects, including function security, data privacy, access management, and protection of sensitive data. By adhering to best practices such as the principle of least privilege, implementing robust encryption mechanisms, and leveraging AWS's comprehensive suite of security services, organizations can build secure and compliant serverless ML pipelines.

Moreover, integrating security into every stage of the ML lifecycle—from data ingestion and preprocessing to model training and deployment—ensures that security is not an afterthought but a foundational component of the architecture. As serverless technologies continue to evolve, maintaining a strong security posture will remain critical to safeguarding data, preserving trust, and ensuring the successful deployment of machine learning applications.

Additional Best Practices and Recommendations

1. **Regular Security Audits and Penetration Testing:**

- Conduct periodic security assessments to identify and remediate vulnerabilities.
- Utilize AWS Inspector for automated security assessments.

1. **Automate Security Compliance:**

- Use AWS Config Rules to enforce compliance standards across resources.
- Integrate security checks into CI/CD pipelines to ensure that deployments adhere to security policies.

1. **Implement Logging and Monitoring:**

- Centralize logs using CloudWatch Logs or third-party tools for comprehensive monitoring.
- Set up dashboards and alerts to monitor security metrics and respond to incidents promptly.

1. **Educate and Train Teams:**

- Ensure that development and operations teams are aware of security best practices.
- Provide training on secure coding, data handling, and incident response procedures.

1. **Stay Updated with Security Patches:**

- Regularly update serverless function runtimes and dependencies to incorporate the latest security patches.

Advanced Topics: Edge Computing and Serverless AI

The convergence of edge computing and serverless architectures is revolutionizing the deployment and scalability of artificial intelligence (AI) applications. Edge AI brings computation closer to data sources, enabling real-time processing and reduced latency, while serverless architectures offer scalability, cost-efficiency, and simplified infrastructure management. This section explores advanced topics at the intersection of edge computing and serverless AI, including an introduction to Edge AI, deploying AI models on edge devices using serverless paradigms, integrating Edge AI with cloud serverless architectures, and examining compelling use cases in the Internet of Things (IoT) landscape.

1. Introduction to Edge AI

Edge AI refers to the deployment of artificial intelligence algorithms and models directly on edge devices—hardware located near the data source, such as smartphones, IoT sensors, drones, and autonomous vehicles—rather than relying solely on centralized cloud-based servers. This paradigm shift enables real-time data processing, reduced latency, enhanced privacy, and decreased bandwidth usage.

1.1. What is Edge AI?

- **Definition:** Edge AI combines edge computing and artificial intelligence, allowing data processing and inference to occur on local devices instead of remote cloud servers.
- **Components:**
- **Edge Devices:** Hardware devices with computing capabilities (e.g., smartphones, IoT devices, gateways).
- **AI Models:** Machine learning models optimized for deployment on resource-constrained devices.
- **Edge Infrastructure:** Software frameworks and tools that facilitate AI deployment and management on edge devices.

1.2. Importance of Edge AI

- **Reduced Latency:** Processing data locally eliminates the delays associated with transmitting data to the cloud, enabling real-time responses crucial for applications like autonomous driving and industrial automation.
- **Bandwidth Efficiency:** By processing data on-device, Edge AI minimizes the amount of data sent to the cloud, conserving network bandwidth and reducing costs.
- **Enhanced Privacy and Security:** Sensitive data can be processed locally without being transmitted over networks, mitigating privacy concerns and potential security breaches.
- **Reliability and Resilience:** Edge AI enables devices to operate independently of cloud connectivity, ensuring continuous functionality even in environments with unreliable or limited internet access.

1.3. Edge AI vs. Cloud AI

FeatureEdge AICloud AI

Latency

Low latency due to local processing

Higher latency due to data transmission

Bandwidth Usage

Reduced, as less data is sent to the cloud
Higher, as large volumes of data are transmitted
Privacy
Enhanced, data remains on local devices
Potential privacy concerns with data in transit and storage
Scalability
Limited by device resources
Highly scalable with cloud infrastructure
Cost
Lower operational costs for data transmission
Potentially higher due to bandwidth and storage costs

1.4. Technologies Enabling Edge AI

- **AI Frameworks:** TensorFlow Lite, PyTorch Mobile, ONNX Runtime, NVIDIA Jetson, AWS IoT Greengrass.
- **Hardware Accelerators:** GPUs, TPUs, FPGAs, and dedicated AI chips designed for efficient inference on edge devices.
- **Serverless Platforms:** AWS Lambda@Edge, Azure Functions on IoT Edge, enabling serverless computing paradigms at the network's edge.

2. Deploying AI Models on Edge Devices Using Serverless

Deploying AI models on edge devices using serverless architectures involves leveraging serverless computing principles to manage the lifecycle of AI models on devices. This approach simplifies deployment, scaling, and maintenance, enabling efficient AI inference directly on edge hardware.

2.1. Serverless Paradigm for Edge AI

- **Definition:** Applying serverless computing principles—such as event-driven execution, automatic scaling, and pay-per-use pricing—to manage AI workloads on edge devices.
- **Benefits:**
- **Simplified Deployment:** Abstracts the underlying infrastructure, allowing developers to focus on AI model development and deployment

logic.
- **Scalability:** Automatically adjusts compute resources based on demand, ensuring optimal performance without manual intervention.
- **Cost-Efficiency:** Charges based on actual usage, reducing costs associated with idle resources.

2.2. Deployment Strategies

1. **Containerization:**

- **Docker Containers:** Package AI models and their dependencies into lightweight containers for consistent deployment across edge devices.
- **Kubernetes on Edge:** Use Kubernetes distributions tailored for edge environments (e.g., K3s) to orchestrate containerized AI workloads.

1. **Serverless Frameworks:**

- **AWS Lambda@Edge:** Extend AWS Lambda functions to edge locations, enabling serverless AI processing closer to end-users.
- **Azure Functions on IoT Edge:** Deploy serverless functions directly on IoT Edge devices for local AI inference.

1. **Managed Services:**

- **AWS IoT Greengrass:** Deploy and manage serverless Lambda functions, machine learning models, and other resources on edge devices.
- **Google Cloud Functions for Edge:** Utilize Google's serverless functions tailored for edge deployments to run AI models locally.

2.3. Steps to Deploy AI Models Using Serverless on Edge Devices
Example: Deploying an Image Classification Model Using AWS IoT Greengrass

ADVANCED TOPICS: EDGE COMPUTING AND SERVERLESS AI

1. **Train and Optimize the Model:**

- Train the image classification model using frameworks like TensorFlow or PyTorch.
- Optimize the model for edge deployment using TensorFlow Lite or ONNX for reduced size and faster inference.

1. **Set Up AWS IoT Greengrass:**

- **Create a Greengrass Group:** In the AWS Management Console, navigate to AWS IoT Greengrass and create a new Greengrass group.
- **Configure Core Device:** Define the edge device as the Greengrass core, ensuring it has the necessary permissions and network access.

1. **Deploy the Serverless Function:**

- **Create a Lambda Function:** Develop a Lambda function that loads the optimized model and performs inference on incoming images.
- **Configure Function in Greengrass:** Add the Lambda function to the Greengrass group, specifying the execution settings and dependencies.

1. **Deploy to Edge Device:**

- **Install Greengrass Core Software:** On the edge device, install the Greengrass core software and associate it with the Greengrass group.
- **Deploy Configuration:** Push the Greengrass group configuration to the edge device, initiating the deployment of the Lambda function.

1. **Invoke the Function:**

- **Event Trigger:** Configure the Lambda function to trigger on specific events, such as new images being uploaded to a local storage directory.
- **Inference:** The function processes the image, performs classification,

and outputs the results locally or to the cloud as needed.

Sample Lambda Function Code:

```python
Copy code
import json
import boto3
import tensorflow as tf
import numpy as np
from PIL import Image

# Load the TensorFlow Lite model
interpreter = tf.lite.Interpreter(model_path='model.tflite')
interpreter.allocate_tensors()
input_details = interpreter.get_input_details()
output_details = interpreter.get_output_details()

def lambda_handler(event, context):
    try:
        # Assume event contains the path to the image
        image_path = event['image_path']

        # Load and preprocess the image
        image = Image.open(image_path).resize((224, 224))
        input_data = np.expand_dims(np.array(image) / 255.0,
        axis=0).astype(np.float32)

        # Perform inference
        interpreter.set_tensor(input_details[0]['index'],
        input_data)
        interpreter.invoke()
        output_data =
        interpreter.get_tensor(output_details[0]['index'])
        prediction = np.argmax(output_data, axis=1)[0]

        # Return the prediction
        return {
            'statusCode': 200,
```

```
        'body': json.dumps({'prediction': int(prediction)})
    }
except Exception as e:
    return {
        'statusCode': 500,
        'body': json.dumps({'error': str(e)})
    }
```

2.4. Tools and Frameworks

- **AWS IoT Greengrass:** Extends AWS services to edge devices, allowing serverless functions and machine learning models to run locally.
- **TensorFlow Lite:** Optimizes TensorFlow models for deployment on mobile and edge devices with limited resources.
- **ONNX Runtime:** Provides cross-platform, high-performance inference for machine learning models on various hardware.
- **Serverless Framework:** Facilitates the deployment of serverless applications across multiple cloud providers, including edge integrations.

3. Combining Edge AI with Cloud Serverless Architecture

Integrating Edge AI with cloud-based serverless architectures creates a hybrid ecosystem that leverages the strengths of both environments. This combination enables comprehensive data processing, seamless scalability, and enhanced functionality, ensuring robust and efficient AI applications.

3.1. Hybrid Architecture Overview

- **Edge Components:**
- **Data Collection:** Sensors and devices collect data locally.
- **Local Processing:** Edge devices perform initial data processing and inference using serverless functions deployed on the edge.
- **Decision Making:** Immediate actions based on local inference results.
- **Cloud Components:**
- **Centralized Storage:** Aggregates data from multiple edge devices for long-term storage and analysis.

- **Advanced Analytics:** Performs complex data processing, model training, and global inference.
- **Management and Orchestration:** Coordinates deployments, updates, and monitoring across edge and cloud environments.

3.2. Benefits of Integration

- **Optimized Performance:** Offloads complex processing to the cloud while handling real-time inference at the edge.
- **Scalability:** Combines the cloud's ability to scale with the edge's capacity to manage localized workloads.
- **Data Synchronization:** Ensures consistent data flow and model updates between edge devices and the cloud.
- **Resilience:** Enhances system reliability by distributing workloads and mitigating single points of failure.

3.3. Implementation Strategies

1. **Model Synchronization:**

- **Version Control:** Maintain consistent versions of AI models across edge and cloud environments.
- **Automated Updates:** Use CI/CD pipelines to deploy model updates to both edge devices and cloud services simultaneously.

1. **Data Flow Management:**

- **Local Aggregation:** Process and aggregate data at the edge before sending summaries to the cloud.
- **Selective Transmission:** Only transmit essential data to the cloud, reducing bandwidth usage and enhancing privacy.

1. **Unified Monitoring and Management:**

- **Central Dashboards:** Monitor performance metrics and operational status of both edge and cloud components from a single interface.
- **Automated Alerts:** Trigger notifications based on anomalies detected in either environment, enabling proactive maintenance.

1. **Security and Compliance:**

- **End-to-End Encryption:** Secure data transmission between edge devices and the cloud.
- **Access Controls:** Implement consistent IAM policies across both environments to manage permissions effectively.

3.4. Example: Smart Agriculture with Edge AI and Cloud Serverless Integration

Objective:

Develop a smart agriculture system that monitors soil conditions and automates irrigation based on real-time data and predictive analytics.

Architecture Components:

- **Edge Devices:**
- **Soil Sensors:** Collect data on moisture levels, temperature, and nutrient content.
- **Edge Compute Nodes:** Run serverless functions to process sensor data and make immediate irrigation decisions.
- **Cloud Services:**
- **Data Lake:** Store aggregated sensor data in Amazon S3 for historical analysis.
- **Analytics and ML:** Use AWS Lambda and Amazon SageMaker to analyze data trends and predict future irrigation needs.
- **Visualization:** Implement Amazon QuickSight dashboards to provide farmers with insights and recommendations.

Workflow Steps:

1. **Data Collection at Edge:**

- Soil sensors transmit data to edge compute nodes.
- AWS IoT Greengrass executes serverless functions that process data locally, determining if irrigation is needed.

1. **Immediate Decision Making:**

- If moisture levels are low, the edge function triggers irrigation systems to water the crops promptly.

1. **Data Aggregation and Storage:**

- Processed data and irrigation actions are sent to the cloud, where they are stored in Amazon S3.

1. **Advanced Analytics and Prediction:**

- AWS Lambda functions analyze historical data to identify patterns and train predictive models using Amazon SageMaker.
- Models forecast future soil conditions and optimize irrigation schedules.

1. **Continuous Improvement:**

- Model updates are deployed to edge devices through automated CI/CD pipelines, ensuring that edge functions benefit from the latest analytics.

1. **Visualization and Reporting:**

- Farmers access real-time dashboards displaying soil conditions, irrigation actions, and predictive insights, enabling informed decision-making.

Benefits:

- **Resource Optimization:** Automated irrigation conserves water and ensures crops receive optimal moisture levels.
- **Scalability:** The system can easily expand to cover additional fields or incorporate more sensors without significant infrastructure changes.
- **Cost-Efficiency:** Leveraging serverless architectures reduces operational costs by eliminating the need for dedicated servers and enabling pay-as-you-go pricing.
- **Enhanced Productivity:** Real-time insights and automated actions improve crop yields and reduce manual labor.

Tools and Services Used:

- **AWS IoT Greengrass**
- **AWS Lambda**
- **Amazon SageMaker**
- **Amazon S3**
- **Amazon QuickSight**
- **AWS CloudWatch**

4. Use Cases for Edge AI in IoT

Edge AI plays a pivotal role in enhancing IoT applications by enabling intelligent, real-time data processing and decision-making directly on edge devices. The following use cases illustrate the transformative impact of Edge AI in various industries.

4.1. Industrial Automation and Predictive Maintenance
Scenario:
Manufacturing facilities utilize IoT sensors to monitor machinery performance, detecting anomalies that may indicate potential failures.
Implementation:

- **Sensors:** Deploy vibration, temperature, and pressure sensors on critical machinery.
- **Edge AI:** Edge devices process sensor data in real-time, using ML models

to identify patterns indicative of wear and tear or impending failures.
- **Actions:** Trigger maintenance alerts or automatically shut down malfunctioning equipment to prevent accidents and reduce downtime.

Benefits:

- **Enhanced Reliability:** Proactively address equipment issues before they escalate.
- **Cost Savings:** Reduce maintenance costs and extend machinery lifespan through timely interventions.
- **Operational Efficiency:** Minimize unplanned downtime and maintain consistent production levels.

4.2. Smart Home Automation
Scenario:

Smart home systems leverage Edge AI to provide personalized and responsive environments for residents.

Implementation:

- **Devices:** Utilize smart thermostats, lighting systems, security cameras, and voice assistants equipped with AI capabilities.
- **Edge AI:** Local processing enables real-time adjustments based on user behavior, preferences, and environmental conditions without relying on cloud connectivity.
- **Integration:** Seamlessly connect edge devices with cloud services for centralized management, data aggregation, and advanced analytics.

Benefits:

- **Personalization:** Offer tailored experiences by learning user preferences and habits.
- **Privacy:** Keep sensitive data processing on-device, enhancing privacy and security.

ADVANCED TOPICS: EDGE COMPUTING AND SERVERLESS AI

- **Reliability:** Ensure continuous functionality even during internet outages.

4.3. Autonomous Vehicles
Scenario:
Self-driving cars and drones rely on Edge AI for navigation, obstacle detection, and real-time decision-making.
Implementation:

- **Sensors:** Incorporate cameras, LIDAR, radar, and GPS systems to gather environmental data.
- **Edge AI:** Onboard AI systems process sensor data instantly, enabling dynamic route planning, obstacle avoidance, and safe maneuvering.
- **Connectivity:** Use cloud services for map updates, software updates, and fleet management without compromising real-time operations.

Benefits:

- **Safety:** Reduce response times to sudden obstacles, enhancing passenger and pedestrian safety.
- **Efficiency:** Optimize routes and driving behaviors for fuel efficiency and reduced emissions.
- **Scalability:** Enable fleets of autonomous vehicles to operate cohesively with minimal latency.

4.4. Healthcare and Wearable Devices
Scenario:
Wearable health monitors utilize Edge AI to track vital signs and detect health anomalies in real-time.
Implementation:

- **Devices:** Equip wearables with sensors for heart rate, blood oxygen levels, activity tracking, and more.

- **Edge AI:** Process data locally to identify irregularities such as arrhythmias, falls, or other health emergencies.
- **Alerts:** Notify users or healthcare providers immediately upon detecting critical conditions, facilitating timely interventions.

Benefits:

- **Immediate Response:** Provide real-time health monitoring and emergency alerts, potentially saving lives.
- **Data Privacy:** Keep sensitive health data on-device, ensuring user privacy and compliance with health data regulations.
- **Continuous Monitoring:** Enable seamless and uninterrupted health tracking without relying on constant cloud connectivity.

4.5. Retail and Customer Experience
Scenario:

Retail stores employ Edge AI to enhance customer experiences through intelligent interactions and personalized services.

Implementation:

- **Devices:** Install smart kiosks, interactive displays, and surveillance cameras with AI capabilities.
- **Edge AI:** Analyze customer behavior, preferences, and interactions in real-time to offer personalized recommendations, targeted promotions, and improved store layouts.
- **Integration:** Connect with cloud-based inventory systems and CRM platforms for holistic customer relationship management.

Benefits:

- **Enhanced Customer Engagement:** Provide personalized experiences that increase customer satisfaction and loyalty.
- **Operational Insights:** Gain real-time insights into customer behaviors

and preferences to inform business strategies.
- **Efficiency:** Optimize store operations, inventory management, and staff allocation based on real-time data analytics.

Conclusion

Edge computing and serverless architectures are pivotal in advancing the deployment and scalability of AI applications across diverse industries. By bringing computation closer to data sources, Edge AI enables real-time processing, reduced latency, and enhanced privacy, while serverless paradigms simplify deployment, scaling, and cost management. The integration of Edge AI with cloud-based serverless services creates a robust and flexible ecosystem capable of addressing complex, data-intensive challenges with efficiency and agility.

Through real-world case studies—from predictive analytics in retail and automated quality inspection in manufacturing to intelligent chatbots in e-commerce and autonomous vehicles—it's evident that the synergy between edge computing and serverless AI drives innovation and operational excellence. As technologies continue to evolve, embracing these advanced paradigms will be essential for organizations seeking to harness the full potential of artificial intelligence, ensuring responsive, scalable, and secure AI-driven solutions.

By leveraging the comprehensive tools and services offered by cloud providers like AWS, organizations can architect sophisticated Edge AI solutions that are not only powerful and efficient but also maintainable and cost-effective. As the demand for intelligent, real-time applications grows, the marriage of Edge Computing and Serverless AI stands as a cornerstone for the next generation of technological advancements.

Serverless Machine Learning Best Practices

Deploying machine learning (ML) models using serverless architectures offers remarkable advantages, including automatic scaling, reduced operational overhead, and cost efficiency. However, to fully leverage these benefits and ensure robust, maintainable, and performant ML applications, it is essential to adhere to best practices tailored specifically for serverless environments. This section outlines key best practices for serverless ML model development, effective management of model versions and rollbacks, strategies for optimizing cost and performance, and explores future trends shaping the landscape of serverless AI and machine learning.

1. Best Practices for Serverless Model Development

Developing ML models for serverless deployment requires thoughtful consideration of the unique constraints and capabilities of serverless platforms. Adhering to best practices ensures that models are efficient, scalable, and maintainable.

1.1. Optimize Model Size and Complexity

- **Lightweight Models:** Choose or design models that are sufficiently lightweight to fit within the memory and execution time constraints of serverless functions. For example, prefer models like Logistic Regression, Decision Trees, or lightweight neural networks over large-scale models like deep CNNs or Transformers when appropriate.

```python
Copy code
from sklearn.linear_model import LogisticRegression
import joblib

# Train a simple Logistic Regression model
model = LogisticRegression()
model.fit(X_train, y_train)

# Serialize the model
joblib.dump(model, 'model.joblib')
```

- **Model Compression:** Apply techniques such as pruning, quantization, or knowledge distillation to reduce the model size without significantly compromising performance.

1.2. Efficient Serialization and Deserialization

- **Use Fast Serialization Formats:** Employ efficient serialization libraries like joblib for scikit-learn models or pickle for Python objects, ensuring quick load and save times.

```python
Copy code
import joblib

# Save the model
joblib.dump(model, 'model.joblib')

# Load the model
model = joblib.load('model.joblib')
```

- **Lazy Loading:** Load models into memory only when necessary, reducing the cold start latency of serverless functions.

```python
Copy code
import joblib
import os

model = None

def load_model():
    global model
    if model is None:
        model_path = '/tmp/model.joblib'
        # Assuming the model is already downloaded to /tmp
        model = joblib.load(model_path)
    return model

def lambda_handler(event, context):
    model = load_model()
    # Proceed with inference
```

1.3. Minimize Dependencies

- **Lightweight Libraries:** Use only essential libraries to keep the deployment package small, reducing cold start times and simplifying maintenance.
- **Lambda Layers:** Utilize Lambda Layers to manage dependencies separately, promoting reuse and reducing redundancy across functions.

```bash
Copy code
# Create a layer with scikit-learn and joblib
mkdir python
pip install scikit-learn joblib -t python/
```

```
zip -r sklearn_layer.zip python
aws lambda publish-layer-version --layer-name sklearn-layer
--zip-file fileb://sklearn_layer.zip --compatible-runtimes
python3.8
```

1.4. Environment Configuration

- **Environment Variables:** Store configuration parameters, such as model S3 bucket names or thresholds, in environment variables. Encrypt sensitive variables using AWS Key Management Service (KMS).

```
bash
Copy code
aws lambda update-function-configuration --function-name
MLInferenceFunction \
    --environment
    "Variables={MODEL_BUCKET=my-models,MODEL_KEY=model.joblib}" \
    --kms-key-arn arn:aws:kms:region:account-id:key/key-id
```

- **Configuration Management:** Use infrastructure as code (IaC) tools like AWS CloudFormation or Terraform to manage environment configurations consistently across environments.

1.5. Stateless Design

- **Avoid Local State:** Design functions to be stateless, ensuring that each invocation is independent. Store any necessary state externally using services like Amazon DynamoDB or Amazon S3.

```python
Copy code
import boto3
import json

dynamodb = boto3.resource('dynamodb')
table = dynamodb.Table('InferenceResults')

def lambda_handler(event, context):
    # Perform inference
    prediction = model.predict([features])[0]

    # Store result in DynamoDB
    table.put_item(Item={'request_id': event['request_id'],
    'prediction': prediction})

    return {
        'statusCode': 200,
        'body': json.dumps({'prediction': prediction})
    }
```

1.6. Security Best Practices

- **Least Privilege:** Assign only the necessary IAM permissions to serverless functions.
- **Secure Data Handling:** Encrypt data at rest and in transit, and implement input validation to prevent injection attacks.
- **Regular Audits:** Periodically review and update security configurations to address emerging threats.

1.7. Example: Developing a Serverless Sentiment Analysis Function
Function Code (lambda_function.py):

```python
Copy code
import json
import joblib
```

```python
import boto3
import os

s3 = boto3.client('s3')

MODEL_BUCKET = os.environ['MODEL_BUCKET']
MODEL_KEY = os.environ['MODEL_KEY']

model = None

def load_model():
    global model
    if model is None:
        model_path = '/tmp/model.joblib'
        s3.download_file(MODEL_BUCKET, MODEL_KEY, model_path)
        model = joblib.load(model_path)
    return model

def lambda_handler(event, context):
    try:
        body = json.loads(event['body'])
        text = body['text']

        if not isinstance(text, str) or not text.strip():
            raise ValueError("Input 'text' must be a non-empty
            string.")

        # Preprocess input (e.g., tokenization)
        processed_text = preprocess(text)

        # Make prediction
        model = load_model()
        prediction = model.predict([processed_text])[0]
        sentiment = 'Positive' if prediction == 1 else 'Negative'

        # Return response
        return {
            'statusCode': 200,
            'body': json.dumps({'sentiment': sentiment})
        }
```

```python
    except Exception as e:
        return {
            'statusCode': 400,
            'body': json.dumps({'error': str(e)})
        }

def preprocess(text):
    # Implement preprocessing steps
    return text.lower().strip()
```

Deployment Steps:

1. **Package the Function and Dependencies:**

```bash
Copy code
mkdir package
cd package
pip install joblib scikit-learn -t .
cp ../lambda_function.py .
zip -r ../sentiment_analysis.zip .
cd ..
```

1. **Create the Lambda Function:**

```bash
Copy code
aws lambda create-function --function-name SentimentAnalysisFunction \
    --runtime python3.8 --role arn:aws:iam::account-id:role/LambdaRole \
    --handler lambda_function.lambda_handler --zip-file
```

```
fileb://sentiment_analysis.zip \
--environment
Variables={MODEL_BUCKET=my-models,MODEL_KEY=sentiment_model.joblib}
\
--memory-size 512 --timeout 30
```

1. **Set Up API Gateway:**

- Create a REST API with a /sentiment POST endpoint integrated with the Lambda function.
- Enable CORS and configure throttling as needed.

1. **Test the Deployment:**

```bash
Copy code
curl -X POST https://your-api-id.execute-api.region.amazonaws.com/prod/sentiment \
-H "Content-Type: application/json" \
-d '{"text": "I am very happy with the service!"}'
```

2. Managing Model Versions and Rollbacks

Effective version control and management of ML models are crucial for maintaining application stability, facilitating updates, and enabling quick recovery from potential issues introduced by new model deployments.

2.1. Model Versioning

- **Immutable Versions:** Treat each deployed model version as immutable. Once a version is deployed, it should not be altered, ensuring consistency across environments.

```bash
Copy code
aws lambda publish-version --function-name SentimentAnalysisFunction
```

- **Semantic Versioning:** Adopt a semantic versioning scheme (e.g., v1.0.0, v1.1.0) to clearly indicate changes, enhancements, or bug fixes.

2.2. Aliases for Version Management

- **Use Aliases:** Implement aliases (e.g., dev, staging, prod) to point to specific model versions. This facilitates smooth transitions between versions and simplifies rollback procedures.

```bash
Copy code
aws lambda create-alias --function-name SentimentAnalysisFunction --name prod --function-version 1
```

- **Traffic Shifting:** Gradually shift a percentage of traffic to a new version using aliases, enabling blue-green deployments and minimizing risk.

```bash
Copy code
aws lambda update-alias --function-name SentimentAnalysisFunction --name prod \
    --function-version 2 --routing-config
    '{"AdditionalVersionWeights": {"3": 0.1}}'
```

2.3. Rollback Strategies

- **Automated Rollbacks:** Integrate rollback mechanisms within CI/CD pipelines to automatically revert to the previous stable version if deployment metrics (e.g., error rates, latency) exceed predefined thresholds.
- **Manual Rollbacks:** In cases where automated rollbacks are insufficient, maintain procedures for manual intervention to switch aliases back to earlier versions.

```bash
Copy code
aws lambda update-alias --function-name SentimentAnalysisFunction
--name prod --function-version 1
```

2.4. Tracking and Documentation

- **Change Logs:** Maintain detailed change logs documenting what changes were made in each model version, including model architecture, hyperparameters, and data sources.
- **Metadata Storage:** Store version metadata alongside the models in repositories or databases to facilitate easy retrieval and auditing.

2.5. Example: Implementing Version Control with AWS Lambda Aliases

1. **Publish a New Model Version:**

```bash
Copy code
aws lambda publish-version --function-name
SentimentAnalysisFunction
```

1. **Create or Update an Alias to Point to the New Version:**

```bash
Copy code
# Create a new alias pointing to version 2
aws lambda create-alias --function-name SentimentAnalysisFunction --name prod --function-version 2

# Or update an existing alias to point to version 3 with traffic shifting
aws lambda update-alias --function-name SentimentAnalysisFunction --name prod \
    --function-version 3 --routing-config
    '{"AdditionalVersionWeights": {"4": 0.1}}'
```

1. **Monitor Deployment Metrics:**

- Use CloudWatch Metrics and Alarms to monitor performance indicators such as error rates and latency.

1. **Trigger a Rollback if Necessary:**

```bash
Copy code
aws lambda update-alias --function-name SentimentAnalysisFunction --name prod --function-version 2
```

3. Optimizing Cost and Performance

Balancing cost and performance is essential for maximizing the efficiency of serverless ML applications. Implementing optimization strategies ensures that resources are utilized effectively without compromising on performance.

3.1. Cost Optimization Strategies

- **Right-Sizing Resources:**
- Allocate appropriate memory and CPU resources based on the function's

requirements. Over-provisioning leads to unnecessary costs, while under-provisioning can degrade performance.

```bash
Copy code
aws lambda update-function-configuration --function-name SentimentAnalysisFunction --memory-size 512
```

- **Utilize Reserved and Provisioned Concurrency:**
- **Reserved Concurrency:** Guarantees a set number of concurrent executions, preventing resource contention.
- **Provisioned Concurrency:** Keeps functions pre-initialized to reduce cold start times, beneficial for high-traffic functions but incurs additional costs.

```bash
Copy code
# Set reserved concurrency
aws lambda put-function-concurrency --function-name SentimentAnalysisFunction --reserved-concurrent-executions 100
```

- **Leverage Lambda Layers:**
- Use Lambda Layers to manage and share common dependencies across multiple functions, reducing deployment package sizes and promoting reuse.
- **Implement Caching Mechanisms:**
- Cache frequent inference results using services like Amazon ElastiCache or API Gateway caching to minimize redundant function invocations.

```bash
Copy code
# Enable API Gateway caching for the /sentiment endpoint
aws apigateway update-stage --rest-api-id your-api-id --stage-name prod --patch-operations op=replace,path=/cacheDataEncrypted,value=true
```

3.2. Performance Optimization Strategies

- **Minimize Cold Start Latency:**
- **Provisioned Concurrency:** Pre-warm function instances to ensure low latency.
- **Optimize Initialization Code:** Reduce the time taken during function initialization by minimizing dependencies and avoiding heavy computations at startup.

```python
Copy code
import joblib
import boto3
import os

s3 = boto3.client('s3')
MODEL_BUCKET = os.environ['MODEL_BUCKET']
MODEL_KEY = os.environ['MODEL_KEY']

model = None

def load_model():
    global model
    if model is None:
        model_path = '/tmp/model.joblib'
        s3.download_file(MODEL_BUCKET, MODEL_KEY, model_path)
        model = joblib.load(model_path)
    return model
```

```
def lambda_handler(event, context):
    model = load_model()
    # Proceed with inference
```

- **Asynchronous Processing:**
- Offload non-critical tasks to asynchronous workflows using AWS Step Functions or Amazon SQS, allowing the main function to respond quickly.
- **Batch Processing:**
- Aggregate multiple inference requests into a single batch to optimize resource utilization and reduce per-request overhead.

```
python
Copy code
def lambda_handler(event, context):
    features = [record['features'] for record in event['records']]
    predictions = model.predict(features)
    return {
        'statusCode': 200,
        'body': json.dumps({'predictions': predictions.tolist()})
    }
```

3.3. Monitoring and Continuous Optimization

- **Use CloudWatch Metrics:**
- Monitor key metrics such as invocation counts, durations, error rates, and throttles to identify optimization opportunities.
- **Automate Scaling Policies:**
- Define auto-scaling policies based on real-time metrics to adjust resources dynamically in response to workload changes.
- **Cost Explorer Analysis:**
- Utilize AWS Cost Explorer to analyze spending patterns and identify cost-saving opportunities.

3.4. Example: Cost and Performance Optimization for a Sentiment Analysis API

1. **Analyze Current Usage:**

- Use CloudWatch to review function invocation counts, average durations, and error rates.

1. **Adjust Memory Allocation:**

- Increase memory if functions are running out of memory or decrease if over-provisioned.

```bash
Copy code
aws lambda update-function-configuration --function-name SentimentAnalysisFunction --memory-size 1024
```

1. **Implement API Caching:**

- Enable caching for frequently requested sentiments to reduce Lambda invocations.

1. **Set Up Reserved Concurrency:**

- Reserve concurrency for the function to ensure availability during peak times.

```bash
Copy code
```

```
aws lambda put-function-concurrency --function-name
SentimentAnalysisFunction --reserved-concurrent-executions 200
```

1. **Enable Provisioned Concurrency:**

- Allocate provisioned concurrency to minimize cold starts for high-traffic periods.

```bash
Copy code
aws lambda put-provisioned-concurrency-config --function-name
SentimentAnalysisFunction --qualifier $LATEST
--provisioned-concurrent-executions 50
```

1. **Monitor and Iterate:**

- Continuously monitor performance metrics and adjust configurations to maintain an optimal balance between cost and performance.

4. Future Trends in Serverless AI and Machine Learning

The intersection of serverless architectures and artificial intelligence is continually evolving, driven by advancements in technology and the growing demand for scalable, efficient, and intelligent applications. Understanding future trends can help organizations stay ahead of the curve and strategically plan their ML deployments.

4.1. Enhanced Serverless ML Frameworks

- **Integrated ML Services:** Expect more integrated services that combine model training, deployment, and monitoring within serverless frameworks, simplifying the ML lifecycle.
- **AutoML on Serverless Platforms:** Automated machine learning

(AutoML) capabilities will become more prevalent, enabling non-experts to develop and deploy models without deep ML expertise.

4.2. Edge Serverless AI Expansion

- **Greater Edge AI Adoption:** Increased deployment of AI models on edge devices using serverless paradigms, facilitating real-time processing in IoT, autonomous systems, and smart devices.
- **Hybrid Deployments:** Seamless integration between edge and cloud serverless architectures, enabling distributed AI workloads with centralized management and coordination.

4.3. Advanced Security and Compliance Features

- **Built-In Security Controls:** Serverless platforms will offer more robust, built-in security features tailored for AI applications, including automated compliance checks and enhanced encryption options.
- **Privacy-Preserving AI:** Techniques like federated learning and differential privacy will gain traction, allowing organizations to train models on sensitive data without compromising privacy.

4.4. Cost Optimization Innovations

- **Granular Billing Models:** More sophisticated billing models that allow for even finer-grained cost control and optimization based on usage patterns and model demands.
- **Resource-Aware AI Models:** Development of AI models that dynamically adjust their resource consumption based on the underlying serverless infrastructure's capabilities and current load.

4.5. AI-Driven Serverless Management

- **Automated Orchestration:** Leveraging AI to automate the orches-

tration of serverless functions, optimizing workflows, and resource allocation in real-time.
- **Predictive Scaling:** AI-driven predictive scaling mechanisms that anticipate workload changes and adjust resources proactively to maintain optimal performance and cost-efficiency.

4.6. Integration with Emerging Technologies

- **Quantum Computing:** Exploration of serverless paradigms in quantum computing environments, enabling the deployment of quantum ML models.
- **Blockchain Integration:** Combining serverless AI with blockchain for decentralized, secure, and transparent AI applications.

4.7. Example: Future-Ready Serverless ML Deployment Strategy

1. **Adopt AutoML Tools:**

- Utilize serverless AutoML services to streamline model development and deployment, reducing the need for extensive manual tuning.

1. **Expand to Edge Devices:**

- Deploy models on edge devices using serverless frameworks like AWS IoT Greengrass, enabling real-time inference and decision-making.

1. **Implement Federated Learning:**

- Train models across multiple decentralized devices without centralizing data, enhancing privacy and compliance.

1. **Leverage AI for Management:**

- Integrate AI-driven tools to automate the orchestration, scaling, and optimization of serverless ML workloads.

1. **Stay Updated with Emerging Standards:**

- Monitor advancements in AI and serverless technologies, adapting strategies to incorporate new tools, frameworks, and best practices as they emerge.

Conclusion

Serverless architectures are fundamentally transforming the deployment and management of machine learning applications, offering unparalleled scalability, cost efficiency, and operational simplicity. By adhering to best practices in serverless model development, effectively managing model versions and rollbacks, and strategically optimizing cost and performance, organizations can build robust and efficient ML applications that meet dynamic business needs.

As the landscape of serverless AI continues to evolve, embracing emerging trends such as enhanced serverless ML frameworks, expanded Edge AI capabilities, advanced security features, and AI-driven management tools will be crucial for maintaining a competitive edge. Organizations that proactively integrate these advancements into their ML strategies will be well-positioned to leverage the full potential of serverless AI, driving innovation and achieving sustained success in a rapidly advancing technological world.

By staying informed and adaptable, businesses can ensure that their serverless ML deployments remain resilient, secure, and optimized, enabling them to harness the transformative power of artificial intelligence with confidence and agility.

Additional Best Practices and Recommendations

1. **Implement Comprehensive Testing:**

- **Unit Tests:** Validate individual components and functions to ensure they work as intended.
- **Integration Tests:** Test the interactions between different services and components within the serverless architecture.
- **Load Testing:** Simulate high traffic scenarios to assess performance and scalability under stress.

1. **Automate Deployment Pipelines:**

- Utilize CI/CD tools like AWS CodePipeline, GitHub Actions, or Jenkins to automate the build, test, and deployment processes, ensuring consistency and reducing manual errors.

1. **Continuous Monitoring and Feedback Loops:**

- Establish continuous monitoring mechanisms using CloudWatch, X-Ray, and third-party tools to gather insights and feedback, enabling ongoing optimizations and rapid issue resolution.

1. **Documentation and Knowledge Sharing:**

- Maintain thorough documentation of serverless ML architectures, deployment processes, and operational procedures to facilitate team collaboration and knowledge transfer.

1. **Stay Updated with Serverless and ML Innovations:**

- Regularly explore updates and new features from cloud providers and the ML community to incorporate cutting-edge technologies and practices into your serverless ML workflows.

Conclusion: The Future of AI and Serverless Computing

As we stand on the brink of a technological revolution, the synergy between Artificial Intelligence (AI) and serverless computing is poised to redefine the landscape of software development and deployment. This convergence promises to unlock unprecedented levels of scalability, efficiency, and innovation, enabling organizations to harness the full potential of AI without the traditional constraints of infrastructure management. In this conclusion, we explore the future trajectory of AI and serverless technologies, highlight emerging trends and innovations, and offer final thoughts to those embarking on their journey in serverless machine learning.

1. The Future of AI and Serverless Technologies

The integration of AI with serverless computing is setting the stage for a new era of intelligent, scalable, and cost-effective applications. Several factors contribute to this promising future:

- **Scalability and Flexibility:** Serverless architectures inherently provide automatic scaling, allowing AI applications to handle varying workloads seamlessly. As AI models become more complex and data-intensive, serverless platforms will evolve to support even larger and more sophisticated models without compromising performance.

- **Cost Efficiency:** The pay-as-you-go pricing model of serverless computing aligns perfectly with the fluctuating demands of AI workloads. Organizations can optimize costs by allocating resources dynamically based on actual usage, eliminating the need for overprovisioning and reducing idle resource expenses.
- **Rapid Deployment and Iteration:** Serverless platforms streamline the deployment process, enabling faster iterations and continuous improvement of AI models. Developers can focus on enhancing model accuracy and functionality without being bogged down by infrastructure concerns.
- **Global Accessibility:** With serverless services available across multiple regions and cloud providers, AI applications can achieve global reach effortlessly. This ubiquity ensures low latency and high availability for end-users worldwide.
- **Integration with Emerging Technologies:** The future will witness deeper integration of serverless AI with other cutting-edge technologies such as Internet of Things (IoT), blockchain, and quantum computing. This integration will foster the development of innovative solutions that leverage the strengths of multiple technological domains.

2. Emerging Trends and Innovations

The landscape of AI and serverless computing is continually evolving, with several emerging trends and innovations shaping its future:

2.1. Enhanced Serverless AI Frameworks

- **Unified Platforms:** Expect the emergence of more integrated platforms that combine model training, deployment, and monitoring within a single serverless framework. These platforms will simplify the end-to-end ML lifecycle, making it more accessible to a broader range of users.
- **AutoML Integration:** Automated Machine Learning (AutoML) capabilities will be increasingly incorporated into serverless environments, allowing users to develop and deploy models without extensive expertise in ML algorithms or hyperparameter tuning.

2.2. Edge Serverless AI Expansion

- **Proliferation of Edge Devices:** As the number of IoT devices and edge computing resources grows, serverless AI will extend its reach to these devices, enabling real-time data processing and inference at the source.
- **Hybrid Deployments:** Combining edge and cloud serverless architectures will become more prevalent, facilitating distributed AI workloads that benefit from both local processing power and centralized analytics.

2.3. Advanced Security and Compliance Features

- **Built-In Security Controls:** Serverless platforms will offer more robust, built-in security features tailored for AI applications, including automated compliance checks and enhanced encryption options to protect sensitive data.
- **Privacy-Preserving AI:** Techniques such as federated learning and differential privacy will gain traction, enabling the training of models on decentralized data sources without compromising individual privacy.

2.4. Cost Optimization Innovations

- **Granular Billing Models:** Enhanced billing models that offer even finer-grained cost control based on usage patterns and specific AI workloads will emerge, allowing for more precise cost management.
- **Resource-Aware AI Models:** Development of AI models that dynamically adjust their resource consumption based on the underlying serverless infrastructure's capabilities and current load will optimize both performance and costs.

2.5. AI-Driven Serverless Management

- **Automated Orchestration:** AI-driven tools will automate the orchestration of serverless functions, optimizing workflows and resource

allocation in real-time to enhance efficiency and performance.
- **Predictive Scaling:** Machine learning algorithms will predict workload changes and adjust resources proactively, ensuring optimal performance and cost-efficiency without manual intervention.

2.6. Integration with Emerging Technologies

- **Quantum Computing:** Serverless paradigms will explore quantum computing environments, enabling the deployment of quantum ML models that can solve complex problems beyond the capabilities of classical computers.
- **Blockchain Integration:** Combining serverless AI with blockchain technology will facilitate decentralized, secure, and transparent AI applications, enhancing trust and accountability in AI-driven processes.

3. Final Thoughts for Beginners in Serverless Machine Learning

Embarking on the journey of serverless machine learning can be both exciting and challenging. To navigate this landscape effectively, consider the following final thoughts and recommendations:

3.1. Start with a Solid Foundation

- **Understand the Basics:** Grasp the fundamental concepts of both serverless architectures and machine learning. Familiarize yourself with key services like AWS Lambda, Amazon SageMaker, and AWS IoT Greengrass.
- **Learn through Practice:** Engage in hands-on projects to apply theoretical knowledge. Building small-scale serverless ML applications can provide invaluable experience and insights.

3.2. Embrace Best Practices

- **Optimize for Performance and Cost:** Always consider the trade-offs between model complexity, resource allocation, and cost. Strive for

CONCLUSION: THE FUTURE OF AI AND SERVERLESS COMPUTING

models that are efficient yet effective.
- **Prioritize Security:** Implement robust security measures from the outset. Adhere to the principle of least privilege, encrypt sensitive data, and regularly audit your deployments for vulnerabilities.
- **Implement CI/CD Pipelines:** Automate your deployment processes using Continuous Integration and Continuous Deployment (CI/CD) tools. This ensures consistency, reduces errors, and accelerates the development lifecycle.

3.3. Leverage Available Resources

- **Utilize Managed Services:** Take advantage of managed services offered by cloud providers to simplify deployment, scaling, and maintenance of serverless ML applications.
- **Stay Updated:** The fields of AI and serverless computing are rapidly evolving. Regularly follow industry blogs, attend webinars, and participate in communities to stay abreast of the latest developments and best practices.

3.4. Experiment and Innovate

- **Explore Different Frameworks:** Experiment with various AI frameworks and serverless platforms to discover what works best for your specific use cases and requirements.
- **Innovate with Edge AI:** Consider integrating Edge AI into your projects to leverage the benefits of real-time processing and enhanced privacy.

3.5. Build a Community and Seek Support

- **Join Communities:** Engage with online forums, attend meetups, and collaborate with peers to exchange knowledge and solve common challenges.
- **Seek Mentorship:** Learning from experienced professionals can acceler-

ate your understanding and help you avoid common pitfalls in serverless ML deployments.

3.6. Focus on Continuous Learning

- **Pursue Certifications:** Consider obtaining certifications in cloud computing and machine learning to validate your skills and enhance your career prospects.
- **Engage in Lifelong Learning:** Commit to ongoing education through courses, workshops, and self-study to keep your skills relevant in a fast-paced technological landscape.

Final Thoughts

The fusion of AI and serverless computing is ushering in a transformative era, enabling the development of intelligent, scalable, and cost-effective applications that were previously unattainable. As these technologies continue to mature, they will unlock new possibilities across various industries, driving innovation and efficiency to unprecedented heights.

For beginners venturing into serverless machine learning, the journey may seem daunting, but the rewards are substantial. By building a strong foundational knowledge, adhering to best practices, embracing continuous learning, and leveraging the wealth of resources and communities available, you can navigate this evolving landscape with confidence and expertise.

As we look to the future, the continued evolution of serverless architectures and AI technologies will undoubtedly present new challenges and opportunities. Staying adaptable, curious, and proactive in your learning and development will ensure that you remain at the forefront of this exciting convergence, ready to harness the full potential of serverless machine learning to drive meaningful and impactful solutions.

www.ingramcontent.com/pod-product-compliance
Lightning Source LLC
Chambersburg PA
CBHW071017240526
45469CB00006BD/1960

www.ingramcontent.com/pod-product-compliance
Lightning Source LLC
Chambersburg PA
CBHW071017240526
45469CB00006BD/1953

THE NEW FOUNDATIONS OF HUMAN PERFORMANCE

workplaces where individuals feel valued, supported, and empowered.

As we embark on this journey, let us remember that the future of work is not predetermined. Our actions, decisions, and commitment to fostering environments prioritizing safety, Efficiency, and sustainability shape it. By working together, we can build a future where human performance and safety go hand in hand, creating workplaces that benefit employees, organizations, and society. The road ahead may be challenging, but with determination, innovation, and collaboration, we can make work environments thrive in the face of change, ensuring a prosperous future for all.

isolation by fostering a sense of connection among remote employees.

2. Adapting to Workforce Demographics
The workforce is becoming increasingly diverse, with different generations bringing unique perspectives and expectations to the Workplace. Organizations must be prepared to address the needs and preferences of a multigenerational workforce.

a) Flexible Work Options
Flexible work arrangements, such as flexible hours and hybrid work models, can accommodate the varying needs of employees. Younger generations often prioritize work-life balance and seek flexibility in their roles. Organizations can attract and retain top talent by providing options that align with employee preferences.

b) Mentorship and Knowledge Sharing
Facilitating mentorship programs that pair experienced employees with younger colleagues promote knowledge sharing and skill development. These programs can foster collaboration and help bridge generational gaps within the workforce. Additionally, organizations can create platforms for employees to share their expertise and learn from one another.

Conclusion: A Vision for the Future
The road ahead for human performance and safety is filled with possibilities. Organizations can create safe, efficient, and sustainable work environments by embracing a holistic approach, prioritizing safety as a core value, leveraging Technology, fostering sustainable practices, and preparing for future workforce trends.

Our challenges are complex, but with a commitment to continuous improvement and a focus on employee well-being, we can pave the way for a brighter future. As organizations strive to enhance human performance and safety, they must recognize that these efforts are not merely about compliance or productivity but about creating

THE NEW FOUNDATIONS OF HUMAN PERFORMANCE

challenges that encourage teamwork and collaboration. These activities not only contribute to environmental goals but also strengthen team dynamics.

b) Recognition and Incentives

Recognizing employees actively participating in sustainability efforts can motivate others to get involved. Organizations can establish incentive programs that reward sustainable behaviours, such as using public transportation or reducing energy consumption. Celebrating these achievements fosters a culture of sustainability.

Preparing for Future Workforce Trends

As the workforce continues to evolve, organizations must remain agile and adaptable. Preparing for future trends, such as the gig economy, remote work, and shifting employee expectations, is essential for maintaining safety and performance.

1. Embracing Remote Work

The rise of remote work has transformed the employment landscape. Organizations must adapt their safety and performance strategies to accommodate remote employees while ensuring safety remains a priority.

a) Remote Safety Protocols

Organizations should develop safety protocols tailored explicitly to remote work. This may include providing guidelines for creating safe home office environments, ergonomic assessments, and resources for mental health support. Ensuring remote employees feel supported in their safety needs is essential for maintaining productivity and morale.

b) Communication and Engagement

Effective communication is crucial for engaging remote employees. Organizations can leverage digital platforms to facilitate regular check-ins, virtual team meetings, and social interactions. Organizations can enhance engagement and reduce feelings of

Fostering Sustainable Practices

As the world increasingly prioritizes sustainability, organizations must consider the environmental impact of their operations. Creating sustainable work environments benefits the planet and enhances employee morale and productivity.

1. Sustainable Facility Design

Organizations should invest in sustainable facility design that promotes energy Efficiency, reduces waste, and prioritizes employee health. Green buildings with natural lighting, ventilation, and eco-friendly materials create a positive work environment.

a) Indoor Air Quality

Improving indoor air quality is essential for employee health and well-being. Organizations can implement ventilation systems that filter out pollutants, reducing the risk of respiratory issues. Additionally, incorporating plants into the workspace can enhance air quality while promoting a calming atmosphere.

b) Ergonomic Workspaces

Sustainable design also encompasses ergonomics. Workspaces should be designed with employee comfort, incorporating adjustable furniture and layouts promoting movement. Organizations reduce the risk of musculoskeletal disorders by prioritizing ergonomics and enchanting productivity.

2. Promoting Sustainable Practices

Encouraging employees to adopt sustainable practices benefits the environment and fosters a sense of responsibility and community. Organizations can implement recycling programs, promote carpooling, and encourage the use of public transportation.

a) Employee Engagement Initiatives

Engaging employees in sustainability initiatives creates a sense of ownership and accountability. Organizations can organize events such as clean-up days, tree-planting initiatives, or sustainability

a) Health Monitoring
Wearable devices can track employees' physiological responses, such as heart rate and stress levels. By monitoring these indicators, organizations can identify signs of Fatigue or stress, allowing for timely interventions. This proactive approach not only enhances safety but also promotes employee well-being.

b) Safety Alerts
Wearable Technology can also be equipped with alert systems that notify employees of hazardous conditions. For example, the device can issue an immediate warning if an employee enters a high-risk area without proper protective equipment. This capability empowers employees to take proactive measures to ensure their safety.

2. Artificial Intelligence and Data Analytics
Artificial intelligence (AI) and data analytics are transforming how organizations approach safety and performance. By harnessing the power of data, organizations can identify trends, predict risks, and implement targeted interventions.

a) Predictive Analytics
Predictive analytics utilize historical data to identify patterns and forecast potential safety incidents. Organizations can analyze past accidents, near misses, and employee behaviour to identify risk factors and implement preventive measures. This data-driven approach enhances decision-making and allows organizations to allocate resources effectively.

b) Continuous Monitoring
AI-powered systems can continuously monitor Workplace conditions, identifying potential hazards in real-time. For instance, sensors can detect changes in environmental factors such as temperature, noise levels, and air quality, alerting management to address any issues promptly. This proactive monitoring contributes to a safer work environment.

2. Implementing Robust Safety Training Programs

Training is a cornerstone of any effective safety strategy. Organizations must provide comprehensive training programs that equip employees with the knowledge and skills to identify hazards and respond to emergencies.

a) Tailored Training Solutions

Training programs should be tailored to meet the specific needs of different job roles and environments. Organizations can leverage Technology to deliver engaging and interactive training modules, making safety training more accessible and practical. Regular refresher courses inform employees about the best practices and emerging safety trends.

b) Real-World Simulations

Incorporating real-world simulations into training programs allows employees to practice safety protocols in a controlled environment. Simulations provide valuable hands-on experience and build confidence in employees' abilities to respond effectively in emergencies. These practical exercises reinforce the importance of safety and prepare employees for real-life scenarios.

Leveraging Technology for Safety and Efficiency

Technology is a powerful tool that can enhance safety and Efficiency in the Workplace. Organizations embracing digital transformation must leverage Technology to create safer and more productive environments.

1. The Role of Wearable Technology

Wearable Technology, such as intelligent helmets and fitness trackers, can provide real-time data on employee health and safety. These devices can monitor vital signs, Fatigue levels, and environmental conditions, alerting employees and supervisors to potential risks.

THE NEW FOUNDATIONS OF HUMAN PERFORMANCE

c) Environmental Conditions

The physical environment in which employees work can either facilitate or hinder performance. Factors such as lighting, noise levels, ergonomics, and overall design contribute to employee comfort and productivity. Organizations must invest in creating environments that support physical and mental well-being, ensuring that employees can perform at their best.

Prioritizing Safety as a Core Value

Safety must be ingrained in the DNA of every organization. It should not be viewed as a compliance requirement or a reactive measure but rather as a core value that drives every decision, action, and initiative. A proactive approach to safety sets the stage for improved performance and employee engagement.

1. Creating a Safety-First Culture

Building a safety-first culture requires a shift in mindset across all levels of the organization. Leaders must model safety behaviours, encourage employee participation in safety initiatives, and recognize individuals prioritizing Workplace safety.

a) Leadership Commitment

Leadership commitment is essential for fostering a safety-first culture. Leaders should actively participate in safety training, engage in safety discussions, and prioritize safety in decision-making processes. Leaders inspire employees to adopt similar attitudes by demonstrating their dedication to safety.

b) Employee Engagement

Engaging employees in safety initiatives empowers them to take ownership of their safety and the safety of their colleagues. Organizations can create platforms for employees to share feedback, report hazards, and participate in safety committees. When employees feel valued and heard, they are more likely to contribute to safety efforts actively.

opportunities. In this conclusion, we will explore the pathways to creating safe, efficient, and sustainable work environments, emphasizing the integral role that human performance plays in achieving these goals.

Embracing a Holistic Approach

To truly enhance human performance and safety, organizations must adopt a holistic approach that considers the physical aspects of work and the cognitive, emotional, and environmental factors that influence employee well-being. This comprehensive perspective allows for developing strategies that foster an integrated and resilient workforce.

1. Understanding Human Performance

Many factors, including individual capabilities, Workplace culture, and environmental conditions, influence human performance. Organizations must prioritize understanding these elements to create safe and efficient work environments.

a) Individual Capabilities

Every employee brings unique skills, experiences, and attributes to the Workplace. Recognizing and harnessing these individual capabilities can lead to improved performance outcomes. Organizations should create opportunities for employees to develop skills through training, mentorship, and ongoing education.

b) Workplace Culture

Workplace culture significantly impacts employee performance and safety. A culture that prioritizes open communication, Trust, and collaboration encourages employees to voice concerns, share ideas, and engage in safety practices. Leaders play a pivotal role in shaping this culture, demonstrating a commitment to safety and well-being through their actions and decisions.

Conclusion: A Future of Possibilities

The future of human performance and safety is filled with possibilities, but it also presents challenges that organizations must confront head-on. By embracing flexibility, prioritizing mental health, leveraging Technology, cultivating a safety-first culture, and addressing diversity and inclusion, organizations can create work environments where employees feel safe, engaged, and empowered.

As we prepare for the challenges of tomorrow's Workplace, let us remember that safety and performance are not just goals but core values that should underpin every aspect of our operations. By investing in the well-being of our employees and fostering a culture of continuous improvement, we can build resilient organizations that thrive in the face of change.

The journey toward a safer and more effective Workplace is ongoing and requires collaboration, innovation, and a shared commitment to excellence. Together, we can create a future where human performance and safety are not just priorities but the very foundation of our work culture. The challenges of tomorrow may be daunting, but with the right strategies and mindset, we can navigate them successfully, ensuring a brighter and safer future for all employees.

The Road Ahead: Creating Safe, Efficient, and Sustainable Work Environments

As we navigate the complexities of the modern Workplace, it becomes increasingly clear that the intersection of human performance and safety is crucial for fostering environments where individuals can thrive. With rapid advancements in Technology, evolving workforce demographics, and a growing emphasis on sustainability, the road ahead presents both challenges and

a) Real-Time Feedback Systems

Implementing real-time feedback systems allows organizations to gather insights on safety performance and employee experience. This can include surveys, suggestion boxes, and regular check-ins with employees. By actively soliciting feedback, organizations can identify areas for improvement and make data-informed decisions that enhance safety and performance.

b) Data Analytics for Performance Insights

Data analytics plays a crucial role in understanding safety performance and identifying trends. Organizations should invest in tools to analyze safety incident data, employee engagement metrics, and training effectiveness. Organizations can make informed decisions that drive continuous improvement and enhance Workplace safety by leveraging data.

7. Preparing for Future Workforce Trends

Organizations must remain agile and responsive to changing workforce trends as we look toward the future. This involves preparing for shifts in employee expectations, technological advancements, and industry demands.

a) Upskilling and Reskilling Initiatives

The rapid pace of technological change means that employees must continuously update their skills. Organizations should invest in upskilling and reskilling initiatives that prepare employees for emerging roles and responsibilities. This may involve offering training programs, mentorship opportunities, and access to online learning platforms.

b) Anticipating Future Challenges

Organizations must remain vigilant in anticipating future challenges impacting safety and performance. This includes staying informed about industry trends, regulatory changes, and economic shifts. By proactively addressing potential challenges, organizations can position themselves for success in an ever-changing landscape.

b) Employee Involvement and Ownership

Engaging employees in safety initiatives fosters a sense of ownership and accountability. Organizations can create platforms for employees to share their safety concerns, suggest improvements, and participate in safety committees. When employees feel empowered to contribute to safety efforts, they are more likely to adhere to safety protocols and promote a culture of care.

5. Addressing Diversity, Equity, and Inclusion (DEI)

Organizations must prioritize diversity, equity, and inclusion (DEI) as integral components of their safety and performance strategies as the workforce becomes increasingly diverse. A diverse workforce brings a wealth of perspectives and ideas, which can enhance safety and performance outcomes.

a) Inclusive Safety Practices

Organizations should ensure that safety practices consider the diverse needs of their workforce. This may involve providing training materials in multiple languages, accommodating various work styles, and recognizing cultural differences in safety practices. By creating inclusive safety programs, organizations can foster a sense of belonging among all employees.

b) Diverse Leadership Representation

Diversity in leadership positions is essential for driving DEI initiatives. Organizations should actively work to promote diverse candidates to leadership roles, ensuring that decision-making reflects the perspectives and needs of all employees. Diverse leadership teams are more likely to prioritize safety and well-being, benefiting the organization.

6. Continuous Improvement Through Data and Feedback

The future of human performance and safety relies on a commitment to continuous improvement. Organizations must continually establish robust feedback mechanisms and data-driven approaches to enhance their safety and performance initiatives.

3. Leveraging Technology for Enhanced Safety and Performance

Technology continues to evolve rapidly, and its role in enhancing Workplace safety and performance cannot be overstated. As organizations prepare for the future, they must harness the power of Technology to create safer, more efficient work environments.

a) Artificial Intelligence and Automation

Artificial intelligence (AI) and automation have the potential to revolutionize Workplace safety. AI-powered systems can analyze vast amounts of data to identify patterns and predict potential risks, allowing organizations to take proactive measures. For instance, AI can monitor equipment performance in real-time, alerting managers to potential failures before accidents occur.

b) Smart Wearables

The rise of smart wearables, such as helmets equipped with sensors and fitness trackers, provides organizations valuable insights into employee health and safety. These devices can monitor Fatigue levels, environmental conditions, and overall well-being. Organizations can implement targeted interventions to prevent accidents and enhance performance by utilizing this data.

4. Cultivating a Safety-First Culture

A strong safety culture is essential for driving performance and minimizing risks. Organizations must prioritize the development of a culture that values safety at every level, from leadership to front-line employees.

a) Leadership Commitment to Safety

Leaders play a pivotal role in shaping safety culture. Leaders can set an example for their teams by visibly committing to safety initiatives. This includes actively participating in safety training, communicating the importance of safety in decision-making, and recognizing employees who prioritize safety in their work.

furniture and access to Technology, and maintaining safety standards in physical workspaces.

b) Tailored Safety Training

Training programs should be adaptable to various work environments. Organizations must invest in online training modules that employees can access regardless of location. These programs should cover essential safety topics while emphasizing the importance of mental well-being in isolation and remote work challenges.

2. Prioritizing Mental Health and Well-Being

As we navigate the complexities of modern work, employees' mental health and well-being must take centre stage. The challenges of remote work, economic uncertainty, and social isolation can lead to increased stress and burnout, ultimately impacting performance and safety.

a) Comprehensive Mental Health Programs

Organizations should develop comprehensive mental health programs that provide employees with access to resources and support. This includes offering counselling services, stress management workshops, and training for managers to recognize and address mental health challenges within their teams. By fostering a culture prioritizing mental well-being, organizations can reduce stigma and create an environment where employees feel comfortable seeking help.

b) Work-Life Balance Initiatives

Promoting work-life balance is essential for preventing burnout and ensuring long-term employee well-being. Organizations can implement policies encouraging employees to disconnect after work hours, take regular breaks, and utilize vacation time. Organizations can help employees recharge and maintain their performance by normalizing these practices.

Preparing for the Challenges of Tomorrow's Workplace

As we move into the 21st century, Workplace dynamics are evolving unprecedentedly. Globalization, rapid technological advancement, and shifting workforce demographics are reshaping how we think about human performance and safety. The challenges of tomorrow's Workplace require a proactive approach, blending traditional safety practices with innovative solutions to create environments where employees can thrive. In this conclusion, we will explore the key elements that organizations must embrace to prepare for the challenges ahead, ensuring that safety and performance remain at the forefront of their operations.

The New Reality of Work

The world of work is no longer confined to the traditional office or factory setting. The rise of remote work, hybrid models, and gig economies has transformed the landscape, requiring organizations to adapt their safety and performance strategies. This new reality brings unique challenges, including ensuring consistent safety standards across diverse work environments, addressing a dispersed workforce's mental health and well-being, and fostering engagement among employees who may feel isolated or disconnected.

1. Embracing Flexibility in Work Arrangements

The COVID-19 pandemic has accelerated the shift towards flexible work arrangements, forcing organizations to rethink their strategies. As we emerge from this crisis, embracing flexibility as a core principle of Workplace safety and performance is crucial.

a) Hybrid Work Models

Hybrid work models will likely become the norm, where employees will alternate between remote and in-office work. Organizations must develop safety protocols for both environments, ensuring employees feel secure working from home or on-site. This includes providing resources for remote work setups, such as ergonomic

THE NEW FOUNDATIONS OF HUMAN PERFORMANCE

organizations can ensure that their workforce remains adaptable and prepared for future challenges.

b) Preparing for the Future of Work

The future of work is characterized by technological advancements, changing workforce dynamics, and evolving customer expectations. Organizations must proactively prepare for these changes by investing in future-oriented skills training, promoting adaptability, and fostering an agile mindset.

7. Conclusion: A Holistic Approach to Human Performance and Safety

The future of human performance and safety lies in a holistic approach that integrates Technology, human behaviour, organizational culture, and employee well-being. As we move forward, we must recognize that safety and performance are interconnected and that organizations must prioritize both to achieve sustainable success.

The emerging trends we have explored in this conclusion highlight the importance of embracing change, leveraging Technology, fostering a culture of safety and performance, and prioritizing employee well-being. By adopting these principles, organizations can enhance safety and performance and create an environment where employees feel valued, engaged, and empowered.

In this rapidly changing world, organizations that commit to continuous improvement, adaptability, and a human-centred approach will be best positioned to navigate the complexities of the future Workplace. As we look ahead, let us embrace the opportunities and work together to build safer, more effective, and more inclusive work environments for all. The future of human performance and safety is bright and a journey worth embarking on.

5. The Role of Data in Driving Performance Improvement

Data-driven decision-making will continue to be a cornerstone of adequate safety and performance management. Organizations can make informed decisions that enhance outcomes as they gather more data on employee performance, safety incidents, and environmental conditions.

a) Real-Time Monitoring

Real-time monitoring of Workplace conditions allows organizations to identify potential hazards and intervene promptly. For instance, sensor Technology can detect unsafe temperature levels, air quality issues, or equipment malfunctions, alerting employees to potential dangers before incidents occur. This proactive approach not only enhances safety but also minimizes downtime and disruptions.

b) Performance Metrics and Key Performance Indicators (KPIs)

Organizations must establish clear performance metrics and KPIs to measure the effectiveness of their safety and performance initiatives. These metrics should be aligned with organizational goals and regularly reviewed to ensure continuous improvement.

Organizations can identify trends, improvement areas, and optimization opportunities by analyzing performance data.

6. Future-Proofing the Workforce

As we look to the future, organizations must focus on future-proofing their workforce. This involves investing in employee development, upskilling, and reskilling to ensure employees have the skills needed for evolving roles and responsibilities.

a) Lifelong Learning Initiatives

Organizations should promote lifelong learning initiatives that encourage employees to develop their skills continuously. This might involve providing access to online courses, workshops, and mentorship opportunities. By fostering a culture of lifelong learning,

mental health challenges by providing resources, support, and training. Initiatives such as mental health days, access to counselling services, and workshops on stress management can foster a healthier work environment.

b) Creating Supportive Work Environments
Creating a supportive work environment prioritizes employee well-being is essential for enhancing performance. This includes promoting work-life balance, providing flexible work arrangements, and encouraging open dialogue about mental health. Organizations prioritizing well-being are more likely to retain talent, reduce absenteeism, and enhance productivity.

4. Emphasizing Diversity, Equity, and Inclusion (DEI)
Organizations must embrace diversity, equity, and inclusion (DEI) as fundamental components of their safety and performance strategies as the workforce becomes increasingly diverse. DEI initiatives promote fairness and equality and enhance Workplace safety and performance.

a) Recognizing Diverse Needs
Different demographic groups may have unique needs and perspectives regarding safety and performance. Organizations must recognize these differences and tailor their safety programs to ensure inclusiveness. For example, providing materials in multiple languages or considering diverse work styles can create a more inclusive environment.

b) Promoting Inclusive Leadership
Inclusive leadership is critical for fostering a diverse workforce. Leaders who value diverse perspectives and actively seek input from all team members create an environment where everyone feels heard and valued. This inclusivity enhances safety by encouraging reporting and collaboration and drives innovation and creativity.

a) Leadership Commitment

Leadership commitment to safety and performance is a fundamental driver of cultural change. Leaders must model safety behaviours, communicate the importance of safety, and hold themselves accountable for creating a safe work environment. By prioritizing safety at the highest levels of the organization, leaders set the tone for the entire workforce.

b) Employee Empowerment and Engagement

Engaging employees in safety initiatives fosters a sense of ownership and responsibility for their safety and the safety of their colleagues. Empowered employees are more likely to report hazards, suggest improvements, and participate actively in safety training. Organizations can encourage engagement by creating platforms for open communication where employees feel comfortable sharing their insights and experiences.

c) Continuous Learning and Adaptability

As we discussed in earlier chapters, the future of human performance is rooted in continuous learning and adaptability. Organizations must invest in ongoing training programs that equip employees with the skills and knowledge to navigate changing work environments. Moreover, fostering a culture that embraces experimentation and learning from mistakes will help organizations adapt to new challenges more effectively.

3. Mental Health and Well-Being as Integral to Performance

The increasing recognition of mental health and well-being as critical components of Workplace performance is a significant trend that will continue to shape the future of work. Organizations are beginning to understand that psychological safety is as important as physical safety.

a) Addressing Mental Health Challenges

Workplace stressors can significantly impact employee performance and safety. Organizations must proactively address

a) Predictive Analytics

Predictive analytics is becoming increasingly vital in safety management. Organizations can forecast potential risks and intervene before incidents by analyzing historical data and identifying patterns. For example, manufacturing companies can use predictive analytics to monitor equipment performance, recognizing signs of wear and tear that may lead to accidents if left unchecked. Organizations can implement preventive measures by anticipating potential failures and enhancing Workplace safety.

b) Wearable Technology

Wearable devices, such as smart helmets, safety vests with sensors, and fitness trackers, are gaining popularity in various industries. These devices collect real-time data on workers' health, safety compliance, and environmental conditions. For instance, wearables can monitor Fatigue levels, alerting supervisors when employees are at risk of exhaustion. This proactive approach enhances safety and improves overall productivity and job satisfaction.

c) Virtual Reality (VR) and Augmented Reality (AR)

Training and simulation technologies, such as VR and AR, are transforming how employees learn and practice safety protocols. These immersive technologies allow workers to experience realistic scenarios in a safe environment, enabling them to develop critical skills without the risks associated with traditional training methods. For example, emergency responders can practice handling crises in simulated environments, improving their decision-making and performance in real-life situations.

2. Fostering a Culture of Safety and Performance

While Technology plays a crucial role in enhancing safety, the human element remains paramount. Building a strong safety culture is essential for achieving sustainable performance improvements. Organizations prioritizing safety as a core value tend to see fewer incidents, higher employee engagement, and improved overall performance.

Conclusion

The Future of Human Performance and Safety

Emerging Trends in Workplace Safety and Performance

As we stand at the intersection of innovation, Technology, and evolving human dynamics, the landscape of Workplace safety and performance is profoundly transforming. The insights gathered throughout this book have illuminated the critical importance of understanding human performance in fostering safe, effective, and thriving work environments. In this conclusion, we will explore the emerging trends shaping the future of human performance and safety while also reflecting on the foundational concepts discussed in previous chapters.

The Changing Nature of Work

The nature of work is changing rapidly, driven by advancements in Technology, globalization, and shifts in workforce demographics. As we look toward the future, we see that the traditional boundaries of work are blurring, leading to new forms of employment and collaboration. Remote work, hybrid models, and gig economies are commonplace, allowing organizations to tap into a global talent pool. This evolution presents unique challenges and opportunities for safety and performance management.

1. Embracing Technology as a Safety Enhancer

One of the most significant trends shaping the future of Workplace safety is the integration of advanced Technology. From artificial intelligence (AI) and machine learning to the Internet of Things (IoT) and big data analytics, Technology is revolutionizing how organizations approach safety and performance.

By fostering leadership that embraces change, organizations can create a work environment where adaptability is valued, and continuous improvement is seen as an integral part of achieving long-term goals.

Conclusion
Adaptability as a Pillar of Continuous Improvement
Adaptability is a crucial pillar of continuous improvement in a world where change is the only constant. By fostering a culture that embraces learning, agility, and data-driven decision-making, organizations can navigate the complexities of today's work environments and position themselves for long-term success.

Continuous improvement is not just about making incremental gains; it's about preparing for the future, anticipating challenges, and building resilience in uncertainty. Organizations that prioritize adaptability in their continuous improvement efforts will be better equipped to thrive in an ever-changing world, ensuring that they remain competitive, innovative, and prosperous for years to come.

but cause other bottlenecks. With this information, leaders can make targeted adjustments to improve Efficiency and address challenges.

Furthermore, data-driven decision-making allows organizations to be more proactive in anticipating changes. By monitoring industry trends, customer behaviour, and employee feedback, organizations can identify potential disruptions before they occur and develop strategies to stay ahead of the curve.

4. Building Long-Term Success through Adaptability
a) Setting Long-Term Goals with Flexibility in Mind

While continuous improvement emphasizes incremental changes, long-term success requires setting clear, measurable goals that align with the organization's vision. However, long-term goals must also be flexible in a constantly changing work environment.

Organizations that can adjust their goals as new opportunities and challenges arise are more likely to sustain success.
For example, an organization might set a long-term goal to reduce Workplace accidents by 20% over five years. As new safety technologies become available, the organization may need to revise its strategy to incorporate these tools and achieve its goal more efficiently. By being open to change and adjusting long-term goals, organizations can remain on track to achieve sustainable success.

b) Fostering Leadership that Embraces Change

Leadership plays a critical role in adaptability and continuous improvement. Leaders who model flexibility, curiosity, and a commitment to learning inspire their teams to do the same.

Moreover, leaders must communicate the importance of adaptability and continuous improvement to their teams, ensuring employees understand how these principles contribute to the organization's long-term success.

b) Promote Agility and Flexibility

Agility refers to an organization's ability to respond quickly to changing circumstances. Flexible work environments allow employees to adjust their workflows, collaborate across teams, and adapt to new challenges. Building agility into the culture of continuous improvement is critical for ensuring that teams can pivot when faced with unexpected changes.

One way to promote agility is by encouraging cross-functional collaboration. When employees from different departments work together to solve problems, they bring diverse perspectives and insights that can lead to more innovative solutions. Cross-functional teams are also better equipped to address complex challenges, as they have a broader understanding of the organization's operations and goals.

In addition to collaboration, flexibility in work schedules, remote work options, and adaptive project management methodologies such as Agile or Scrum can help organizations respond more effectively to changing conditions. By building flexibility into the organization's fabric, businesses can create a work environment that is responsive, adaptable, and prepared for the future.

c) Emphasize Data-Driven Decision Making

In a continuous improvement culture, data plays a central role in decision-making. As work environments change, organizations must be able to analyze performance data, track key metrics, and adjust strategies based on real-time insights. Data-driven decision-making ensures that organizations can make informed choices about where to focus their improvement efforts and how to allocate resources most effectively.

By integrating data analysis into continuous improvement processes, organizations can better understand how changes in the work environment impact performance. For example, data might reveal that new technologies improve productivity in certain areas

Continuous improvement provides a pathway for addressing these shifts by fostering a culture of inclusion, engagement, and flexibility. In a constant improvement culture, employees are encouraged to provide input on creating a more supportive and productive work environment. This might involve rethinking communication strategies, implementing new collaboration tools, or adjusting workflows to accommodate remote teams.

Furthermore, continuous improvement emphasizes the importance of leadership in driving cultural change. Leaders who model adaptability and encourage a growth mindset can help create a work environment that supports innovation, collaboration, and high performance, regardless of how the workforce evolves.

3. Strategies for Building Adaptability into Continuous Improvement
a) Encourage a Learning Culture
Learning culture encourages employees to seek new knowledge, learn from their mistakes, and continuously develop their skills. In a rapidly changing work environment, fostering a learning culture is essential for ensuring employees can keep pace with new developments and adapt to evolving expectations.

Organizations can support a learning culture by offering continuous training and development opportunities. This might include formal training programs, mentorship opportunities, and access to online learning platforms. Additionally, leaders can encourage employees to take ownership of their professional growth by setting aside time for reflection, learning, and skill-building.

When employees are empowered to learn and grow, they are more likely to adapt to changes in the work environment with confidence and enthusiasm. Moreover, a learning culture helps organizations remain agile, as employees constantly seek new ways to improve processes, increase Efficiency, and stay ahead of industry trends.

THE NEW FOUNDATIONS OF HUMAN PERFORMANCE

of change. When employees are encouraged to actively participate in identifying areas for improvement and implementing new strategies, they are more likely to embrace change as part of the Process rather than something imposed from the top.

b) Keeping Pace with Technological Advancements

As technological advancements continue to accelerate, organizations must find ways to integrate new tools and systems into their operations while maintaining productivity and Efficiency. The challenge lies in balancing the adoption of new technologies with the need for training, support, and the refinement of processes.

Continuous improvement can help organizations manage this balance by encouraging an incremental approach to Technology integration. Instead of implementing new systems simultaneously, teams can pilot technologies on a small scale, gather feedback, and make necessary adjustments before full-scale adoption. This iterative approach allows organizations to adapt to new technologies without overwhelming employees or disrupting operations.

Additionally, continuous improvement in cultures prioritizes ongoing training and development, ensuring employees have the skills to succeed in a tech-driven work environment. By making learning a constant Process, organizations can stay ahead of technological advancements and ensure that their workforce remains agile and capable of handling new tools and systems.

c) Navigating Shifts in Workforce Dynamics

Workforce dynamics are constantly evolving, particularly in response to generational shifts, changes in labour markets, and the increasing prevalence of remote and hybrid work models.

Organizations must adapt to new work-life balance, collaboration, and communication expectations as the workforce becomes more diverse and flexible.

introducing cutting-edge Technology to improve safety and performance. Innovation requires a mindset of curiosity and openness to change—qualities fostered in a continuous improvement culture.

c) Resilience: A Key Component of Adaptability

Resilience refers to the ability to recover quickly from setbacks, overcome challenges, and remain focused on long-term goals, even in adversity. In an ever-changing work environment, resilience is critical for individuals and organizations. Continuous improvement fosters resilience by encouraging employees to view challenges as opportunities for growth and learning. Instead of being discouraged by obstacles, resilient teams use continuous improvement principles to find creative solutions and keep moving forward.

Organizations that embrace continuous improvement as a strategy for adaptability are better equipped to handle unexpected disruptions, whether in the form of new regulations, economic downturns, or global pandemics. Resilience ensures that the organization can continue to innovate, evolve, and achieve success even in difficult times.

2. Challenges of Adapting to Changing Work Environments
a) Overcoming Resistance to Change

One of the most common barriers to adapting to changing work environments is resistance to change. People naturally favour stability and predictability; altering established routines can be daunting. This resistance can manifest in many ways in organizations, from employees needing more time to adopt new technologies to managers hesitating to update long-standing procedures.

To overcome resistance, it's essential to communicate the benefits of change clearly and involve employees in the Process. Continuous improvement provides a framework for addressing these challenges by emphasizing collaboration, transparency, and shared ownership

1. The Need for Continuous Improvement in a Changing Landscape

a) Why Adaptability Is Key to Long-Term Success

Adaptability is more than the ability to survive in changing conditions; it's the capacity to thrive and capitalize on new opportunities that arise in these conditions. In a business context, adaptability means pivoting quickly when faced with new challenges, adjusting strategies to meet evolving customer needs, and integrating new technologies that improve Efficiency.

The future work environment will be characterized by increased uncertainty and complexity. Technological advancements such as artificial intelligence (AI), machine learning, and automation are expected to redefine roles, reshape industries, and change the skills required for work. At the same time, external pressures like climate change, economic instability, and global health crises will continue to affect how businesses operate. In this constantly shifting environment, organizations that remain rigid in doing things will need help to stay competitive.

Continuous improvement enables organizations to remain adaptable by fostering learning, innovation, and growth culture. Instead of reacting to change only when it becomes unavoidable, organizations that emphasize continuous improvement can proactively anticipate shifts in the work environment and adjust accordingly.

b) The Role of Innovation in Continuous Improvement

One of the driving forces behind continuous improvement is innovation, finding new and better ways to solve problems, meet customer needs, and achieve business goals. In a constantly changing work environment, innovation is essential. Organizations must be willing to experiment with new ideas, embrace emerging technologies, and rethink traditional processes to stay competitive.

In the context of continuous improvement, innovation can take many forms. It might involve the development of new products and services, implementing more efficient operational processes, or

Adapting to Changing Work Environments for Long-Term Success

Introduction: The Power of Adaptation in a Rapidly Changing World

In the early 2000s, the world of work looked significantly different than it does today. Smartphones were just beginning to emerge, remote work was a rarity, and automation had yet to transform industries at the level we see now. Fast forward to the 2020s, and we're amid an unprecedented pace of change. Technology, globalization, and societal shifts are constantly reshaping how these operate. From new technological advancements to changing workforce dynamics and customer demands, today's work environments are marked by unpredictability.

In such a landscape, the ability to adapt is not just an advantage—it's a necessity. Organizations that can adjust quickly to changing circumstances, whether those changes come from technological innovations or global crises, are more likely to thrive. The question then becomes, how can businesses create a culture of continuous improvement that is flexible enough to adapt to these constant changes and maintain long-term success?

This chapter explores the critical role of continuous improvement in helping organizations navigate and succeed in ever-evolving work environments. It delves into the importance of adaptability, the challenges organizations face in changing landscapes, and practical strategies for fostering a culture that is resilient, agile, and prepared for the future.

THE NEW FOUNDATIONS OF HUMAN PERFORMANCE

individuals and teams who have made improvements helps to maintain enthusiasm and engagement.

Setting Long-Term Goals: Continuous improvement is a long-term strategy. Organizations should set clear, measurable goals for their improvement initiatives and regularly track progress.

Conclusion

Building a culture of continuous improvement is a transformative Process that requires commitment, leadership, and an organization-wide mindset shift. Organizations can create an environment where continuous improvement thrives by empowering employees, fostering open communication, embracing mistakes, prioritizing training, and making data-driven decisions.

The journey is not without challenges, but the rewards are significant: improved safety, enhanced performance, increased employee engagement, and a more agile organization that is better equipped to meet the demands of the future. A culture of continuous improvement is not just about improving things—it's about creating a Workplace where everyone is invested in achieving success, one improvement at a time.

workloads. Leaders must address these fears by communicating the benefits of change and providing reassurance.

- Involving Employees in the Process: Employees are more likely to embrace change when they feel involved. Leaders can reduce resistance and foster buy-in by actively seeking input and involving employees in decision-making.

b) Balancing Improvement with Daily Operations

Another challenge is balancing the pursuit of continuous improvement with the demands of day-to-day operations. Employees may feel they need more time or resources to focus on improvements when they are already stretched thin by their regular responsibilities.

- Dedicated Time for Improvement: Some organizations address this challenge by setting aside dedicated time for improvement initiatives. For example, Toyota's famous "Kaizen" approach includes regular improvement sessions where employees work together to identify and solve problems.

- Embedding Improvement into Daily Work: Continuous improvement shouldn't be seen as an additional task—it should be embedded into daily work processes. Leaders can encourage this by rewarding minor, incremental improvements and making them part of the typical workflow.

c) Sustaining Momentum

Once an organization has started building a culture of continuous improvement, the challenge becomes sustaining that momentum. With ongoing commitment from leadership and employees, improvement efforts can stay strong.

- Celebrating Wins: One way to sustain momentum is by celebrating big and small wins. Recognizing the contributions of

THE NEW FOUNDATIONS OF HUMAN PERFORMANCE

e) Data-Driven Decision Making

In a culture of continuous improvement, decisions are based on data rather than assumptions. Data provides a clear picture of current performance, identifies trends, and highlights areas that need attention. Organizations that embrace data-driven decision-making are better equipped to make informed choices about where to focus their improvement efforts.

- **Tracking Key Metrics:** Continuous improvement requires tracking performance metrics such as Efficiency, safety incidents, customer satisfaction, and employee engagement. By analyzing this data, organizations can identify patterns and areas for improvement.

- **Regular Review of Data:** Establishing regular data reviews to assess progress and adjust strategies as needed is essential. These reviews should be part of the continuous feedback loop, allowing teams to course correctly in real time.

- **Technology Integration:** Modern Technology, such as AI and automation, can enhance data collection and analysis, providing real-time insights into performance. Organizations should leverage these tools to support their continuous improvement initiatives.

3. Challenges in Building a Continuous Improvement Culture

While the benefits of a continuous improvement culture are evident, building and sustaining such a culture is challenging. Organizations must be prepared to address these obstacles to create an ongoing growth and improvement environment.

a) Resistance to Change

One of the biggest challenges to continuous improvement is resistance to change. Employees and leaders may be reluctant to embrace new working methods, especially if they are comfortable with the status quo. Overcoming this resistance requires clear communication, education, and strong leadership.

- **Addressing Fear:** Change can be intimidating, especially if employees fear improvements might lead to job cuts or increased

- Celebrating Failures: Some organizations take this approach a step further by celebrating failures and the lessons learned from them. For example, post-mortem meetings or "fail fast" sessions can help teams dissect what went wrong and develop strategies for preventing similar issues in the future.

- Root Cause Analysis: When mistakes occur, it's essential to conduct a thorough root cause analysis to understand what led to the error and how it can be prevented. This Process helps to ensure that mistakes lead to meaningful improvements.

d) Commitment to Training and Development

Continuous improvement of culture prioritizes ongoing learning and development. Employees need to be equipped with the skills and knowledge necessary to identify opportunities for improvement and implement changes effectively. Training and development should be continuous, allowing employees to expand their skill sets and adapt to new challenges.

- Skills Training: Regular training sessions on problem-solving, Lean methodologies, safety protocols, and communication can help employees develop the necessary skills to contribute to continuous improvement initiatives.

- Cross-Training: Cross-training employees to understand different organizational roles can foster collaboration and provide fresh perspectives on improving processes. When employees understand the bigger picture, they are better equipped to suggest improvements that benefit the entire organization.

- Leadership Development: Leaders, too, must continue to develop their skills. Leadership training should focus on fostering the qualities that support continuous improvement, such as active listening, emotional intelligence, and the ability to coach and mentor others.

THE NEW FOUNDATIONS OF HUMAN PERFORMANCE

b) Open Communication and Feedback

Open communication is the lifeblood of a continuous improvement in culture. In a Workplace where improvement is valued, communication must flow freely between all levels of the organization. Employees should feel comfortable sharing their observations, ideas, and feedback with their peers and supervisors.

Feedback loops are essential for continuous improvement. These loops allow teams to reflect on what's working and what isn't and to adjust their strategies accordingly. This feedback can come in many forms, including informal conversations, structured team meetings, and formal evaluations.

- Two-Way Communication: Continuous improvement requires both giving and receiving feedback. Leaders must be open to feedback from their teams and should actively seek input on improving processes and safety measures.

- Continuous Feedback Loops: Instead of relying on periodic reviews or evaluations, continuous improvement cultures thrive on ongoing feedback. This enables immediate course corrections and allows teams to respond quickly to changing circumstances.

c) Embracing Mistakes as Learning Opportunities

A culture of continuous improvement views mistakes not as failures but as opportunities to learn and grow. In such an environment, employees are encouraged to experiment, innovate, and test new ideas without fear of being to blame. This attitude is critical to fostering a culture of innovation and creativity.

When mistakes are seen as part of the learning Process, employees are more likely to take risks that can significantly improve processes, safety, and performance. Leaders can reinforce this mindset by creating a "no blame" culture where mistakes are openly discussed and analyzed to extract valuable lessons.

Leadership commitment also involves providing the necessary resources, training, and support for continuous improvement initiatives. This might include investing in professional development, introducing tools and Technology that enhance Efficiency, or creating cross-functional teams to tackle specific challenges. Leaders prioritizing continuous improvement help create an adaptive, resilient, and forward-thinking organization.

2. Key Elements of a Continuous Improvement Culture
a) Empowerment of Employees

A fundamental element of a continuous improvement in culture is the empowerment of employees. When employees feel empowered, they take ownership of their work and are more likely to engage in problem-solving and innovation. Empowerment comes from giving employees the autonomy to make decisions, the authority to implement changes, and the confidence that their voices will be heard.

- **Autonomy:** Employees need freedom to decide how they perform their tasks. This leads to greater job satisfaction and fosters creativity and innovation. Employees who have control over their work processes are more likely to identify areas for improvement.

- **Authority to Implement Changes:** It's not enough to encourage employees to develop ideas—they must also be given the authority to implement them. This means creating a streamlined Process for testing and applying improvements. Empowered employees can make real-time adjustments that can enhance productivity and safety.

- **Psychological Safety:** Employees must feel safe to share their ideas without fear of punishment or ridicule for continuous improvement to thrive. Psychological safety, where individuals feel comfortable taking risks and making suggestions, is essential for innovation.

Creating such a culture requires deliberate action, leadership commitment, and a systemic approach that embeds the values of growth, learning, and adaptation into the organization's very fabric.

This chapter explores how to build and sustain a culture of continuous improvement, the challenges and rewards of doing so, and practical steps for embedding these values into day-to-day operations.

1. The Foundation of Continuous Improvement
a) What Is a Culture of Continuous Improvement?
At its core, a continuous improvement of culture fosters an environment where everyone is encouraged and empowered to look for ways to enhance their work. This means seeking opportunities to increase Efficiency, improve safety, and drive innovation. In such a culture, improvement is not viewed as a top-down directive but as a collaborative effort involving all employees.

This mindset encourages employees to be curious, to ask questions, and to think critically about their work processes. It fosters a proactive attitude where individuals are motivated to prevent problems before they arise rather than simply reacting to issues after they occur. In a continuous improvement culture, everyone contributes to success, making the Workplace more agile, safe, and productive.

b) The Importance of Leadership in Shaping Culture
Leadership plays a crucial role in creating a culture of continuous improvement. Leaders must model the behaviours and attitudes they wish to see in their teams. This means embracing change, encouraging innovation, and being open to feedback. Leaders must be willing to challenge the status quo and create an environment where employees feel safe to suggest improvements without fear of reprimand.

In human performance and Workplace safety, feedback and evaluation are particularly important for identifying risks, enhancing Efficiency, and fostering a culture of accountability. When organizations actively seek out and act on feedback, they empower employees, improve processes, and ultimately create a safer and more productive work environment.

Pursuing continuous improvement is never-ending, but by prioritizing feedback and evaluation, organizations can stay ahead of the curve and ensure long-term success.

How to Create a Culture of Continuous Improvement

Introduction

Imagine a Workplace where every individual is not only committed to doing their best but is also consistently striving to improve. The work environment is dynamic, safety is paramount, and every team member feels empowered to suggest better ways to perform their tasks. Mistakes are viewed as learning opportunities rather than setbacks, and innovation flows freely from all levels of the organization. This is the essence of a culture of continuous improvement.

In today's fast-paced, competitive, and safety-conscious world, building a culture of continuous improvement is more than a strategy—it is a survival tool. The concept of continuous improvement, often associated with methodologies such as Lean, Six Sigma, and Kaizen, extends far beyond formal processes. It encompasses an organizational mindset where everyone, from the

leadership to the front-line workers, actively enhances work processes, safety protocols, and overall performance.

THE NEW FOUNDATIONS OF HUMAN PERFORMANCE

5. Case Studies of Feedback and Evaluation Driving Continuous Improvement

a) Case Study: Manufacturing

The management team noticed a high rate of minor safety incidents in a manufacturing plant, such as slips and falls, impacting productivity. After conducting an evaluation and gathering feedback from employees, it was revealed that the layout of the factory floor was contributing to the problem.

Based on this feedback, the plant managers reorganized the workstations to minimize clutter and installed additional safety signage. They also introduced a real-time feedback loop where employees could report any new safety concerns.
As a result of these changes, the plant saw a significant reduction in safety incidents, and employee morale improved as they felt their concerns were being heard and addressed.

b) Case Study: Healthcare

In a healthcare setting, staff turnover was high, and patient care suffered. After conducting staff evaluations and gathering feedback, it was discovered that many employees felt overwhelmed by their workload and needed to be more appreciated by management.

The hospital implemented a new peer feedback system that allowed staff to recognize each other's contributions. They also revised their evaluation Process to include more frequent, informal check-ins with management. These changes helped reduce staff turnover and improve patient care outcomes, as employees felt more supported and engaged.

6. Conclusion

Feedback and evaluation are indispensable components of continuous improvement in any organization. By embedding feedback loops and regular evaluations into the culture, organizations create an environment where growth, safety, and performance are constantly optimized.

4. The Benefits of Feedback and Evaluation in Continuous Improvement

a) Improved Safety and Performance

Regular feedback and evaluations help organizations identify and address potential risks before they become serious issues. This proactive approach to safety reduces incidents, improves compliance with regulations, and fosters a culture of accountability.

Regarding performance, feedback and evaluations, it provides employees with the guidance they need to improve continuously. Employees who receive regular feedback are more likely to be engaged, productive, and aligned with organizational goals.

b) Increased Employee Engagement

Employees who feel their voices are heard and their contributions are valued are likelier to be engaged and motivated. Feedback and evaluations create opportunities for employees to share their ideas, express concerns, and receive recognition for their efforts.

When employees feel, they are actively contributing to the organization's success, they are more likely to take ownership of their performance and safety practices.

c) Fostering a Learning Culture

Feedback and evaluations create a culture of continuous learning and improvement. In such environments, employees are encouraged to view mistakes as learning opportunities rather than failures. This fosters innovation, resilience, and a growth mindset.

- **Learning from Mistakes:** Organizations that embrace feedback and evaluation as part of their continuous improvement Process create a safe space for employees to learn from their mistakes and develop new skills.

- **Encouraging Innovation:** Feedback-driven organizations are more likely to encourage innovation because they constantly seek new ways to improve and adapt to changing conditions.

- Self-Evaluation: Encouraging employees to evaluate their performance fosters self-awareness and accountability. It can also provide valuable insights into how employees perceive their strengths and areas for improvement.

- Peer Evaluations: Peer evaluations allow coworkers to provide input on each other's performance. This can be particularly useful in team-oriented environments, where collaboration and communication are essential.

- Safety Audits: In safety-critical industries, regular safety audits are essential for evaluating the effectiveness of safety protocols and identifying potential risks.

c) Effective Evaluation Practices

Organizations must ensure that the Process is fair, transparent, and actionable to maximize the impact of evaluations. Here are some best practices for conducting effective evaluations:

- Clear Criteria: Evaluations should be based on clear, objective criteria aligned with the organization's goals. This ensures that employees understand what is expected of them and how their performance will be measured.

- Regular Evaluations: Organizations should conduct regular evaluations to monitor progress and provide ongoing feedback rather than relying solely on annual reviews.

- Two-Way Dialogue: Evaluations should not be one-sided. Encourage employees to share their thoughts on their performance and the support they need to succeed.

- Follow-Up: Following up with an action plan is essential after an evaluation. This ensures that feedback is carried out, and employees have the resources and support they need to improve.

- **Peer-to-Peer Feedback:** Cultivating a culture where peers provide feedback to one another fosters collaboration and strengthens team dynamics.
- **Leadership by Example:** Leaders should model the behaviour they expect from their teams by seeking feedback on their performance and showing how they act.

3. The Role of Evaluation in Continuous Improvement
a) Why Evaluation Is Critical
Evaluation systematically assesses performance to determine whether goals are being met and where improvements are necessary. Evaluation is critical to continuous improvement because it offers a structured, objective way to measure progress and identify gaps.

In a safety context, evaluation helps assess the effectiveness of safety protocols, compliance with regulations, and overall safety culture within an organization. Regarding human performance, evaluations can provide insights into productivity, skill levels, and employee engagement.
- **Benchmarking:** Evaluations allow organizations to benchmark their performance against industry standards, competitors, or internal goals.
- **Identifying Strengths and Weaknesses:** Through evaluation, organizations can pinpoint what works well and where improvements are needed.
- **Informed Decision-Making:** Evaluations provide data and insights that enable leaders to make informed decisions about training, resource allocation, and operational changes.

b) Methods of Evaluation
There are various methods for conducting evaluations, each with its benefits and limitations:
- **Performance Reviews:** Performance reviews are among the most common evaluation forms. These structured reviews typically occur annually or biannually and provide an opportunity to assess employee performance against predefined criteria.

employees and supervisors and provides real-time insights and immediate course corrections.

- 360-Degree Feedback: This type of feedback involves gathering input from various source supervisors, peers, subordinates, and sometimes even customers. It provides a well-rounded view of an individual's performance and behaviour in the Workplace.

c) Effective Feedback Practices

For feedback to be effective and support continuous improvement, it must be delivered constructively and actionable. Here are some critical practices for delivering effective feedback:

- Timeliness: Feedback should be as close to the event or behaviour as possible. Delayed feedback can lead to missed learning opportunities and diminished impact.

- Specificity: Vague feedback could be more helpful. The more specific the feedback, the easier it is for the recipient to understand what they need to improve or continue doing.

- Constructiveness: Feedback should be focused on behaviours and outcomes, not personal attributes. Constructive feedback helps employees see areas for growth without feeling attacked or devalued.

- Balanced Approach: While addressing areas for improvement is essential, it's equally important to recognize successes and strengths. A balanced approach to feedback helps maintain morale and motivation.

d) Fostering a Feedback Culture

Organizations that excel in continuous improvement often have a robust feedback culture. In these organizations, feedback is a two-way street where employees and management feel comfortable giving and receiving input.

- Open Communication: Encourage an open-door policy where employees can freely share their concerns, ideas, and feedback with management.

a powerful tool for driving change, boosting performance, and fostering a culture of accountability.

2. The Role of Feedback in Continuous Improvement
a) Why Feedback Matters
Feedback is the lifeblood of continuous improvement. With it, organizations can avoid stagnation, repeating mistakes, and missing opportunities for optimization. Constructive feedback allows individuals and teams to recognize their strengths and weaknesses, offering them clear guidance on improving.

In safety and human performance, feedback is crucial for reducing Workplace hazards, enhancing productivity, and improving morale. Employees who receive regular, meaningful feedback tend to be more engaged, motivated, and committed to personal and organizational success.
- **Clarity and Direction:** Feedback helps individuals understand how their work aligns with organizational goals. Clear and actionable feedback enables employees to correct courses, if necessary, and align their efforts with the organization's broader objectives.
- **Empowerment:** Employees who receive feedback feel empowered to take control of their development. Constructive feedback fosters a sense of ownership and responsibility for personal performance and safety practices.

b) Types of Feedback
There are different types of feedback, each serving a unique role in the Process of continuous improvement:
- **Formal Feedback:** This is structured feedback typically provided during performance reviews or evaluations. It often takes the form of written reports or scheduled meetings where employees are assessed against specific criteria.
- **Informal Feedback:** Informal feedback happens spontaneously and is often verbal. It can occur in day-to-day interactions between

THE NEW FOUNDATIONS OF HUMAN PERFORMANCE

1. What Is Continuous Improvement?
a) The Philosophy of Continuous Improvement
Continuous improvement is more than just a Process—it's a mindset that embraces the idea that no system, procedure, or individual performance is ever truly perfect. It is rooted in the belief that there is always room to grow, refine, and optimize. This philosophy is often encapsulated in methodologies such as Lean,
Six Sigma, or Kaizen, but its principles can be applied universally across industries and functions.

For organizations to thrive in a continuous improvement culture, they must foster an environment where feedback is accepted and encouraged, evaluations are seen as opportunities for growth rather than criticism, and learning is a perpetual endeavour.

b) The Importance of Feedback Loops
Feedback loops are essential for continuous improvement. They create a cycle where employees and management can communicate, reflect, and make informed decisions about adjusting behaviours and processes. Feedback loops help identify inefficiencies, safety concerns, and potential areas of innovation.
- **Positive Feedback Loops:** These occur when the feedback reinforces current behaviours and encourages them to continue. For example, positive feedback on a new safety initiative can motivate teams to maintain or enhance that behaviour.
- **Negative Feedback Loops:** Negative feedback identifies areas that need adjustment or change. It's not about assigning blame but pinpointing areas where improvements are necessary to avoid repeating mistakes or inefficiencies.

c) Evaluation as a Driver for Change
Evaluation is the structured Process of assessing performance against predefined goals, standards, or criteria. It allows organizations to systematically review how well employees, teams, and processes function and where changes must be made. When evaluations are conducted regularly and transparently, they become

Chapter 15

Continuous Improvement: The Path to Sustainable Success

The Role of Feedback and Evaluation in Performance

Introduction

In today's rapidly changing work environment, pursuing continuous improvement is not just a nice to have; it's necessary for organizations aiming to remain competitive, efficient, and safe. Constant improvement consistently refining operations, processes, and human performance to meet evolving demands and mitigate potential risks. At the heart of this Process lies a critical component: feedback and evaluation.

Feedback provides the necessary insights into what's working and what isn't, while evaluation allows organizations to assess performance based on set criteria. Together, they form the foundation of a performance-driven culture where employees, teams, and leadership align their goals for growth, safety, and excellence.

This chapter explores the central role of feedback and evaluation in driving continuous improvement. We'll discuss how feedback can be effectively collected, delivered, and acted upon, how evaluations should be conducted for maximum impact, and the tangible benefits of embedding these processes into the organizational fabric. We'll also look at case studies of organizations successfully leveraging feedback and evaluation to transform their Workplace and performance.

data-driven approach to enhance safety protocols and promote a culture of accountability.

They began collecting data on safety incidents, training completion rates, and employee engagement scores. Analyzing this data, they identified specific sites with higher incident rates and developed targeted interventions, such as increased safety training and frequent safety meetings.

Over time, the company saw a significant decline in safety incidents and improved employee engagement. This success reinforced the importance of data-driven decision-making in promoting safety and performance in the construction industry.

7. Conclusion

Measuring human performance through data is essential for driving Workplace Safety and Efficiency. Organizations can gain valuable insights that inform decision-making and enhance operational outcomes by collecting, analyzing, and applying performance data. Integrating quantitative and qualitative data allows organizations to create a holistic view of human performance, fostering a culture of continuous improvement.

As demonstrated in the case studies presented, organizations across various industries have successfully leveraged data to enhance safety, streamline processes, and boost employee engagement. By prioritizing data-driven decision-making, leaders can build resilient organizations that thrive in an ever-evolving work environment.

Ultimately, measuring human performance is not a one-time effort but an ongoing Process requiring commitment and adaptability. By embracing data as a foundational element of performance measurement, organizations can navigate the complexities of modern work and drive safety and Efficiency in the long term.

Celebrating achievements motivates employees and encourages them to prioritize safety and Efficiency.

6. Case Studies of Data-Driven Performance Measurement
a) Manufacturing Industry: Lean Principles and Safety
A leading manufacturing company implemented a data-driven performance measurement system to enhance safety and Efficiency. The organization focused on eliminating waste and optimizing processes by adopting lean principles. They began collecting data on production rates, downtime, and safety incidents.

Through their analysis, they identified equipment failure patterns that contributed to production delays and safety risks. Implementing preventive maintenance schedules based on data insights significantly reduced downtime and improved safety outcomes. This approach enhanced operational Efficiency and fostered a culture of continuous improvement.

b) Healthcare Sector: Reducing Patient Risks
Leaders in a large healthcare organization recognized the need to enhance patient safety and improve overall performance. They implemented a comprehensive data collection and analysis strategy to measure clinical outcomes, patient satisfaction, and staff performance.

The organization identified common areas of concern by analyzing incident reports and patient feedback, such as medication errors and communication breakdowns. They developed targeted training programs for staff and implemented standardized protocols for high-risk procedures. As a result, the organization experienced a notable decrease in adverse events and improved patient satisfaction scores.

c) Construction Industry: Enhancing Safety Protocols
A significant construction firm faced challenges related to safety incidents and employee engagement. The leadership team adopted a

THE NEW FOUNDATIONS OF HUMAN PERFORMANCE

- **Incident Analysis:** Analyzing incident reports and near misses allows organizations to identify common factors contributing to accidents. Organizations can develop targeted safety interventions and training programs by addressing these factors.
- **Risk Assessment:** Organizations can use data to conduct comprehensive risk assessments, evaluating potential hazards in the Workplace. This proactive approach helps organizations prioritize safety initiatives and allocate resources effectively.

b) Improving Training Programs

Data-driven insights can also inform the development of effective training programs. Organizations can identify skill gaps and tailor training initiatives by analyzing performance metrics and employee feedback to meet their needs.

- **Targeted Training:** Performance data can reveal areas where employees may require additional training or support. Tailoring training programs to address these areas enhances employee competency and safety.
- **Evaluating Training Effectiveness:** After implementing training programs, organizations can assess their effectiveness by tracking changes in performance metrics. This data-driven approach ensures that training initiatives yield tangible results.

c) Enhancing Employee Engagement

Employee engagement is a critical factor influencing performance and safety. Organizations can create a work environment that fosters motivation and commitment. by measuring engagement levels and analyzing feedback

- **Engagement Surveys:** Regular employee engagement surveys allow organizations to assess employees' perceptions of their work environment, leadership, and safety culture. This data can guide initiatives to enhance engagement and morale.
- **Recognizing and Rewarding Performance:** Utilizing performance data to recognize and reward high-performing employees fosters a culture of appreciation and accountability.

4. Analyzing Data for Insights
a) Statistical Analysis Techniques

Once data is collected, organizations must analyze it to uncover insights that drive safety and Efficiency. Statistical analysis techniques can help organizations identify trends, correlations, and potential areas for improvement.

- **Descriptive Statistics:** Descriptive statistics summarize data to provide an overview of performance metrics. Measures such as mean, median, and standard deviation help organizations understand central tendencies and variability in performance.

- **Inferential Statistics:** Inferential statistics allow organizations to make predictions or generalizations about a larger population based on sample data. Techniques such as regression analysis can help identify relationships between variables, providing valuable insights into factors that influence performance.

b) Data Visualization

Data visualization tools enable organizations to present performance data in an accessible and understandable format. Effective visualization helps leaders quickly identify trends, patterns, and areas for improvement.

- **Dashboards and Reports:** Dashboards that visualize KPIs and performance metrics allow leaders to track progress briefly. Customizable reports can provide deeper insights into specific performance areas, facilitating data-driven decision-making.

- **Interactive Data Tools:** Interactive data tools enable users to explore data sets and conduct analyses. These tools empower employees at all levels to engage with performance data and identify opportunities for improvement.

5. Practical Applications of Data-Driven Decision-Making
a) Identifying Safety Hazards

Data-driven performance measurement is crucial for identifying safety hazards and implementing preventive measures. Organizations can uncover trends that indicate potential risks by analyzing safety data and taking proactive steps to mitigate them.

THE NEW FOUNDATIONS OF HUMAN PERFORMANCE

techniques can help organizations draw meaningful conclusions from survey results.

b) Performance Management Software

Performance management software provides a centralized platform for tracking and analyzing performance data. These tools streamline the data collection Process and enable organizations to generate real-time insights into employee performance.

- **Integrated Metrics Dashboard:** Performance management software typically includes dashboards that visualize KPIs and other performance metrics. This visual representation makes it easier for leaders to track progress and identify areas that require attention.
- **Goal Setting and Tracking**: Organizations can use performance management software to set individual and team goals, monitor progress, and provide ongoing feedback. This dynamic approach fosters accountability and encourages continuous improvement.

c) Safety Reporting Systems

Safety reporting systems allow organizations to collect data on incidents, near misses, and safety compliance. These systems are essential for identifying hazards and implementing preventive measures.

- **Incident Reporting:** Employees should have access to a user-friendly system for reporting incidents and near miss. Collecting detailed information about these events enables organizations to analyze trends and identify potential risks.
- **Safety Audits and Inspections:** Regular safety audits and inspections allow organizations to assess compliance with safety protocols and identify areas for improvement. Documenting findings helps track progress over time and ensures accountability.

- **Surveys and Assessments:** Employee surveys can gather quantitative data on various aspects of human performance, such as job satisfaction, engagement, and perceived safety. Scoring these surveys allows organizations to quantify employee sentiments and track changes over time.

b) Qualitative Data

Qualitative data provides rich, descriptive insights into employee experiences, behaviours, and motivations. While it may not be as easily quantifiable as numerical data, qualitative data plays a critical role in understanding the context behind performance metrics.

- **Interviews and Focus Groups:** Conducting interviews or focus groups can yield valuable qualitative insights into employee perspectives on safety, Workplace culture, and performance challenges. These insights can help organizations identify underlying issues that may not be evident from quantitative data alone.

- **Observational Data:** Direct observations of employee behaviours can provide qualitative insights into Workplace dynamics, safety practices, and teamwork. This data can complement quantitative metrics by adding context and depth to performance assessments.

3. Methods for Collecting Data
a) Surveys and Questionnaires

Surveys and questionnaires are potent tools for collecting both quantitative and qualitative data. They can assess employee satisfaction, engagement, safety perceptions, and performance outcomes.

- **Designing Effective Surveys:** Organizations should focus on crafting straightforward, concise questions that align with their measurement goals. Using a mix of closed-ended and open-ended questions allows for a comprehensive understanding of employee sentiments and experiences.

- **Analyzing Survey Results:** After collecting survey responses, organizations can analyze the data to identify trends, correlations, and areas for improvement. Employing statistical analysis

evidence and subjective opinions, allowing them to develop targeted strategies that enhance performance and mitigate risks.

b) Driving Safety and Efficiency

The relationship between safety and Efficiency is profound. Organizations prioritizing safety tend to experience fewer accidents and incidents, enhancing overall Efficiency. Conversely, when safety is compromised, productivity can suffer due to disruptions, injuries, and increased insurance costs. Data-driven performance measurement allows organizations to identify the key factors influencing safety and Efficiency, enabling them to implement strategies supporting both objectives.

- **Enhancing Safety:** Organizations can identify patterns and trends that reveal potential hazards by collecting and analyzing safety data—such as incident reports, near misses, and compliance checks. This insight enables proactive measures to mitigate risks and improve safety outcomes.

- **Improving Efficiency:** Performance data, including productivity metrics and employee engagement scores, clearly show how effectively team's work. Organizations can streamline processes and improve resource allocation by identifying bottlenecks and inefficiencies.

2. Types of Data for Measuring Human Performance
a) Quantitative Data

Quantitative data consists of numerical values that can be measured and analyzed statistically. This data type is crucial for tracking performance metrics, identifying trends, and making data-driven decisions.

- **Key Performance Indicators (KPIs):** KPIs are specific, measurable values that reflect the success of an organization in achieving its objectives. Examples include productivity rates, incident rates, and employee turnover rates. Organizations can regularly monitor KPIs to assess their performance against predefined goals and benchmarks.

Using Data to Drive Safety and Efficiency

Introduction

Understanding human performance is more critical than ever in today's fast-paced and increasingly complex work environments. Organizations recognize that effective measurement is the key to enhancing productivity, improving safety, and fostering employee well-being. By leveraging data to drive decisions, businesses can create a culture prioritizing safety and promoting Efficiency and continuous improvement.

This chapter will explore the essential role of data in measuring human performance, focusing on how it can be used to drive safety and Efficiency in the Workplace. We will discuss the different types of data, the methods for collecting and analyzing this data, and the practical applications of performance measurement tools. Additionally, we will examine case studies that illustrate how organizations have successfully used data to transform their operations and enhance overall performance.

1. The Importance of Data in Human Performance Measurement

a) Understanding Human Performance

Human performance encompasses various behaviours and outcomes that contribute to Workplace success. It includes not only the physical capabilities of employees but also their cognitive abilities, emotional well-being, and interpersonal skills. By measuring these factors, organizations can gain valuable insights into how their workforce operates and how it can be optimized.

Data serves as the backbone of this measurement Process. It provides objective evidence to be analyzed and used to make informed decisions about training, resource allocation, and safety protocols. With data, organizations can move beyond anecdotal

c) Continuous Improvement

A performance measurement system should not be static but evolve as the organization grows and changes. Organizations must regularly review and update their measurement systems to ensure continued relevance and effectiveness.

- **Regular Reviews:** Schedule regular reviews of performance measurement metrics and tools. Assess whether the chosen KPIs align with organizational goals and whether data collection methods yield meaningful insights.

- **Feedback Mechanisms:** Establish feedback mechanisms to gather employee input regarding the performance measurement Process. Employees can provide valuable insights into what works well and what needs improvement.

- **Adapting to Change:** As organizations evolve, so should their performance measurement systems. Be open to adapting methodologies, tools, and KPIs in response to changing business environments, employee needs, and industry standards.

Conclusion

Measuring human performance is a multifaceted endeavour that requires a blend of traditional and innovative tools and techniques. By implementing effective measurement systems, organizations can gain valuable insights into employee performance, identify areas for improvement, and foster a culture of continuous development.

From surveys and performance reviews to cutting-edge wearable technology and performance management software, various tools are available to organizations seeking to enhance human performance. The essential lies in developing a comprehensive measurement framework that engages employees, fosters transparency and promotes continuous improvement.

A robust performance measurement system will empower organizations to make informed decisions, drive safety, and optimize performance, leading to tremendous success in today's dynamic Workplace.

4. Implementing Performance Measurement Systems

a) Developing a Performance Measurement Framework

Organizations should develop a comprehensive framework to successfully implement a performance measurement system that outlines the goals, objectives, and methodologies for measuring human performance.

- **Defining Goals and Objectives:** Begin by clearly defining the organization's goals and objectives related to human performance. These should align with the organization's overall mission and vision.
- **Selecting Relevant KPIs:** Choose KPIs that accurately reflect the desired outcomes and performance metrics. Involve employees in the selection Process to ensure KPIs resonate with their daily responsibilities.
- **Establishing Data Collection Methods:** Determine the methods and tools for collecting performance data. This may involve a combination of surveys, observations, technology, and qualitative assessments.

b) Engaging Employees in the Process

Employee engagement is crucial for the success of any performance measurement system. When employees feel involved and valued in the Process, they are more likely to embrace the measurement initiatives and take ownership of their performance.

- **Communication and Transparency:** Communicate the purpose and benefits of the performance measurement system to employees. Transparency about how data will be used and the potential for personal development fosters Trust and buy-in.
- **Involving Employees in KPI Selection:** Engage employees in selecting KPIs, allowing them to voice their perspectives on what constitutes successful performance. This involvement enhances accountability and creates a sense of shared responsibility.
- **Celebrating Successes:** Recognize and celebrate achievements based on performance metrics. Highlighting individual and team successes fosters a positive work environment and reinforces the value of performance measurement.

THE NEW FOUNDATIONS OF HUMAN PERFORMANCE

experiences. Methods for collecting qualitative data include interviews, open-ended survey questions, focus groups, and narrative assessments.

- **Quantitative Data:** Quantitative data is numerical and objective, allowing for statistical analysis and trend identification. Standard methods for collecting quantitative data include surveys with Likert scale questions, performance metrics, and observational checklists.

- **Balancing Both Types of Data:** A well-rounded performance measurement system should incorporate qualitative and quantitative data. Qualitative data adds context to quantitative metrics, while quantitative data provides a solid foundation for analyzing trends and making data-driven decisions.

b) Statistical Analysis Techniques

Once data is collected, organizations must employ statistical analysis techniques to draw meaningful conclusions and insights from performance metrics. This analysis helps identify trends, correlations, and areas for improvement.

- **Descriptive Statistics:** Descriptive statistics summarize data, providing insights into central tendencies (mean, median, mode) and variability (standard deviation, range). This foundational analysis is crucial for understanding overall performance levels.

- **Inferential Statistics:** Inferential statistics allow organizations to make predictions or generalizations about a larger population based on a sample of data. Regression analysis, t-tests, and ANOVA can help identify relationships between variables and inform decision-making.

- **Data Visualization:** Utilizing data visualization tools enables organizations to present performance data. Graphs, charts, and dashboards enhance communication and make it easier to identify trends and insights briefly.

- **Data-Driven Insights:** Advanced performance management tools often employ data analytics and machine learning to generate insights from performance data. This enables organizations to identify correlations, predict outcomes, and make proactive adjustments to enhance performance.

c) Learning Management Systems (LMS)

Learning Management Systems (LMS) provides a platform for delivering training and educational content while tracking employee progress. This technology is instrumental in measuring the effectiveness of training programs and ensuring that employees acquire the necessary skills for optimal performance.

- **Tracking Training Completion:** Organizations can monitor employee participation in training programs through an LMS. This data helps ensure that employees receive the necessary training to perform their jobs safely and effectively.

- **Assessing Knowledge Retention:** Many LMS platforms offer assessment tools to measure knowledge retention following training. Organizations can evaluate whether employees successfully apply the skills learned during training to their daily tasks.

- **Customized Learning Paths:** An LMS can enable organizations to create personalized employee learning paths based on their specific performance needs. Tailoring training to individual requirements enhances employee engagement and improves overall performance.

3. Data Collection and Analysis Techniques
a) Qualitative vs. Quantitative Data

Measuring human performance involves both qualitative and quantitative data collection techniques. Understanding the distinction between these two data types is essential for creating a comprehensive performance measurement system.

- **Qualitative Data:** Qualitative data is descriptive and subjective, providing insights into employees' thoughts, feelings, and

THE NEW FOUNDATIONS OF HUMAN PERFORMANCE

2. Technology-Driven Measurement Techniques
a) Wearable Technology
The advent of wearable technology has revolutionized how organizations measure human performance. Devices such as smartwatches, fitness trackers, and specialized safety wearables provide real-time data on various performance metrics.

- **Monitoring Physical Activity:** Wearable devices can track employees' physical activity levels, heart rates, and Fatigue. This data can help organizations assess whether workers manage their physical demands effectively and provide insights into potential fatigue-related issues.

- **Enhanced Safety Monitoring:** Wearables with sensors can monitor environmental conditions, detect falls, or alert workers to hazards. This technology empowers organizations to prioritize employee safety and respond to real-time incidents.

- **Data Analysis and Feedback:** Collecting and analyzing data from wearable devices enables organizations to identify patterns and make informed decisions. For example, if data shows high Fatigue levels among workers in a specific role, adjustments can be made to shift patterns or workload distribution.

b) Performance Management Software
Performance management software consolidates various performance metrics and provides organizations with a centralized platform for tracking, analyzing, and reporting on human performance. This technology streamlines the performance measurement Process and enhances decision-making.

- **Integrated Metrics Dashboard:** Performance management software typically includes dashboards that provide real-time insights into performance metrics. These dashboards allow leaders to track KPIs, identify trends, and monitor progress toward goals.

- **Goal Setting and Tracking:** Organizations can use performance management software to set individual and team goals, track progress, and provide ongoing feedback. This dynamic approach promotes accountability and encourages continuous improvement.

- **Setting Clear Objectives:** For performance reviews to be effective, organizations must establish clear objectives aligning with broader organizational goals. These objectives should be communicated to employees immediately, ensuring they understand what is expected of them.
- **Structured Evaluation Criteria:** A standardized evaluation framework helps maintain consistency and fairness across performance reviews. Organizations can develop rating scales to assess employees based on specific competencies, behaviours, and outcomes.
- **Feedback and Development Plans:** Performance reviews should assess past performance and focus on future development. Constructive feedback can guide employees on areas for improvement, and organizations can create personalized development plans to foster growth.

c) Observational Methods
Observation is a powerful technique for measuring human performance, particularly in high-risk environments where behaviours directly impact safety. Through direct observation, leaders can assess employees' adherence to safety protocols, teamwork dynamics, and overall performance.
- **Structured Observation Checklists:** Developing structured checklists can help observers focus on specific behaviours or actions relevant to performance metrics. These checklists can cover safety compliance, communication effectiveness, and problem-solving skills.
- **Peer Observations:** Encouraging peer observations fosters a culture of accountability and collaboration. Employees can observe one another's performance and provide constructive feedback, creating an environment of mutual support.
- **Regular Observation Reviews:** Regularly reviewing observation data enables organizations to identify performance trends and improvement areas. This information can inform targeted training and interventions to enhance safety and Efficiency.

1. Traditional Measurement Techniques
a) Surveys and Questionnaires

Surveys and questionnaires are widely used for gathering qualitative and quantitative data about employee performance, satisfaction, and engagement. These instruments allow organizations to assess various aspects of human performance, including emotional well-being, stress levels, and perceptions of safety.

- **Designing Effective Surveys:** To maximize the usefulness of surveys, organizations should focus on creating straightforward, concise, and relevant questions. Questions should be tailored to address specific performance metrics, ensuring they accurately capture the desired data. Using a mix of open-ended and closed-ended questions can provide both quantitative data and rich qualitative insights.

- **Frequency and Timing:** The timing of surveys is crucial. Organizations should conduct them regularly—such as quarterly or bi-annually—to track changes over time. Additionally, surveys can be administered after significant events, such as training sessions or major organizational changes, to gather immediate feedback.

- **Analyzing Survey Results:** After collecting survey responses, organizations should analyze the data thoroughly. Employing statistical analysis methods can help identify trends, correlations, and areas that require attention. Qualitative data can also provide deeper insights into employee sentiments, revealing underlying issues that may not be evident through quantitative metrics alone.

b) Performance Reviews

Performance reviews often conducted annually or bi-annually provide structured feedback on individual and team performance. These reviews can encompass various performance metrics, such as productivity, collaboration, adherence to safety protocols, and personal development.

Conclusion

KPIs for human performance are essential for understanding, improving, and sustaining Workplace Safety and Efficiency. By measuring physical, cognitive, emotional, and behavioural factors, organizations can create a comprehensive view of how well their teams are performing. More importantly, well-defined KPIs provide the data necessary to make informed decisions, improve processes, and foster a culture of continuous improvement. Leaders who harness the power of KPIs will be better equipped to drive safely, performance, and long-term success.

Tools and Techniques for Performance Measurement

Introduction

To optimize Workplace safety and enhance performance, organizations must adopt systematic methods for measuring human performance. While Key Performance Indicators (KPIs) are invaluable for tracking progress, they represent just one facet of a comprehensive performance measurement system. The tools and techniques employed to measure human performance are critical in collecting data, analyzing trends, and facilitating continuous improvement.

This chapter delves into various tools and techniques for measuring human performance, exploring traditional and innovative approaches. From qualitative assessments to advanced technologies, we will highlight how these methods can create a more informed, effective, and engaged workforce. By the end of this chapter, readers will have a robust understanding of the diverse array of performance measurement tools available and how to implement them in their organizations effectively.

KPIs are not just abstract metrics but are meaningful to the business's overall success.

- **SMART Goals:** KPIs should follow the SMART framework, meaning they should be Specific, Measurable, Achievable, Relevant, and Time-bound. This approach makes it easier to track progress and adjust strategies when needed.

b) Involving Employees in KPI Development

Employees actively involved in creating KPIs are more likely to understand and buy into the metrics being used to measure their performance. Leaders should engage employees in reprocesses, especially in safety and human performance areas.

- **Collaboration and Feedback:** Collect employee feedback to ensure that KPIs are realistic and relevant to their daily tasks. Involving workers in developing these indicators creates a sense of ownership and responsibility.

- **Clear Communication:** It's essential to communicate the purpose and value of KPIs to employees. They need to understand how their performance will be measured and why these metrics are critical for their safety and the organization's success.

c) Regularly Reviewing and Updating KPIs

The Workplace is constantly evolving, and so should KPIs. Regularly reviewing and updating KPIs ensures they remain relevant, actionable, and aligned with organizational goals. Outdated KPIs can lead to skewed insights and ineffective management strategies.

- **Dynamic KPIs**: Human performance KPIs should be flexible enough to change as organizational priorities shift or new safety challenges arise. For example, during a high-stress period such as a significant project, cognitive performance KPIs may become more relevant than physical ones.

-**Feedback Loops:** Implementing a feedback loop where KPI data is continuously reviewed allows for real-time adjustments in training, workload distribution, or safety measures. Leaders can use the data gathered from KPIs to refine processes, reduce risks, and drive continuous improvement.

This can include emotional exhaustion, depersonalization, feelings of reduced accomplishment, and critical aspects of burnout syndrome.

d) Behavioral KPIs
Behavioural KPIs focus on how well employees follow established safety protocols and contribute to the organization's safety culture. These indicators are significant for industries with stringent safety regulations.
- **Compliance with Safety Protocols:** One of the most straightforward and critical behavioural KPIs is tracking how consistently employees adhere to safety rules and guidelines. Non-compliance can lead to accidents and injuries, making it a crucial area of focus.
- **Participation in Safety Training:** This KPI measures employees' engagement in ongoing safety training programs. High participation rates often correlate with better overall safety performance.
- **Proactive Hazard Reporting:** Employees who take the initiative to report potential safety hazards before they result in incidents contribute to a safer Workplace. Monitoring the number of proactive hazard reports can indicate a strong safety culture.
- **Incident Investigation Participation:** Following Workplace incidents, it is essential for employees to engage in the investigation and root cause analysis. This KPI tracks employees' involvement in learning from mistakes and improving safety protocols.

3. Setting Effective KPIs: Best Practices
a) Aligning KPIs with Organizational Goals
When defining KPIs for human performance, it's essential to ensure they are aligned with the organization's broader goals. Safety and performance KPIs should directly support the company's mission, values, and objectives, such as reducing incident rates, increasing productivity, or fostering a more engaged workforce.
- **Strategic Alignment:** Make sure that KPIs reflect the specific outcomes the organization tries to achieve, whether it's enhanced safety, higher Efficiency, or better team dynamics. This ensures that

aviation, or manufacturing, where minor errors can have significant consequences.

- **Task Completion Time:** The time it takes to complete complex cognitive tasks can indicate how healthy employees are handling their workload. Increases in task completion times may suggest cognitive Fatigue or information overload.

- **Error Rates in Cognitive Tasks:** Tracking the number of errors made in cognitive tasks—such as data entry errors, calculation mistakes, or procedural oversights—provides insight into the mental sharpness of employees.

- **Attention Span and Focus:** In environments where distractions are prevalent, monitoring the ability of employees to maintain focus on their tasks is essential. Tools such as attention span tests or real-time task tracking can help me measure this KPI.

c) Emotional and Psychological KPIs

Human performance is not solely about physical strength or cognitive ability. Emotional factors like stress, anxiety, and resilience play a crucial role in determining how well employees perform, particularly in high-pressure environments.

- **Stress Levels:** Stress can impair both cognitive and physical performance. Tracking stress levels through employee surveys, physiological data (like heart rate variability), or direct feedback can offer insights into Workplace conditions that may contribute to underperformance.

- **Emotional Resilience:** This KPI measures how well employees bounce back from setbacks, errors, or high-pressure situations. It can be tracked through psychological assessments, supervisor feedback, or even employee self-evaluations.

- **Workplace Satisfaction and Engagement:** While not directly linked to emotional intelligence, Workplace satisfaction surveys provide a valuable proxy for overall emotional well-being. A happy, engaged workforce is likelier to perform well, stay focused, and maintain a strong safety record.

- **Burnout Indicators**: Monitoring KPIs that track burnout can help prevent employees' long-term emotional and psychological decline.

in risk mitigation. Behavioural KPIs are crucial in fostering a safety-oriented culture.

2. Defining Key KPIs for Human Performance
a) Physical Performance KPIs
Physical KPIs provides an understanding of how healthy employees handle their job's physical demands. These indicators can include direct and indirect physical capacity measurements, such as endurance, injury rates, and response to Fatigue.

- **Injury Rates:** One of the most straightforward physical KPIs is tracking the frequency of Workplace injuries. A high injury rate could indicate poor ergonomics, lack of safety training, or other systemic issues that need addressing.

- **Absenteeism Due to Injury:** This KPI monitors the number of workdays lost due to injury. High absenteeism rates can contribute to excessive physical strain or poor safety practices.

- **Fatigue-Related Incidents:** Fatigue can significantly impair physical performance, leading to mistakes and accidents. Tracking the number of incidents related to Fatigue can help organizations assess whether their work-rest cycles or shift patterns need adjustment.

- **Reaction Time and Task Efficiency:** In physically demanding jobs, the speed and Efficiency of completing tasks can serve as important indicators. For example, KPIs might measure how quickly workers react to safety alarms or complete time-sensitive tasks without compromising quality.

b) Cognitive Performance KPIs
Cognitive KPIs measure employees' mental agility and accuracy, particularly when split-second decisions or high concentration levels are required. Cognitive overload, Fatigue, and stress can harm performance, so monitoring these aspects is critical.

- **Decision-Making Accuracy:** This KPI measures the percentage of correct decisions made in time-sensitive situations. It is particularly relevant in high-stakes environments like healthcare,

THE NEW FOUNDATIONS OF HUMAN PERFORMANCE

training, and enhanced productivity. KPIs make performance visible and measurable, helping leaders identify areas that need attention and enabling them to provide feedback based on actual data.

- **Benchmarking Performance:** KPIs are a reference point for comparing current performance with previous results or industry standards. These benchmarks are necessary to gauge whether performance is improving, stagnating, or declining.

- **Identifying Trends and Issues:** Organizations can spot patterns and trends over time with KPIs in place. For instance, a sudden drop in attention-related KPIs might indicate rising Fatigue among workers, prompting schedule adjustments or work-rest cycles.

- **Supporting Continuous Improvement:** KPIs are about tracking and learning. Leaders can use performance data to identify areas for improvement, ensure corrective actions are implemented, and continuously refine processes to boost safety and Efficiency.

b) The Multidimensional Nature of Human Performance KPIs

Human performance involves physical capacity, cognitive skills, emotional intelligence, and behavioural consistency. A robust KPI framework for human performance must capture these diverse elements, creating a comprehensive picture of what contributes to individual and team success.

- **Physical KPIs:** These might measure attributes like strength, stamina, or reaction times, all of which are essential in industries that require physical labour. They can also include metrics like the number of safety-related incidents (e.g., slips, trips, and falls) to ensure workers perform physical tasks safely.

- **Cognitive KPIs:** Metrics that evaluate decision-making speed, accuracy, focus, and attention are essential in high-pressure environments where cognitive overload can lead to costly mistakes.

- **Emotional KPIs:** While more challenging to quantify, emotional KPIs assess factors like stress levels, resilience, and emotional regulation under pressure. These can be gauged through surveys, assessments, and psychological metrics.

- **Behavioral KPIs:** These measure compliance with safety protocols, participation in training sessions, and proactive behaviour

Chapter 14

Measuring Human Performance

Key Performance Indicators (KPIs) for Human Performance

Introduction

In the realm of Workplace safety and performance, measurement is essential. The adage, "What gets measured, gets managed," holds, particularly regarding human performance. Organizations must have clear metrics to track, analyze, and improve performance to ensure that team's function at their best and maintain safety standards. Enter Key Performance Indicators (KPIs), the quantitative benchmarks for evaluating human performance.

However, KPIs in the context of human performance are not one-dimensional. They encompass a variety of factors, from physical and cognitive abilities to emotional resilience and decision-making under pressure. Leaders who understand how to measure these dimensions effectively can drive better outcomes, foster safer environments, and create high-performing teams. This chapter delves into how to identify, implement, and monitor KPIs to measure human performance, ultimately supporting a culture of continuous improvement in the Workplace.

1. Understanding the Importance of KPIs in Human Performance
a) Why KPIs Matter
KPIs provide a way to track progress and performance objectively. These indicators are crucial for human performance because they offer insights into how individuals and teams' function on multiple levels, allowing for more informed decision-making, improved

- Making the Business Case for Safety: Leaders should be prepared to make the business case for safety investments, demonstrating that the long-term benefits—such as fewer accidents, reduced absenteeism, and lower insurance premiums—outweigh the short-term costs.

b) Handling Resistance to Change

Some organizations may resist new safety initiatives, particularly if they are perceived as slowing production or adding unnecessary complexity. Leaders must be prepared to address this resistance head-on, communicating the importance of safety and the benefits of the changes.

- Engaging Employees in the Process: Involving employees in developing and implementing safety initiatives can help overcome resistance. When employees feel they have a say in the Process, they are more likely to buy into the changes.

- Providing Ongoing Education: Leaders should offer ongoing education and training to help employees understand the rationale behind safety initiatives and their role in protecting everyone on the team.

Conclusion

Integrating safety into leadership is more than just policies and procedures; it's about setting a standard through action. By leading by example, communicating the importance of safety, and creating a culture of accountability, leaders can ensure that safety becomes a core value that drives performance and well-being.

Leaders who consistently prioritize safety through their actions, decisions, and communications create environments where employees feel valued, trusted, and empowered to take ownership of their safety. This commitment to safety reduces risks and enhances overall performance, making it a critical factor in long-term success. As the Workplace evolves, leaders must prioritize safety as a foundational element of effective leadership.

b) Creating a System of Accountability

Leaders should implement systems that make it easy to track and measure accountability for safety. These systems might include safety audits, regular inspections, and transparent reporting mechanisms for safety violations or near misses.

- **Safety Metrics:** Leaders should establish key safety metrics regularly monitored and reported on. These metrics can include the number of days without incidents, the number of safety training sessions completed, or the percentage of safety audits passed.

- **Accountability Reviews:** Regular reviews of safety performance can help ensure that accountability is maintained. Leaders can conduct quarterly or annual reviews that assess the safety performance of individuals and teams, offering opportunities for recognition and improvement.

c) Encouraging Peer Accountability

Peer accountability is a powerful tool in fostering a strong safety culture. Leaders should encourage team members to hold each other accountable for safety practices, creating a sense of shared responsibility.

- **Peer Safety Checks:** Leaders can implement peer safety check programs, where employees are responsible for checking each other's adherence to safety protocols. This not only enhances safety but also strengthens team cohesion and shared accountability.

- **Recognizing Peer Leadership in Safety:** Leaders should recognize employees who take the initiative to hold their peers accountable for safety. This recognition can be formal or informal but should constantly reinforce the value of peer accountability.

4. Overcoming Challenges to Leading by Example in Safety
a) Navigating Time and Budget Constraints

One of the most significant challenges leaders face in prioritizing safety is balancing it with the demands of tight schedules and limited budgets. However, compromising safety for speed or cost-cutting is a false economy that can lead to accidents, injuries, and costly delays.

d) Encouraging Open Dialogue Around Safety

Creating an open, transparent culture where employees feel comfortable discussing safety concerns is crucial for preventing accidents and improving safety outcomes. Leaders play a significant role in encouraging this dialogue and ensuring it's acted upon.

- **Creating a No-Blame Culture:** Employees should never fear retaliation for reporting safety concerns or incidents. Leaders must foster a no-blame culture where employees feel safe to speak up about potential hazards or mistakes without fearing punitive consequences.

- **Listening to Employee Feedback**: Employees on the ground often have the best insights into potential safety risks. Leaders should regularly solicit feedback from their teams on safety issues and be willing to implement changes based on that feedback.

- **Responding Quickly to Safety Concerns:** When safety issues are raised, leaders should immediately address them. A swift response reduces the risk of accidents and reinforces to employees that their safety concerns are taken seriously.

3. Cultivating a Culture of Accountability
a) Holding Everyone to the Same Standard

Accountability is essential for ensuring that safety remains a priority. Leaders must hold themselves and their teams accountable to the same high standards. Safety rules apply equally to everyone, from entry-level employees to top executives.

- **Leading by Example in Accountability:** Leaders must demonstrate accountability by making their mistakes and being transparent about safety decisions. When leaders hold themselves accountable, it encourages employees to do the same.

- **Addressing Safety Violations Consistently:** Leaders should address them consistently and fairly when safety violations occur. This reinforces the importance of safety and ensures employees understand the consequences of failing to follow safety procedures.

- **One-on-One Conversations:** Leaders should use one-on-one meetings with employees to check in on their safety concerns. This approach helps to identify potential risks early and shows employees that their safety is a personal priority for leadership.
- **Public Acknowledgment of Safe Behaviors:** Recognizing employees who consistently demonstrate safe behaviours reinforces the importance of safety. Leaders should publicly celebrate safety achievements, whether it's a safety milestone, an employee suggestion that improved safety protocols, or proactive hazard identification.

c) Making Safety a Core Value in Decision-Making

Leaders who integrate safety into their leadership consider it in every decision. Whether it's a decision about project timelines, resource allocation, or operational strategies, safety should always be a central consideration.

- **Prioritizing Safety Over Speed:** There is often pressure to complete tasks quickly in industries where time is money. However, leaders must demonstrate that safety always precedes speed or cost savings. For example, if a project is running behind schedule, a leader prioritizing safety might extend the timeline to ensure safety protocols are not compromised.
- **Risk Assessment and Mitigation:** Leaders should involve themselves in the risk assessment Process, showing that safety risks are considered at the highest levels of decision-making. They should also actively mitigate these risks by approving new safety equipment, investing in employee training, or implementing new safety procedures.
- **Balancing Safety with Innovation**: Leaders should encourage innovation but ensure that new processes, technologies, or equipment do not compromise safety. By considering safety early in the innovation Process, leaders can avoid implementing solutions that may introduce new risks.

- Employee Engagement and Retention: Employees who feel safe and see their leaders prioritizing their well-being are more likely to be engaged and remain with the company long term. This reduces turnover and increases team cohesion.

2. Practical Ways Leaders Can Integrate Safety Into Their Leadership
a) Consistently Demonstrating Safe Behaviors
One simplest yet most powerful way to lead by example is to follow safety procedures and protocols in all situations consistently. Leaders should never exempt themselves from safety practices and should always adhere to the same rules that apply to everyone else.

- Wearing Protective Equipment: Whether it's a hard hat, safety goggles, or other PPE, leaders should always use the appropriate safety gear when required. This shows employees that no one is above the rules and reinforces the importance of safety measures.

- Following Safety Procedures: Leaders should follow all safety protocols and procedures, even when it might be tempting to cut corners. For example, taking the time to properly lock out/tag out equipment, conducting safety checks, or following proper lifting techniques demonstrates a commitment to safety.

- Participating in Safety Drills and Training: Leaders should actively participate in safety drills and training sessions alongside their teams. This involvement shows that safety is a priority for everyone, not just those on the front lines.

b) Communicating the Importance of Safety
Leadership is not just about action, it's also about communication. Leaders who regularly communicate the importance of safety reinforce its value to their teams. Effective communication around safety involves both formal and informal channels; ensuring safety is always part of conversation.

- Safety in Team Meetings: Safety should be a standing agenda item in team meetings, not an afterthought. Leaders can start each meeting with a safety moment, sharing a safety tip, discussing a recent incident, or highlighting a safety success story.

help embed it into the organization's DNA, ensuring that future leaders and employees uphold these values.

b) Building Trust Through Integrity
Trust is essential for effective leadership, and integrity is a crucial driver of Trust. When leaders consistently demonstrate that they value safety by adhering to the same standards they expect of their teams, they build Trust. This Trust is crucial for fostering a culture where employees feel comfortable speaking about safety concerns and where accountability thrives.

- **Walking the Talk:** Leaders who "walk the talk" by embodying safety practices earn the respect and Trust of their teams. Employees are more likely to believe in and adhere to safety protocols when they see their leaders doing the same.

- **Avoiding Double Standards**: If leaders expect employees to follow strict safety guidelines but fail to follow them themselves, they risk creating a culture of distrust and disengagement. Consistency is critical to maintaining the integrity of safety initiatives.

- **Empowering Employees:** Trust built through leading by example empowers employees to take ownership of safety. When they Trust that their leaders prioritize their well-being, employees feel more confident in bringing up potential hazards or concerns.

c) Enhancing Organizational Reputation and Success
Organizations prioritizing safety through strong leadership will likely enjoy long-term success regarding safety metrics, performance, and productivity. Leading by example enhances the organization's reputation internally and externally, attracting top talent and securing loyalty from employees, customers, and stakeholders.

- **External Perception:** Clients, investors, and regulators view companies with a strong safety culture more favourably. Leaders who emphasize safety by example help build a reputation for responsibility, reliability, and care.

Leading by Example—Integrating Safety into Leadership

Introduction

In any organization, leadership is pivotal in shaping the work environment, influencing team culture, and driving performance. One of the most critical aspects of leadership, particularly in industries where safety is paramount, is leading by example. Integrating safety into leadership is not just about making rules and policies about embodying those principles in everyday actions, decisions, and behaviours. This chapter explores how leaders can exemplify safety, ensuring it becomes deeply ingrained in their team's operations and culture. By leading by example, leaders foster a culture of accountability, Trust, and high performance where safety is not a separate consideration but an integral part of success.

1. Why Leading by Example Matters
a) The Influence of Leadership on Team Behavior

Employees often take cues from their leaders on how to behave, what to prioritize, and what standards to uphold. Leaders who exemplify safety in their day-to-day actions send a powerful message to their teams: safety matters, and it's non-negotiable.

- **Role Modeling**: When leaders consistently demonstrate safe behaviours, such as wearing personal protective equipment (PPE), following safety protocols, and prioritizing safety over speed or Efficiency, employees are more likely to follow suit. This role modelling establishes safety as a core value rather than an afterthought.

- **Setting the Tone:** The tone from the top is critical. A leader's attitude toward safety influences how employees perceive its importance. If leaders neglect safety or make exceptions to safety rules, employees may feel empowered to do the same, leading to increased risk.

- **Long-Term Impact**: Leading by example has long-term effects on organizational culture. Leaders who consistently prioritize safety

- Holding Difficult Conversations: While it's essential to offer support, leaders must also be willing to hold difficult conversations when necessary. These conversations should be framed as opportunities for growth, focusing on solutions rather than blaming.

c) Cultivating Trust Through Accountability

Trust and accountability reinforce one another. Trust will naturally grow as leaders hold employees accountable somewhat, consistently, and supportive. Employees will feel secure knowing their leaders will support them in meeting expectations, and leaders will Trust their teams to perform at their best.

Conclusion

Trust and accountability are the cornerstones of high-performance teams. In safety-driven environments, these elements take on even greater importance, as they directly influence both individual performance and overall team safety. Leaders who prioritize building Trust through transparency, empathy, and empowerment while simultaneously fostering accountability through clear expectations and structured systems can create teams that are resilient, high-performing, and committed to maintaining the highest safety standards.

As the modern Workplace evolves, leaders must remain vigilant in nurturing these critical qualities. Through intentional leadership, they can build teams that are not only productive but also safe, engaged, and empowered—ultimately driving performance excellence and long-term organizational success.

THE NEW FOUNDATIONS OF HUMAN PERFORMANCE

- **Peer Accountability:** Encouraging peer accountability can further strengthen a culture of responsibility. When team members hold each other accountable, it creates a supportive yet high-performing team dynamic where everyone is committed to shared goals.

4. Building a Culture of Accountability and Trust
a) Recognizing and Rewarding Accountability
One of the most effective ways to foster accountability is to recognize and reward it. Leaders can build a culture of accountability by celebrating employees who consistently meet or exceed expectations. This motivates the individual and signals to the team that accountability is valued and appreciated.

-Public Acknowledgment: Recognizing employees in team meetings or company-wide announcements helps reinforce the importance of accountability. Public recognition can motivate others to take responsibility for their performance.

- **Incentive Programs:** Leaders can create incentive programs that reward accountability in safety and performance, providing tangible rewards for employees who consistently meet high standards.

- **Personal Growth Opportunities:** Providing personal and professional growth opportunities for accountable team members can further reinforce the value of taking responsibility for one's actions.

b) Addressing Accountability Gaps
While celebrating success is essential, leaders must also address accountability gaps. When employees fail to meet expectations, leaders must intervene constructively, fostering improvement rather than discouragement.

- **Identifying Root Causes:** Leaders should investigate the underlying reasons for accountability gaps, whether due to unclear expectations, lack of resources, or personal challenges.

- **Providing Support and Guidance**: Leaders should offer support and guidance instead of immediately resorting to punitive measures to help employees get back on track. This might include additional training, mentorship, or resources.

feedback that helps team members understand their performance and where to improve.

b) Leading by Example

Leaders must embody the behaviours they expect from their teams. When leaders hold themselves accountable, they model the standards they expect their employees to follow. This "leading by example" approach is one of the most effective ways to instill team accountability.

- **Demonstrating Accountability in Actions**: Leaders who take responsibility for their actions, acknowledge mistakes, and follow through on their commitments set a powerful example for their teams.
- **Emphasizing Personal Responsibility**: When leaders demonstrate personal responsibility, it encourages team members to do the same. Leaders can foster this by being transparent about their goals and deadlines, showing how they hold themselves accountable.
- **Creating a Culture of Ownership:** By emphasizing the importance of ownership of one's work and outcomes, leaders encourage a culture where employees feel accountable to their managers, peers, and themselves.

c) Implementing Accountability Systems

While personal accountability is essential, leaders must establish formal systems to ensure accountability is ingrained in the organization's processes. These systems help create a structured environment where accountability is expected, tracked, and reinforced.

- **Performance Metrics and KPIs:** Leaders can implement key performance indicators (KPIs) and metrics to track team performance and safety outcomes. Regularly reviewing these metrics helps keep accountability at the forefront.
- **Regular Performance Reviews:** Formal performance reviews provide a structured opportunity to assess accountability and provide feedback on how healthy team members meet expectations.

c) Building Personal Relationships

Strong, trusting relationships between leaders and team members are essential for high-performing teams. Leaders who invest time in building relationships demonstrate that they care about their employees as workers and people.

- **Regular One-on-One Meetings:** Leaders can build personal connections by holding regular one-on-one meetings with team members. These meetings provide opportunities to discuss performance, challenges, and personal goals, strengthening the leader-employee relationship.
- **Showing Empathy:** Empathy is a powerful tool for building Trust. Leaders who show understanding and compassion during difficult times can create lasting bonds with their teams.
- **Recognizing Personal and Professional Milestones:** Recognizing personal achievements, life events, and professional successes can deepen Trust and demonstrate that leaders care about their employees as whole individuals.

3. The Role of Leaders in Fostering Accountability
a) Setting Clear Expectations

Accountability begins with clarity. Leaders must set clear, achievable expectations for their teams, particularly about safety and performance. When expectations are clear, employees may feel confident about their roles, which can lead to mistakes or underperformance.

- **Defining Roles and Responsibilities:** Leaders should clearly define each team member's role and responsibilities, ensuring everyone understands their part in the team's overall performance.
- **Setting SMART Goals:** Leaders can improve accountability by setting SMART goals—goals that are Specific, Measurable, Achievable, Relevant, and Time-bound. These goals provide a clear roadmap for success and allow leaders and employees to track progress.
- **Providing Regular Feedback**: Feedback is essential for accountability. Leaders should provide ongoing, constructive

- **Open Communication:** Leaders should prioritize clear, honest, and frequent communication. Sharing good and bad news openly helps teams Trust that they are getting the whole picture, not just a curated version of the truth.

- **Consistency in Actions:** Leaders must align their actions with their words. Consistency in decision-making and actions demonstrates integrity and builds Trust. If a leader says that safety is the top priority but consistently ignores safety protocols for productivity, Trust will quickly erode.

- **Vulnerability and Humility:** Admitting mistakes and demonstrating vulnerability as a leader can also strengthen Trust. When leaders acknowledge their errors, they show that it's okay for others to do the same, creating an environment where continuous learning is possible.

b) Empowering Team Members

Empowering team members is a critical strategy in building Trust. When leaders give employees autonomy, they send a clear message: "I Trust you to make the right decisions and perform your tasks effectively." This empowerment fosters Trust and promotes ownership and accountability among team members.

- **Delegating Responsibility**: Leaders who delegate important tasks and decisions to team members show that they Trust their abilities. This delegation encourages employees to take initiative and take responsibility for the outcomes of their work.

- **Encouraging Input:** Leaders should encourage input from all team members, fostering a culture where every voice is heard. This inclusive approach builds Trust, as employees feel their opinions and insights are valued.

- **Providing Support, Not Micromanaging**: Trust grows when leaders support their teams without hovering. Leaders should resist the urge to micromanage and provide guidance and resources while allowing employees to make decisions independently.

b) Accountability as the Catalyst for Performance

While Trust sets the foundation, accountability ensures that standards are met. Accountability in the Workplace is the expectation that team members will take responsibility for their actions, performance, and contributions to the team's goals. Leaders play a crucial role in fostering accountability by setting clear expectations and holding individuals responsible for meeting those standards.

- **Clarity of Roles:** Each member understands their role and responsibilities in highly accountable teams. This clarity reduces confusion, improves Efficiency, and ensures critical safety tasks are noticed.

- **Responsibility for Outcomes:** Accountability doesn't just mean acknowledging failures; it also involves recognizing successes. When leaders and teams embrace accountability, they celebrate achievements and learn from mistakes, creating a cycle of continuous improvement in performance and safety.

c) The Symbiotic Relationship Between Trust and Accountability

Trust and accountability are mutually reinforcing. Teams that Trust one another are more likely to hold each other accountable because they know feedback will be received constructively. Similarly, accountability fosters Trust by demonstrating team members' dedication to their tasks and each other. Together, they create an environment where performance and safety can thrive.

2. The Role of Leaders in Building Trust
a) Leading with Transparency and Integrity

Transparency and integrity are essential for building Trust in any team. Leaders who communicate openly and act consistently with their values earn the Trust of their teams. This Trust becomes the foundation upon which safety practices and performance standards are built.

Building Trust and Accountability in Teams

Introduction

In human performance and safety, leadership is the linchpin that holds teams together, fostering an environment where Trust and accountability are not just ideals but practices that guide everyday interactions. As workplaces evolve to become more dynamic and complex, the role of leaders in building Trust and fostering accountability becomes even more critical. These two components—Trust and accountability—are the bedrock of effective teamwork, safety, and high performance. This chapter delves deep into leaders' strategies to cultivate Trust and accountability within their teams, ensuring a safe and productive work environment.

1. The Connection Between Trust, Accountability, and Team Performance

a) Trust as the Foundation of Team Dynamics

Trust is the invisible glue that binds teams together. It forms the foundation for open communication, collaboration, and innovation. In high-risk or performance-driven environments, Trust is essential for ensuring that team members feel secure in their roles and are confident in the support of their colleagues and leaders.

- **Psychological Safety:** Trust creates an atmosphere of psychological safety, where employees are free to express ideas, share concerns, and admit mistakes without fear of retribution. This safety is paramount in safety-critical industries, where unspoken concerns or errors can lead to dangerous outcomes.

- **Collaboration and Innovation:** With Trust, teams are more likely to collaborate effectively. Employees are willing to share knowledge and resources, leading to improved problem-solving and innovation. This is particularly important in safety-driven environments where new ideas can lead to safer and more efficient practices.

THE NEW FOUNDATIONS OF HUMAN PERFORMANCE

3. Encouraging Work-Life Balance: Promoting work-life balance demonstrates a commitment to employee well-being and contributes to higher levels of engagement and performance.

c) Investing in Leadership Development
To prepare for the future, organizations must invest in leadership development programs. This investment can help identify and nurture future leaders who can effectively drive performance and safety initiatives. Critical components of leadership development include:

1. Mentorship Programs: Pairing emerging leaders with experienced mentors can provide valuable guidance and support.

2. Training and Workshops: Training focused on leadership skills, communication, and emotional intelligence can enhance leadership effectiveness.

3. 360-Degree Feedback: Implementing 360-degree feedback processes allows leaders to gain insights into their strengths and areas for improvement.

Conclusion
Leadership is a critical driver of human performance and safety in the Workplace. By embodying effective leadership styles, fostering a strong safety culture, and adapting to changing landscapes, leaders can create an environment where employees feel valued, engaged, and empowered to perform at their best. As organizations navigate the complexities of the modern Workplace, the role of leaders in shaping a culture of safety and performance will become increasingly vital. By investing in leadership development and prioritizing employee well-being, organizations can cultivate a thriving workforce, achieving operational excellence and a commitment to safety. Strong leadership is the linchpin of success, driving the future of human performance and safety in the Workplace.

2. Highlighting Individual Contributions: Celebrating individual contributions reinforces the idea that every employee plays a vital role in organizational success.

3. Sharing Success Stories: Sharing success stories with the entire organization can inspire others and promote a culture of continuous improvement.

6. The Future of Leadership in Performance and Safety
a) Adapting to Changing Landscapes

The future of work is marked by rapid changes driven by technology, globalization, and evolving workforce demographics. Leaders must adapt to these changes by:

1. Embracing Technological Advancements: Leaders should stay informed about advancements that enhance performance and safety.

2. Fostering Diversity and Inclusion: A diverse and inclusive workforce brings varied perspectives, driving innovation and enhancing organizational performance.

3. Prioritizing Employee Well-Being: As mental health becomes increasingly recognized as a critical aspect of Workplace success, leaders must prioritize employee well-being and mental health support.

b) Leading with Empathy

Empathetic leadership is becoming increasingly important in today's Workplace. Leaders who demonstrate empathy can create a supportive environment where employees feel valued and understood. Key aspects include:

1. Understanding Employee Needs: Leaders must actively seek to understand the needs and concerns of their employees, fostering open dialogue and trust.

2. Providing Support During Challenges: Leaders should be proactive in providing support to employees facing personal or professional challenges, whether through resources, flexibility, or mental health support.

THE NEW FOUNDATIONS OF HUMAN PERFORMANCE

5. Leaders as Change Agents
a) Driving Change in Human Performance
Influential leaders serve as change agents, driving initiatives that enhance human performance. They can achieve this by:

1. Identifying Opportunities for Improvement: Leaders must assess current practices and identify areas where performance can be enhanced.

2. Implementing Change Initiatives: Leaders should develop and implement change initiatives to improve processes, safety protocols, and employee engagement.

3. Monitoring and Evaluating Change Efforts: Continuous monitoring of change initiatives allows leaders to assess their impact and make necessary adjustments.

b) Navigating Resistance to Change
Resistance to change is a common challenge in any organization. Leaders can navigate this resistance by:

1. Involving Employees in the Change Process: Engaging employees in the change process fosters a sense of ownership and reduces resistance.

2. Communicating the Benefits of Change: Leaders should clearly articulate the benefits of proposed changes, helping employees understand their rationale.

3. Providing Support and Resources: Leaders must ensure employees have the support and resources to adapt to changes successfully.

c) Celebrating Successes
Celebrating big and small successes reinforces the importance of performance and safety initiatives. Leaders can celebrate successes by:

1. Acknowledging Team Achievements: Recognizing team achievements fosters a sense of pride and motivates employees to continue performing at their best.

2. Providing Feedback: Regular feedback helps employees understand their performance and areas for improvement. Constructive feedback should be specific, timely, and actionable.

3. Encouraging Two-Way Communication: Leaders must create an environment where employees feel comfortable sharing their ideas, concerns, and suggestions.

b) Tailoring Communication to the Audience

Different stakeholders may require different communication approaches. Leaders should tailor their communication to meet the needs of various audiences, including:

1. Frontline Employees: Communication with frontline employees should be straightforward and practical, focusing on specific safety protocols and performance expectations.

2. Management and Executives: Communication with higher management may require a more strategic approach, emphasizing data-driven insights and performance metrics.

3. Stakeholders and Regulatory Agencies: When communicating with external stakeholders, leaders must be transparent and ensure compliance with safety regulations.

c) Utilizing Technology for Communication

In today's digital age, technology is vital in enhancing communication. Leaders can leverage various tools to improve communication and collaboration:

1. Collaboration Platforms: Platforms like Slack, Microsoft Teams, or Asana can facilitate real-time communication and collaboration among team members.

2. Video Conferencing Tools: These tools allow leaders to connect with remote employees, fostering a sense of presence and engagement.

3. Data Dashboards: Implementing data dashboards can help leaders visualize key performance metrics and safety data, enabling informed decision-making.

b) Leadership Commitment to Safety

Leadership commitment to safety is essential for establishing a robust safety culture. This commitment can be demonstrated through:

1. Allocating Resources: Leaders must allocate the necessary resources, including time, training, and equipment, to support safety initiatives.

2. Participating in Safety Programs: Leaders should actively participate in safety training and programs to show their commitment and involvement.

3. Setting an Example: Leaders must model safe behaviours in their actions, demonstrating that safety is a priority.

c) Building a Culture of Continuous Improvement

A safety culture is not static; it requires continuous improvement. Leaders can drive this process by:

1. Encouraging Learning from Incidents: When accidents occur, leaders should promote a culture of learning rather than blame. Analyzing incidents to identify root causes and implement corrective actions is crucial.

2. Facilitating Ongoing Training: Leaders should ensure employees receive ongoing training and development opportunities to enhance their knowledge and skills.

3. Engaging Employees in Safety Initiatives: Involving employees in safety committees and initiatives fosters a sense of ownership and accountability for safety.

4. Leadership Communication: A Catalyst for Performance
a) The Importance of Communication

Effective communication is at the heart of successful leadership. Leaders must communicate clearly and consistently to ensure performance and safety. Key aspects include:

1. Setting Clear Goals: Leaders should establish precise performance and safety goals aligned with the organization's vision.

3. Focus on Team Success: Servant leaders emphasize collective success, fostering a sense of belonging and collaboration.

c) Authentic Leadership

Authentic leaders are true to themselves and their values, fostering a culture of transparency and integrity. Their impact on performance and safety includes:

1. Building Trust: Authentic leaders establish trust through honesty and consistency in their actions and decisions.

2. Encouraging Open Communication: They create an environment where employees feel comfortable expressing their concerns and ideas.

3. Modeling Safety Behaviors: Authentic leaders consistently model safety behaviours, reinforcing the importance of safety in daily operations.

3. The Role of Leaders in Shaping Safety Culture
a) Understanding Safety Culture

Safety culture refers to the shared beliefs, practices, and attitudes that shape how safety is prioritized and addressed within an organization. Leaders play a crucial role in establishing and nurturing a positive safety culture through various actions:

1. Communicating Safety Expectations: Leaders must communicate safety expectations to their teams, ensuring everyone understands their roles and responsibilities.

2. Promoting Reporting and Feedback: Encouraging a culture of reporting near misses and safety concerns without fear of retribution is vital. Leaders should actively seek feedback from employees about safety practices.

3. Recognizing and Rewarding Safe Behavior: Leaders should acknowledge and reward employees who demonstrate safe behaviours, reinforcing the importance of safety as a core value.

THE NEW FOUNDATIONS OF HUMAN PERFORMANCE

b) The Safety-Performance Connection

The relationship between safety and performance is intricately linked. Organizations that prioritize safety often see significant improvements in overall performance. A safe Workplace fosters employee morale, reduces turnover, and enhances productivity. Conversely, neglecting safety can lead to increased accidents, decreased Efficiency, and compromised employee well-being. Leaders must recognize this connection and champion a culture that integrates safety into every performance aspect.

2. The Leadership Styles that Drive Performance
a) Transformational Leadership

Transformational leaders inspire and motivate their teams by creating a shared vision and fostering an environment of trust and collaboration. They are characterized by their ability to:

1. Communicate a Clear Vision: Transformational leaders articulate a compelling vision for safety and performance that resonates with employees.

2. Encourage Innovation: They promote a culture of creativity and innovation, encouraging employees to contribute ideas for improving safety and performance.

3. Foster Relationships: These leaders build strong relationships with their team members, ensuring open lines of communication and mutual respect.

b) Servant Leadership

Servant leaders prioritize the needs of their employees and the organization's needs. They lead by example and demonstrate empathy and humility. Key characteristics include:

1. Listening and Empathy: Servant leaders actively listen to their team members, demonstrating empathy and understanding of their challenges.

2. Empowerment: They empower employees to take ownership of their roles, encouraging them to contribute to safety and performance initiatives.

Part IV: Leadership and Organizational Success

Chapter 13

Leadership in Human Performance and Safety

The Role of Leaders in Driving Performance

Introduction

Leadership is often considered the backbone of any organization, shaping its culture, driving performance, and influencing the well-being of its employees. In the context of human performance and safety, the role of leaders transcends traditional management functions; they become architects of an environment where safety, Efficiency, and well-being thrive. This chapter explores the multifaceted role of leaders in enhancing human performance and safety, emphasizing how effective leadership can transform workplaces into safe and productive environments.

1. The Essence of Leadership in Performance and Safety
a) Defining Leadership in Human Performance

Leadership is not just about directing tasks or managing people; it involves inspiring, motivating, and guiding individuals toward a shared vision. In human performance, influential leaders understand that their influence extends beyond operational metrics. They are pivotal in shaping attitudes, behaviours, and practices that directly impact safety and performance outcomes.

complex interpersonal dynamics and contribute positively to Workplace culture.

Conclusion

In an era of constant change, the importance of ongoing learning and adaptability in the Workplace cannot be overstated. Organizations prioritizing continuous learning empower their employees to develop the skills and mindset necessary to thrive in uncertainty. Organizations can enhance employee engagement, improve performance, and drive innovation by fostering a culture of ongoing learning.

As the future of work unfolds, organizations that embrace continuous learning as a core value will be best positioned to navigate challenges, adapt to change, and achieve sustainable success. Ultimately, investing in ongoing learning is an investment in the future that pays dividends in employee satisfaction, organizational performance, and long-term growth.

c) Continuous Improvement

Organizations should use the data collected from KPIs and employee feedback to drive continuous improvement in their learning initiatives. Regularly review and update training programs to ensure they remain relevant and effective in meeting the evolving needs of the workforce.

6. The Future of Continuous Learning and Adaptability
a) Embracing a Culture of Lifelong Learning

As workplaces evolve, organizations must embrace a culture of lifelong learning. This means recognizing that learning does not stop after formal education or initial training; it is an ongoing journey. Organizations prioritizing continuous learning will better adapt to future challenges and seize new opportunities.

b) Preparing for Technological Advancements

Technological advancements will heavily influence the future of work. Organizations must prepare their workforce for emerging technologies like artificial intelligence, machine learning, and automation. Ongoing learning will equip employees with the skills to work alongside these technologies effectively.

c) Fostering Inclusivity and Diversity in Learning

As organizations become more diverse, it is crucial to create inclusive learning environments that cater to the unique needs of all employees. This includes recognizing different learning styles, backgrounds, and experiences. Organizations can enhance employee engagement and performance across the board by fostering inclusivity in learning.

d) Emphasizing Soft Skills Development

While technical skills remain essential, the demand for soft skills— such as communication, problem-solving, and emotional intelligence—is rising. Organizations should prioritize the development of these skills to ensure their employees can navigate

THE NEW FOUNDATIONS OF HUMAN PERFORMANCE

2. Mobile Learning Solutions: Provide mobile learning options that allow employees to access training resources anytime, anywhere, enhancing flexibility and accessibility.

3. Virtual Collaboration Tools: Virtual collaboration tools facilitate remote learning and teamwork, enabling employees to share knowledge and learn from one another.

5. Measuring the Impact of Continuous Learning
a) Key Performance Indicators (KPIs)

To assess the effectiveness of ongoing learning initiatives, organizations should establish key performance indicators (KPIs) that align with their goals. These KPIs may include:

1. Employee Engagement Scores: Measure employee engagement through surveys assessing the impact of learning initiatives on motivation and commitment.

2. Training Completion Rates: Track the percentage of employees completing training programs to evaluate participation and interest in ongoing learning.

3. Performance Metrics: Analyze performance metrics, such as productivity levels and error rates, to determine the impact of continuous learning on operational Efficiency.

b) Employee Feedback

Collecting feedback from employees is vital for understanding the effectiveness of learning initiatives. Organizations can gather feedback through:

1. Surveys and Questionnaires: Use surveys to solicit input on training content, delivery methods, and overall satisfaction with learning experiences.

2. Focus Groups: Conduct focus groups to facilitate in-depth discussions about employees' learning needs and preferences.

3. Exit Interviews: Gather feedback during exit interviews to assess the role of continuous learning in employees' decisions to leave the organization.

1. Formal Training Programs: Offer structured training programs focusing on specific skills or competencies related to employee roles.

2. Online Learning Platforms: Leverage technology to provide access to online courses, webinars, and other learning resources that employees can use at their own pace.

3. Mentorship Programs: Establish mentorship opportunities for experienced employees to share their knowledge and insights with newer team members.

4. Cross-functional collaboration: Encourage employees to work on cross-functional teams, exposing them to different perspectives and approaches.

c) Encouraging a Growth Mindset

Fostering a growth mindset is essential for promoting ongoing learning and adaptability. Organizations can encourage this mindset by:

1. Promoting a Positive Attitude Toward Failure: Create an environment where employees view failures as learning opportunities rather than setbacks.

2. Emphasizing Continuous Improvement: Encourage employees to seek ways to improve their performance and develop new skills regularly.

3. Providing Constructive Feedback: Offer regular feedback on growth and development rather than merely evaluating performance.

d) Leveraging Technology for Learning

Technology plays a crucial role in facilitating ongoing learning. Organizations can leverage various tools to enhance learning experience:

1. Learning Management Systems (LMS): Implement an LMS to organize and deliver training content, track employee progress, and assess learning outcomes.

THE NEW FOUNDATIONS OF HUMAN PERFORMANCE

3. Improved Decision-Making: Adaptability enables employees to make informed decisions even in ambiguous situations. By leveraging their continuous learning experiences, adaptable individuals can analyze information, weigh options, and take calculated risks.

c) Cultivating Adaptability Through Continuous Learning

Organizations can cultivate adaptability by prioritizing ongoing learning initiatives. Training programs emphasizing flexibility, critical thinking, and problem-solving can help employees develop the skills to adapt to changing circumstances. Additionally, providing opportunities for cross-training and job rotation allows employees to broaden their skill sets and enhance their adaptability.

4. Strategies for Fostering Ongoing Learning and Adaptability
a) Leadership Commitment

Leadership plays a pivotal role in fostering a culture of continuous learning and adaptability. Leaders must model the behaviours they wish to see in their employees by actively engaging in ongoing learning. This commitment can take various forms:

1. Participating in Training Programs: Leaders should participate in training and development initiatives to demonstrate their dedication to learning.

2. Encouraging Open Communication: Create an environment where employees feel comfortable sharing their ideas, challenges, and learning experiences.

3. Recognizing and Rewarding Learning: Acknowledge employees' efforts to learn and adapt to change continuously. Recognition can motivate others to pursue their development.

b) Creating Learning Opportunities

Organizations should provide diverse learning opportunities to cater to different learning styles and preferences. This may include:

c) Improving Performance and Productivity

Ongoing learning directly correlates with improved performance. Employees engaged in continuous learning are better equipped to handle their responsibilities, make informed decisions, and contribute effectively to their teams. As skills improve, so do productivity levels, enhancing overall organizational performance.

d) Fostering Innovation

A culture of ongoing learning fosters innovation by encouraging employees to think creatively and challenge the status quo. Organizations can cultivate a more innovative workforce when individuals are empowered to explore new ideas, experiment with different approaches, and learn from their failures. Continuous learning fuels a cycle of creativity, problem-solving, and growth.

3. The Role of Adaptability in the Workplace
a) Understanding Adaptability

Adaptability is not merely a trait but a skill that can be developed and enhanced through continuous learning. Adaptable employees can navigate uncertainty, embrace change, and remain open to new ideas and experiences. This adaptability is crucial in a world where organizations must pivot quickly to meet market demands and respond to disruptions.

b) The Benefits of Adaptability

1. Resilience in the Face of Change: Adaptable employees are more resilient in the face of change. They can quickly adjust their strategies and approaches when faced with new challenges or unexpected circumstances.

2. Enhanced Collaboration: Adaptable individuals are often more open to collaboration and teamwork. They can work effectively with diverse teams, adapting their communication and problem-solving styles to meet the needs of others.

b) The Shift Towards a Learning Culture

Historically, many organizations viewed training as a one-time event, often relegated to onboarding new employees. However, the rapid pace of change in the business world has necessitated a shift toward a learning culture that encourages ongoing education and growth. Organizations must embrace a mindset recognizing learning as a dynamic, ongoing process rather than a finite event.

c) The Role of Adaptability

Adaptability is the ability to adjust to new conditions and challenges. In the Workplace, adaptability is closely tied to continuous learning. Employees engaged in ongoing learning develop the skills and mindset needed to navigate change effectively. Adaptability allows individuals to respond to evolving circumstances, innovate solutions, and contribute positively to their teams and organizations.

2. The Importance of Ongoing Learning
a) Keeping Pace with Change

The speed of technological advancement is unprecedented. From artificial intelligence and automation to remote work and digital collaboration, the Workplace is constantly in flux. Ongoing learning equips employees with the knowledge and skills to keep pace with these changes. Organizations foster a learning culture to ensure their workforce remains relevant and competitive.

b) Enhancing Employee Engagement

Continuous learning is a powerful driver of employee engagement. Employees who feel their organization is invested in their growth and development are more likely to be motivated, productive, and committed to their work. Engaged employees contribute positively to Workplace culture, leading to higher retention rates and reduced turnover.

As the modern work environment evolves, embracing continuous learning as a core organizational value will be crucial for sustaining success. By cultivating a culture that prioritizes skills development for safety and Efficiency, organizations can navigate the challenges of today's workforce, ultimately achieving their strategic goals while fostering a healthier and more productive work environment for all employees.

The Role of Continuous Learning in the Importance of Ongoing Learning and Adaptability

Introduction

Change itself is the only constant in the rapidly changing landscape of modern workplaces. Technological advancements, shifting market demands, and evolving employee expectations challenge organizations to adapt continually. At the heart of this adaptability lies a critical concept: ongoing learning. The ability to learn continuously empowers employees, enhances organizational performance, and fosters a culture that thrives in uncertainty. This chapter explores the significance of ongoing learning and adaptability in the Workplace, highlighting its impact on employee engagement, performance, and overall organizational success.

1. The Landscape of Continuous Learning
a) Understanding Continuous Learning
Continuous learning is the lifelong process of acquiring new knowledge, skills, and competencies through various means. It encompasses formal education, on-the-job training, self-directed learning, and experiential learning. In today's Workplace, continuous learning is not just an option but a necessity for individuals and organizations.

THE NEW FOUNDATIONS OF HUMAN PERFORMANCE

b) Personalization of Learning Experiences

The future of training lies in personalized learning experiences that cater to individual employee needs and preferences. Organizations can achieve this by:

- **Adaptive Learning Technologies:** Implement adaptive learning technologies that customize training content based on employee performance and learning styles.
- **Individual Development Plans:** Encourage employees to create individualized development plans that outline their learning goals and aspirations.

c) Focus on Soft Skills Development

As workplaces become more collaborative and dynamic, the importance of soft skills development is increasingly recognized. Organizations should prioritize training in:

- **Emotional Intelligence:** Training in emotional intelligence enhances employees' ability to navigate interpersonal relationships and manage stress.
- **Communication Skills:** Effective communication is vital for collaboration and Efficiency; training programs should enhance verbal and written communication skills.
- **Problem-Solving and Critical Thinking**: Employees should be equipped with problem-solving and critical thinking skills to address challenges creatively and effectively.

Conclusion

The role of continuous learning and skills development in enhancing safety and Efficiency cannot be overstated. Organizations prioritizing performance training improve operational outcomes and foster a safety and employee engagement culture. By investing in ongoing learning initiatives, organizations empower employees to adapt to change, develop essential skills, and contribute to a high-performing Workplace.

b) Assessing Learning Needs

Organizations should regularly assess the learning needs of their workforce to ensure training initiatives align with employee and organizational goals. This assessment can involve:

- **Surveys and Feedback:** Conduct surveys to gather employee feedback on training needs and preferences.
- **Performance Evaluations:** Use performance evaluations to identify skills gaps and areas for development.
- **Industry Trends:** Stay informed about industry trends and best practices to ensure training programs remain relevant and practical.

c) Evaluating Training Effectiveness

To measure the effectiveness of training programs, organizations should implement evaluation mechanisms, including:

- **Pre- and Post-Training Assessments:** Assess employee knowledge and skills before and after training to measure learning outcomes.
- **Performance Metrics:** Analyze performance metrics to determine the impact of training on safety and Efficiency.
- **Employee Feedback:** Gather employee feedback about their training experiences and the relevance of the skills learned to their roles.

6. Future Trends in Training for Performance
a) Embracing Technology in Training

The integration of technology into training programs is revolutionizing skills development. Organizations should consider:

- **E-Learning Platforms:** Leverage e-learning platforms that offer employees flexible, on-demand training resources.
- **Virtual Reality (VR) Training:** Explore VR training simulations that provide immersive experiences for skills development, particularly in high-risk industries.
- **Gamification:** Incorporate gamification elements into training programs to enhance employee engagement and motivation.

can contribute to a safer work environment by minimizing distractions and streamlining workflows.

b) Case Studies of Safety and Efficiency Integration
1. Manufacturing Sector: In manufacturing, companies implementing rigorous safety training often experience decreased accident rates and increased productivity. For example, a leading automotive manufacturer integrated safety protocols into its Lean manufacturing processes, improving safety records and higher production Efficiency.

2. Healthcare Industry: Hospitals prioritizing continuous learning in safety protocols and efficient patient care processes demonstrate improved patient outcomes and employee satisfaction. Training healthcare professionals in emergency response and communication enhances safety and Efficiency in high-pressure environments.

3. Construction Industry: Construction firms that invest in safety training and Efficiency practices, such as pre-job safety planning and workflow optimization, see reduced accident rates and increased project completion rates.

5. Implementing a Continuous Learning Framework
a) Developing a Learning Culture
To foster continuous learning and skills development, organizations must develop a learning culture emphasizing the importance of ongoing education. Key elements include:
- **Leadership Commitment:** Leaders should model a commitment to continuous learning by participating in training programs and advocating for employee development.
- **Accessible Learning Resources**: Provide employees with various learning resources, including online courses, workshops, and mentorship opportunities.
- **Encourage Peer Learning:** Foster a culture where employees share knowledge and learn from one another, creating an environment of collaboration and support.

b) Training Methods for Efficiency Skills Development
1. Time Management Workshops: Offer workshops that teach employees effective time management strategies, such as setting priorities and minimizing distractions.

2. Process Improvement Training: Provide training in methodologies like Lean and Six Sigma to equip employees with tools for analyzing processes and implementing improvements.

3. Team-Building Activities: Facilitate team-building exercises that foster employee collaboration and communication skills.

4. Performance Metrics and Feedback: Implement systems for measuring performance metrics, providing employees with feedback on their Efficiency and areas for improvement.

c) Creating an Efficient Work Environment
To support skills development for Efficiency, organizations should create an environment conducive to productivity:
- **Implement Flexible Workspaces:** Design workspaces that encourage collaboration while allowing for focused, individual work.
- **Provide Access to Technology:** Equip employees with the tools and technology necessary to perform their tasks efficiently.
- **Encourage Continuous Feedback:** Foster a culture of ongoing feedback, where employees receive regular input on their performance and opportunities for improvement.

4. The Interplay Between Safety and Efficiency
a) The Synergy of Safety and Efficiency
While safety and Efficiency may seem like separate priorities, they are intrinsically linked; an organization that prioritizes safety will likely experience enhanced Efficiency, as employees who feel safe are more engaged and productive. Conversely, efficient processes

3. Workshops and Seminars: Interactive workshops led by safety experts can provide employees valuable insights into best practices and the latest safety standards.

4. Safety Drills: Regular safety drills ensure employees are familiar with emergency procedures, enhancing their preparedness and confidence in handling crises.

c) Building a Safety Culture
Creating a culture of safety goes beyond skills development; it requires a holistic approach involving leadership commitment and employee involvement. Organizations can foster a safety culture by:
- **Encouraging Open Communication:** Create an environment where employees feel comfortable reporting safety concerns and discussing potential hazards.
- **Recognizing Safety Achievements:** Acknowledge and reward employees for their contributions to safety initiatives, reinforcing the importance of a safety-first mindset.
- **Integrating Safety into Performance Reviews:** Incorporate safety metrics into performance evaluations, emphasizing the expectation of safe practices in daily operations.

3. Skills Development for Efficiency
a) Identifying Key Efficiency Skills
Efficiency is a critical component of organizational success. Employees must possess skills that enable them to work effectively and efficiently. Essential skills for Efficiency development can include:
- **Time Management:** Employees should be trained in prioritizing tasks and managing their time effectively to enhance productivity.
- **Process Improvement**: Training in process optimization techniques, such as Lean and Six Sigma, empowers employees to identify areas for improvement and streamline operations.
- **Collaboration and Teamwork:** Encouraging collaboration enhances communication and coordination among team members, leading to more efficient workflows.

4. Competitive Advantage: Companies prioritizing continuous learning are better positioned to adapt to market changes and maintain a competitive edge in their industry.

c) The Role of Skills Development

Skills development is vital to continuous learning, encompassing training initiatives to enhance employees' capabilities. In safety and Efficiency, skills development focuses on equipping employees with the knowledge and competencies necessary to perform their jobs safely and effectively.

2. Development Skills for Safety
a) Identifying Key Safety Skills

To create a culture of safety, organizations must identify the critical skills required for employees to perform their tasks safely. These skills can include:

- **Risk Assessment:** Employees should be trained to identify potential hazards in their work environment and assess the associated risks.
- **Emergency Response**: Training in emergency protocols, first aid, and evacuation procedures ensures employees are prepared to respond effectively in crises.
- **Safe Equipment Operation:** Employees must receive training in the safe operation of machinery and equipment to prevent accidents and injuries.

b) Training Methods for Safety Skills Development

1. On-the-Job Training: Hands-on training allows employees to learn safety protocols in real-world scenarios, reinforcing their understanding and application of safety procedures.

2. Simulation Training: Virtual simulations and scenarios can replicate high-risk situations, enabling employees to practice their response without the dangers of real-life emergencies.

The Role of Continuous Learning in Skills Development for Safety and Efficiency

Introduction

In a world characterized by rapid technological advancements, evolving Workplace dynamics, and increasingly complex tasks, the need for continuous learning and skills development has never been more critical. Organizations prioritizing performance training enhance their operational Efficiency and cultivate a culture of safety and employee engagement. This chapter delves into the role of continuous learning in developing skills for safety and Efficiency, exploring its impact on workforce performance, organizational resilience, and overall success.

1. Understanding the Importance of Continuous Learning
a) The Landscape of Modern Work

Today's Workplace is marked by constant change. Emerging technologies, shifting regulations, and evolving industry standards necessitate an adaptable workforce with the latest skills and knowledge. Continuous learning enables employees to keep pace with these changes, fostering an environment where they can thrive.

b) The Benefits of Continuous Learning

1. Enhanced Skills and Knowledge: Continuous learning equips employees with the skills to perform their roles effectively, reducing errors and enhancing overall productivity.

2. Improved Safety Standards: Ongoing safety protocol and procedure training reduces Workplace accidents and injuries, creating a safer environment for all employees.

3. Increased Employee Engagement: Organizations that invest in their employees' development demonstrate commitment to their growth, fostering loyalty and engagement.

and artificial intelligence (AI) create immersive and personalized learning experiences that enhance engagement and retention.

b) Focus on Soft Skills
In addition to technical skills, organizations will increasingly recognize the importance of soft skills, such as communication, emotional intelligence, and adaptability. Training programs must incorporate these skills to prepare employees for the evolving demands of the Workplace.

c) Lifelong Learning Mindset
The future workforce will need to embrace a lifelong learning mindset. Organizations that encourage employees to seek knowledge and develop new skills continuously will be better positioned to thrive in a rapidly changing environment.

6. Conclusion
Performance training is vital to organizational success in today's dynamic Workplace. Continuous learning fosters adaptability, enhances employee engagement, and drives productivity.
Organizations can cultivate a culture of growth and innovation by developing effective training programs that align with organizational goals and employee needs.

Leadership commitment, resource allocation, and a focus on knowledge sharing are essential for creating a learning culture. Moreover, organizations must evaluate training effectiveness and embrace continuous improvement to ensure training programs remain relevant and impactful.

As organizations look to the future, prioritizing continuous learning will be vital to unlocking the full potential of their workforce and achieving sustainable success. By investing in training for performance, organizations can build a resilient and high-performing workforce capable of thriving in the face of challenges and opportunities.

- Pre- and Post-Training Assessments: Conducting assessments before and after training helps gauge knowledge retention and skill improvement. This provides tangible evidence of the training's effectiveness.

- Employee Feedback: Gathering participant feedback about their training experience can provide valuable insights into what worked well and what could be improved.

- Performance Metrics: Analyzing performance metrics after training can help organizations determine whether the training has improved performance outcomes, such as increased productivity or reduced errors.

b) Continuous Improvement

Training programs should be dynamic and adaptable. Organizations must be willing to adjust based on feedback and performance data. Continuous improvement can be achieved by:

- Regularly Reviewing Training Content: Organizations should periodically update training materials to ensure they remain relevant and align with industry trends.

- Soliciting Ongoing Feedback: Encouraging ongoing employee feedback about training programs allows organizations to make real-time adjustments and improvements.

- Investing in New Technologies: Staying abreast of emerging training technologies can enhance training programs and provide innovative learning experiences for employees.

5. The Future of Training for Performance

As organizations navigate the complexities of the modern Workplace, continuous learning will only become more critical. The future of performance training is likely to be shaped by:

a) Technology-Enhanced Learning

Advancements in technology will continue to transform how training is delivered. Virtual reality (VR), augmented reality (AR),

- **Modeling Lifelong Learning:** Leaders who commit to learning inspire employees to embrace growth. Sharing personal learning experiences can make learning more relatable.

b) Providing Resources for Learning

Organizations must provide the necessary resources to support continuous learning. This includes:

- **Training Budgets:** Allocating budgets for training and development ensures that employees can access valuable resources and opportunities.
- **Learning Management Systems (LMS):** Implementing an LMS allows organizations to streamline training processes, track employee progress, and provide access to various learning materials.
- **Access to Knowledge Repositories:** Creating a centralized repository of training materials, articles, and resources allows employees to access information as needed.

c) Encouraging Knowledge Sharing

Fostering an environment where employees feel comfortable sharing their knowledge and experiences contributes to a learning culture. Organizations can encourage knowledge sharing by:

-**Facilitating Cross-Department Collaboration:** Encouraging employees from different departments to work together on projects fosters the exchange of ideas and expertise.
- **Hosting Knowledge Sharing Sessions:** Organizing regular sessions where employees can share insights, lessons learned, and best practices encourage collaboration and continuous learning.
- **Creating Internal Networks:** Establishing internal networks or forums allows employees to connect and engage with one another, facilitating sharing knowledge and experiences.

4. Evaluating Training Effectiveness
a) Measuring Training Outcomes

To ensure that training programs are effective, organizations must assess their impact. Measuring training outcomes can be done through:

THE NEW FOUNDATIONS OF HUMAN PERFORMANCE

approaches to cater to different learning styles and preferences. Some effective training methods include:

- **On-the-Job Training:** This hands-on approach allows employees to learn by doing. It provides practical experience and helps employees apply new skills immediately.
- **Classroom Training:** Traditional classroom training can effectively impart knowledge and skills in a structured environment. In-person or virtual classroom sessions can facilitate interaction and discussion.
- **E-Learning:** Online training modules offer flexibility and convenience. Employees can complete e-learning courses at their own pace, making it easier to balance training with work responsibilities.
- **Mentorship Programs:** Pairing employees with experienced mentors fosters a culture of learning and development. Mentorship can provide personalized guidance and support.
- **Simulation and Role-Playing:** Simulations and role-playing exercises allow employees to practice skills in a controlled environment. This approach is efficient for training in high-stakes situations.

3. Creating a Learning Culture
a) Leadership Commitment to Learning

Leadership plays a crucial role in establishing a culture of continuous learning. When leaders prioritize learning, it sets a powerful example for employees. Organizations can foster a learning culture by:

- **Encouraging Professional Development:** Leaders should actively support and encourage employees to pursue training opportunities, certifications, and workshops that align with their career goals.
- **Celebrating Learning Achievements:** Recognizing and celebrating employees who engage in continuous learning reinforces the value of training and encourages others to follow suit.

- **Performance Evaluations:** Analyzing performance evaluations can reveal skill gaps and areas for improvement. Organizations should regularly review performance metrics to inform training decisions.

- **Industry Benchmarking:** Comparing organizational performance against industry standards can highlight areas for improvement. This helps organizations align their training initiatives with best practices.

b) Setting Clear Objectives
Once training needs have been identified, it is essential to establish clear training objectives. These objectives should be specific, measurable, achievable, relevant, and time-bound (SMART). Clear objectives provide direction for the training program and help evaluate its effectiveness.
- **Specific:** Training objectives should be well defined. For example, instead of stating that employees will "improve customer service skills," a specific purpose might be "employees will be able to resolve customer complaints within five minutes."
- **Measurable:** Objectives should be quantified to track progress. This allows organizations to assess whether the training has achieved its intended outcomes.
- **Achievable:** Setting realistic objectives ensures that employees can attain them. Unrealistic goals can lead to frustration and disengagement.
- **Relevant:** Training objectives should align with organizational goals and employee needs. This ensures that the training is meaningful and applicable.
- **Time-Bound:** Establishing a timeline for achieving training objectives creates urgency and helps keep the training program on track.

c) Choosing Appropriate Training Methods
Different training methods can be employed to meet the diverse needs of employees. Organizations should consider various training

- Industry Regulations: Many industries are subject to regulatory changes that require employees to stay informed and compliant. Continuous learning helps employees adapt to these changes effectively.

b) The Impact of Continuous Learning on Employee Performance

Continuous learning significantly impacts employee performance and engagement. Organizations that foster a culture of learning tend to experience:

- Enhanced Skill Sets: Ongoing training ensures that employees remain competent in handling their responsibilities. This leads to higher quality work and increased productivity.

- Greater Adaptability: Employees engaged in continuous learning are better equipped to navigate change. They are more flexible and can quickly adjust to new processes or systems.

- Increased Job Satisfaction: Opportunities for growth and development contribute to higher job satisfaction. Employees who feel their skills are nurtured are likelier to remain engaged and committed to their work.

- Improved Retention Rates: Organizations that invest in training and development often enjoy lower turnover rates. Employees are more likely to stay with an organization that values their growth.

2. Key Principles for Developing Effective Training Programs
a) Assessing Training Needs

Before developing a training program, organizations must assess their training needs. This involves identifying the skills and knowledge gaps within the workforce. Practical assessment can be achieved through:

- Surveys and Feedback: Gathering feedback from employees about their training needs can provide valuable insights. Surveys can help identify specific areas where employees feel they need additional training.

Chapter 12

Training for Performance

The Role of Continuous Learning in Developing Effective Training Programs

In today's fast-paced and ever-evolving Workplace, the demand for continuous learning has never been more crucial. Organizations that prioritize training and development are not just investing in their employees; they are investing in their future success. As the work landscape shifts due to technological advancements, changes in consumer behaviour, and evolving industry standards, performance training has emerged as a fundamental pillar of organizational effectiveness. This chapter explores the critical role of continuous learning in developing effective training programs that enhance employee performance, engage in engagement, and foster a culture of growth within organizations.

1. Understanding the Importance of Continuous Learning
a) The Changing Nature of Work

The nature of work is changing at an unprecedented rate. Employees must adapt and learn continuously with new technologies, automation, and globalization. The once-sufficient skills may become obsolete quickly, necessitating a commitment to ongoing learning and development.

- **Technological Advancements:** From artificial intelligence to machine learning, technology is reshaping how work is done. Employees must stay updated with the latest tools and technologies relevant to their roles.

- **Evolving Consumer Expectations:** Organizations must adapt their approaches to meeting changing demands as consumers become more informed and discerning. This requires employees to develop new skills and knowledge continually.

THE NEW FOUNDATIONS OF HUMAN PERFORMANCE

organizations can implement strategies that foster a culture of openness, provide valuable resources, and create a supportive atmosphere.

Leaders are crucial in prioritizing mental health, and their commitment sets the tone for the entire organization. Encouraging open communication, implementing comprehensive mental health programs, and fostering resilience and coping strategies contribute to a healthier Workplace.
The benefits of prioritizing mental health are profound.

Organizations that invest in their employees' mental well-being experience increased productivity, reduced turnover rates, and enhanced Workplace morale. Promoting a healthy Workplace environment is not just a moral obligation; it is a strategic advantage that unlocks the full potential of a workforce dedicated to success and well-being.

-**Physical Activity:** Promoting physical wellness through gym memberships, fitness classes, or walking groups can enhance mental well-being.

- **Mindfulness Practices:** Mindfulness programs or meditation sessions can help employees manage stress and improve focus.

-**Healthy Eating Initiatives**: Providing healthy food options in the Workplace and promoting nutrition education can contribute to overall well-being.

5. Measuring the Impact of Mental Health Initiatives
a) Employee Surveys
Regularly conducting employee surveys can provide valuable insights into the effectiveness of mental health initiatives. Surveys assess employee satisfaction, mental health awareness, and the perceived effectiveness of support programs. Analyzing survey results allows organizations to identify areas for improvement and adjust their strategies accordingly.

b) Performance Metrics
Monitoring key performance metrics, such as absenteeism rates, productivity levels, and employee engagement scores, can help organizations gauge the impact of their mental health initiatives.
Decreased absenteeism and increased productivity and engagement can indicate that mental health programs are having a positive effect.

c) Feedback Mechanisms
Establishing feedback mechanisms allows employees to share their experiences with mental health initiatives. This can include focus groups, suggestion boxes, or open forums where employees can provide input on what is working and what needs improvement.

6. Conclusion
Promoting a healthy Workplace environment is essential for supporting employee mental health and enhancing Workplace performance. By recognizing the importance of mental health,

THE NEW FOUNDATIONS OF HUMAN PERFORMANCE

- **Promotional Materials**: Distributing brochures, posters, and online resources highlighting mental health resources and strategies for maintaining well-being can help raise awareness.

c) Flexible Work Arrangements
Flexible work arrangements play a crucial role in supporting mental health. Organizations can promote flexibility by:
- **Remote Work Options:** Allowing employees to work remotely can reduce the stress associated with commuting and provide a more comfortable work environment.
- **Flexible Hours:** Allowing employees to adjust their work hours can help them manage personal commitments and reduce stress.
- **Compressed Workweeks:** Implementing compressed workweeks allows employees to work longer hours over fewer days, giving them extended time off to recharge.

4. Fostering Resilience and Coping Strategies
a) Resilience Training
Building resilience among employees is essential for coping with stress and mental health challenges. Organizations can implement resilience training programs that teach employees how to:
- **Manage Stress:** Providing employees with tools and techniques to manage stress effectively, such as mindfulness practices and time management skills, empowering them to navigate challenges.
- **Cultivate Positive** Relationships: Encouraging teamwork and collaboration helps employees build strong support networks, fostering resilience through shared experiences.
- **Set Realistic Goals:** Teaching employees to set achievable goals and celebrate small victories can boost confidence and motivation.

b) Promoting Self-Care
Organizations should encourage employees to prioritize self-care as part of their mental health strategy. Self-care can include:

-**Creating Safe Spaces:** Establishing forums, workshops, or informal gatherings where employees can share their experiences and concerns without judgment fosters a sense of belonging and understanding.

- **Anonymous Feedback Channels:** Anonymous feedback allows employees to express their mental health concerns without fear of repercussions, ensuring that leadership remains informed about employee needs.

- **Regular Check-Ins:** Encouraging managers to conduct regular one-on-one check-ins with employees to help identify mental health challenges early on, allowing for timely support.

3. Implementing Comprehensive Mental Health Programs
a) Employee Assistance Programs (EAPs)
EAPs are essential resources that provide employees with confidential support for personal or work-related challenges. These programs typically offer counselling services, resources for mental health issues, and guidance on work-life balance. EAPs can significantly reduce the stigma surrounding mental health and provide employees with the tools they need to manage their well-being.

b) Mental Health Awareness Campaigns
Organizations can initiate mental health awareness campaigns to educate employees about the importance of mental health and available resources. These campaigns can include:
- **Workshops and Training:** Offering workshops on stress management, resilience building, and mental health awareness equips employees with coping strategies and promotes a culture of understanding.

- **Information Sessions:** Hosting information sessions led by mental health professionals can provide employees with insights into mental health issues and available support.

THE NEW FOUNDATIONS OF HUMAN PERFORMANCE

- **Decreased Productivity:** Mental health challenges can reduce focus, creativity, and overall work output, adversely impacting the organization's bottom line.
- **Higher Healthcare Costs:** Mental health issues often result in increased healthcare claims and expenses, further straining organizational resources.
- **Legal Liabilities:** Failing to address mental health concerns can lead to legal issues, particularly if an employee experiences discrimination or harassment related to their mental health struggles.

2. Creating a Supportive Organizational Culture
a) Leadership Commitment to Mental Health
The commitment of organizational leadership to mental health is paramount in promoting a healthy Workplace environment. When leaders prioritize mental well-being, it sets the tone for the entire organization. This commitment can be demonstrated through:
- **Visible Support:** Leaders should openly discuss mental health, share their experiences, and participate in mental health initiatives. This visibility can normalize conversations about mental health and create an atmosphere of openness.
- **Investment in Resources:** Organizations should allocate resources to mental health programs, employee assistance programs (EAPs), and training for managers to equip them with the skills to support employees effectively.

- **Policy Development:** Establishing clear policies that support mental health, such as flexible work arrangements, mental health days, and anti-discrimination policies, demonstrates a commitment to creating a healthy work environment.

b) Encouraging Open Communication
Promoting open communication is crucial for fostering a supportive Workplace culture. Organizations can encourage open dialogue about mental health by:

1. Understanding the Importance of Mental Health in the Workplace

a) The Link Between Mental Health and Productivity

Mental health is integral to an individual's well-being, impacting their thoughts, feelings, and behaviour. A mentally healthy workforce is essential for a productive and efficient organization. Studies have consistently shown that mental health challenges such as anxiety, depression, and stress significantly hinder employee performance. According to the World Health Organization (WHO), mental health disorders are a leading cause of disability worldwide, affecting individuals' capacity to work effectively.

Conversely, when mental health is prioritized, organizations witness several benefits, including:
- **Increased Productivity:** Employees who feel supported and valued are likelier to be engaged in their work, leading to higher productivity and creativity.

- **Enhanced Employee Retention:** A Workplace that promotes mental well-being fosters loyalty and reduces turnover rates. Employees are more inclined to stay with organizations that care about their well-being.
- **Reduced Absenteeism:** Prioritizing mental health leads to fewer sick days and decreased presenteeism, where employees are physically present but mentally disengaged.
- **Improved Workplace Morale:** Focusing on mental health fosters a positive organizational culture, boosting employee morale and collaboration.

b) The Cost of Ignoring Mental Health

Ignoring mental health in the Workplace comes with significant costs. Organizations that neglect mental well-being may occur:
- **High Turnover Rates:** Employees who feel unsupported in their mental health are more likely to leave, increasing recruitment and training costs.

THE NEW FOUNDATIONS OF HUMAN PERFORMANCE

5. Conclusion

Mental health is crucial in Workplace performance, influencing productivity, safety, and overall employee well-being. By recognizing and addressing mental health challenges, organizations can create a culture of support that fosters mental well-being.

Implementing strategies to reduce stigma, providing resources, promoting work-life balance, and fostering a supportive Workplace culture can significantly improve employee mental health outcomes.

Ultimately, prioritizing mental health is a moral obligation and a strategic advantage for organizations. By investing in the mental well-being of their employees, companies can unlock the full potential of their workforce, enhance productivity, and create a safer, more engaged Workplace for everyone.

Promoting a Healthy Workplace Environment

In an era where productivity and Efficiency are the cornerstones of organizational success, mental health has emerged as a pivotal element influencing Workplace performance. The correlation between mental well-being and productivity is undeniable; when employees feel mentally supported, they are more engaged, innovative, and committed to their work. However, promoting a healthy Workplace environment is not simply a matter of providing resources; it requires a comprehensive approach that intertwines organizational culture, employee engagement, and proactive mental health initiatives. This chapter explores the vital role of mental health in Workplace performance and outlines strategies for creating a healthy Workplace environment.

- Promoting Mindfulness and Stress Reduction: Workshops on mindfulness, meditation, and stress reduction techniques can help employees develop coping strategies to manage stress and improve their mental well-being.

- Encouraging Physical Activity: Regular physical activity is linked to improved mental health. Organizations can promote physical wellness by offering gym memberships, organizing group fitness classes, or encouraging walking meetings.

- Fostering Healthy Eating Habits: Providing resources on nutrition and healthy eating can help employees make better food choices that support their mental health.

4. Measuring the Impact of Mental Health Initiatives
a) Tracking Employee Well-Being
Organizations should regularly assess the effectiveness of their mental health initiatives by tracking employee well-being. This can involve conducting surveys, focus groups, or feedback sessions to gather insights into employees' mental health needs and experiences.

b) Monitoring Performance Metrics
Monitoring performance metrics, such as productivity levels, absenteeism rates, and employee engagement scores, can help organizations evaluate the impact of their mental health initiatives. By analyzing these metrics, companies can identify areas for improvement and make data-driven decisions to enhance employee well-being.

c) Adjusting Strategies as Needed
Organizations should be willing to adjust their mental health strategies based on employee feedback and performance data. Flexibility and adaptability are essential for creating a supportive environment that meets employees' evolving needs.

to equip employees with the skills to cope with challenges effectively.

b) Encouraging Work-Life Balance

Work-life balance is a critical factor in supporting mental health in the Workplace. Organizations can promote work-life balance by:
- **Flexible Work Arrangements:** Offering flexible work hours, remote work options, or compressed workweeks can help employees manage their responsibilities and reduce stress.
- **Encouraging Time Off:** Encouraging employees to take their vacation time and mental health days can prevent burnout and promote overall well-being.
- **Setting Realistic Expectations**: Organizations should set realistic performance expectations and avoid creating a culture of overwork. This can involve reviewing workloads, providing additional resources, or adjusting deadlines.

c) Fostering a Supportive Workplace Culture

Creating a supportive Workplace culture is essential for addressing mental health challenges. Organizations can foster a positive culture by:
- **Building Strong Relationships**: Encouraging teamwork and collaboration can create employees' sense of belonging and support. Employees who feel connected to their colleagues are more likely to seek help.
- **Promoting Inclusivity:** An inclusive Workplace culture that values diversity and recognizes employees' unique experiences can help create a sense of safety and support.
- **Recognizing and Rewarding Contributions:** Regularly recognizing and rewarding employee contributions can boost morale and promote a positive work environment.

d) Encouraging Self-Care Practices

Encouraging employees to prioritize self-care is vital for maintaining mental health. Organizations can support self-care by:

- **Training for Managers:** Providing training for managers and supervisors on how to identify signs of mental health struggles and how to approach employees in a supportive manner is essential. Managers should be equipped with the tools to facilitate conversations about mental health and understand when to refer employees to additional resources.

- **Encouraging Open Communication:** Organizations should create channels for employees to communicate their mental health concerns without fear of retribution. This can involve regular check-ins, anonymous feedback forms, or mental health awareness campaigns that promote dialogue.

- **Normalizing Mental Health Conversations:** Leaders should openly discuss mental health and share their experiences to demonstrate that it is a shared concern. Normalizing these conversations can help reduce stigma and encourage employees to seek help.

3. Addressing Mental Health Challenges
a) Providing Resources and Support
Organizations must offer resources and support to employees facing mental health challenges. This can include:

- **Employee Assistance Programs (EAPs):** EAPs provide confidential counselling and support services to employees dealing with personal or work-related challenges. They can be invaluable for employees seeking help with mental health issues.

- **Access to Mental Health Professionals:** Companies can partner with mental health organizations or provide access to therapists and counsellors specializing in Workplace issues. This ensures that employees have access to the support they need.

- **Workshops and Training:** Organizations can offer workshops on stress management, resilience training, and mental health awareness

experiencing burnout may struggle to maintain their usual level of performance and may even consider leaving their jobs.

- Post-Traumatic Stress Disorder (PTSD): PTSD can develop after an individual experience or witnesses a traumatic event. Symptoms may include flashbacks, nightmares, and severe anxiety, which can impact an employee's ability to concentrate and perform effectively.

b) Signs and Symptoms to Watch For
Recognizing the signs and symptoms of mental health challenges in the Workplace is crucial for timely intervention. Common indicators that an employee may be struggling include:

- **Changes in Behavior:** Sudden changes in an employee's behaviour, such as increased irritability, withdrawal from colleagues, or reduced engagement in meetings, may signal mental health issues.

- **Decline in Performance:** A noticeable decline in work quality, missed deadlines, or decreased productivity can indicate an employee facing mental health challenges.

- **Physical Symptoms:** Mental health issues can manifest physically, leading to symptoms such as Fatigue, headaches, stomach problems, or other unexplained ailments.

- **Increased Absenteeism**: Frequent absenteeism or a pattern of taking sick days may suggest that an employee is struggling with mental health challenges.

- **Difficulty Concentrating:** Employees experiencing mental health issues may find it challenging to concentrate, leading to forgetfulness, difficulty making decisions, or a lack of attention to detail.

c) Creating a Culture of Awareness
Organizations should foster a culture of awareness and openness to recognize mental health challenges. This includes:

b) The Stigma Surrounding Mental Health

Despite increasing awareness, stigma remains a significant barrier to open discussions about mental health in the Workplace. Many employees may fear being perceived as weak or incompetent if they disclose their struggles, leading them to suffer in silence. This stigma can be exacerbated by Workplace cultures that prioritize performance over well-being, creating an environment where employees feel compelled to hide their mental health issues.

Organizations must actively work to dismantle stigma by promoting mental health awareness and fostering a culture of openness and acceptance. By normalizing conversations about mental health and encouraging employees to seek help, businesses can create a supportive atmosphere where everyone feels valued and understood.

2. Recognizing Mental Health Challenges
a) Common Mental Health Issues in the Workplace

Several mental health conditions can manifest in the Workplace, affecting an employee's performance and overall well-being. Some of the most common issues include:

- **Anxiety Disorders:** Anxiety can lead to excessive worry, restlessness, and difficulty concentrating, making it challenging for employees to perform their duties effectively. Anxiety disorders can manifest in various ways, including generalized anxiety disorder (GAD), panic disorder, and social anxiety disorder.

- **Depression:** Depression can cause persistent feelings of sadness, hopelessness, and Fatigue. Employees struggling with depression may experience decreased motivation and energy, leading to reduced productivity and engagement.

- **Burnout:** Burnout is a state of emotional, physical, and mental exhaustion caused by prolonged stress. It often manifests as feelings of cynicism, detachment, and a lack of accomplishment. Employees

Recognizing and Addressing Mental Health Challenges

In the modern Workplace, the conversation surrounding mental health is evolving from one of stigma and misunderstanding to one of recognition and proactive engagement. As organizations increasingly realize that mental well-being is integral to performance, productivity, and safety, the emphasis on addressing mental health challenges has never been more critical. This chapter delves into the importance of recognizing mental health challenges in the Workplace, the signs and symptoms that may indicate an employee is struggling, and the strategies organizations can employ to create a supportive environment that prioritizes mental health.

1. Understanding Mental Health in the Workplace
a) The Impact of Mental Health on Performance

Mental health is not merely the absence of mental illness; it encompasses overall emotional, psychological, and social well-being. It affects how individuals think, feel, and behave, influencing their ability to cope with stress, relate to others, and make choices. Consequently, mental health significantly impacts Workplace performance.

When employees experience mental health challenges, their ability to focus, communicate effectively, and maintain productivity can deteriorate. Research indicates that poor mental health is linked to increased absenteeism, presenteeism (being physically present but mentally disengaged), and turnover rates. According to the World

Health Organization (WHO), depression and anxiety disorders cost the global economy an estimated $1 trillion each year in lost productivity. Therefore, recognizing and addressing mental health challenges is a moral imperative and a sound business strategy.

programs that teach coping mechanisms, stress management techniques, and emotional intelligence skills.

Resilience training helps employees develop the mental tools to navigate challenges without becoming overwhelmed. This, in turn, enhances their ability to maintain focus, make sound decisions, and stay productive, even in high-pressure situations.

- **Example:** A financial firm introduced a "Resilience at Work" program, where employees attended workshops on mindfulness, stress management, and emotional regulation. As a result, employees reported feeling more equipped to handle the demands of their roles, and the company saw a noticeable decrease in stress-related absenteeism.

4. Conclusion
Mental health is a critical factor that directly impacts Workplace productivity and safety. By fostering a mentally healthy work environment, reducing the stigma around mental health issues, and providing employees with the tools they need to manage stress; companies can unlock the full potential of their workforce. When mental health is prioritized, employees are better equipped to focus, make sound decisions, and contribute to a safer, more productive Workplace.

THE NEW FOUNDATIONS OF HUMAN PERFORMANCE

programs, and resilience training, to help employees manage stress and maintain their mental well-being.

Example: A large tech company implemented a "Mental Health First Aid" program, where employees received training to identify signs of mental health struggles in their colleagues and offer immediate support. This program significantly reduced the stigma surrounding mental health and provided employees with the tools they needed to support one another.

c) Creating a Mentally Healthy Work Environment

A mentally healthy work environment promotes balance, well-being, and stress management. There are several ways companies can create a culture that prioritizes mental health:

- **Work-Life Balance:** Encouraging work-life balance by offering flexible work hours, remote work options, and reasonable workloads can help prevent burnout and reduce stress.

- **Breaks and Downtime:** Providing employees with regular breaks throughout the workday gives them time to recharge, refocus, and reduce cognitive overload. This is particularly important for high-pressure workers requiring sustained focus and decision-making.

- **Recognition and Support:** Recognizing employees for their hard work and providing support during challenging times can help build a positive Workplace culture that fosters mental health. Acknowledging accomplishments, offering positive feedback, and showing empathy during difficult periods can boost morale and improve overall well-being.

d) Building Resilience in Employees

Resilience is the ability to bounce back from adversity, stress, or challenges, and it plays a critical role in maintaining mental health. Employers can help employees build resilience by offering training

3. Strategies to Improve Mental Health and Performance in the Workplace
a) Reducing the Stigma Around Mental Health
One of the most significant barriers to addressing mental health in the Workplace is the stigma that surrounds it. Many employees feel uncomfortable discussing their mental health challenges for fear of being judged, labelled as weak, or facing discrimination.

This reluctance to seek help only exacerbates the problem, leading to worsened mental health and a decline in performance.
Employers play a crucial role in reducing the stigma around mental health. By creating an open, supportive environment where mental health is treated with the same importance as physical health, organizations can encourage employees to seek help when needed.

Open Dialogue: Managers should be trained to recognize signs of mental health challenges and initiate conversations with employees in a compassionate, nonjudgmental way. By normalizing discussions around mental health, employees are more likely to feel comfortable seeking support.

- Mental Health Awareness Campaigns: Companies can launch awareness campaigns that educate employees about mental health, reduce misconceptions, and encourage people to prioritize their well-being.

b) Providing Mental Health Resources
Providing employees access to mental health resources is vital to improving Workplace mental health. This can include offering mental health benefits as part of the company's health insurance plan, providing access to counselling services, or offering Employee Assistance Programs (EAPs) that provide confidential support for various issues.
In addition to external resources, companies can implement internal initiatives, such as mental health days, meditation or mindfulness

THE NEW FOUNDATIONS OF HUMAN PERFORMANCE

other hand, poor mental health can impair cognitive function, decrease awareness, and lead to risky behaviours that compromise safety.

For employees working in high-risk environments, such as construction sites, factories, or transportation hubs, mental health challenges can significantly increase the likelihood of accidents and injuries. Depression, anxiety, and stress can cause workers to lose focus, overlook safety protocols, or engage in impulsive behaviours that put themselves and others at risk.

- **Example:** A construction worker experiencing depression may have difficulty concentrating on their tasks, which could result in them forgetting to secure their safety harness or miscalculating the stability of a scaffold. These oversights, caused by impaired mental health, could lead to a severe fall or injury.

b) The Role of Stress in Workplace Accidents

Stress is one of the most common mental health issues affecting workers today, and its impact on safety cannot be overstated. Chronic stress leads to physiological changes, such as increased heart rate and elevated cortisol levels, which can impair judgment, slow reaction times, and make it challenging to stay focused on tasks. In high-risk environments, these effects can be disastrous.

Moreover, workers experiencing high stress levels are likelier to engage in unsafe behaviours, such as rushing through tasks, ignoring safety protocols, or cutting corners to meet deadlines. These behaviours increase the likelihood of accidents and create a culture where safety is deprioritized for speed or Efficiency.

- **Example:** In a manufacturing plant, a worker under intense stress might rush to finish their shift without properly shutting down a machine, leading to a malfunction or injury. In such cases, the stress-driven decision to skip safety checks can have far-reaching consequences for the Individual and the organization.

unwell, which can significantly hamper their productivity and potentially spread a hostile atmosphere to their colleagues.

For employees dealing with mental health issues, presenteeism often stems from a desire to avoid being seen as weak or uncommitted. They may fear taking time off will result in negative perceptions from their managers or peers. However, presenteeism can lead to even more significant losses in productivity than absenteeism because employees are unable to perform at their best while struggling with mental health challenges.

c) Cognitive Overload and Decision Fatigue

Mental health issues like stress and anxiety often lead to cognitive overload, where the brain becomes overwhelmed by the sheer volume of information and decisions it must process. This may result in decision Fatigue, a condition when workers lose their ability to make wise judgments due to mental exhaustion.

Cognitive overload not only reduces productivity but also compromises the quality of work. When stressed or mentally fatigued, employees are more likely to make mistakes, overlook critical details, and struggle with problem-solving. Decision Fatigue can have profound safety implications in high-risk industries, such as healthcare, construction, or transportation, potentially leading to accidents or even fatalities.

- **Example:** A nurse working in a busy hospital may become mentally overwhelmed after working several consecutive 12-hour shifts. As their cognitive resources are depleted, they might miss essential cues from patients or administer the wrong medication, leading to potentially life-threatening consequences.

2. Mental Health and Workplace Safety
a) The Link Between Mental Health and Safety

Mental health and Workplace safety are inextricably linked. When employees are mentally healthy, they can better focus on tasks, make sound decisions, and react swiftly to potential hazards. On the

1. Mental Health and Workplace Productivity
a) The Cost of Poor Mental Health on Productivity

Mental health issues, such as depression, anxiety, and burnout, are often referred to as "invisible" ailments because they do not manifest physically in the same way that other illnesses do. However, the impact of poor mental health on productivity is far from invisible. Employees who struggle with mental health issues often struggle to focus, remain motivated, and sustain their energy levels throughout the workday. Consequently, there is a decline in overall job quality, a rise in mistakes, and a drop in productivity.

- Example: Consider an employee who is dealing with high levels of anxiety. Even though they may physically be present at work, their mental energy is consumed by worrying thoughts and feelings of panic, making it nearly impossible for them to focus on their tasks entirely. As a result, they might miss important details, make mistakes, or fall behind on their work. Over time, these issues compound, reducing productivity and increasing feelings of inadequacy and stress.

Research has shown that poor mental health costs businesses billions of dollars each year due to lost productivity, absenteeism, presenteeism (where employees are physically present but not fully engaged), and increased turnover rates. According to a study by the World Health Organization (WHO), depression and anxiety alone cost the global economy an estimated $1 trillion per year in lost productivity. This staggering figure highlights the urgent need for businesses to prioritize mental health initiatives in the Workplace.

b) Presenteeism: The Hidden Productivity Killer

While absenteeism (missing work due to illness or other reasons) is a well-known issue in the Workplace, presenteeism is an equally, if not more, detrimental problem. Presenteeism occurs when employees come to work despite being physically or mentally

Chapter 11

The Role of Mental Health in Workplace Performance

Mental Health's Impact on Productivity and Safety

In today's fast-paced work environments, where Efficiency and performance are highly valued, mental health has often been relegated to the sidelines. However, mental health plays a critical role in shaping productivity and safety in the Workplace. With increased awareness surrounding mental health issues, it has become clear that fostering a mentally healthy work environment is no longer optional—it's essential for the success of both employees and organizations.

The Workplace is a dynamic space where employees encounter various pressures. Meeting deadlines, interacting with colleagues, and handling personal responsibilities can all lead to stress, anxiety, or even more severe mental health challenges. These factors can take a heavy toll on workers, directly affecting their productivity, decision-making abilities, and overall safety. As more studies emerge on the relationship between mental health and Workplace performance, it has become increasingly evident that organizations must adopt a proactive approach to mental well-being to optimize Efficiency, minimize errors, and ensure the long-term success of their workforce.

This chapter explores the intricate connections between mental health, Workplace productivity, and safety and offers strategies for fostering a mentally healthy work environment.

THE NEW FOUNDATIONS OF HUMAN PERFORMANCE

Example: A manufacturing plant introduced a hydration challenge. Employees tracked their daily water intake, and those who met the recommended hydration levels were entered into a monthly raffle for a prize. This program increased overall water consumption and reduced the number of dehydration-related incidents on the factory floor.

5. Conclusion

Hydration is a powerful tool for optimizing physical and cognitive performance in the Workplace. By implementing tailored hydration strategies, businesses can ensure their employees perform at their best, reducing Fatigue, minimizing errors, and enhancing overall Efficiency. In an environment where even small mistakes can have significant consequences, staying properly hydrated is one of the most effective ways to maintain safety, performance, and long-term success.

THE NEW FOUNDATIONS OF HUMAN PERFORMANCE

in break rooms and providing education on the importance of hydration.

4. Practical Workplace Hydration Strategies
a) Hydration Stations and Accessibility

One of the simplest yet most effective ways to encourage proper hydration in the Workplace is by providing easy access to water. Installing hydration stations or water coolers throughout the work environment ensures workers have convenient access to clean drinking water.

- Hydration Stations: In large workplaces or outdoor job sites, strategically placing hydration stations in high-traffic areas can promote regular water intake. For workers who spend most of their time on the move, such as construction workers or delivery drivers, portable water bottles or hydration packs can ensure they stay hydrated throughout the day.

b) Educating Employees on Hydration

Educating employees about hydration and the sign of dehydration is essential for fostering a hydration-conscious Workplace. Employers can offer workshops or distribute educational materials on hydration strategies and the effects of dehydration on performance.

- Signs of Dehydration: Employees should be familiar with typical signs of dehydration, including dry mouth, dark urine, headaches, dizziness, and Fatigue. Encouraging workers to monitor their hydration status empowers them to take control of their performance and well-being.

c) Incentivizing Hydration Habits

Some workplaces have introduced innovative programs encouraging hydration, such as hydration challenges or rewards for meeting daily water intake goals. Providing reusable water bottles with company branding or offering incentives for staying hydrated can motivate employees to prioritize hydration.

Staying hydrated is crucial for individuals in cognitively demanding roles, such as emergency responders, surgeons, air traffic controllers, or executives making high-stakes decisions. Even mild dehydration can lead to decreased alertness, increased feelings of Fatigue, and impaired short-term memory.

Example: In a high-pressure environment like an operating room, even a tiny lapse in concentration due to dehydration could result in a critical error. Staying properly hydrated ensures that cognitive functions remain sharp and that decisions are made with clarity and precision.

b) Mental Hydration Breaks

One of the most effective strategies for optimizing cognitive performance is incorporating hydration into regular mental breaks. These breaks serve two purposes: they allow workers to rehydrate and give their brains a chance to rest and refocus.

- **Structured Hydration Breaks:** Encouraging employees to take brief hydration breaks every hour helps maintain fluid balance and improves overall mental performance. Even a short pause for a drink of water allows workers to reset their focus and return to their tasks with renewed energy.

c) The Role of Caffeine and Hydration

Many workplaces rely on caffeine as a stimulant to enhance mental focus and energy levels. While caffeine can boost alertness, it is also a diuretic, increasing urine production and contributing to dehydration if consumed in excess.

- **Balancing Caffeine and Hydration:** Workers who consume caffeine should balance it with increased water intake. For every cup of coffee or caffeinated beverage, an additional 8 ounces of water should be consumed to offset the dehydrating effects of caffeine. Employers can encourage this practice by offering coffee and water

or coconut water, can also help restore balance, particularly after prolonged or intense exertion.

c) Electrolyte Balance: The Key to Sustained Physical Performance

While water is essential, it's not the only factor in hydration. Electrolytes—such as sodium, potassium, calcium, and magnesium—are critical for maintaining fluid balance, muscle function, and nerve signaling. These minerals are lost through sweat; failing to replace them can lead to muscle cramps, Fatigue, and diminished performance.

For workers engaging in prolonged physical activity, particularly in hot environments, electrolyte replacement is as necessary as water intake. In some cases, consuming too much water without replenishing electrolytes can lead to a dangerous condition known as hyponatremia, where sodium levels in the body become dangerously low.

- Electrolyte Replacement Strategies: Workers can incorporate electrolyte-rich drinks, such as sports drinks or specially formulated hydration powders, into their hydration routine. Foods like bananas (rich in potassium), leafy greens, and dairy products can also help maintain electrolyte balance.

3. Hydration Strategies for Cognitive Performance Optimization
a) Hydration and Mental Focus
Hydration is not just about optimizing physical performance; it is equally vital in mental focus and cognitive function. Dehydration affects brain function, impair concentration, slower reaction times, and decreased problem-solving ability. These effects are particularly detrimental in high-risk work environments where quick thinking and precision are essential.

to listen to their bodies, drink when thirsty, and monitor signs of dehydration, such as dry mouth, dark-colored urine, or Fatigue.

For those engaging in physically demanding tasks, it may be helpful to calculate hydration needs based on body weight and sweat rate. A standard formula consumes approximately 0.5 to 1 ounce of water per pound of body weight daily. This means a 150-pound worker should aim for 75-150 ounces of water daily, with higher amounts during physical exertion or heat exposure.

b) Hydration Timing: Pre-, During, and Post-Activity
Just as athletes follow a specific hydration schedule to maximize performance, workers in physically demanding jobs can benefit from structured hydration strategies. Proper hydration before, during, and after activity is essential for maintaining performance levels and reducing the risk of dehydration-related issues.

- Pre-Activity Hydration: Hydration should begin well before any physical task. Workers should aim to start their day well-hydrated, consuming water throughout the morning before engaging in physical tasks. A guideline is to drink 16-20 ounces of water 2-3 hours before starting work and another 8-12 ounces 20-30 minutes before activity begins.

- During Activity Hydration: Replacing fluids lost through sweat is essential for tasks lasting more than an hour. A general recommendation is to drink 7-10 ounces of water every 20 minutes during physical activity. For jobs that involve heavy physical exertion or heat exposure, electrolyte-replacement drinks can help replenish sodium, potassium, and other minerals lost through sweat.

Post-Activity Hydration: After physical exertion, replacing fluids and electrolytes lost during work is essential. Workers should aim to drink 16-24 ounces of water for every pound of body weight lost during the activity. Electrolyte-rich beverages, such as sports drinks

b) Dehydration and Its Effects on Workplace Performance

Dehydration, even in its mild form, significantly impacts Workplace performance. Physically, dehydration reduces endurance, increases Fatigue, and a higher likelihood of injury. It also slows down reaction times and motor coordination, which is particularly dangerous in jobs that involve machinery or other high-risk activities.

Dehydration impairs concentration, short-term memory, and cognitive decision-making abilities. Workers may become irritable, less able to handle stress, and more prone to mistakes, leading to decreased productivity and increased Workplace accidents.

- Example: A factory worker operating heavy machinery in a hot environment without adequate hydration may experience slower reaction times, making them more prone to accidents. Similarly, an office worker engaged in complex tasks may need help concentrating or making effective decisions if they are dehydrated, reducing overall Efficiency.

Understanding these physiological and cognitive impacts highlights why hydration is critical to Workplace success. When adequately hydrated, employees perform better, make fewer errors, and are more resilient to stress.

2. Hydration Strategies for Physical Performance Optimization
a) Tailoring Hydration Needs to the Individual

Hydration needs are not one-size-fits-all. Factors such as body weight, activity level, environment, and diet influence how much water an individual needs. For example, a physically active worker in a hot environment will have much higher hydration needs than someone working in an air-conditioned office.

A basic guideline is the "8x8 rule" (eight 8-ounce glasses of water per day), which may be insufficient for individuals with higher activity levels or in hot conditions. Workers should be encouraged

optimization. Our bodies comprise about 60% water, making it a foundational resource for every biological function—from regulating temperature and maintaining blood pressure to ensure that cells function optimally.

Hydration is not merely about quenching thirst; it's about fueling the body and mind to achieve maximum Efficiency. Hydration plays a pivotal role in performance optimization, whether you are managing employees in a physically demanding environment, overseeing high-pressure decision-making scenarios, or simply aiming to improve overall Workplace productivity.

In this chapter, we explore the science behind hydration and its effects on performance, delve into practical hydration strategies, and examine how proper hydration habits can significantly enhance individual and organizational success.

1. The Science of Hydration and Its Impact on Performance
a) The Role of Water in the Human Body
Water is involved in nearly every human body function, making it essential for physical and mental performance. Critical roles of water include:

- **Regulation of body temperature:** Water helps dissipate heat through sweat, critical in maintaining core body temperature during physical activity.
- **Lubrication of joints:** Proper hydration ensures that the joints remain lubricated, reducing friction and preventing wear and tear, particularly during physically demanding tasks.
- **Transportation of nutrients:** Water is a medium for transporting essential nutrients, oxygen, and hormones throughout the body.
- **Cognitive function:** The brain is susceptible to dehydration. Even mild dehydration (as little as 1-2% body water loss) can impair cognitive performance, including memory, attention, and decision-making.

THE NEW FOUNDATIONS OF HUMAN PERFORMANCE

hydrated. Encouraging employees to bring reusable water bottles can also promote regular hydration.

Education and Awareness: Offering workshops or seminars on nutrition and hydration can raise awareness about the impact of diet on Workplace Efficiency. Employers can also provide resources, such as meal planning guides or hydration tips, to help employees make informed choices.

- Structured Breaks: Encouraging employees to take regular breaks for meals and snacks can prevent energy crashes and promote sustained focus. Structured breaks also give workers time to hydrate and recharge, enhancing physical and cognitive performance.

5. Conclusion
The connection between diet, hydration, and Workplace Efficiency is clear: what we eat, and drink profoundly impacts our performance. A well-nourished and hydrated workforce is more focused, energized, and productive, leading to fewer mistakes and higher overall Efficiency.

Employers prioritizing nutrition and hydration invest in their employees' health and their organization's success. By creating a Workplace culture that values balanced nutrition, regular hydration, and education on healthy habits, companies can unlock the full potential of their workforce and set the stage for long-term success.

Hydration Strategies for Performance Optimization

In the quest for peak performance, both in physical and cognitive tasks, the importance of hydration is often overshadowed by other factors like training, nutrition, or mental focus. However, water is one of the most critical elements of human survival and performance

need more to compensate for fluid loss through sweat in physically demanding jobs or hot environments.

Employers can promote hydration by providing easy access to water and encouraging regular hydration breaks. Workers should also be educated on the importance of staying hydrated and the signs of dehydration, such as dry mouth, dizziness, and dark-colored urine.

c) The Benefits of Hydration for Cognitive Function
Staying well-hydrated not only supports physical endurance but also enhances cognitive function. Proper hydration improves focus, memory, and reaction times, which are critical for jobs that require mental agility and quick thinking.

- **Example:** In a corporate setting, employees who stay hydrated throughout the day may notice improved concentration during meetings, better problem-solving skills, and more efficient task completion. Encouraging hydration in the Workplace can lead to a noticeable improvement in productivity and employee well-being.

4. Practical Strategies for Integrating Nutrition and Hydration into the Workplace
a) Creating a Culture of Health
Employers play a crucial role in promoting nutrition and hydration in the Workplace. Companies can boost employee Efficiency and well-being by creating a culture prioritizing health. Practical steps include:

- **Healthy Food Options:** Providing nutritious food options in the Workplace, such as fruits, vegetables, whole grains, and lean proteins, can encourage employees to make healthier choices. Replacing sugary snacks and drinks in vending machines with healthier alternatives can reduce energy crashes and improve focus.

- **Hydration Stations**: Installing hydration stations or water coolers throughout the Workplace makes it easy for employees to stay

Consuming balanced meals and snacks throughout the day is essential to avoid these energy dips. Combining complex carbohydrates with proteins and healthy fats helps stabilize blood sugar levels and gives the brain a steady supply of glucose.

- **Example:** A nurse working a 12-hour shift may benefit from small, balanced snacks like an apple with peanut butter or a whole-grain sandwich with turkey and avocado. These foods provide a mix of macronutrients that stabilize blood sugar and support sustained mental focus.

3. The Role of Hydration in Workplace Efficiency
a) Cognitive and Physical Effects of Dehydration
Dehydration is one of the most overlooked factors in Workplace performance. Even mild dehydration, defined as a 1-2% loss of body water, can lead to noticeable declines in cognitive and physical performance. Studies have shown that dehydration can impair attention, short-term memory, and motor coordination, which are critical for efficient work.

Dehydration also affects mood, increasing irritability and reducing motivation. In a high-pressure work environment, such as healthcare or emergency services, where quick decision-making is essential, dehydration can lead to errors, slower reaction times, and poor judgment.
- **Example:** A construction worker operating heavy machinery in the heat may experience slower reflexes and impaired decision-making if dehydrated, increasing the risk of accidents and inefficiency.

b) How Much Water Is Enough?
Individual water needs vary depending on body size, activity level, and environmental conditions. However, the Institute of Medicine recommends that men drink about 3.7 litres (125 ounces), and women drink 2.7 litres (91 ounces) of water daily. Workers may

- **Example:** A manager who regularly consumes omega-3-rich foods may notice improved problem-solving skills and faster decision-making during high-stress situations, leading to excellent Workplace Efficiency.

b) The Role of Micronutrients in Mental Clarity

While macronutrients provide the body's primary energy sources, micronutrients—vitamins and minerals—are equally essential for maintaining cognitive performance and Workplace Efficiency. Specific vitamins and minerals directly support brain function, mood regulation, and stress management.

B vitamins, particularly B6, B12, and folate, are critical for energy production and neurotransmitter function. They help convert food into energy and support mental clarity, focus, and mood stability. A deficiency in B vitamins can lead to Fatigue, irritability, and difficulty concentrating.

- **Iron is** essential for oxygen transport in the blood, and iron deficiency can lead to Fatigue, brain fog, and impaired cognitive function. Workers who are iron deficient may find it harder to stay focused and may experience a decrease in productivity.

Magnesium helps regulate muscle and nerve function and cognitive processes. It has also been shown to reduce stress and anxiety, both of which can negatively impact Workplace performance. Foods rich in magnesium, such as leafy greens, nuts, and seeds, can help improve mental clarity and reduce Workplace stress.

c) Blood Sugar Stability and Cognitive Function

Maintaining stable blood sugar levels is critical for cognitive function, particularly in jobs that require sustained attention, quick decision-making, and creative problem-solving. Cognitive performance declines when blood sugar drops too low, leading to mistakes, missed opportunities, and decreased Workplace Efficiency.

- Proteins are essential for muscle repair, tissue maintenance, and enzyme production. In addition to supporting physical performance, proteins help regulate mood and cognitive function. A steady intake of lean proteins from sources like poultry, fish, beans, and plant-based alternatives can help workers stay focused and energized throughout the day.

- Fats are a concentrated energy source and are especially important for brain function. Healthy fats, such as those found in nuts, seeds, avocados, and fatty fish, provide sustained energy and support cognitive performance, particularly in tasks that require decision-making and concentration.

Incorporating all three macronutrients into meals and snacks is crucial for maintaining Workplace Efficiency, as each plays a unique and complementary role in keeping the body and mind functioning at peak levels.

2. The Connection Between Diet and Cognitive Function
a) Brain Power: The Influence of Nutrition on Cognition
The brain is one of the most energy-demanding organs in the body, consuming approximately 20% of our daily caloric intake. It relies heavily on glucose for energy, and cognitive performance suffers when blood sugar levels drop. Workers may have trouble concentrating, slower reaction times, and impaired memory, which hinder Workplace Efficiency.

The type of food consumed can profoundly impact cognitive function. Omega-3 fatty acids, for example, are essential for brain health and have been shown to improve memory, learning, and overall cognitive function. These fats, found in foods like salmon, flaxseeds, and walnuts, support the structure of brain cells and facilitate communication between neurons, enhancing brain power and decision-making capabilities.

a diet rich in complex carbohydrates, lean proteins, and healthy fats promotes steady energy levels, enhances focus, and supports sustained physical performance.

b) The Glycemic Index and Energy Stability

One of the most essential concepts in understanding how diet affects Workplace Efficiency is the glycemic index (GI). GI measures how quickly foods raise blood glucose levels. Foods with a high GI, such as sugary snacks and refined carbohydrates, cause rapid spikes in blood sugar, followed by sharp declines. These fluctuations can lead to energy crashes, irritability, and difficulty concentrating—nonconductive to Workplace Efficiency.

In contrast, foods with a low GI, such as whole grains, fruits, vegetables, and legumes, provide a slow and steady release of glucose. This promotes sustained energy throughout the workday, leading to better focus, improved mood, and greater overall productivity.

- **Example:** A worker who starts the day with a high-GI breakfast, such as sugary cereal or a pastry, may experience a brief surge of energy followed by a mid-morning energy slump. In contrast, a worker who eats a balanced breakfast with low-GI foods, such as oatmeal, fruit, and nuts, will likely maintain steady energy levels and mental clarity throughout the morning.

c) The Role of Macronutrients in Workplace Performance

Each macronutrient plays a specific role in supporting Workplace Efficiency:

- **Carbohydrates provide** the primary source of fuel for the brain and muscles. Complex carbohydrates in whole grains, vegetables, and legumes release glucose slowly, providing long-lasting energy that prevents Fatigue and keeps workers alert and focused.

THE NEW FOUNDATIONS OF HUMAN PERFORMANCE

The Connection Between Diet and Workplace Efficiency

In the Modern Workplace, where Efficiency and productivity are highly valued, one critical factor often flies under the radar: nutrition. While training, technology, and strategic planning undoubtedly play pivotal roles in enhancing Workplace Efficiency, the fuel that drives human performance—diet and hydration—remains a key, yet sometimes neglected, element. This chapter explores how what we eat, and drink influences our energy levels, cognitive abilities, mood, decision-making, and overall Workplace Efficiency.

To understand the connection between diet and Workplace Efficiency, we must consider how the human body operates like a finely tuned machine. For a machine to perform optimally, it needs the right input. In the same way, the human body, from the brain to muscle, relies on balanced nutrition and hydration to function at its best. These essential inputs are necessary for even the most skilled worker to avoid decreased productivity, increased Fatigue, and a higher likelihood of errors.

1. The Science of Fueling Workplace Efficiency
a) Understanding Energy Metabolism

At the core of nutrition's impact on Workplace Efficiency is the process of energy metabolism. Our bodies convert food into energy through a series of metabolic reactions. The primary source of energy is glucose, which is derived from carbohydrates. Glucose is the fuel that powers our brains, muscles, and cells. Other macronutrients—proteins and fats—also contribute to energy production, particularly in long-term tasks and endurance-related activities.

The Efficiency with which the body converts food into energy directly affects how we perform at work. If our diet lacks balance or essential nutrients, energy metabolism slows down, leading to sluggishness, Fatigue, and impaired cognitive function. Conversely,

b) Hydration Stations

Installing hydration stations or water coolers throughout the Workplace makes it easy for employees to stay hydrated. Encourage workers to bring reusable water bottles to refill throughout the day and offer electrolyte drinks for those in physically demanding roles.

c) Structured Breaks for Nutrition and Hydration

Employers should encourage regular breaks for meals and hydration. Structured snack breaks can help prevent blood sugar crashes and maintain energy levels, while hydration breaks ensure workers stay alert and focused.

5. Conclusion

Fueling the body with the proper nutrients and maintaining hydration are critical elements of Workplace performance and safety. Whether it's cognitive tasks requiring mental clarity or physically demanding work that strains the muscles, nutrition and hydration are vital to sustaining energy, focus, and well-being.

By adopting strategies that prioritize balanced diets, regular hydration, and employee education, organizations can enhance their workers' performance, reduce Fatigue, and foster a healthier, more productive environment. In the long run, investing in nutrition and hydration isn't just about preventing mistakes or accidents, it's about creating a culture of care that enables employees to thrive at their best.

The body is a finely tuned machine, and by fueling it properly, we can unlock its full potential and drive success both individually and organizationally.

rule, the Institute of Medicine recommends 3.7 litres (or about 13 cups) of water per day for men and 2.7 litres (about 9 cups) for women. However, workers in hot or physically demanding environments may need more to compensate for fluid lost through sweat.

1. Monitoring Hydration Levels

A straightforward way to monitor hydration is to pay attention to urine color. Pale yellow indicates good hydration, while darker yellow or amber suggests dehydration. Employers can encourage workers to monitor their hydration and provide easy access to water throughout the day.

2. Breaks for Hydration

Employers should ensure that workers take regular breaks to hydrate, especially in physically demanding environments or heat exposure. Encouraging hydration breaks can reduce Fatigue, prevent accidents, and improve overall performance.

4. Practical Strategies for Maintaining Optimal Nutrition and Hydration

a) Workplace Nutrition Programs

Employers can significantly support employee nutrition by offering Workplace programs that provide healthy food options and nutritional education.

- **Healthy Vending Machines:** Stock vending machines with nutritious snacks like nuts, granola bars, and fresh fruit instead of sugary drinks and processed snacks.
- **Cafeterias and Meal Programs:** If the Workplace has a cafeteria, offering healthy meal options such as salads, lean proteins, and whole grains can encourage employees to make healthier choices.
- **Nutrition Workshops:** Educational workshops on meal planning, balanced diets, and hydration can empower employees to make better nutritional choices at work and home.

- **Example:** A busy manager juggling multiple projects can benefit from foods rich in B vitamins, such as eggs, leafy greens, and fortified cereals, to stay sharp and manage stress effectively.

3. Hydration and Performance: Quenching the Body's Thirst

While proper nutrition is essential, hydration is equally important for maintaining peak performance. Water makes up about 60% of the human body, and it's involved in every cellular function, including transporting nutrients, removing waste, and regulating temperature. Hydration is critical to performance and safety in a work environment, particularly physical exertion.

a) Hydration for Cognitive Function

Dehydration impairs cognitive function, leading to slower reaction times, reduced concentration, and poor decision-making. Workers in high-risk or detail-oriented jobs, such as construction, manufacturing, or healthcare, must stay hydrated to avoid costly mistakes or accidents.

Example: A healthcare worker who experiences dehydration may struggle with focus and memory, potentially leading to medical errors. They can maintain the mental clarity needed for patient care by staying hydrated.

b) Hydration for Physical Performance

Dehydration increases the risk of muscle cramps, heat exhaustion, and injuries for physically active workers. Sweat depletes water and essential electrolytes like sodium, potassium, and chloride, which need to be replenished to maintain muscle function.

Example: A warehouse worker who lifts heavy boxes for hours may experience muscle Fatigue and cramps if they don't drink enough water and replenish electrolytes. Drinking water infused with electrolytes or consuming sports drinks can help prevent this.

c) How Much Water Is Enough?

The recommended daily water intake varies depending on age, gender, physical activity level, and environmental conditions. As a

3. Fats for Brain Function and Long-Term Energy

Healthy fats, such as those found in avocados, olive oil, and fish, provide concentrated energy and support brain function. They are handy for workers who need long-term energy and mental clarity, as fats are digested slowly and provide a sustained energy source.

Example: An office worker preparing for a day of back-to-back meetings and high-level decision-making might eat almonds or a salad with olive oil to keep their brain sharp and focused.

b) Micronutrients for Enhanced Focus and Stamina
1. Iron for Oxygen Transport

Iron is crucial for transporting oxygen in the blood, directly impacting energy levels. Iron deficiency, common in workers who don't consume enough red meat or leafy greens, can lead to Fatigue, weakness, and impaired cognitive function.

- Example: Workers in high-altitude environments or those with physically demanding jobs should focus on iron-rich foods, such as spinach, lentils, and red meat, to maintain their energy and performance levels.

2. Magnesium for Muscle and Nerve Function

Magnesium supports muscle relaxation, nerve function, and energy production. Low magnesium levels can lead to muscle cramps, Fatigue, and poor concentration.

For example, Athletes or workers in physically strenuous jobs can benefit from incorporating magnesium-rich foods like nuts, seeds, and leafy greens into their diets to reduce muscle soreness and improve endurance.

3. B-Vitamins for Energy Metabolism

The B-vitamin family, including B6, B12, and folate, plays a vital role in converting food into energy. B vitamins also support brain health and mood regulation, making them essential for workers in high-stress or cognitively demanding roles.

2. Nutrition and Performance: The Right Fuel for the Job

Different types of work require different nutritional strategies. For workers in physically demanding jobs, the body needs more fuel for muscle endurance and recovery. At the same time, those in cognitive-focused roles require a diet that supports sustained concentration and mental agility. Regardless of the job type, nutrition should be viewed as a strategic tool to enhance performance and prevent burnout.

a) Balancing Macronutrients for Optimal Energy
1. Carbohydrates for Sustained Energy

Carbohydrates are often the most misunderstood macronutrient. While simple sugars from sweets and processed foods can cause energy spikes and crashes, complex carbohydrates provide a slow and steady release of glucose, the brain's and muscles' preferred fuel source. Incorporating whole grains, fruits, vegetables, and legumes into meals helps maintain a stable blood sugar level, preventing Fatigue and energy slumps.

- **Example:** A construction worker on a 10-hour shift might start the day with a breakfast rich in complex carbohydrates, such as oatmeal with fruit and nuts, to provide a long-lasting energy source. This meal will help sustain their energy levels throughout the morning, reducing the need for frequent breaks or sugary snacks.

2. Protein for Muscle Maintenance and Recovery

Protein is essential for muscle repair and recovery in physically demanding jobs, especially after heavy lifting or repetitive motions. Even in less physically intensive roles, protein supports cognitive functions by providing the amino acids needed for neurotransmitter production.

- **Example:** A factory worker who spends long hours on their feet and lifting heavy objects can benefit from protein-rich meals and snacks, such as grilled chicken, beans, or Greek yoghurt, to aid muscle recovery and prevent soreness.

THE NEW FOUNDATIONS OF HUMAN PERFORMANCE

- **Carbohydrates are** the body's primary energy source, particularly for the brain and muscles. Foods rich in complex carbohydrates, such as whole grains, vegetables, and legumes, provide a steady energy supply by slowly releasing glucose into the bloodstream.

- **Proteins** are vital for muscle repair, tissue regeneration, and the production of enzymes and hormones. Lean meats, fish, beans, and plant-based protein sources help maintain muscle mass and support recovery from physical exertion.

- **Fats are** essential for brain function, cell structure, and long-term energy storage. Healthy fats, such as those found in nuts, seeds, avocados, and fatty fish, provide sustained energy and support cognitive performance.

Vitamins and minerals are critical micronutrients that support various bodily functions, including energy metabolism, immune function, and mental clarity. For example, iron supports oxygen transport in the blood, while magnesium helps regulate muscle function.

b) Hydration: The Body's Cooling and Transport System

Water is essential to nearly every bodily function. It serves as the medium for transporting nutrients, flushing out waste, regulating body temperature, and supporting cognitive and physical performance. The body loses water constantly through sweat, urine, and respiration, so regular hydration is crucial to maintaining optimal function.

Dehydration, even in its mild form, can have immediate and detrimental effects on performance. Studies have shown that losing 1-2% of body water can impair concentration and reduce cognitive performance, Fatigue, and muscle weakness. In physical tasks, dehydration can increase the risk of injury due to muscle cramps, decreased coordination, and slower reaction times.

Chapter 10

Nutrition and Hydration for Peak Performance

Fueling the Body for Sustained Work

In the fast-paced world of modern work, where deadlines loom and Efficiency is paramount, one critical element is often overlooked: how we fuel our bodies. The human body is a remarkable machine, but like any machine, it requires the right fuel to function at its best. Whether you're an office worker trying to stay focused during long meetings or a construction worker facing physically demanding tasks, nutrition and hydration play a central role in sustaining performance, energy, and overall well-being.

This chapter will delve into the importance of proper nutrition and hydration for peak performance in the Workplace, exploring how the right balance of nutrients and water can lead to increased energy, better cognitive function, enhanced physical stamina, and improved safety. Through real-life examples and scientific insights, we'll uncover the building blocks of a performance-oriented diet and hydration strategy designed to keep workers energized and focused throughout the day.

1. The Science Behind Nutrition and Hydration
a) Nutrition: The Body's Fuel
At the most basic level, nutrition refers to the process by which the body takes in and uses food to function. Our food is broken down into essential nutrients, including carbohydrates, proteins, fats, vitamins, and minerals, which serve various roles in maintaining our health and supporting physical and cognitive performance.

THE NEW FOUNDATIONS OF HUMAN PERFORMANCE

5. Conclusion

Managing Fatigue in the Workplace is crucial for maintaining high levels of performance and safety. Organizations must adopt a proactive approach to address the multifaceted nature of Fatigue, incorporating various strategies that promote employee well-being.

Organizations can create a culture that values and promotes well-being by prioritizing sleep hygiene, implementing effective work-rest cycles, fostering a supportive environment, leveraging technology, and continuously evaluating strategies.

As we move into an increasingly demanding world, addressing Fatigue must become a core component of Workplace safety and performance initiatives. By acting today, organizations can protect their most valuable asset—their employees—while enhancing productivity and fostering a safer, more engaged Workplace. The future of work is one where Fatigue is recognized, managed, and ultimately reduced, allowing employees to thrive and succeed.

THE NEW FOUNDATIONS OF HUMAN PERFORMANCE

Several companies have successfully implemented Fatigue management programs in the transportation industry, where Fatigue can have severe consequences. One such company introduced a comprehensive training program focusing on sleep hygiene, work-rest cycles, and stress management. They also implemented a

Fatigue monitoring system encouraging drivers to report their Fatigue levels and take breaks as needed.

As a result of these initiatives, the company reported a 30% reduction in fatigue-related accidents and improved overall driver performance.

b) Healthcare Sector

In healthcare, where long shifts and high-stress environments are standard, one hospital implemented a Fatigue management program that included regular training on recognizing Fatigue and its impact on patient care. The hospital introduced structured breaks, mandatory rest periods, and designated nap areas for staff during shifts.

After implementing these strategies, the hospital saw a significant decrease in medical errors, improved patient outcomes, and higher staff satisfaction ratings.

c) Manufacturing Industry

Management recognized that Fatigue was impacting productivity and safety in a manufacturing plant. They conducted workload assessments and adjusted schedules to ensure a more balanced distribution of tasks. They also implemented mandatory break times and provided resources for stress management and Fatigue education.

Following these changes, the plant experienced a 25% increase in productivity and a marked decrease in Workplace accidents.

3. Data Analytics

Utilize data analytics to identify patterns of Fatigue within the organization. Analyzing trends in absenteeism, productivity, and employee feedback can help organizations identify areas needing improvement and evaluate the effectiveness of Fatigue management strategies.

f) Create Physical Spaces for Recovery
1. Designated Rest Areas

Create designated areas within the Workplace where employees can take short breaks or naps. Providing a comfortable and quiet space for rest can help employees recharge and reduce Fatigue.

2. Encourage Movement

Incorporate opportunities for physical activity throughout the workday. Encouraging employees to stretch or take short walks can increase circulation, improve energy levels, and combat Fatigue.

g) Regularly Evaluate and Adjust Strategies
1. Feedback Mechanisms

Implement feedback mechanisms that allow employees to provide input on Fatigue management strategies. Regularly assess the effectiveness of these strategies and make necessary adjustments based on employee feedback.

2. Ongoing Enhancement

Managing Fatigue is a continuous process. Strategies for managing tiredness must be examined and revised regularly to stay relevant and valuable. An organization's commitment to employee well-being is shown by its pursuit of continual improvement.

4. Case Studies:
Successful Fatigue Management Initiatives

To illustrate the effectiveness of Fatigue management strategies, let's explore a few case studies from various industries.

a) The Transportation Industry

THE NEW FOUNDATIONS OF HUMAN PERFORMANCE

2. Encourage Open Communication

Create a culture of open communication where employees feel comfortable discussing their workloads and Fatigue levels. Please encourage them to speak up when they feel overwhelmed or fatigued, allowing for timely interventions.

d) Foster a Supportive Work Environment
1. Build a Culture of Well-Being

Organizations should actively promote a culture of well-being. This includes providing resources for mental health support, stress management, and Fatigue education. Encourage employees to prioritize their well-being and take advantage of available resources.

2. Provide Employee Assistance Programs (EAPs)

EAPs can be valuable resources for employees experiencing stress, burnout, or Fatigue. These programs often offer confidential counselling, mental health resources, and stress management strategies.

3. Leadership Training

Train leaders and managers to recognize the signs of Fatigue in their teams and respond appropriately. Organizations can foster a more supportive environment by equipping leaders with the knowledge and skills to address Fatigue.

e) Leverage Technology
1. Wearable Technology

Implement wearable devices that monitor employees' sleep patterns, activity levels, and Fatigue. These devices can provide valuable insights, allowing employees to understand their Fatigue levels better and make necessary adjustments.

2. Mobile Apps

Encourage employees to use mobile applications to promote healthy sleep habits, mindfulness, and stress management. Many apps offer guided relaxation exercises, sleep tracking, and break reminders.

3. Flexible Work Hours

Allowing flexible work hours can help employees align their work schedules with their natural circadian rhythms. This flexibility enables individuals to prioritize sleep, particularly those who work night shifts or have irregular hours.

b) Effective Work-Rest Cycles
1. Design Structured Breaks

Incorporating regular, structured breaks into the workday can significantly reduce Fatigue. Research suggests brief breaks (5-10 minutes) every hour can improve focus and overall performance. Encourage employees to step away from their workstations during breaks to recharge.

2. Use the 90-Minute Rule

The body naturally cycles through periods of heightened alertness and Fatigue. Encourage employees to work in focused bursts of about 90 minutes, followed by a 15- to 30-minute break. This method allows for optimal performance and recovery based on the ultradian rhythm.

3. Shift Scheduling

For organizations with rotating shifts or extended hours, develop a shift scheduling system that minimizes Fatigue. Avoid back-to-back night shifts and provide ample recovery time between shifts. For instance, rotating shifts forward (day to evening to night) are generally less disruptive to the body's circadian rhythms than backward rotations.

c) Monitor Workloads
1. Conduct Workload Assessments

Assess workloads regularly to ensure that employees are well-rested. High workloads can lead to chronic Fatigue and decreased performance. Use data analytics to identify trends in employee workload and make necessary adjustments.

abilities decline, and their attention wanes. This poses a risk to themselves, their coworkers, and the organization.

b) Impact on Productivity
Fatigue adversely affects productivity. Research has shown that fatigued workers are 61% less productive than their well-rested counterparts. The result is increased costs for employers due to lost productivity, higher rates of absenteeism, and increased turnover.

c) Impact on Employee Well-Being
Chronic Fatigue can lead to burnout, mental health issues, and a general decline in employee well-being. By managing Fatigue effectively, organizations can promote a healthier work environment, leading to greater employee satisfaction and retention.

3. Strategies for Reducing Fatigue
Organizations must adopt a proactive approach to mitigating Fatigue's effects. Here are several effective strategies for reducing Fatigue in the Workplace.

a) Promote Sleep Hygiene
1. Educate Employees on Sleep Importance
Understanding the value of sleep is crucial for managing Fatigue. Organizations can provide training sessions or workshops emphasizing sleep's importance for physical and mental health. Topics might include the effects of sleep deprivation on cognitive function, emotional regulation, and overall performance.

2. Encourage Healthy Sleep Habits
Organizations can promote healthy sleep habits by encouraging employees to:
- Maintain a consistent sleep schedule, go to bed, and wake up at the same time daily.
- Create a restful sleep environment, including comfortable bedding, appropriate temperature, and minimal noise or light disturbances.
- Limit caffeine and alcohol consumption, especially in the hours leading up to bedtime.

chapter will explore practical strategies for reducing Fatigue in the Workplace, enhancing employee performance, and promoting a healthier work environment.

1. Understanding Fatigue
a) Defining Fatigue
Fatigue is a state of physical and/or mental exhaustion resulting from prolonged exertion, stress, or inadequate recovery. It can affect various aspects of performance, including cognitive function, emotional well-being, and physical capabilities. Understanding Fatigue's nature and impact is the first step toward effective management.

b) The Causes of Fatigue
Fatigue can be categorized into several types:
- **Physical Fatigue:** Resulting from physical exertion, it can impair muscle performance and endurance.
- **Mental Fatigue:** This occurs from extended cognitive activity, leading to diminished focus and decision-making abilities.
- **Emotional Fatigue:** Often seen in high-stress environments, it can lead to feelings of burnout and disengagement.
Recognizing the different sources of Fatigue enables organizations to implement tailored strategies that address specific issues.

2. The Importance of Fatigue Management
Effective Fatigue management is essential for maintaining high levels of performance and safety in the Workplace. Neglecting Fatigue can have severe consequences, impacting not only individual workers but also organizational productivity and culture.

a) Impact on Safety
Fatigue is a significant contributor to Workplace accidents and incidents. According to the National Safety Council (NSC), Fatigue is involved in roughly 13% of Workplace injuries. When employees are fatigued, their reaction times slow, their decision-making

- **Data Analytics:** Leverage data analytics to identify Fatigue patterns within the organization and assess the effectiveness of Fatigue management strategies.

6. Conclusion

Fatigue is a complex phenomenon that significantly impacts Workplace safety and performance. As organizations strive for greater Efficiency and productivity, addressing Fatigue must be a priority. Organizations can create a safer, more productive work environment by understanding the science of Fatigue management, recognizing its manifestations, and implementing effective strategies.

The journey toward effective Fatigue management requires commitment from leadership, open communication among employees, and a culture that values well-being. By fostering a Workplace where Fatigue is recognized and managed, organizations can protect their most asset—their employees—and enhance overall performance and safety. As we move forward, it is crucial to prioritize Fatigue Management for productivity and the health and well-being of individuals and the organization. Through a proactive and comprehensive approach, organizations can mitigate the impacts of Fatigue, ensuring a brighter, safer future for all.

Strategies for Reducing Fatigue in the Workplace

Fatigue is an invisible force that can significantly undermine Workplace performance, safety, and overall employee well-being. It creeps in silently, often unnoticed, until it manifests as decreased productivity, increased errors, or even accidents. In an age where businesses constantly strive for excellence, understanding, and managing Fatigue, Fatigue is not just a luxury but a necessity. This

- **Shift Rotation:** Implement shift rotation policies that prevent prolonged night shifts or back-to-back long shifts, minimizing the impact on circadian rhythms.
- **90-Minute Work Cycles:** Base work schedules on the ultradian rhythm, encouraging 90 minutes of focused work followed by a 15- to 30-minute break.

c) Monitor Workloads

Organizations should regularly assess workloads to ensure employees are well-rested. Excessive workloads can lead to chronic Fatigue, reducing overall performance and safety. Monitoring tools can help identify employees at risk of burnout or Fatigue and allow for proactive interventions.

d) Foster a Supportive Work Environment

Creating a supportive work environment is essential for managing Fatigue. This can include:
- **Open Communication:** Encourage employees to speak openly about fatigue-related concerns without fear of stigma or repercussions.
- **Employee Assistance Programs (EAPs):** Provide access to EAPs that offer mental health support and resources for managing stress and Fatigue.
- **Leadership Training:** Equip leaders and managers with the skills to recognize signs of team Fatigue and respond effectively.

e) Invest in Technology

Utilizing technology can aid in Fatigue management efforts. This can include:
- **Wearable Devices:** Implement wearable technology that tracks sleep patterns and Fatigue levels, allowing for real-time monitoring and intervention.
- **Mobile Apps:** Encourage using mobile applications that promote healthy sleep habits, stress management, and mindfulness practices.

THE NEW FOUNDATIONS OF HUMAN PERFORMANCE

When Fatigue is left unaddressed, organizations face increased liability, costs related to workers' compensation, and damage to their reputation.

d) Financial Costs

The financial implications of Workplace Fatigue can be staggering. Organizations can incur significant costs due to increased accident rates, healthcare expenses, and diminished productivity. According to the Centers for Disease Control and Prevention (CDC), fatigue-related Workplace injuries cost employers around $136 billion annually in lost productivity.

5. Mitigating Fatigue: Strategies for Organizations

Understanding the impact of Fatigue on safety and performance is the first step toward effective management. Organizations must implement comprehensive Fatigue management strategies to mitigate its effects and enhance Workplace safety.

a) Promote Sleep Hygiene

Organizations should actively promote sleep hygiene among employees. This can include:
- **Education and Awareness:** Conduct workshops or training sessions that educate employees on the importance of sleep and practical tips for improving sleep quality.
- **Flexible Scheduling:** Allow for flexible work schedules that accommodate employees' natural circadian rhythms and enable them to prioritize sleep.
- **Rest Areas:** Create designated rest areas where employees can take short naps or breaks to recharge during their shifts.

b) Implement Work-Rest Cycles

Designing effective work-rest cycles can significantly reduce Fatigue levels. Organizations should consider:
- **Regular Breaks:** Encourage employees to take regular, scheduled breaks throughout the workday for mental and physical recovery.

b) Impact on Decision-Making

Fatigue can impair judgment and decision-making abilities. Research indicates that fatigued individuals are more likely to engage in riskier behaviours and make poor decisions. This is particularly concerning in safety-critical industries, where the consequences of subpar decision-making can be catastrophic.

For instance, fatigued pilots in aviation may misjudge their altitude or speed, leading to potential crashes. Similarly, a tired worker in construction may need to pay attention to safety protocols, resulting in accidents or injuries.

4. The Organizational Impact of Fatigue

Fatigue affects not only individual workers but has broader implications for organizations.

a) Reduced Productivity

Fatigue leads to decreased productivity, impacting an organization's bottom line. When employees are fatigued, their performance declines, resulting in slower work processes and lower output. A study by the American Psychological Association (APA) found that fatigued workers are 61% less productive than their well-rested counterparts.

b) Increased Absenteeism and Turnover

Fatigue is a significant contributor to absenteeism and turnover in the Workplace. Employees who experience chronic Fatigue are more likely to take sick leave, increasing organizational costs. Additionally, high levels of Fatigue can lead to employee burnout, prompting individuals to leave their jobs in search of less demanding positions.

c) Safety Incidents

The impact of Fatigue on safety is perhaps the most critical concern for organizations. According to the National Safety Council (NSC), Fatigue is a factor in approximately 13% of Workplace injuries.

THE NEW FOUNDATIONS OF HUMAN PERFORMANCE

b) Cognitive Effects

Fatigue adversely affects cognitive performance, leading to lapses in attention and increased error rates. A fatigued brain struggles with processing information efficiently and making sound decisions. This decline in mental function can have dire consequences, especially in jobs where quick, accurate decisions are crucial.

A significant body of research has shown that mental Fatigue leads to:
- Diminished attention spans
- Increased susceptibility to distractions
- Impaired memory and recall abilities

For example, in healthcare settings, a fatigued nurse may overlook critical patient information or fail to follow safety protocols, potentially endangering lives. In manufacturing, an operator may misinterpret machine signals due to Fatigue, leading to machinery malfunctions or accidents.

3. The Psychological Impact of Fatigue

Beyond its physical effects, Fatigue also carries significant psychological implications that can compromise Workplace safety and performance.

a) Stress and Fatigue

Fatigue can exacerbate feelings of stress and anxiety, creating a vicious cycle. High-stress levels can lead to mental Fatigue, which, in turn, can heighten stress levels, causing a downward spiral that impacts overall well-being and performance.

When employees are fatigued, they are less able to cope with stressors. As a result, their emotional regulation may decline, leading to irritability, reduced motivation, and conflict with colleagues. Such emotional disturbances can create a toxic work environment, reducing morale and increasing turnover rates.

processing speeds, and impaired decision-making abilities. It can be especially prevalent in roles that require sustained concentration, such as in healthcare or technical fields.

- **Emotional Fatigue:** Emotional Fatigue, often experienced in high-stress environments, can lead to feelings of burnout and disengagement. Workers in caregiving roles or those dealing with conflict may be emotionally drained, impacting their overall performance.

Understanding the different types of Fatigue allows organizations to develop targeted interventions that address specific issues impacting employee performance and safety.

2. The Physiological Impact of Fatigue
Fatigue has profound physiological effects on the body, influencing a worker's ability to perform tasks safely and effectively.

a) The Role of Sleep
Sleep plays a vital role in managing Fatigue. During sleep, the body undergoes various restorative processes, including muscle repair, memory consolidation, and hormone regulation. Chronic sleep deprivation has a cumulative effect, significantly impairing cognitive and physical functions.

Research shows that just one night of poor sleep can lead to:
- Decreased alertness and slower reaction times
- Impaired decision-making and problem-solving abilities
- Reduced ability to concentrate and stay focused

A study by the National Highway Traffic Safety Administration (NHTSA) estimated that drowsy driving causes approximately 100,000 crashes annually in the United States alone. This statistic underscores the importance of adequate sleep to maintain safety and performance levels, particularly in high-risk environments.

How Fatigue Impacts Safety and Performance

Fatigue is often an invisible menace lurking in the corners of our workplaces, manifesting in diminished productivity, increased error rates, and higher accident rates. As organizations strive for enhanced Efficiency and safety, understanding the science of Fatigue management becomes paramount. This chapter will explore how Fatigue impacts safety and performance in the

Workplace, delving into the physiological, psychological, and organizational factors that contribute to Fatigue and providing actionable strategies to mitigate its effects.

1. Understanding Fatigue
a) What is Fatigue?
Fatigue is not merely a feeling of tiredness; it is a complex, multi-dimensional state characterized by reduced physical and mental performance. Fatigue can arise from various sources, including long work hours, lack of sleep, extended periods of concentration, and even stress. The World Health Organization (WHO) defines Fatigue as a state of tiredness that can be either physical or mental, resulting from prolonged exertion, inadequate recovery, or sleep disturbances.

b) Types of Fatigue
Fatigue manifests in different forms, and recognizing these types is crucial for understanding its impact on safety and performance.

- **Physical Fatigue:** This type results from prolonged physical activity, decreasing muscle strength and endurance. Workers in physically demanding jobs, such as construction or manufacturing, may experience physical Fatigue, leading to slower reaction times and increased risk of injury.

- **Mental Fatigue:** Mental Fatigue arises from prolonged cognitive exertion and is characterized by diminished attention, slower

Organizations can leverage this data to implement targeted interventions, such as personalized work-rest schedules or stress reduction programs. By harnessing technology, organizations can create a more responsive approach to fatigue management.

b) Holistic Approaches to Well-Being
The future of fatigue management will involve a holistic approach that encompasses physical, mental, and emotional well-being. Organizations will need to address the multifaceted nature of Fatigue, recognizing that physical exhaustion is often intertwined with mental and emotional factors.

Programs that promote overall well-being, such as mindfulness training, stress management workshops, and physical fitness initiatives, will become increasingly important. By fostering a culture of well-being, organizations can support employees in managing Fatigue more effectively.

Conclusion
Fatigue management is critical to creating a safe and productive work environment. Organizations can enhance employee performance, well-being, and safety by understanding the science behind work-rest cycles and implementing effective fatigue management strategies.

The journey toward effective fatigue management requires a collective commitment from leadership, employees, and organizational culture. By prioritizing fatigue management, organizations can cultivate a Workplace where employees thrive, contributing to overall success and resilience. As we move forward, integrating technology, open communication, and focusing on well-being will shape the future of fatigue management, enabling organizations to navigate the complexities of the modern work landscape while ensuring the health and safety of their most asset: their employees.

foster open lines of communication, allowing employees to voice their experiences and suggest improvements to work-rest cycles. Regular feedback sessions or surveys can provide valuable insights into employee perceptions of fatigue management practices. By actively seeking employee input, organizations can make informed decisions that align with their needs and preferences.

c) Employee Involvement

Involving employees in developing and implementing fatigue management strategies can enhance engagement and buy-in. Employees with a say in their work-rest cycles are likelier to feel empowered and committed to their well-being.

For example, organizations can establish fatigue management committees comprising employees from various departments. These committees can assess existing practices, identify areas for improvement, and recommend strategies to enhance work-rest cycles. By involving employees in decision-making, organizations create a sense of ownership and accountability for fatigue management.

5. The Future of Fatigue Management

As we look toward the future, the importance of fatigue management will only grow. Rapid technological advancements, coupled with the evolving nature of work, will necessitate innovative approaches to managing Fatigue.

a) Technology-Enabled Solutions

Technology will play a pivotal role in the future of fatigue management. Wearable devices, mobile applications, and data analytics will provide organizations valuable insights into employee fatigue levels and work patterns. For example, wearable devices can monitor sleep quality, physical activity, and stress levels, providing employees and supervisors with real-time data on Fatigue.

c) Training and Education

Educating employees about the science of Fatigue and the importance of work-rest cycles is vital for fostering a culture of fatigue management. Organizations should provide training programs emphasizing sleep hygiene, stress management, and effective time management.

Workshops or seminars can help employees understand their fatigue patterns, recognize signs of Fatigue, and implement strategies to mitigate its effects. By equipping employees with the knowledge and tools they need to manage Fatigue, organizations empower them to take proactive steps toward their well-being.

4. Creating a Culture of Safety and Well-Being

Fatigue management is not solely the responsibility of individual employees; it requires a collective effort to create a culture that prioritizes safety and well-being.

a) Leadership Commitment

Leadership commitment is essential for fostering a culture of fatigue management. Leaders should prioritize employee well-being and safety and ensure that fatigue management is integrated into organizational policies and practices. This commitment should be reflected in Workplace expectations, resource allocation, and support for employee initiatives.

For example, leaders can promote work-life balance by modelling healthy behaviours, encouraging employees to take breaks, and prioritizing mental health resources. Leaders can inspire a similar commitment among their teams by demonstrating a commitment to employee well-being.

b) Open Communication

Creating an environment where employees feel comfortable discussing fatigue-related concerns is crucial. Organizations should

employees to recharge during these breaks, organizations can enhance productivity and reduce the risk of fatigue-related errors.

3. Implementing Effective Fatigue Management Strategies
Organizations can implement strategies tailored to their work environments and employees need to combat Fatigue and optimize work-rest cycles.

a) Flexible Work Schedules
Flexible work schedules allow employees to tailor their work hours to align with their natural rhythms. For instance, some individuals may be more productive in the morning, while others may perform better in the afternoon or evening. Organizations that offer flexible scheduling empower employees to work during peak performance times, enhancing overall productivity and job satisfaction.

Additionally, flexible schedules can help employees manage their responsibilities, improve work-life balance, and reduce stress. Organizations can cultivate a more engaged and motivated workforce by fostering a culture that values flexibility.

b) Regular Breaks
Encouraging regular breaks throughout the workday is essential for managing Fatigue. Short, frequent breaks can help employees recharge, improve concentration, and reduce the risk of burnout. Organizations can implement policies that promote break-taking, such as scheduled rest periods or designated break areas.

During breaks, employees should be encouraged to engage in restorative activities that promote relaxation and rejuvenation. This could include stretching exercises, brief walks, or mindfulness practices. By incorporating regular breaks into the workday, organizations can help employees sustain their energy levels and performance.

cognitive performance, reaction times, and decision-making abilities. Consequently, organizations must prioritize sleep hygiene as part of their fatigue management strategies.

2. Understanding Work-Rest Cycles
The concept of work-rest cycles is fundamental to fatigue management. These cycles refer to the balance between work and rest or recovery periods. Understanding how to optimize these cycles can help organizations minimize Fatigue and enhance overall employee performance.

a) The Biological Basis of Work-Rest Cycles
Human performance is influenced by circadian rhythms, which are natural, internal processes that follow roughly 24-hour cycle. These rhythms regulate sleep-wake cycles, hormone release, and other physiological processes. Disruptions to these rhythms can lead to Fatigue, reduced alertness, and impaired performance.

For instance, workers on night shifts may experience a misalignment between their circadian rhythms and work schedules, leading to chronic sleep deprivation and increased Fatigue. Understanding these biological rhythms is essential for designing effective work-rest cycles that align with employees' natural patterns.

b) The 90-Minute Work Cycle
Research suggests that human cognitive and physical performance follows a 90-minute cycle, after which attention and performance may decline. This cycle is often referred to as the ultradian rhythm. A work-rest schedule based on this rhythm can help employees maintain focus and energy levels throughout the workday.

For example, a typical work cycle might involve 90 minutes of focused work followed by a 15—to 30-minute break. During these breaks, employees can engage in restorative activities such as stretching, walking, or practising mindfulness. By allowing

a) Types of Fatigue

Fatigue can be categorized into several types, each with its causes and effects:

- **Physical Fatigue:** This type results from prolonged physical activity or exertion. It is characterized by a decrease in muscle strength and endurance, leading to feelings of exhaustion and reduced physical performance.

- **Mental Fatigue:** This occurs when cognitive tasks demand significant mental effort. It can lead to diminished concentration, slower reaction times, and increased susceptibility to errors. Mental Fatigue often manifests after long periods of sustained attention or decision-making.

- **Emotional Fatigue:** Emotional or psychological Fatigue is often experienced by individuals in high-stress environments. It can arise from interpersonal conflicts, job-related stress, or an overwhelming workload, leading to feelings of burnout and disengagement.

Understanding these different types of Fatigue is crucial for organizations seeking to implement effective fatigue management strategies. By recognizing the specific kinds of Fatigue that employees may experience, organizations can tailor interventions to address their unique needs.

b) The Role of Sleep

Sleep is a critical component of fatigue management, serving as the body's natural recovery mechanism. The relationship between sleep and Fatigue is well-documented; insufficient sleep leads to increased fatigue levels, reduced cognitive function, and impaired physical performance.

Sleep deprivation can result from various factors, including long work hours, shift work, stress, and lifestyle choices. Research indicates that even a night of poor sleep can significantly impair

Part III

Optimizing Human Performance for Success

Chapter 9

The Science of Fatigue Management

Understanding Work-Rest Cycles

Fatigue is an insidious adversary in the Workplace, silently creeping in and impacting productivity, safety, and overall employee well-being. In industries ranging from manufacturing to healthcare and aviation, the repercussions of Fatigue can be severe, often leading to mistakes, accidents, and long-term health issues.

In this chapter, we will delve into the science of fatigue management, focusing on the importance of understanding work-rest cycles. By comprehensively grasping these cycles, organizations can implement effective strategies to mitigate Fatigue and enhance performance.

1. The Nature of Fatigue
Before we can effectively manage Fatigue, it is essential to understand its nature and the factors that contribute to it. Fatigue is not merely a state of tiredness; it is a complex phenomenon influenced by various factors, including physical exertion, mental strain, sleep quality, and even environmental conditions.

THE NEW FOUNDATIONS OF HUMAN PERFORMANCE

Conclusion: A Vision for the Future

As we envision the future of safety-performance integration, technology will continue to reshape how organizations approach Workplace safety. Wearables, AI, automation, and data analytics will be powerful tools that enhance safety practices, reduce risks, and optimize human performance.

However, this future is not solely about technology but about creating a culture that prioritizes safety, fosters collaboration, and empowers individuals. By integrating safety into the fabric of organizational operations, we can build workplaces where employees feel valued, protected, and motivated to contribute to a safer, more efficient work environment.

The journey towards safety-performance integration will require dedication, innovation, and a commitment to continuous improvement. Together, we can harness the power of technology to create a future where safety is not just a priority but a fundamental value that drives success, resilience, and well-being in the Workplace.

tools but also on understanding their limitations and the importance of human oversight.

For instance, when implementing AI-powered safety systems, organizations should provide training on interpreting AI-generated alerts and understanding when to escalate issues to human supervisors. This blend of technology and human judgment will create a more robust safety environment.

b) Fostering a Safety Mindset
The future of safety-performance integration will require organizations to foster a safety mindset among employees. This involves promoting a culture where safety is viewed as a shared responsibility, and employees feel empowered to speak up about concerns, suggest improvements, and contribute to safety initiatives.

Leadership plays a crucial role in establishing this culture. Leaders should model safe behaviours, recognize and reward employees who prioritize safety, and encourage open communication regarding safety issues. Organizations can enhance employee engagement and overall safety performance by creating an environment where safety is valued.

c) Balancing Automation with Human Oversight
Organizations must balance automated systems and human oversight as automation becomes more prevalent. While computerized systems can enhance Efficiency and reduce risks, situations will always require human judgment and decision-making.

For example, an automated system may alert operators to an anomaly in equipment performance. However, trained employees must investigate further, as they may possess the context and expertise necessary to assess the situation accurately. This collaborative approach between humans and technology will be essential for achieving optimal safety outcomes.

b) Collaboration with Technology Providers

Collaboration with technology providers will be crucial as organizations adopt new safety technologies. Organizations should work closely with vendors to ensure the technology meets their safety needs and goals. This collaboration can facilitate the customization of solutions and provide seamless integration into existing processes.

For instance, when implementing wearable devices, organizations should involve employees in the selection process to ensure they are user-friendly and meet their requirements. Engaging employees in this way can enhance acceptance and utilization of technology.

c) Regulatory Partnerships and Compliance

Regulatory bodies will play a vital role in shaping the future of safety-performance integration. Organizations should actively engage with regulatory agencies to stay informed about emerging standards, best practices, and compliance requirements.

By fostering partnerships with regulatory bodies, organizations can contribute to developing industry standards that promote safety and innovation. Additionally, staying ahead of compliance requirements can position organizations as leaders in Workplace safety.

5. The Human Element in Technology-Driven Safety

While technology will undoubtedly play a central role in the future of safety-performance integration, the human element remains paramount. Organizations must recognize that technology is a tool that should complement, rather than replace, human judgment, intuition, and experience.

a) Training for Technology Utilization

As organizations embrace new technologies, comprehensive training programs must ensure employees can use them effectively. Employees should receive training not only on how to operate new

c) Virtual and Augmented Reality for Training

Virtual reality (VR) and augmented reality (AR) will revolutionize safety training by providing immersive learning experiences. These technologies enable employees to practice safety protocols in simulated environments, allowing them to experience potential hazards without the associated risks.

For example, a utility company might use VR simulations to train employees to work with high-voltage equipment. Trainees can practice safety procedures, learn to identify hazards, and develop muscle memory in a controlled setting. This hands-on experience prepares them for real-world situations, enhancing their confidence and competence.

4. Cultivating a Collaborative Safety Ecosystem

As technology evolves, the future of safety-performance integration will require collaboration among various stakeholders, including employees, management, technology providers, and regulatory bodies. Creating a collaborative ecosystem will be essential for fostering a safety culture and ensuring the successful implementation of safety technologies.

a) Engaging Employees in Safety Initiatives

Employee engagement will be a cornerstone of effective safety-performance integration. Organizations must actively involve employees in safety initiatives, seeking their input, feedback, and insights. When employees feel valued and empowered, they are more likely to contribute to safety efforts and take ownership of their well-being.

For example, safety committees composed of employees from various departments can be established to assess safety practices, review incident reports, and recommend improvements. By fostering shared responsibility, organizations can create a culture where safety is prioritized at every level.

3. Integration of Advanced Technologies
The future of safety-performance integration will also be shaped by the continued advancement of technologies such as artificial intelligence, automation, virtual reality, and augmented reality. These technologies offer innovative solutions to enhance safety practices and improve human performance.

a) AI-Powered Safety Solutions
Artificial intelligence will continue revolutionizing Workplace safety by automating tasks, analyzing data, and providing insights. AI systems can monitor Workplace environments in real-time, detecting unsafe conditions and providing immediate alerts to employees and supervisors.

For example, in a chemical manufacturing plant, AI-powered cameras can monitor leaks or spills in real time, automatically triggering safety protocols and alerting workers to evacuate the area if necessary. By leveraging AI to enhance situational awareness, organizations can respond to hazards more effectively and minimize the risk of accidents.

b) Automation of Hazardous Tasks
Automation will play a crucial role in reducing human exposure to hazardous tasks. As technology advances, organizations will increasingly deploy robots and automated systems to perform dangerous jobs, freeing human workers to focus on tasks that require critical thinking and creativity.

In a mining operation, for instance, automated vehicles can transport materials through hazardous environments, eliminating the need for human operators in high-risk areas. This enhances safety and improves operational Efficiency, as automated systems can work around the clock without Fatigue.

THE NEW FOUNDATIONS OF HUMAN PERFORMANCE

For instance, a construction company may utilize wearable sensors to monitor workers' vital signs and environmental conditions. Suppose the data indicates a rise in heart rates or increased temperatures on a scorching day. In that case, supervisors can intervene to ensure that workers take breaks and hydrate, preventing heat-related illnesses. This proactive approach is not only beneficial for workers' health but also enhances overall productivity.

b) Predictive Analytics for Risk Mitigation

Predictive analytics will play a pivotal role in safety-performance integration by allowing organizations to anticipate potential safety issues before they escalate into incidents. By analyzing historical data and applying machine learning algorithms, organizations can identify risk factors and develop strategies to mitigate them.

For example, a transportation company might analyze past accidents, driver behaviour, weather conditions, and traffic patterns to identify trends contributing to incidents. With this information, they can implement targeted training programs, adjust routes during adverse weather conditions, and enhance driver monitoring systems to improve safety outcomes.

c) Data-Driven Culture

As organizations increasingly rely on data to inform their safety strategies, cultivating a data-driven culture will be essential. Employees at all levels must be trained to understand and interpret data, fostering a mindset where safety decisions are based on evidence rather than intuition.

For instance, safety meetings could incorporate data presentations that highlight key performance indicators (KPIs), trends, and success stories. By making data accessible and relevant, organizations can empower employees to take ownership of safety initiatives and contribute to continuous improvement.

For example, organizations might leverage predictive analytics to anticipate potential hazards based on historical data and emerging trends. By analyzing factors such as employee behaviour, environmental conditions, and equipment performance, organizations can take preemptive action to mitigate risks. This proactive approach reduces the likelihood of accidents and fosters a Safety culture where employees feel empowered to contribute to safety initiatives.

b) Emphasizing Employee Well-Being

As we move into the future, the focus on safety will increasingly expand beyond physical hazards to encompass the holistic well-being of employees. Organizations are beginning to recognize that mental health, emotional well-being, and work-life balance are essential to a safe Workplace.

Imagine a manufacturing facility that implements mental health initiatives alongside traditional safety protocols. Employees can access counselling services, stress management workshops, and resources for maintaining work-life balance. Organizations can enhance overall safety and performance outcomes by addressing the mental and emotional aspects of employee well-being.

2. Harnessing the Power of Data and Analytics

Integrating safety technology and human performance will heavily rely on data and analytics. In the future, organizations will harness the vast amounts of data generated by various safety technologies to drive informed decision-making and continuous improvement.

a) Real-Time Data for Informed Decision-Making

Wearable technology, IoT devices, and AI-powered systems will provide organizations real-time data on employee health, environmental conditions, and equipment performance. This data will be instrumental in identifying trends, patterns, and anomalies that could indicate potential risks.

to create workplaces where safety is not just a priority but a core value that drives success and innovation.

The Future of Safety-Performance Integration

As we stand at the crossroads of unprecedented technological advancement and evolving Workplace demands, the future of safety-performance integration presents a landscape rich with possibilities. No longer can we view safety as a mere compliance issue or a checkbox on an organizational to-do list; it has become a pivotal driver of operational excellence and human performance.

This chapter will explore the dynamic interplay between safety technology and human performance, envisioning a seamlessly integrated future to create safer workplaces and environments that nurture employee well-being, productivity, and innovation.

1. The Shift in Safety Paradigms

Historically, Workplace safety has often been approached reactively, focusing on compliance, inspections, and incident investigations. However, as organizations recognize the profound impact of safety on overall performance, a paradigm shift is underway. Safety is now viewed as a proactive, integral component of business strategy rather than an afterthought.

a) A Proactive Approach to Safety

The future of safety-performance integration lies in proactively identifying risks and implementing preventive measures before incidents occur. This shift requires a cultural transformation where safety is embedded in every aspect of organizational operations.

c) Ensuring Accessibility and Usability

For technology to be effective, it must be accessible and user-friendly for all employees. Organizations should consider the diverse needs of their workforce, including varying levels of technical proficiency and physical abilities.

For example, organizations should provide training when implementing wearable devices to ensure all employees can use the technology effectively. Additionally, devices should be designed to accommodate individuals with disabilities, ensuring that safety solutions are inclusive for everyone.

Conclusion: Embracing Technology for a Safer Future

In conclusion, integrating wearables, AI, and automation into Workplace safety practices represents a paradigm shift in how organizations approach safety management. These technologies offer powerful tools for monitoring health, predicting risks, and enhancing operational Efficiency.

By embracing these innovations, organizations can create safer work environments, prioritizing employee well-being and fostering a safety culture. However, successful implementation requires careful consideration of data privacy, user accessibility, and the importance of maintaining a human touch in safety practices.

As we move toward an increasingly technology-driven future, organizations must remain proactive in adapting their safety strategies to leverage the full potential of these advancements. Doing so can protect their employees, minimize risks, and drive sustainable success in a rapidly evolving Workplace.

This journey towards a safer future is not merely about technology but about empowering individuals, enhancing collaboration, and building a resilient organizational culture prioritizing safety in every aspect of work. Together, we can harness the power of technology

THE NEW FOUNDATIONS OF HUMAN PERFORMANCE

For instance, safety meetings can include discussions on how technology is being used to improve safety outcomes, highlight success stories, and encourage employees to adopt new practices. This reinforces that safety is a shared responsibility and that technology is a valuable ally in achieving a safer Workplace.

5. Addressing Challenges and Limitations

While wearables, AI, and automation substantially benefit Workplace safety, organizations must also be aware of the challenges and limitations associated with these technologies.

a) Data Privacy and Security Concerns

Wearable technology and AI in safety management raise significant data privacy and security concerns. Organizations must protect and use employee data responsibly, adhering to privacy regulations and ethical guidelines.

For example, if an organization collects health data from wearables, it must implement stringent data protection measures to prevent unauthorized access or misuse. Transparency about how data will be used and shared is essential for building employee trust.

b) Over-Reliance on Technology

While technology can enhance safety, organizations must avoid over-reliance on these tools. Technology is powerful, but more is needed than human judgment and experience. Employees should be trained to use technology effectively while remaining vigilant about potential hazards.

For instance, an organization should not assume that an automated hazard detection system will catch every issue. Instead, workers must remain proactive in identifying and reporting risks to supervisors. A culture of safety should emphasize personal responsibility alongside technological solutions.

c) Automating Hazardous Tasks

Automation is vital in industries where workers are exposed to hazardous materials or environments. Remote-controlled robots can be deployed to handle dangerous tasks, such as cleaning up chemical spills or conducting maintenance in toxic areas, keeping workers out of harm's way.

For example, a chemical manufacturing plant might use automated robots to manage hazardous waste disposal. The organization significantly reduces the risk of accidents and health hazards by eliminating human workers from these dangerous tasks.

4. Integrating Technology into Safety Culture

While wearable technology, AI, and automation substantially benefit Workplace safety, their effectiveness depends on how well they are integrated into the organization's safety culture. Technology should complement and enhance existing safety practices rather than replace them.

a) Fostering Employee Engagement and Training

Organizations must engage employees in the process to maximize the impact of safety technology. Providing training on how to use wearables, AI tools, and automated systems is essential for fostering a culture of safety.

Employees should be encouraged to provide feedback on the technology and share their experiences. By involving workers in decision-making and encouraging their input, organizations can ensure that technology is tailored to their needs and concerns.

b) Promoting a Safety-First Mindset

Integrating technology into a safety culture requires promoting a safety-first mindset. Leaders must emphasize the importance of safety and demonstrate their commitment to leveraging technology to enhance employee well-being.

THE NEW FOUNDATIONS OF HUMAN PERFORMANCE

3. Automation: Reducing Human Error and Enhancing Efficiency

Automation has been a game-changer in various industries, significantly reducing the potential for human error while enhancing operational Efficiency. In the context of safety, automation plays a crucial role in mitigating risks associated with human performance limitations.

a) Automated Machinery and Equipment

Automated machinery has become commonplace in manufacturing and construction environments. These machines are programmed to perform tasks that would otherwise require human intervention, reducing the risk of accidents caused by Fatigue, distraction, or error.

For example, robots can take over repetitive tasks in an assembly line, such as lifting heavy materials or assembling components, which are physically demanding and potentially hazardous for human workers. By automating these processes, organizations can minimize the risk of Workplace injuries while improving productivity.

b) Drones for Safety Inspections

Drones are increasingly used for construction, oil and gas, and infrastructure safety inspections. Equipped with cameras and sensors, drones can conduct thorough assessments of hard-to-reach areas, such as roofs, towers, and pipelines, without harming workers.

For instance, a construction company might use drones to inspect a building's structural integrity from above, allowing them to identify potential hazards without requiring workers to scale scaffolding or climb ladders. This approach enhances safety, saves time, and reduces labour costs.

For example, a mining company could use AI to analyze data from past accidents, weather conditions, equipment performance, and employee schedules to identify periods of heightened risk. The organization can implement preventative measures by forecasting potential incidents, such as adjusting work schedules or increasing supervision during high-risk periods.

b) Enhancing Training and Simulation
AI can also enhance training programs by creating realistic simulations that prepare employees for potential hazards. Virtual reality (VR) and augmented reality (AR) are increasingly integrated with AI to develop immersive training experiences that allow workers to practice safety protocols in lifelike scenarios.

Imagine a firefighter undergoing training using a VR system powered by AI. The trainee can experience simulated fires, smoke conditions, and various emergency scenarios, all tailored to their skill level. This type of training allows for hands-on experience in a controlled environment, improving preparedness for real-life situations.

d) Automating Inspections for Safety
AI can expedite safety inspections by automating risk assessment and hazard detection. Artificial intelligence (AI) systems may examine photos or videos of the Workplace using computer vision and machine learning algorithms to spot dangerous elements like missing safety equipment, poor material storage, or exposed edges.

For instance, an AI system installed in a warehouse may examine security camera video to ensure safety procedures are followed. It may notify managers in real time if it notices employees are not wearing the proper personal protective equipment (PPE), allowing for prompt remedial action.

THE NEW FOUNDATIONS OF HUMAN PERFORMANCE

b) Real-Time Health Monitoring

One of the most significant benefits of wearable technology is its ability to monitor workers' health metrics in real time. Devices can track heart rate, body temperature, hydration levels, and other vital signs, alerting supervisors and employees when immediate action is needed.

Imagine a construction worker laboring under the scorching sun. Their smartwatch vibrates, indicating a rising heart rate and elevated body temperature. Heeding the alert, the worker takes a break to hydrate and cool down, preventing potential heat stroke. This is one example of how wearables can save lives by enabling proactive health management.

c) Enhancing Communication and Coordination

Wearable technology also enhances communication among workers. Many devices come equipped with features allowing quick communication between team members, ensuring everyone remains connected, even in noisy environments.

For example, in a manufacturing plant, workers can use voice-activated wearables to communicate hands-free while operating machinery. If a safety issue arises, they can instantly alert their teammates or supervisors, facilitating rapid responses to potential hazards.

2. Artificial Intelligence: Predicting and Preventing Risks

Artificial intelligence transforms how organizations approach Workplace safety. By leveraging advanced algorithms and machine learning, AI can analyze vast amounts of data to predict potential safety risks and enhance decision-making.

a) Predictive Analytics for Safety Management

Predictive analytics is one of the most promising applications of AI in Workplace safety. By analyzing historical data on incidents, near-misses, and employee behaviour, AI can identify patterns that indicate increased risk.

Wearables, AI, and Automation in the Workplace

The Workplace is profoundly transforming in an era of rapid technological advancement. Organizations are harnessing the power of technology to enhance safety, boost productivity, and optimize human performance. Among the most significant innovations are wearable technology, artificial intelligence (AI), and automation. These tools are changing how work is performed and reshaping the landscape of Workplace safety.

This chapter explores the impact of wearables, AI, and automation on safety and Workplace safety, examining their applications, benefits, and challenges. Through engaging narratives and real-world examples, we will uncover how these technologies can be leveraged to create safer, more efficient work environments.

1. Wearable Technology: Revolutionizing Safety Monitoring
Wearable technology has made significant strides in recent years, emerging as a powerful tool for enhancing safety and performance. These devices, which can be worn on the body, collect real-time data on various health and environmental factors.

a) The Evolution of Wearable Devices
Wearable technology encompasses many devices, including smartwatches, fitness trackers, and specialized equipment designed for industrial applications. Initially popularized in the consumer market, wearables are now integrated into Workplace safety protocols.

For instance, a construction company might provide its workers with smart helmets with sensors to monitor vital signs and environmental conditions. These helmets can detect excessive heat, monitor fatigue levels, and provide real-time alerts about nearby hazards. This proactive approach to worker health and safety can prevent accidents before they occur.

THE NEW FOUNDATIONS OF HUMAN PERFORMANCE

help alleviate concerns and foster buy-in. Open communication about the benefits of technology can also encourage acceptance.

Conclusion: Embracing Technology for a Safer Future

In conclusion, modern technology plays a vital role in improving safety and enhancing human performance in the Workplace. From wearable devices that monitor health metrics to data analytics that predict hazards, technology is transforming how organizations approach safety.

By embracing these technological advancements, organizations can create a culture of safety that prioritizes employee well-being, enhances operational Efficiency, and minimizes risks. However, to fully leverage technology's benefits, organizations must address its challenges, ensuring data privacy, balancing automation with human oversight, and managing resistance to change.

Organizations must remain proactive in integrating innovative safety solutions as technology evolves. By doing so, they can build safer work environments that protect employees and foster a culture of excellence and continuous improvement. Embracing technology is about enhancing safety and empowering employees to thrive and contributes to the organization's overall success.

a) Ensuring Data Privacy and Security

Data privacy and security become paramount as organizations collect and analyze large amounts of employee data through wearables and analytics. Organizations must implement robust data protection measures to safeguard sensitive information and comply with privacy regulations.

For instance, organizations should use encryption, access controls, and secure cloud storage solutions to protect employee health data collected through wearable devices. Transparent communication about data usage and privacy policies is essential to build employee trust.

b) Balancing Automation with Human Oversight

While automation can enhance safety practices, balancing technology and human oversight is crucial. More reliance on technology can lead to complacency, where employees may become disengaged or overlook their responsibilities.

Organizations should emphasize that technology is a tool to support, not replace, human judgment. Training programs should educate employees on effectively using safety technology while reinforcing the importance of vigilance and personal responsibility in maintaining safety.

c) Managing Resistance to Change

Introducing new technology can result in resistance from employees who may be accustomed to traditional safety practices.

Organizations should involve employees in adopting technology to overcome this resistance and provide adequate training and support.

For example, if an organization implements a new safety management system, involving employees in the selection process, gathering their feedback, and offering comprehensive training can

photos, and track corrective actions. This centralized approach ensures that safety data is consistently recorded, analyzed, and acted upon.

b) Facilitating Compliance and Reporting
Technology can help organizations streamline compliance with safety regulations and reporting requirements. Automated systems can track compliance metrics, generate reports, and send reminders for safety inspections and training renewals.

For instance, an organization can use automated reminders to ensure employees complete the required safety training before their certifications expire. By minimizing administrative burdens, technology allows safety personnel to focus on proactive safety measures rather than reactive compliance.

c) Enhancing Collaboration and Communication
Effective safety management requires collaboration and communication among various stakeholders. Technology can facilitate this by providing platforms for sharing information, discussing safety concerns, and collaborating on safety initiatives.

For example, an organization might implement a mobile app that allows employees to report hazards, share safety tips, and participate in safety discussions. This collaborative approach encourages a sense of ownership and accountability among employees, fostering a safety culture.

5. Addressing Challenges and Concerns with Safety Technology
While technology presents numerous benefits for improving safety, it also comes with challenges and concerns that organizations must address to maximize effectiveness.

For instance, VR training can immerse employees in a simulated construction site, where they can practice safety protocols, navigate potential hazards, and respond to emergencies in a controlled environment. This hands-on experience enhances learning retention and prepares employees to handle real-world challenges more effectively.

c) Predicting Employee Behavior and Fatigue

AI can analyze employee behaviour patterns to predict potential safety risks. By monitoring data from wearables, work schedules, and performance metrics, AI systems can identify signs of Fatigue or declining performance, allowing organizations to intervene before incidents occur.

For example, an AI system might flag an employee who consistently works long hours without adequate breaks, prompting a supervisor to check in and encourage the worker to rest. By addressing Fatigue proactively, organizations can reduce the risk of accidents and improve overall employee well-being.

4. Integrating Safety Management Systems with Technology

Safety management systems (SMS) are essential for organizing, managing, and improving safety practices within an organization. Organizations can streamline processes, enhance data collection, and improve communication by integrating technology into SMS.

a) Centralizing Safety Data and Documentation

Integrating technology into safety management systems allows organizations to centralize safety data and documentation. Cloud-based platforms enable easy access to safety policies, training materials, incident reports, and inspection checklists, making it more straightforward for employees and management to stay informed.

For example, a construction company might use a cloud-based SMS that allows workers to report real-time safety incidents, attach

format, allowing supervisors and safety personnel to monitor safety performance and make informed decisions on the flight.

For example, if a dashboard indicates an uptick in near-misses, safety personnel can quickly investigate the underlying causes and implement corrective actions before they escalate into serious incidents. This agility in decision-making is crucial in dynamic work environments where conditions can change rapidly.

3. The Impact of Artificial Intelligence on Safety Practices
Artificial Intelligence (AI) is reshaping safety practices by automating processes, enhancing training, and improving hazard detection. Organizations can leverage AI to create safer work environments while reducing human error.

a) Automating Hazard Detection and Risk Assessment
AI-powered systems can automate hazard detection by analyzing data from various sources, including cameras, sensors, and environmental monitoring devices. These systems can identify potential risks—such as equipment malfunctions, hazardous conditions, or unsafe behaviours—and alert supervisors in real time.

For example, an AI system deployed in a manufacturing facility can analyze camera video feeds to detect unsafe practices, such as workers not wearing the required PPE or engaging in risky behaviours. Organizations can promptly address safety concerns by providing immediate feedback to workers and supervisors.

b) Enhancing Training through Virtual Reality
AI is also revolutionizing training programs through immersive technologies such as virtual reality (VR) and augmented reality (AR). These technologies enable organizations to create realistic training scenarios that simulate hazardous situations without exposing employees to natural risks.

2. Leveraging Data Analytics for Predictive Safety Management

Data analytics is a game-changer in Workplace safety. By collecting and analyzing vast amounts of data, organizations can gain valuable insights into potential hazards, employee behaviour, and safety performance.

a) Identifying Trends and Patterns

Data analytics allows organizations to identify trends and patterns related to safety incidents. By analyzing historical data on accidents, near-misses, and unsafe behaviours, organizations can pinpoint areas of concern and develop targeted interventions.

For example, suppose data reveals a higher incidence of slips and falls in a particular department. In that case, the organization can investigate the root causes—such as inadequate lighting or wet floors—and implement solutions to mitigate these risks. This data-driven approach enables organizations to be proactive rather than reactive in their safety efforts.

b) Predictive Modeling for Risk Assessment

Predictive modelling is another powerful tool in safety analytics. By applying statistical techniques and machine learning algorithms to historical data, organizations can develop models that predict the likelihood of future incidents based on various factors.

For instance, a manufacturing facility might analyze data on equipment failures, employee fatigue levels, and environmental conditions to identify patterns that precede accidents. Organizations can take preventative measures by understanding these risk factors, such as scheduling maintenance or adjusting work schedules, to reduce the likelihood of incidents.

c) Enhancing Decision-Making with Real-Time Insights

Real-time data analytics can enhance decision-making in safety management. Organizations can utilize dashboards and visualization tools that present safety data in an easily digestible

THE NEW FOUNDATIONS OF HUMAN PERFORMANCE

workers and supervisors to signs of Fatigue, dehydration, or heat stress before they escalate into serious incidents.

For example, a construction worker wearing a smartwatch that monitors heart rate could receive an alert if their heart rate exceeds a certain threshold, prompting them to take a break or seek medical attention. Organizations can create a more responsive and health-conscious work environment by integrating this technology into safety protocols.

b) Enhancing Communication and Location Tracking

Wearable technology can also facilitate communication and location tracking, crucial for ensuring worker safety, especially in hazardous environments. Devices equipped with GPS can provide real-time location data, enabling supervisors to track employee movements and respond quickly in emergencies.

For instance, a wearable device can alert safety personnel and the worker's precise location in an accident. This rapid response can be critical in minimizing injury severity and ensuring timely medical attention.

c) Promoting Behavioral Change through Feedback

Wearable technology can promote behavioural change by providing real-time feedback to workers. For example, devices can remind employees to engage in safe practices, such as wearing PPE or taking breaks to avoid Fatigue. This immediate feedback loop encourages individuals to adopt safer behaviours and make informed decisions that enhance their well-being.

Some organizations have implemented gamification elements within wearable technology, rewarding employees for safe behaviours and adherence to safety protocols. By making safety engagement and rewarding, organizations can foster a culture of safety that resonates with employees.

Chapter 8

Safety Technology and Human Performance

How Modern Technology Is Improving Safety

In today's rapidly evolving work environment, integrating technology into safety practices is no longer a luxury, it's a necessity. As organizations strive to improve safety outcomes, modern technology has emerged as a powerful ally, providing innovative solutions that enhance human performance and mitigate risks. Technology is transforming the landscape of Workplace safety from wearable devices that monitor health metrics to advanced data analytics that predict hazards.

This chapter delves into how modern technology improves safety, exploring its applications, benefits, and challenges. By understanding these elements, organizations can better harness technology's potential to create safer, more efficient work environments.

1. The Role of Wearable Technology in Enhancing Safety
Wearable technology has revolutionized how organizations approach employee safety. These devices provide real-time data about workers' health and safety, allowing organizations to respond proactively to potential hazards.

a) Monitoring Vital Signs and Health Metrics
Wearable devices, such as smartwatches or fitness trackers, can monitor various health metrics, including heart rate, body temperature, and blood oxygen levels. In high-risk industries such as construction, mining, or manufacturing, these devices can alert

culture where everyone works together to ensure the well-being of their colleagues and themselves.

A safety-driven environment is more than just a safe Workplace; it's a foundation for long-term success. When safety is prioritized, employees feel valued, productivity increases, and the organization thrives. Building a lasting safety culture is an investment that pays dividends in fewer incidents, healthier employees, and a more vital, more resilient organization.

to be appropriately maintained. Addressing these issues promptly can prevent accidents and reinforce the importance of safety.

b) Encourage the Culture of Learning from Mistakes

No organization is immune to accidents or errors, but the key to fostering a safety-driven environment is how the organization responds to these incidents. A culture of continuous improvement embraces mistakes as opportunities for learning. Instead of assigning blame, organizations should focus on identifying root causes and implementing corrective actions.

For instance, after a near-miss or incident, thorough investigation should be conducted to determine what went wrong and how similar situations can be prevented. The lessons learned should be shared openly with employees so everyone can benefit from the insights.

c) Use Data to Drive Improvements

Data is a powerful tool for improving safety performance. Organizations should track and analyze safety data, such as incident rates, near-misses, and safety audit results, to identify trends and areas for improvement. By using data to make informed decisions, organizations can allocate resources more effectively and target their safety efforts where they are needed most.

For example, suppose data shows increased slips and falls in a particular department. In that case, the organization can investigate the root cause—wet floors, poor lighting, or inadequate signage— and implement targeted interventions to address the issue.

Conclusion: Building a Lasting Safety-Driven Environment

Fostering a safety-driven environment requires commitment, collaboration, and continuous effort. It involves leadership that leads by example, employees who are empowered to speak up, open communication, ongoing training, and constant improvement. By following these practical steps, organizations can create a Workplace where safety is ingrained in every aspect of operational

c) Ongoing and Refresher Training

Safety training should not be a one-time event. Ongoing training and refresher courses are essential to reinforce safety knowledge and keep up with changing regulations, technologies, and work conditions. For example, in industries like healthcare or construction, where standards and technologies constantly evolve, periodic training ensures that employees stay updated on best practices.

Organizations should schedule regular safety courses and provide employees with opportunities to improve their skills. For example, an annual safety training day could include workshops, guest speakers, and hands-on demonstrations that allow employees to practice safety techniques in a collaborative and educational environment.

5. Step 5: Implement a System of Continuous Improvement

Safety culture is not static; it requires continuous improvement to remain effective. A safety-driven environment thrives when organizations actively seek ways to refine their safety practices, reduce risks, and learn from incidents and near-misses. The goal should always be to improve safety performance, reduce accidents, and create a more resilient organization.

a) Conduct Regular Safety Audits and Inspections

A proactive approach to safety requires regular audits and inspections. These audits should assess compliance with safety standards, identify potential hazards, and evaluate the effectiveness of safety protocols. Inspections should be thorough and cover all Workplace areas, including equipment, processes, and employee behaviour.

By identifying hazards early, organizations can take corrective actions before incidents occur. For example, an audit might reveal that employees must consistently wear PPE or that equipment needs

4. Step 4: Provide Continuous Safety Training and Development
Training is one of the most critical aspects of building a safety-driven environment. Safety training should go beyond the basics and evolve into an ongoing learning and development process. Employees need to be equipped with the knowledge and skills to identify, assess, and mitigate risks, and training is the foundation of this competence.

a) Customized and Relevant Training Programs
Practical safety training should be customized to the organization's needs and risks. Generic, one-size-fits-all training programs may not address the unique hazards faced by workers in different industries. For example, safety training in a chemical plant will look vastly different from safety training in an office environment.
By tailoring training programs to specific roles and risks, organizations can ensure that employees receive relevant, practical information that they can immediately apply in their daily work. For example, forklift operators should receive hands-on training on safe operation techniques, while office workers might benefit from ergonomics training to reduce the risk of repetitive strain injuries.

b) Interactive and Hands-On Training
Hands-on, interactive training is often more effective than passive, lecture-based learning. When employees actively engage in training—through simulations, role-playing, or practical demonstrations, they are more likely to retain and apply the information. Scenario-based training can be efficient for high-risk industries. Workers can practice responding to emergencies, such as fires, chemical spills, or equipment malfunctions, in a controlled environment.

Moreover, organizations can integrate technology into training using virtual reality (VR) simulations or augmented reality (AR) tools to create immersive, real-world safety scenarios. These cutting-edge training methods allow employees to experience hazardous situations without exposure to danger.

THE NEW FOUNDATIONS OF HUMAN PERFORMANCE

construction or manufacturing might require daily safety huddles to review job-specific hazards and mitigation strategies.

Employees should be encouraged to participate actively during these meetings. Instead of simply receiving information, workers can share their observations, experiences, and suggestions for improving safety. This promotes a sense of shared responsibility and keeps communication channels open.

b) Transparent Reporting of Incidents and Near-Misses

Transparency is critical when reporting incidents, accidents, and near-misses. Employees should be confident that it will be addressed promptly and thoughtfully when they report an issue. A transparent reporting system ensures that the root causes of incidents are identified, corrective actions are taken, and lessons are shared across the organization.

For instance, an organization might create a safety bulletin that outlines recent incidents and the measures taken to prevent future occurrences. This openness demonstrates that the organization is committed to continuous improvement and that employee safety is paramount.

c) Leveraging Technology for Safety Communication

Technology offers powerful tools to improve safe communication in today's digital age. Many organizations use safety apps that allow workers to report hazards, access safety protocols, and receive real-time updates on safety alerts. These tools make it easier for employees to stay informed and engaged in safety efforts.

Additionally, digital platforms such as intranet portals, email newsletters, and social media channels can disseminate safety information, share success stories, and reinforce key safety messages. By leveraging technology, organizations can enhance the reach and effectiveness of their safety communication efforts.

These committees can regularly discuss safety performance, review incidents or near-misses, and brainstorm ways to improve safety practices. By actively involving employees in safety decision-making, organizations can cultivate a collaborative environment where everyone contributes to safety solutions.

c) Recognizing and Rewarding Safe Behavior
Positive reinforcement plays a crucial role in fostering a safety-driven environment. Recognizing and rewarding employees who consistently adhere to safety standards, report hazards, or contribute to safety improvements sends a clear message that safety is valued.

This can be verbal recognition, awards, bonuses, or public acknowledgement during company meetings.
For example, an organization might implement a "Safety Hero" program where employees are nominated by their peers for demonstrating exceptional commitment to safety. Regular recognition motivates employees and reinforces the importance of safety as part of the organizational culture.

3. Step 3: Foster Open and Transparent Communication
Communication is the lifeblood of a strong safety culture. When information about safety flows freely across all levels of the organization, employees are better equipped to make informed decisions and take appropriate actions to mitigate risks. A safety-driven environment thrives on open, honest, and transparent communication channels.

a) Regular Safety Meetings and Briefings
One of the most effective ways to keep safety top-of-mind is through regular safety meetings or briefings. These meetings provide a platform for discussing safety performance, reviewing incidents, sharing best practices, and addressing concerns. Safety meetings should be held frequently—weekly or bi-weekly—depending on the nature of the work environment. High-risk industries like

THE NEW FOUNDATIONS OF HUMAN PERFORMANCE

technology—such as fall protection systems in construction or ergonomic assessments in offices—demonstrates that the organization prioritizes the physical well-being of its workforce.

2. Step 2: Engage Employees at Every Level

A safety-driven environment is not achieved through top-down directives alone; it requires employees' active involvement and engagement at all levels. Workers on the frontline often have the best understanding of the risks and hazards they face, making their input invaluable to developing effective safety practices.

a) Empowering Workers to Speak Up

To foster a strong safety culture, employees must feel empowered to speak up about safety concerns, report hazards, and suggest improvements without fear of retaliation. Creating a "no-blame" environment encourages openness and communication. Employees who believe their concerns will be taken seriously and won't be penalized for reporting hazards or near-misses are more likely to contribute to a safer work environment.

For instance, an anonymous safety reporting system allows workers to report unsafe conditions without fear of retribution. In organizations where employees are encouraged to voice concerns, leaders often discover potential hazards before they result in incidents, allowing for proactive prevention.

b) Involving Employees in Safety Committees

One practical way to engage employees in safety efforts is by creating safety committees or teams. These groups should consist of representatives from various departments and levels of the organization. Employees involved in safety committees gain a sense of ownership over the process, which can result in more effective safety strategies. Involvement also fosters a sense of pride and responsibility toward maintaining a safe Workplace.

safety ceases to be a checkbox for regulatory compliance and becomes a core component of organizational culture.

1. Step 1: Establish Strong Leadership Commitment
A safety culture starts at the Top, with management and leadership setting the tone. Leaders must not simply endorse safety but demonstrate their commitment to it through visible actions and decisions. This leadership commitment acts as the cornerstone upon which the entire safety culture is built.

a) Leading by Example
Leaders must actively demonstrate their commitment to safety by following safety protocols and standards. Whether wearing personal protective equipment (PPE) on the job site, conducting regular safety walks, or attending safety briefings, leaders should embody the behaviours they want to see in their employees. This sets a powerful precedent for the rest of the organization. For example, a construction site manager who always wears a helmet and adheres to safety regulations models the expected behaviour of workers, reinforcing the message that safety is non-negotiable.

b) Setting safety as a Core Value
Safety should be positioned as a core organizational value, on par with quality, Efficiency, and profitability. When safety is seen as a fundamental value rather than a compliance obligation, employees are more likely to integrate safe behaviours into their daily routines. Leaders should communicate this value clearly and consistently, embedding it into the company's mission statement, business strategies, and performance metrics.

c) Allocating Resources for Safety
A genuine commitment to safety requires an investment of time, money, and resources. Leaders should ensure that adequate resources are allocated for safety training, equipment, hazard mitigation, and incident investigations. By doing so, they signal that safety is a top priority. For instance, investing in modern safety

Conclusion: Leading the Way to a Safer, More Productive Future

In conclusion, the role of management in shaping safety culture cannot be overstated. Leadership sets the tone for safety, enforces accountability, fosters open communication, and invests in the development of employees. When management takes an active role in building and sustaining a safety culture, the organization benefits—not only in reduced accidents and injuries but also in improved performance, morale, and long-term success.

A strong safety culture is the foundation of any high-performing Workplace. It is built on trust, accountability, and shared values that prioritize the well-being of employees. Management has the power to create this culture, and in doing so, they set the stage for a safer, more efficient, and ultimately more successful organization.

Practical Steps to Foster a Safety-Driven Environment

Building a strong safety culture is not just about slogans or safety policies but about creating an environment where safety becomes second nature. It's about embedding safety into an organization's DNA—where every decision, action, and behaviour is influenced by the commitment to ensure the well-being of employees, customers, and stakeholders. The importance of fostering a safety-driven environment cannot be overstated: it not only prevents accidents and injuries but also boosts overall performance, improves morale, reduces absenteeism, and enhances productivity.

This chapter explores practical steps organizations can take to cultivate a safety-driven environment. These steps focus on leadership, employee engagement, communication, training, and continuous improvement. When these principles are implemented,

5. Measuring and Celebrating Success: Reinforcing Positive Safety Behaviors

To maintain a solid safety culture, management must also recognize and celebrate successes in safety performance. Positive reinforcement is a powerful motivator, encouraging employees to follow safety protocols and contribute to a safe work environment.

a) Recognizing Safety Achievements

Managers should implement systems for recognizing and rewarding safety achievements, whether it's through formal recognition programs, bonuses, or public acknowledgement of employees who go above and beyond in promoting safety. For example, a company might have a "Safety Champion of the Month" award to highlight employees who demonstrate exceptional commitment to safety.

Celebrating safety milestones—such as achieving a certain number of days without an accident—also reinforces the importance of safety. These celebrations remind us that safety is a collective effort, and that the organization values the contributions of its workforce.

b) Using Metrics to Drive Improvement

In addition to recognition, management should use data and metrics to drive continuous improvement in safety performance. Tracking key safety indicators—such as the number of near-misses, incidents, and safety audits—provides valuable insights into areas where improvements are needed.

Managers can use this data to identify trends, pinpoint potential risks, and develop targeted interventions. By regularly reviewing safety metrics and sharing them with employees, management is committed to transparency and accountability.

4. Training and Development: Empowering Employees Through Education

An organization's safety culture is only as strong as its employees' knowledge and skills. Management is crucial in ensuring workers have the training and resources to perform their jobs safely. This goes beyond the essential compliance training many companies provide; it involves ongoing education that keeps safety in mind and empowers employees to take proactive steps to maintain a safe work environment.

a) Continuous Learning and Improvement

Safety training shouldn't be a one-time event but an ongoing process. Management must invest in regular safety training programs that update employees on the latest safety practices, technologies, and regulations. This continuous learning approach ensures that safety knowledge is not outdated or stale.

For example, in industries such as construction or healthcare, where new tools, equipment, and procedures are constantly being introduced, regular safety training is essential to keeping employees informed about potential hazards. Managers should ensure that safety training is interactive, practical, and tailored to the workforce's needs.

b) Encouraging Skill Development

In addition to formal training, management should encourage skill development that enhances employees' ability to perform their jobs safely. This might involve supervisor leadership training, ergonomic assessments for office workers, or specialized safety certifications for high-risk tasks.

When employees feel that management is invested in their development, they are likelier to take ownership of their roles in maintaining a safe work environment. This sense of empowerment contributes to a more robust safety culture where everyone is committed to reducing risks and preventing accidents.

two-way street, with managers listening to employees' concerns and acting on them promptly.

a) Creating Platforms for Employee Feedback
A hallmark of an influential safety culture is the ability of employees to provide feedback about safety without fear of retribution. Managers must create platforms for employees to voice concerns, report unsafe conditions, and suggest improvements. This can be regular safety meetings, anonymous reporting systems, or even informal check-ins with supervisors. By giving employees a voice in safety matters, management can gain valuable insights into potential hazards that may not be visible from the Top.

For example, a manufacturing plant might implement a "Safety Suggestion Box" where employees can anonymously submit ideas or concerns. Management then reviews these submissions and provides feedback to the workforce, demonstrating that employees' input is valued and acted upon. This transparency builds trust and fosters a sense of collective ownership over safety.

b) The Importance of Consistent and Clear Communication
Managers must also ensure that safety communication is consistent and clear across the organization. Mixed messages about safety can lead to confusion and complacency. For example, if management says that safety is a top priority but rewards workers for meeting production targets at the expense of safe practices, employees may feel pressured to cut corners.

Consistent communication about the importance of safety should be embedded in daily operations. This can include regular safety briefings, clear hazard signage, and frequent reminders about safe work practices. Managers should ensure that safety messages are aligned with organizational goals and that employees understand how safety contributes to overall performance.

THE NEW FOUNDATIONS OF HUMAN PERFORMANCE

functioning safety culture, accountability isn't punitive but a mechanism for continuous improvement.

For instance, managers can implement regular safety audits and inspections to monitor compliance with safety procedures. Employees should understand that safety violations will be addressed swiftly and fairly and that identifying hazards and suggesting safety improvements are encouraged and rewarded. When accountability is enforced consistently, employees understand that safety is a shared responsibility.

b) Addressing Unsafe Behaviors Without Blame

One key aspect of shaping a strong safety culture is addressing unsafe behaviours without creating a culture of blame. When management emphasizes learning over punishment, employees feel more comfortable reporting hazards, mistakes, and near-misses.

This approach, known as a "just culture," recognizes that humans make mistakes, but it also emphasizes the importance of learning from those mistakes to prevent future incidents.

In a just culture, managers don't punish employees for honest errors or near-misses but instead focus on identifying the root causes of those errors and improving systems and processes to prevent recurrences. For example, suppose a forklift driver in a warehouse accidentally damages a pallet because of an unclear traffic route. In that case, management's response should focus on revisiting the layout and providing additional training rather than reprimanding the driver.

3. The Role of Communication: Open Dialogues About Safety

Open and honest communication is one of the most powerful tools managers have in fostering a safety culture. When management encourages continuous dialogue about safety, it promotes a sense of shared responsibility and encourages employees to speak up about hazards before they lead to incidents. Communication must be a

employees will likely feel justified in doing the same, leading to an erosion of safety culture.

b) The Power of Visibility: Management's Presence on the Frontline

Managers who are actively present and engaged in day-to-day operations send a powerful message about the importance of safety. When leadership regularly visits job sites, talks with workers about safety concerns, and participates in safety meetings, it reinforces the idea that safety is an organization-wide priority. This visibility shows employees that safety isn't just a policy written on paper but a living, breathing part of the company's operations.

For example, a CEO who visits the manufacturing floor and discusses safety protocols with workers shows genuine concern for their well-being. Such actions humanize management and foster trust between employees and leadership. Employees who see that their leaders are invested in safety are likelier to follow safety guidelines, report potential hazards, and create safer work conditions.

2. Creating a Culture of Accountability: Management's Role in Enforcing Safety

Accountability must be integral to the organization for a safety culture to thrive. Management plays a crucial role in establishing systems of accountability that reinforce safety behaviours and ensure that safety protocols are followed consistently. Safety initiatives can quickly become diluted without accountability, with workers viewing safety protocols as optional rather than essential.

a) Accountability at Every Level

Managers must ensure that safety accountability permeates all levels of the organization, from top executives to frontline workers. This involves setting clear expectations around safety performance, defining roles and responsibilities, and holding everyone accountable for maintaining a safe work environment. In a well-

1. The Foundation: Why Leadership Sets the Tone for Safety Culture

The relationship between leadership and safety culture is well-documented. Studies consistently show that the attitudes and behaviours of managers and supervisors profoundly influence an organization's safety performance. Leaders set the tone—if they prioritize safety, the rest of the organization will follow suit.

However, employees will likely adopt the same attitude if safety is considered a secondary concern or a regulatory requirement.

Leadership defines what the company stands for. When managers address safety concerns, prioritize safety training, or model safe behaviour, they communicate that safety matters. Employees take cues from leadership about what is truly important. Therefore, the success of any safety culture starts at the Top. A manager who emphasizes safety creates a ripple effect throughout the organization, empowering employees to take safety seriously and encouraging them to identify and report hazards.

a) Leading by Example: Setting Safety Standards Through Actions

One of the managers' most potent tools is leading by example in shaping a safety culture. When leaders demonstrate commitment to safety in their daily activities—such as adhering to safety protocols, wearing appropriate protective gear, and encouraging open discussions about hazards, they show that safety is a non-negotiable part of the job. This reinforces the idea that safety is an organizational responsibility for frontline workers.

Consider a construction site where a site manager refuses to bypass safety measures even when facing tight deadlines. The manager sets a standard for the team by stopping work to address unsafe conditions. This shows that safety is something other than something that can be sacrificed for expediency. In contrast, if managers are seen cutting corners or ignoring safety protocols,

securing contracts, or entering new markets. Clients and customers want to do business with organizations committed to safety and well-being.

In the following sections of this chapter, we'll explore the various elements of a strong safety culture, from leadership's role in fostering safety to the critical importance of ongoing training and open communication. Safety culture is more than just a buzzword, it's the foundation of sustainable, high-performance workplaces. When safety becomes a shared value, everyone wins.

The Role of Management in Shaping Culture

In any organization, management's role extends far beyond the immediate tasks of overseeing productivity and Efficiency. Management's influence is pivotal in shaping a culture—particularly a safety culture. The culture within an organization manifests shared values, beliefs, and behaviours that define how work is done. When it comes to safety, leadership is the key driver in developing an environment where the well-being of employees is prioritized, hazards are proactively managed, and everyone takes accountability for maintaining a safe workspace.

Organizations successfully integrate safety into their everyday operations. This doesn't happen by accident; it results from deliberate actions, policies, and—most importantly—leadership. Whether in a manufacturing plant, a construction site, a healthcare facility, or an office environment, management can shape, reinforce, or derail a safety culture. This chapter explores the vital role of management in establishing, fostering, and sustaining a culture of safety and how this, in turn, enhances both performance and long-term success.

their safety or burdened by the physical and emotional toll of frequent accidents or injuries. As a result, they can focus entirely on their tasks, leading to better performance and higher productivity.

2. Fewer Accidents and Less Downtime

A strong safety culture significantly reduces the likelihood of accidents, which can be costly and time-consuming. When an accident occurs, it doesn't just affect the injured worker—it disrupts the entire operation. Other employees may have to stop work, investigations must be conducted, and repairs or cleanups may be required. This downtime can have a ripple effect, delaying projects and reducing overall output.

Organizations with a strong safety culture avoid costly disruptions by preventing accidents. They can maintain steady, uninterrupted operations, which leads to better outcomes and higher profitability.

3. Improved Employee Morale and Retention

When employees know their well-being is a top priority, they are more likely to feel valued and respected. This sense of belonging fosters greater loyalty to the company, reducing turnover and helping the organization retain its best talent. High turnover can harm performance, leading to the constant need for recruiting, hiring, and training new workers.

A strong safety culture promotes a stable, positive work environment where employees feel secure. This, in turn, leads to higher levels of job satisfaction, improved morale, and a more committed workforce. Workers are more likely to stay with a company that prioritizes their safety, leading to lower turnover and better retention of institutional knowledge.

4. Enhanced Reputation and Competitive Advantage

Companies with a strong safety culture gain a reputation as responsible, ethical employees. This reputation can be a significant competitive advantage, particularly when attracting new talent,

safety training—employees take notice. They understand that safety isn't just lip service; it's a core component of the organization's success.

Conversely, employees will likely follow suit when leaders ignore or downplay safety issues. If a manager disregards shortcuts on the job or fails to address safety concerns, workers may believe that safety is insignificant. This is why it's essential for leaders to model safe behaviours and to hold themselves accountable for safety just as much as they do their teams.

Some of the world's safest companies, like **Alcoa** under the leadership of Paul O'Neill, have demonstrated how decisive leadership can be in transforming safety culture. When O'Neill took over as CEO of Alcoa, he made safety his top priority, famously stating that his goal was to "never see another person hurt at Alcoa." His unyielding focus on safety dramatically reduced Workplace injuries and improved overall organizational performance, proving that safety and success are not mutually exclusive.

Why Safety Culture Matters: The Impact on Performance
A strong safety culture doesn't just protect employees from harm it also enhances overall performance. Companies with robust safety cultures tend to be more efficient, innovative, and resilient in facing challenges. Here's why:

1. Increased Productivity
It might seem counterintuitive, but focusing on safety can boost productivity. In a well-established safety culture, tasks are performed more efficiently because employees are not constantly dealing with interruptions caused by accidents, injuries, or equipment failures. Workflows become smoother, and teams can operate without fear of harm.

When workers feel safe and supported, they are more likely to stay engaged and motivated. They aren't distracted by concerns about

THE NEW FOUNDATIONS OF HUMAN PERFORMANCE

where accidents were common, and safety was often secondary to productivity.

However, as industries evolved and workplaces became more complex, it became clear that more than simply complying with regulations was needed. Major disasters like the Chornobyl nuclear accident and the Challenger space shuttle explosion highlighted the devastating consequences of systemic failures in safety culture.

These incidents were turning points, prompting a broader reevaluation of organizations' safety management. Companies began recognizing that they needed to foster a culture where safety was deeply ingrained in every decision and action to prevent accidents.

1. From Rules to Values
The shift from compliance-based to culture-driven safety represented a transformation from simply following rules to embedding safety as a fundamental organizational value. Rules can ensure compliance, but they do not necessarily foster the proactive thinking needed to anticipate and prevent accidents before they occur.

In a compliance-driven environment, employees may follow safety procedures only when they are being watched or when inspections are imminent. However, in a culture-driven climate, safety becomes internalized. Workers are constantly vigilant, not because they fear punishment, but because they genuinely believe in protecting themselves and their colleagues.

2. The Role of Leadership in Shaping Safety Culture
Leadership is critical to the development of a strong safety culture. Leaders set the tone for how safety is perceived and prioritized in the organization. When leaders demonstrate a genuine commitment to safety through their actions—whether by conducting regular safety walk-throughs, attending safety meetings, or investing in

3. Open Communication and Reporting Without Fear

One of the cornerstones of an influential safety culture is open communication. In organizations with robust safety cultures, employees feel comfortable reporting potential hazards, near-misses, and even mistakes. Importantly, they can do so without fear of punishment or blame. This sense of psychological safety encourages transparency, which helps the organization address issues before they escalate into serious problems.

Leaders in a safety-oriented organization encourage this kind of openness by clarifying that reporting hazards or errors is a positive action, not a failure. Employees aren't stigmatized for making mistakes—instead, mistakes are viewed as learning opportunities that help strengthen the overall safety system. For example, a worker in a construction company who accidentally drops a tool from a height isn't reprimanded but encouraged to analyze what went wrong and how to prevent it from happening again, fostering continuous improvement.

The Evolution of Safety Culture: From Compliance to Commitment

The idea of safety culture as we know it today is relatively new, having gained prominence in the latter half of the 20th century. Historically, safety in the Workplace was often viewed in purely regulatory terms, with companies primarily concerned with adhering to government regulations and avoiding fines. Safety protocols existed but were usually rigid and viewed as bureaucratic necessities rather than dynamic components of organizational success.

In the past, organizations may have taken a "check-the-box" approach to safety: ensuring fire extinguishers were installed, emergency exits were labelled, and hard hats were worn. However, this compliance-based mindset led to a reactive approach only addressing safety when something went wrong. This was particularly evident in industries like manufacturing and mining,

they view its importance relative to other organizational priorities, and how much effort they put into maintaining a safe environment.

1. A Culture of Shared Responsibility

A strong safety culture creates a shared responsibility for preventing accidents and hazards. It's not just the job of safety officers or management, it's a collective effort. Employees across all levels feel empowered to contribute to safety and look out for one another. In this environment, everyone proactively identifies potential risks and communicates them without fear of retribution.

For example, in a factory setting, a worker who notices a loose railing or a wet floor immediately reports or fixes the issue, knowing that it's not just about avoiding an individual injury but protecting the entire team. Similarly, in a hospital, a nurse who spots an inconsistency in a medication dosage might bring it up immediately, understanding that patient safety is always a shared responsibility, not just the doctor's duty.

2. Safety as a Core Value, Not a Priority That Shifts

One of the key distinguishing features of an authentic culture is that safety is a core value, not simply a shifting priority. Priorities can change depending on external pressures—such as production demands, deadlines, or cost-cutting measures—but values remain constant. In a safety culture, protecting people's well-being is considered non-negotiable. No matter what business pressures arise, compromising safety to meet targets is out of the question.

Contrast this with a Workplace where safety is considered a "priority" only when things are going well. In such environments, safety rules might be ignored or downplayed during busy periods or when profitability is at stake, leading to increased accidents, injuries, or even fatalities. In a strong safety culture, the message is clear: Safety always comes first, no matter what the circumstances.

Chapter 7

Safety Culture: Building a Performance-Oriented Environment

What Is a Safety Culture?

Safety must always be considered in today's increasingly complex and high-pressure work environments, where performance and productivity are critical to success. Whether in the manufacturing sector, construction sites, healthcare, or office-based professions, a genuine commitment to safety is essential for maintaining the well-being of employees and the organization's overall efficiency and success. Central to this commitment is a **safety culture**—an organizational mindset that prioritizes safety at every level, embeds it into daily operations, and holds everyone accountable.

But what exactly is a **safety culture**? How does it emerge within organizations, and why is it critical to performance? This chapter will explore the concept of safety culture, its defining characteristics, and its vital role in creating a performance-oriented environment. We will examine why developing a strong safety culture goes beyond compliance with regulations and how it strengthens an organization's resilience, effectiveness, and success.

Understanding Safety Culture: Beyond Rules and Regulations
At its most fundamental level, safety culture can be defined as the collective attitude, beliefs, and values that people within an organization share regarding Workplace safety. It's not merely about compliance with safety protocols or following standard operating procedures—although these are essential components. Instead, safety culture encompasses how seriously people, from leadership down to frontline employees, take safety in their daily work, how

THE NEW FOUNDATIONS OF HUMAN PERFORMANCE

employees to share their ideas and participate in decision-making. Whether through suggestion programs, innovation labs, or regular feedback sessions, leaders can tap into the collective wisdom of their workforce to continuously improve systems and reduce errors.

b. Tracking and Measuring improvement

Finally, leaders must track and measure the success of error-reduction strategies. By regularly reviewing key performance indicators (KPIs) related to safety, quality, and error rates, leaders can assess the effectiveness of their interventions and make data-driven decisions to improve performance.

Conclusion: Leadership's Essential Role in Error Reduction

Reducing human error in the Workplace is not just the responsibility of individual employees, leaders have a vital role to play in creating the conditions that prevent mistakes and promote safety. By modelling safe behaviour, fostering a culture of accountability, investing in training, and implementing systematic error reduction strategies, leaders can shape an organization that minimizes mistakes and maximizes performance.

Leaders who recognize the importance of their influence in reducing errors will protect their employees from harm and enhance the organization's overall productivity and success. In the next chapter, we will explore specific case studies that highlight the power of leadership in transforming Workplace safety and reducing human error across various industries.

These strategies involve designing systems, processes, and environments that make it easier for employees to succeed and harder for them to make mistakes.

1. Designing for Human Factors

Human factors engineering focuses on designing systems that account for human users' limitations and capabilities. Leaders can work with human factors experts to create systems and processes that minimize the likelihood of human error.

a. Simplifying Processes and Interfaces

Complex systems and processes are more likely to result in errors. Leaders should work to simplify workflows, reduce unnecessary steps, and create intuitive interfaces that guide employees through tasks. For example, color-coded components or visual cues in an assembly line can help employees identify the correct parts and assembly sequence, reducing the risk of mistakes.

b. Implementing Fail-Safes and Redundancies

Leaders should also implement fail-safes and redundancies to catch errors before they cause harm. In healthcare, medication administration systems may require multiple checks or electronic verification to ensure the right patient is given the correct medication.

2. Encouraging Continuous Improvement

Leaders should foster a culture of continuous improvement where employees are encouraged to identify and propose changes that can reduce errors. This could involve using Lean or Six Sigma methodologies to streamline processes and eliminate waste or creating cross-functional teams to brainstorm and test new approaches.

a. Empowering Frontline Employees to Innovate

Frontline employees often have the most insight into the sources of errors in their work. Leaders should create opportunities for these

THE NEW FOUNDATIONS OF HUMAN PERFORMANCE

b. Ongoing Professional Development
Learning should not stop after boarding. Leaders must ensure that employees receive ongoing training and professional development opportunities to keep their skills sharp and up to date. By offering refresher courses and advanced training, organizations can ensure that employees remain competent and aware of any changes in processes or regulations.

2. Training in Cognitive and Emotional Resilience
Beyond technical training, leaders can also reduce errors by investing in cognitive and emotional resilience training. Mistakes often occur when employees are under stress, fatigued, or distracted. By providing training that enhances focus, stress management, and emotional regulation, leaders can help employees maintain peak performance even in high-pressure situations.

a. Mindfulness and Stress Management Programs
Incorporating mindfulness and stress management programs into the Workplace can help employees stay focused and avoid errors caused by cognitive overload. Leaders should encourage participation in these programs, recognizing that mental well-being is as important as technical proficiency.

b. Promoting Work-Life Balance
Leaders who prioritize work-life balance can reduce the risk of errors due to employee burnout or fatigue. When employees are overworked or exhausted, their cognitive abilities are diminished, leading to mistakes. Leaders should implement policies that promote reasonable workloads, adequate breaks, and opportunities for time off to ensure employees remain physically and mentally sharp.

Leadership in Implementing Systematic Error Reduction Strategies
Beyond shaping culture and providing training, leaders play a critical role in implementing systematic error-reduction strategies.

of operational errors, prompting the organization to invest in better maintenance protocols.

b. Using Data to Predict and Mitigate Risks
Leaders can also leverage data analytics to predict potential risks and prevent errors. Organizations can identify patterns that may indicate systemic issues by analyzing trends in error reports, absenteeism, or equipment failures. This data-driven approach allows leaders to implement targeted interventions, such as additional training or equipment upgrades, to reduce the likelihood of future mistakes.

Empowering Employees Through Training and Development
One of the most effective ways leaders can reduce errors is by investing in employee training and development. Training equips employees with the knowledge and skills they need to perform their tasks and instils confidence and competence in their roles. Well-trained employees are less likely to make mistakes because they understand the processes and procedures that govern their work.

1. Comprehensive Onboarding Programs
Leaders must ensure that new employees receive comprehensive onboarding programs, introducing them to the organization's safety protocols, systems, and procedures. A rushed or inadequate onboarding process can lead to confusion and errors later.

a. Job-Specific Training
In addition to general onboarding, leaders should provide job-specific training tailored to each role's unique responsibilities. For example, a new employee in a chemical plant should receive specialized training on handling hazardous materials, while a software engineer should receive training on secure coding practices.

THE NEW FOUNDATIONS OF HUMAN PERFORMANCE

b. Promoting Open Communication and Error Reporting

Errors should not be seen as personal failings but as opportunities for learning and systemic improvement. Leaders must foster an environment where employees feel comfortable reporting mistakes without fear of punishment. Open communication channels are critical in identifying errors and near-misses—instances where a mistake was narrowly avoided.

By encouraging transparency, leaders can uncover underlying issues in processes or systems that may contribute to errors. For instance, a technician who feels safe reporting a near-miss involving equipment failure may provide critical information that prevents a future catastrophic failure.

The Role of Leadership in Risk Identification and Management

Influential leaders are proactive in identifying risks that could lead to errors. Rather than waiting for mistakes to occur, they work to anticipate potential problems and address them before they escalate.

Risk identification and management are essential in reducing human error, particularly in high-risk industries such as aviation, healthcare, and manufacturing.

1. Implementing Robust Risk Assessment Processes

Leaders must implement comprehensive risk assessment processes that identify potential sources of errors within the organization. These assessments should evaluate employee workload, communication protocols, equipment functionality, and environmental conditions.

a. Conducting Regular Safety Audits

Safety audits are a powerful tool for identifying risks and vulnerabilities in the Workplace. By regularly conducting audits, leaders can uncover hidden dangers and address them before they lead to errors or accidents. For example, a manufacturing plant may identify that poorly maintained machinery increases the likelihood

a. Modeling Safe Behavior

Leaders must actively demonstrate the behaviours they expect from their employees. For instance, leaders should consistently follow safety protocols if a company prioritizes safety, even if it slows down their work. When employees see that leadership is unwilling to compromise on safety, they are more likely to uphold these standards.

b. Communicating a Clear Vision

Leaders should communicate a clear vision of the organization's commitment to minimizing errors. This vision must emphasize that errors are opportunities for learning and improvement rather than reasons for punishment. By establishing this mindset, leaders can create an environment where employees feel comfortable reporting mistakes and working collaboratively to address them.

2. Creating a Culture of Accountability and Transparency

A strong culture of accountability is essential in reducing Workplace errors. When employees take ownership of their tasks and responsibilities, they are likelier to pay attention to detail and follow established protocols. Leadership plays a crucial role in fostering this sense of accountability by ensuring that clear expectations are set, and everyone understands their role in preventing errors.

a. Encouraging Ownership of Tasks

Leaders should encourage employees to own their work by clearly defining roles and responsibilities. When employees understand they are accountable for their tasks, they are more likely to exercise diligence and follow procedures.

For example, nurses taking ownership of patient care in healthcare are more likely to double-check medication orders or ensure all safety protocols are followed. By instilling a sense of personal responsibility, leaders can minimize the risk of errors due to negligence or oversight.

The Role of Leadership in Reducing Errors

Human error is a reality that every organization must contend with, regardless of industry. Mistakes in healthcare, manufacturing, and office-based professions can significantly affect safety, productivity, and financial performance. Yet, while errors are often viewed as individual failures, they frequently arise from systemic weaknesses, including poor communication, inadequate training, or suboptimal working conditions. Leadership plays a pivotal role in shaping the environment where errors proliferate or are minimized.

Leaders set the tone for organizational culture and influence the processes, systems, and policies that can prevent or reduce mistakes. In this chapter, we will explore the essential role of leadership in reducing Workplace errors. From fostering a culture of accountability and safety to implementing robust error-prevention strategies, leaders are critical in creating an environment where employees can thrive and minimize mistakes.

The Power of Leadership in Shaping Organizational Culture

Organizational culture is the backdrop for every company decision, action, and interaction. When leaders emphasize safety, communication, and continuous improvement, employees are more likely to align with these values. Conversely, if leaders tolerate carelessness or prioritize speed over quality, employees may feel pressured to cut corners, resulting in increased errors.

1. Setting the Tone at the Top

Leadership behaviour has a profound impact on organizational culture. Employees look to their leaders to understand what is expected of them and what behaviours will be rewarded or punished. If leaders demonstrate a commitment to safety, transparency, and accountability, employees will likely adopt similar values in their work.

giving medicine to ensure correctness, significantly reducing medication mistakes.

5. Important Takeaways for Designing Error-Resistant Systems

1. Prioritize simplicity and consistency – Simplified processes and standardized procedures decrease cognitive strain, making activities simpler and less error-prone.

2. Use automation judiciously - Automation can handle repetitive activities and eliminate many mistakes, but explicit feedback systems and fail-safes must accompany it to enable human supervision.

3. Design for user-friendliness - Intuitive designs, straightforward communication tools, and visual indications enable people to engage more successfully with Technology, lowering the chance of errors.

4. Prioritize ongoing training and education - Skill reinforcement via scenario-based training and frequent refreshers ensure that employees are well-prepared for their jobs.

5. Promote an open and learning culture - AA Workplace encourages mistake reporting and analysis and fosters continuous improvement and systemic learning.

This chapter on human mistakes emphasizes the significance of seeing faults not as isolated instances but as signs of opportunities for development in system design and Workplace culture.

Understanding and proactively addressing the causes of human mistakes allows firms to build safer, more robust systems that maximize human potential while minimizing risk. The ideas and tactics covered here are critical for any sector seeking to create systems that align with human capabilities and limits.

causes of mistakes, such as a design defect, a lack of training, or an environmental problem.

Share Lessons Learned: Ensure insights acquired from mistake reports and analysis are disseminated across the company. By disseminating lessons learned, other teams and departments may apply these insights to their operations, reducing the likelihood of repeating errors.

4. Case Studies: Effective Error Reduction in Action.

Real-world examples may show how these techniques play out across various industries. Here are two instances.

Case Study 1

Aviation Industry, Standardized Checklists

The aircraft sector has an excellent safety record, largely thanks to standardized processes, particularly checklists. Pilots and crew employ thorough checklists before, during, and after flights to reduce cognitive burden and ensure that each step is performed correctly. Standardized communication methods are also in place, which reduces the possibility of miscommunication during vital periods.

Case Study 2

Healthcare, Reducing Medication Errors with Barcoding Systems

Because of the complexities of prescribing and delivering pharmaceuticals, hospitals often suffer from medication mistakes. Many healthcare institutions increasingly use barcoding systems for patient bracelets and medicine packaging. Before providing medicine, nurses scan the patient's wristband and medication before

memory mistakes. In workplaces where workers must follow consecutive processes, displaying visual reminders immediately in their line of sight may help them stay focused on the job.

d. Invest in training and education.

Scenario-Based Training for Critical Thinking Single training sessions sometimes need to be improved to teach the complex abilities required in fast-paced, high-stakes scenarios. Investing in scenario-based training allows staff to practice dealing with important events in a controlled setting. This training helps people get acquainted with the system, predict possible problems, and create appropriate solutions.

Promote a Learning Culture: Encourage employees to see faults as learning opportunities rather than failures. When errors are treated with a developmental mentality, workers are more likely to report them and seek assistance in preventing them from happening again.

Memory recall declines with time. Thus, frequent training refreshers may assist in understanding processes and system changes. Furthermore, monthly skill evaluations enable supervisors to identify areas for further training, allowing for focused improvements.

f. Create a robust error reporting and analysis system.

Encourage the open reporting of errors and near misses. Create a culture where workers feel free to disclose mistakes or near misses without fear of repercussions. Open reporting promotes openness and gives valuable information about where errors are likely.

Implement Root Cause Analysis (RCA): When an error happens, it is vital to understand why it occurred rather than who was to blame. Root cause analysis allows businesses to address the fundamental

THE NEW FOUNDATIONS OF HUMAN PERFORMANCE

scheduling, or alarm monitoring. To avoid overreliance, which may lead to errors in crucial circumstances, automation should be used in conjunction with human judgment rather than as a replacement for it.

Feedback Mechanisms in Automation: Systems should have feedback loops to ensure operators get confirmation when operations are done correctly, or problems are detected. For example, a warehouse's automated order-picking system may include a confirmation screen to ensure that each item is correct.

Automation failures: It is critical to incorporate fail-safes in automated systems that offer unambiguous instructions in the case of failure. In this manner, if automation fails, human operators will be prepared to make educated judgments rather than getting disoriented in a chaotic circumstance.

b. Design for Intuitive Use and Clear Communication.

User-Centered Design (UCD): The user-centered design approach prioritizes end-user demands, preferences, and restrictions throughout the design Process. When systems are simple to comprehend and use, the likelihood of mistakes is reduced. For example, an intuitive control panel with clear labeling and consistent symbols decreases the possibility of an operator hitting the wrong button or choosing the incorrect choice.

Clear labeling and color-coded warnings help to prevent uncertainty. In an industrial setting, separate color-coded indicators indicating danger zones or emergency stop buttons allow workers to respond quickly and precisely. In addition, signage with succinct instructions or step-by-step images may improve clarity and prevent misunderstanding.

Reduce Reliance on Memory with Visible Cues: Cognitive aids like prompts, reminders, and checklists may help individuals avoid

3. Designing Systems to Reduce Human Error.

Once we understand the causes of human mistakes, the next step is to apply design concepts that may assist in lessening their frequency and severity. Here are a few significant approaches:

a. Simplify and streamline processes.

Design with simplicity in mind: Reducing superfluous stages or choices in a Process reduces the likelihood of mistakes. Complex systems with several branching routes increase cognitive stress and create more potential for error. Simplifying these stages helps employees to concentrate on their primary responsibilities without feeling overwhelmed.

Poka-Yoke is an error-proofing technique. Error-proofing is a design concept that was created in the manufacturing industry to prevent mistakes from occurring. Poka-yoke approaches entail incorporating measures into the system that either avoid or instantly highlight improper behaviors when they occur. For example, an item that only fits in one orientation might prevent positioning mistakes in assembly.

Procedure Standardization: Ensure that procedures are uniform across all jobs and staff to eliminate variance and the possibility of mistakes. A standard checklist, for example, may be used to guarantee that each step is completed in the proper sequence, lowering the likelihood of inadvertent omissions.

a. Use automation to assist, rather than replace, human judgment.

Assistive Automation: Automation is beneficial for tackling repetitive, low-value chores, allowing people to concentrate on more complicated, high-stakes choices. Automated systems may decrease mistakes by handling jobs prone to lapses, such as data input,

Mistakes are more complicated blunders that include incorrect logic or planning. Mistakes occur when individuals make bad judgments due to misconceptions, a lack of knowledge, or poor judgment.

2. Why do human errors occur?

Understanding the causes of human mistakes is critical for developing solutions that may help reduce them. While errors may happen for a variety of reasons, typical ones include:

Cognitive Overload: When people are overwhelmed with knowledge, they are more likely to make mistakes. Cognitive overload occurs when the task demands surpass a person's ability to comprehend information, resulting in errors, lapses, or omissions.

Stress and Fatigue: Physical and mental exhaustion raises the risk of mistakes. Prolonged exposure to stress, tight deadlines, or a lack of sleep impairs attention and cognitive function, affecting decision-making accuracy and reaction times.

Ambiguous or Complex Instructions: Instructions that are difficult to understand or follow may lead to confusion, particularly in fast-paced work contexts. Clear, precise directions minimize the possibility of misunderstanding and mistakes.

Routine and Monotony: Repetitive work may lead to complacency and decreased alertness, with little but crucial aspects being forgotten. Such jobs may also lead to "automation bias," in which individuals depend on automation without confirming its correctness.

Individuals are more prone to mistakes when they need more training or are unfamiliar with a job. Skilled jobs require a certain amount of experience and familiarity to be executed correctly.

Workplace where employees thrive, and errors are minimized. The following chapters will explore strategies and practices to reduce human error and enhance Workplace performance.

How to Design Systems That Minimize Human Error

Human mistakes have been studied extensively in various industries, including aviation, health, manufacturing, and software engineering. Mistakes occur in many industries, but the aim remains to reduce these mistakes to maintain Efficiency, safety, and production. In Chapter 6, we'll look at the subtleties of human mistakes, how and why they happen, and how to create practical systems that lower the possibility of such errors, resulting in safer and more successful work environments.

1. The Nature of Human Error.

A human mistake is an unintentional action or omission resulting in an undesirable consequence. Unlike mechanical or technical flaws, human errors are unavoidable in human interaction with Technology. They result from a complicated interaction between cognitive limits, contextual circumstances, and system design. Understanding the core causes of mistakes allows us to design systems more appropriate to human capabilities and limits.

Human mistakes are often categorized into two major categories:

Slips and Lapses: Unintended acts or oversights often occur in highly familiar situations. For example, a worker may inadvertently push the incorrect button or pay attention to a vital step in a standard operation.

THE NEW FOUNDATIONS OF HUMAN PERFORMANCE

1. Modeling Safe Behavior

Leaders must lead by example, demonstrating safe behaviours and practices. When employees observe their leader's prioritizing safety, they are more likely to adopt similar attitudes and behaviours.

2. Encouraging Reporting and Learning

Creating an environment where employees feel safe reporting errors and near-misses without fear of retribution is essential for reducing mistakes. Leaders should encourage open dialogue and emphasize that errors are opportunities for learning and improvement.

3. Providing Resources and Support

Leaders should ensure employees can access the resources, tools, and training to perform their jobs effectively. This support can empower employees to take ownership of their tasks and minimize the likelihood of errors.

Conclusion: Transforming Errors into Opportunities for Growth

Human error is inherent in the Workplace but must not be insurmountable. Organizations can foster a culture of continuous improvement and safety by understanding the common causes of Workplace errors and implementing targeted strategies.

Leaders must actively participate in shaping Workplace culture, promoting open communication, and emphasizing the importance of safety. By doing so, organizations can transform errors into opportunities for growth, ultimately enhancing performance and ensuring the well-being of their employees.

As we move forward, we must recognize that human error is not solely a reflection of individual shortcomings but a product of the complex interplay between cognitive, environmental, and organizational factors. By addressing these root causes and fostering a culture of safety and accountability, organizations can create a

Example
A nurse working long shifts may experience fatigue that affects her ability to focus on patient care. This fatigue could lead to errors in medication administration or vital sign assessments.

Mitigation Strategies
Organizations should prioritize employee well-being by implementing policies that promote work-life balance, such as reasonable shift lengths and regular breaks. Providing access to mental health resources and stress management programs can help employees cope with stressors.

6. Lack of Accountability and Ownership
Employees who do not feel a sense of ownership over their tasks may be less inclined to adhere to established procedures and protocols. This lack of accountability can lead to violations and careless mistakes.

Example
In a manufacturing plant, workers who perceive their tasks as repetitive and unimportant may skip safety checks or cut corners in production, believing that their actions will not be scrutinized.

Mitigation Strategies
Organizations should foster a culture of accountability by clearly defining roles and responsibilities. Encouraging employees to take ownership of their work and recognizing their contributions can enhance engagement and reduce the likelihood of errors.

The Role of Leadership in Reducing Errors
Leaders are crucial in shaping Workplace culture and establishing a safety-driven environment. By promoting a culture that values safety and learning, leaders can inspire employees to prioritize safety and take proactive steps to reduce errors.

THE NEW FOUNDATIONS OF HUMAN PERFORMANCE

Mitigation Strategies
Organizations must invest in comprehensive training programs that equip employees with the knowledge and skills to perform their jobs effectively. Ongoing training and assessments can help ensure employees remain competent and aware of procedure updates.

4. Poor Communication
Effective communication is the backbone of any successful organization. When communication breaks down, misunderstandings can occur, leading to errors. This can happen at various levels, including between team members, departments, and management.

Example
Miscommunication between architects and contractors in a construction project can result in significant errors, such as using incorrect materials or dimensions. These mistakes can lead to costly delays and safety hazards.

Mitigation Strategies
Organizations should foster open communication, encouraging employees to ask questions, seek clarification, and provide feedback. Regular team meetings and collaborative platforms can facilitate better communication and ensure everyone is on the same page.

5. Stress and Fatigue
High stress levels and fatigue can severely impair an individual's cognitive functions, leading to errors. In demanding work environments, employees may experience chronic stress or exhaustion, making it challenging to concentrate and perform at their best.

Encouraging breaks and allowing employees to focus on single tasks can reduce mental strain and improve overall performance.

2. Environmental Factors

The physical environment in which employees operate can significantly impact their performance and susceptibility to errors. Factors such as noise, lighting, and workspace organization can create distractions or hinder focus, leading to mistakes.

Example

Excessive noise from machinery in a manufacturing facility can prevent workers from hearing safety alarms or verbal instructions. This distraction can result in critical oversights and dangerous situations.

Mitigation Strategies

Organizations should regularly assess the Workplace environment to identify and address factors contributing to errors. Implementing ergonomic designs, reducing noise levels, and ensuring adequate lighting can create a more conducive atmosphere for focused work.

3. Inadequate Training and Knowledge Gaps

Employees who need more training or knowledge about their tasks are more prone to making mistakes. When individuals are adequately prepared for their roles, they may need help understanding complex processes or following established protocols.

Example

A new employee in a healthcare setting may need to become more familiar with the specific protocols for administering medication. This knowledge gap could lead to mistakes, such as administering the wrong dosage or medication type.

THE NEW FOUNDATIONS OF HUMAN PERFORMANCE

Lapses are memory-related errors when individuals forget to perform a task or overlook a critical step in a process. For example, a nurse might need to remember to administer medication due to distractions or a busy environment.

- **Mistakes:** arise from a lack of knowledge or understanding, leading individuals to make incorrect decisions. For instance, an engineer might choose the wrong specifications for a project due to insufficient training or information.

-**Violations** are deliberate deviations from established protocols or rules. Employees may violate for various reasons, including time pressure, perceived inefficiency, or a lack of confidence in existing procedures.

Understanding these categories helps organizations pinpoint the underlying causes of errors and develop targeted interventions to reduce their occurrence.

Common Causes of Workplace Errors
1. Cognitive Overload

In our fast-paced work environments, employees often juggle multiple tasks and responsibilities. This cognitive overload can lead to lapses in attention and memory, resulting in errors. The brain has a limited capacity for processing information, and when overwhelmed, it is more likely to overlook important details or make poor decisions.

Example

Consider a warehouse worker responsible for managing inventory while simultaneously assisting customers. The mental demands of switching between these tasks can lead to slips, such as forgetting to log an item after it has been restored.

Mitigation Strategies

Organizations can combat cognitive overload by implementing task prioritization, simplified processes, and workload management.

Chapter 6

Human Error: Understanding and Reducing Mistakes

Common Causes of Workplace Errors

In the intricate tapestry of Workplace dynamics, human error emerges as a prominent thread, often unravelling the fabric of efficiency and safety. Despite our best intentions, mistakes are an inevitable part of human behaviour. Understanding the causes of these errors is not just an academic exercise; it is a crucial step in enhancing organizational performance, safety, and overall employee well-being. This chapter delves into the common causes of Workplace errors, exploring the psychological, environmental, and organizational factors contributing to mistakes. By unravelling these causes, we can develop effective strategies to mitigate human error and foster a culture of continuous improvement.

The Nature of Human Error
Human error can be broadly defined as an unintended act or omission that leads to adverse outcomes. While some may view errors as a reflection of individual incompetence or negligence, this perspective fails to recognize the complex interplay of various factors that influence human behaviour. Errors can be classified into several categories, including slips, lapses, mistakes, and violations, each with distinct causes and implications.

-Slips: These errors occur when individuals intend to do one thing but accidentally do another. For instance, a worker might intend to enter data into a computer but accidentally enter it into the wrong field due to a momentary lapse in attention.

THE NEW FOUNDATIONS OF HUMAN PERFORMANCE

operational efficiency. Employees felt valued and motivated to contribute to the organization's success.

- **Financial Turnaround:** Alcoa's focus on safety and operational excellence resulted in a significant turnaround in financial performance. The company reported increased profits and enhanced shareholder value.

Lessons Learned

Alcoa's case exemplifies the power of leadership commitment to safety. By embedding safety in the organizational culture and empowering employees, companies can achieve remarkable safety and performance outcomes.

Conclusion: The Imperative of Safety-Driven Performance

These case studies demonstrate that safety is not a standalone concept but an integral component of organizational performance.

Companies prioritizing safety cultivate a culture of trust, engagement, and accountability, leading to enhanced productivity and long-term success.

As organizations navigate the complexities of modern business, the safety-performance link will continue to be a critical area of focus.

By learning from the experiences of industry leaders, organizations can implement effective safety strategies that protect employees and drive performance and profitability.

In the following chapters, we will explore strategies and practices that organizations can adopt to enhance safety and performance, ultimately fostering a harmonious culture of safety and excellence.

THE NEW FOUNDATIONS OF HUMAN PERFORMANCE

Case Study 5
Alcoa: A Turnaround Story
Overview
Alcoa, a global leader in aluminum production, faced significant challenges related to safety and performance in the early 2000s. After experiencing a series of Workplace incidents, the company recognized the urgent need to prioritize safety as a core value.

Implementation of Safety Initiatives
Alcoa's transformation began with a renewed focus on safety, spearheaded by then-CEO Paul O'Neill:

1. Safety as a Core Value: O'Neill declared that safety would be Alcoa's top priority. This commitment set the tone for a cultural shift within the organization, emphasizing the importance of safety at all levels.

2. Behavior-Based Safety Programs: Alcoa implemented behavior-based safety programs to encourage employees to take ownership of safety. Employees were trained to identify unsafe behaviours and practices, fostering a culture of accountability.

3. Data-Driven Approach: The company adopted a data-driven approach to safety, analyzing incidents and near misses to identify trends and areas for improvement. This focuses on data-enabled Alcoa to make informed decisions regarding safety initiatives.

Results and Impact on Performance
Alcoa's commitment to safety yielded transformative results:
- **Dramatic Reduction in Incident Rates:** Alcoa experienced a remarkable decline in Workplace incidents, achieving a safety record that surpassed industry averages. This achievement was a testament to the effectiveness of its safety initiatives.
- **Increased Productivity:** A strong safety culture improves employee morale and engagement, increasing productivity and

2. Standardized Work Practices: Toyota establishes standardized work practices prioritizing safety. Clear procedures and guidelines ensure employees know safety protocols and can execute their tasks safely.

3. Investment in Training: The company invests significantly in training programs that educate employees on safety practices, risk management, and emergency preparedness. Ongoing training reinforces the importance of safety in the Workplace.

Results and Impact on Performance

Toyota's safety-driven approach has yielded remarkable outcomes:

- **Exceptional Safety Record:** Toyota boasts an impressive safety record, with incident rates significantly lower than industry averages. This achievement is a testament to the effectiveness of its safety initiatives.

-**Improved Production Efficiency:** A strong safety culture enhances production efficiency, as employees feel confident and focused on their tasks. This efficiency contributes to higher-quality vehicles and improved customer satisfaction.

- **Reputation for Quality and Reliability:** Toyota's commitment to safety and quality has solidified its reputation as a trusted automotive manufacturer. Customers prioritize safety features, and Toyota's track record enhances its competitive edge.

Lessons Learned

Toyota's case underscores the importance of embedding safety into the organizational culture. Organizations can achieve exceptional safety and performance outcomes by empowering employees, standardizing practices, and fostering continuous improvement.

- Reduction in Adverse Events: The organization has successfully reduced the incidence of adverse events in patient care, improving overall patient outcomes and enhancing the quality of care.

- Increased Employee Engagement: Focusing on employee wellness and safety has led to higher job satisfaction and engagement among healthcare professionals. Engaged employees are likelier to provide exceptional care and contribute to a positive patient experience.

- Cost Savings: By minimizing adverse events and enhancing patient outcomes, Kaiser Permanente has achieved cost savings associated with reduced hospital readmissions and malpractice claims.

Lessons Learned

Kaiser Permanente's case demonstrates that safety is integral to delivering high-quality care. By prioritizing employee wellness and fostering a culture of continuous improvement, healthcare organizations can achieve exceptional performance and patient satisfaction.

Case Study 4
Toyota: Safety in Automotive Manufacturing
Overview

Toyota, a global leader in automotive manufacturing, is renowned for its commitment to quality and safety. The company's production system, the Toyota Production System (TPS), emphasizes safety as a critical component of operational excellence.

Implementation of Safety Initiatives

Toyota's safety strategy is grounded in several principles:

1. Continuous Improvement (Kaizen): Toyota embraces the philosophy of continuous improvement, encouraging employees to identify safety concerns and implement solutions. This culture of Kaizen empowers employees at all levels to contribute to safety enhancements.

leveraging data, organizations can cultivate a culture of safety that enhances overall performance and reputation.

Case Study 3
Kaiser Permanente: A Healthcare Paradigm
Overview
Kaiser Permanente, one of the largest healthcare organizations in the United States, is a beacon of excellence in patient care and employee safety. In the healthcare sector, where the stakes are high, Kaiser Permanente emphasizes safety as a fundamental aspect of its operational philosophy.

Implementation of Safety Initiatives
Kaiser Permanente's safety strategy encompasses several key components:

1. Patient Safety Programs: The organization has implemented various programs to minimize medical procedures and treatment risks. These programs include protocols for medication administration, infection control, and surgical safety.

2. Employee Wellness Initiatives: Kaiser Permanente prioritizes employee well-being by offering wellness programs, mental health support, and ergonomic assessments. A healthy workforce is crucial for delivering high-quality patient care.

3. Continuous Improvement: The organization fosters a culture of continuous improvement, encouraging employees to identify safety concerns and suggest solutions. Regular training and workshops inform staff about the best practices and emerging safety trends.

Results and Impact on Performance
Kaiser Permanente's commitment to safety has resulted in significant benefits:

THE NEW FOUNDATIONS OF HUMAN PERFORMANCE

Implementation of Safety Initiatives
The following elements characterize Boeing's safety strategy:

1. Safety Management System (SMS): Boeing employs a comprehensive Safety Management System that integrates safety practices into its operations. This systematic approach allows for proactive risk identification and mitigation.

2. Employee Empowerment: Boeing encourages employees to take ownership of safety by giving them the authority to halt operations if they identify safety concerns. This empowerment fosters a culture where safety is everyone's responsibility.

3. Data-Driven Decision Making: The company leverages data analytics to assess safety performance and identify trends. Boeing can make informed decisions to enhance safety protocols and processes by analyzing data from various sources.

Results and Impact on Performance
Boeing's commitment to safety has yielded significant outcomes:
- Improved Safety Metrics: Boeing has achieved a remarkable safety record, with incident rates consistently below industry benchmarks. This achievement is a testament to the effectiveness of its safety initiatives.
- Enhanced Operational Efficiency: A strong safety culture contributes to streamlined operations, as employees feel more confident and focused on their tasks. This efficiency translates into faster production cycles and improved product quality.
- Reputation and Customer Trust: Boeing's commitment to safety has solidified its reputation as a trusted leader in the aerospace industry. Clients and customers prioritize safety, and Boeing's track record enhances its competitive edge.

Lessons Learned
Boeing's case highlights the importance of a proactive and systematic approach to safety. By empowering employees and

3. Use of Technology: DuPont employs advanced technologies like wearable devices and safety management software to monitor safety performance and identify potential hazards. This data-driven approach enables the company to make informed decisions about safety improvements.

Results and Impact on Performance

The impact of DuPont's safety initiatives is profound:

- **Reduction in Incident Rates:** DuPont has seen a remarkable decrease in Workplace incidents since implementing its safety programs. The company boasts a total incident rate significantly lower than industry averages.

- **Increased Productivity:** By fostering a culture of safety, DuPont has created an environment where employees feel valued and engaged. This has increased productivity and innovation, with employees more willing to share ideas and collaborate.

- **Financial Performance:** DuPont's commitment to safety has translated into substantial financial benefits. The company's focus on safety has reduced costs associated with accidents, insurance claims, and legal liabilities, contributing to its overall profitability.

Lessons Learned

DuPont's case exemplifies that safety and performance are not mutually exclusive but are intertwined. Organizations can achieve remarkable performance outcomes by prioritizing safety and cultivating a culture that values employee well-being.

Case Study 2
Boeing: Safety in Aerospace Engineering
Overview

As a leader in the aerospace industry, Boeing recognizes the paramount importance of safety. The stakes are incredibly high in aviation, where safety failures can have catastrophic consequences. Boeing has developed a robust safety culture emphasizing continuous improvement and employee engagement.

THE NEW FOUNDATIONS OF HUMAN PERFORMANCE

The Importance of Case Studies in Understanding Safety-Performance Links

Case studies serve as powerful tools for understanding the real-world implications of theories and principles. They provide concrete examples of how organizations successfully implement safety measures and the tangible benefits they reap. Each case study highlights the best practices and reveals the common challenges organizations face when prioritizing safety. By analyzing these case studies, readers can glean insights into practical strategies and the transformative power of a safety-focused approach.

Case Study 1
DuPont: A Legacy of Safety Excellence
Overview

DuPont, a global leader in science and technology, is renowned for its unwavering commitment to safety. With a legacy dating back over two centuries, DuPont has consistently emphasized safety as a cornerstone of its operational strategy. The company's approach to safety is comprehensive, focusing not only on compliance but also on cultivating a culture of safety that permeates every level of the organization.

Implementation of Safety Initiatives

DuPont's safety strategy is built on several key pillars:

1. Behavior-Based Safety Programs: DuPont introduced behavior-based safety programs to foster a proactive safety culture. Employees are encouraged to observe and provide feedback on each other's safety practices, creating a sense of shared responsibility.

2. Safety Training and Education: The company invests significantly in training programs that educate employees on safety protocols, risk management, and emergency preparedness. These programs are tailored to specific job functions, ensuring relevance and applicability.

Conclusion: The Imperative of Safety in the Workplace

In an era where productivity is paramount, organizations must recognize that safety is not a mere regulatory obligation but a foundational component of successful operations. Ignoring safety can lead to dire consequences, impacting not only employees but also organizational performance and reputation.

The costs associated with neglecting safety are vast, encompassing direct expenses like medical and legal fees and indirect consequences such as decreased morale, increased absenteeism, and reputational damage. Organizations can unlock the potential for enhanced productivity and long-term success by understanding and addressing the safety-performance link.

Investing in safety is an investment in the future. It is a commitment to fostering a culture where employees can thrive, innovate, and contribute to the organization's goals without fear. As we move forward, let us prioritize safety as an integral part of our organizational ethos, paving the way for sustainable success in an increasingly competitive landscape.

Case Studies of Safety-Driven Workplaces

In the contemporary landscape of organizational management, the nexus between safety and performance is gaining unprecedented recognition. As businesses navigate the complex interplay of risk and reward, understanding how safety can drive performance is vital for sustaining productivity and fostering employee well-being. This chapter explores compelling industry case studies, illustrating how safety-driven initiatives have led to remarkable performance, culture, and profitability outcomes.

The Long-Term Benefits of Prioritizing Safety
1. Improved Financial Performance
Investing in safety leads to tangible financial benefits for organizations. The reduction of Workplace incidents results in the following:

-Decreased Costs: Healthier profit margins result from lower medical costs, workers' compensation claims, and legal expenditures. Businesses that put safety first often discover that their initial expenditure on safety measures result in long-term savings.

-Increased Productivity: A safe Workplace enhances employee morale and productivity, resulting in higher output levels and improved overall performance.

2. Enhanced Employee Retention
A strong safety culture contributes to higher employee retention rates. When employees feel safe and valued, they are more likely to stay with the organization, reducing turnover costs and fostering a more experienced workforce.

3. Stronger Team Dynamics
Safety fosters teamwork and collaboration. Employees who work together to identify and address safety concerns develop stronger relationships and trust, enhancing overall team dynamics.

4. Greater Adaptability to Change
Organizations that prioritize safety are better equipped to adapt to Workplace changes. A culture of safety encourages flexibility, innovation, and resilience, enabling organizations to navigate challenges and seize opportunities effectively.

5. Positive Organizational Culture
Ultimately, prioritizing safety creates a positive organizational culture where employees feel valued, respected, and engaged. This culture fosters a sense of belonging and commitment, driving performance and success.

-**Regular Audits:** Conduct regular safety audits to evaluate compliance with safety protocols and identify areas for improvement.

3. Leveraging Technology for Safety

Advancements in technology can significantly enhance Workplace safety. Organizations can leverage technology by:

- **Utilizing Safety Management Software:** Implement software solutions to track incidents, conduct audits, and analyze safety data to identify trends and areas for improvement.
- **Wearable Technology:** Consider using wearable technology that monitors employees' health and safety conditions, providing real-time feedback and alerts.

4. Fostering Open Communication

Open communication is crucial for addressing safety concerns. Organizations can promote open communication by:

- **Establishing Reporting Mechanisms:** Create anonymous reporting mechanisms where employees can share safety concerns without fear of retaliation.
- **Regular Safety Meetings:** Conduct regular safety meetings to discuss safety issues, share updates, and encourage employee feedback.

5. Recognizing and Rewarding Safety Initiatives

Recognizing and rewarding safety initiatives can motivate employees to prioritize safety. Organizations should:

- **Celebrate Safety Achievements:** Acknowledge teams and individuals who demonstrate exceptional commitment to safety through awards and public recognition.
- **Incentivize Participation:** Implement incentive programs that reward employees for participating in safety training, reporting hazards, or contributing to safety initiatives.

THE NEW FOUNDATIONS OF HUMAN PERFORMANCE

Decreased Organizational Resilience
Resilience refers to an organization's ability to adapt to challenges and thrive amid uncertainty. Ignoring safety can hinder resilience, resulting in:
- **Inability to Recover from Setbacks:** Organizations that do not prioritize safety may struggle to recover from incidents, leading to prolonged disruptions and financial losses.
- **Difficulty in Navigating Change:** A lack of emphasis on safety can make it harder for organizations to pivot in response to market changes or crises.

Strategies for Prioritizing Safety to Enhance Productivity
1. Cultivating a Safety Culture
Creating a culture that prioritizes safety involves:
- **Leadership Commitment:** Leadership must demonstrate a genuine commitment to safety through actions, communications, and investments in safety initiatives. This includes allocating resources for training, safety equipment, and employee well-being programs.
- **Employee Involvement:** Engage employees at all levels in safety initiatives. Please encourage them to share their ideas, experiences, and concerns related to safety. This involvement fosters a sense of ownership and responsibility for Workplace safety.
- **Regular Training and Education:** Provide ongoing training and education on safety protocols, risk assessment, and emergency preparedness. Regular training ensures that employees are equipped to identify and mitigate potential hazards.

2. Implementing Effective Safety Protocols
Organizations should establish and enforce safety protocols that address various risks. This includes:
- **Risk Assessments:** Conduct regular risk assessments to identify potential hazards and implement preventive measures.

-Clear Procedures: Develop procedures for reporting incidents, conducting investigations, and addressing safety concerns.

- **Loss of Business Opportunities:** Clients and customers are increasingly concerned about the ethical practices of their partner companies. A reputation for neglecting safety can deter potential clients and affect market competitiveness.
- **Public Scrutiny and Backlash:** Media coverage of Workplace incidents can damage an organization's reputation, leading to public scrutiny and loss of consumer trust. Rebuilding a tarnished reputation can take years and significant resources.

The Ripple Effect of Ignoring Safety
Impact on Customer Satisfaction
Safety impacts not only on employees but also customers. When organizations experience incidents or negative publicity related to safety, customer satisfaction can decline. For example:
- **Service Disruptions:** Workplace accidents can lead to service interruptions that affect customers. If a manufacturing plant experiences a significant incident, production may halt, impacting supply chains and customer deliveries.
- **Quality Concerns:** A workforce preoccupied with safety fears may produce lower-quality work. This can lead to customer dissatisfaction, damaging the brand's reputation.

Impaired Innovation
A culture that ignores safety stifles innovation. Employees who feel unsafe are less likely to take risks, share ideas, or collaborate effectively. This results in:
- **Decreased Creativity:** Innovation thrives in environments where employees feel comfortable expressing themselves. Safety concerns can inhibit creative thinking and problem-solving.
- **Resistance to Change:** Organizations that neglect safety may struggle to adapt to new technologies, processes, or practices, as employees fear that changes could introduce new risks.

Replacement Costs
When an employee is injured and unable to work, organizations often face the need to replace them. This can lead to:
- **Recruitment and Training Expenses:** Hiring and training new employees incur costs related to recruitment, onboarding, and skill development, which can be particularly burdensome in specialized roles.
- **Loss of Productivity:** New hires typically take time to reach the productivity levels of their more experienced counterparts, resulting in decreased output during the transition.

Indirect Costs of Neglecting Safety
Reduced Employee Morale
Neglecting safety can significantly impact employee morale. When workers perceive their Workplace as unsafe, they may experience:
- **Increased Anxiety and Stress:** Fear of injury or unsafe conditions can lead to heightened stress levels, which in turn diminish productivity and focus.
- **Disengagement:** Employees who feel unsafe are likelier to disengage from their work, leading to lower quality output and diminished performance.

Increased Absenteeism
Safety-related incidents can contribute to increased absenteeism. When employees are injured or experience stress due to unsafe conditions, they may miss work, resulting in:
- **Lost Productivity:** Absenteeism leads to disruptions in workflow and reduced overall productivity as teams may be left short-staffed.
- **Team Dynamics Disruption:** Frequent absenteeism can disrupt team dynamics and collaboration, affecting morale and performance.

Negative Impact on Organizational Reputation
Organizations that neglect safety may face significant reputational damage. This can have far-reaching consequences, including:

The Link Between Safety and Productivity

The connection between safety and productivity is profound. A safe Workplace fosters an environment where employees can focus on their tasks without the distractions or fears that stem from unsafe conditions. When safety is prioritized, organizations witness improved employee morale, lower absenteeism rates, and increased productivity. Conversely, neglecting safety can result in accidents, injuries, and other issues that undermine productivity.

The High Cost of Ignoring Safety
Direct Costs of Workplace Accidents
Medical Expenses

One of the most immediate costs associated with Workplace accidents is the medical expenses injured employees incur. These costs can accumulate rapidly, particularly in industries with high physical demands. Organizations may face:

- **Workers' Compensation Claims:** Injured employees often file claims for medical treatment and lost wages. These claims can place a significant financial burden on organizations, affecting cash flow and profitability.

- **Insurance Premium Increases:** A history of Workplace incidents can lead to increased insurance premiums, further straining an organization's financial resources.

Legal Costs

Ignoring safety can expose organizations to legal repercussions. If an employee is injured due to unsafe working conditions, the organization may face:

- **Litigation Costs:** Legal fees associated with defending against lawsuits can quickly add up, diverting resources from other essential business areas.

- **Settlements and Fines:** Organizations may be required to pay settlements or fines if found negligent regarding safety regulations. These costs can have long-term financial implications.

link, organizations can unlock their full potential and achieve sustainable success in today's competitive business environment.

The Cost of Ignoring Safety in Productivity

In today's high-stakes business environment, the drive for productivity often takes centre stage. Organizations strive for efficiency, aiming to maximize output while minimizing costs. However, Workplace safety still needs to be appreciated amid this relentless pursuit. Ignoring safety endangers employees and can severely affect organizational productivity and profitability. This chapter delves into the intricacies of the safety-performance link, highlighting the hidden costs associated with neglecting safety and the detrimental impact on productivity.

Understanding the Safety-Performance Relationship
The Definition of Safety in the Workplace
Workplace safety encompasses many practices to protect employees from physical, psychological, and emotional harm. It involves implementing protocols and measures to prevent accidents, injuries, and health hazards, creating an environment where employees can work without fear. Safety is not merely a regulatory requirement but a fundamental component of a thriving Workplace culture.

The Importance of Productivity
Productivity refers to the efficiency with which an organization transforms inputs—labour, materials, and capital—into outputs, such as products and services. High productivity is essential for organizational success; it drives profitability, enhances competitiveness, and improves customer satisfaction. However, productivity is not solely about the quantity of output but also the quality of work, employee engagement, and overall Workplace morale.

Case Study 2
DuPont's Safety-Driven Culture
DuPont, a science and technology company with a long history in chemical manufacturing, has built a global reputation for its strong safety culture. DuPont's safety philosophy, known as the DuPont Safety Management System, emphasizes that all accidents are preventable, and that safety is a shared responsibility.

DuPont has consistently demonstrated that a commitment to safety leads to better performance. The company's focus on safety has reduced injury rates, improved operational efficiency, and enhanced employee engagement. DuPont has found that its safest plants are also their most productive, further reinforcing the link between safety and performance.

By embedding safety into its organizational culture, DuPont has protected its workers, improved its financial performance, and maintained its position as a leader in the industry.

Conclusion: Safety as a Performance Multiplier
The evidence is clear: safety is not a cost but an investment that pays dividends in improved performance, productivity, and profitability. When organizations prioritize safety, they create an environment where employees can perform at their best, operations run smoothly, and long-term success is achievable.

Safety is the foundation of high-performing organizations. It enhances focus, fosters innovation, reduces costs, and attracts top talent. In short, safety is not a separate goal from performance, it is integral to achieving it.

In the chapters, we will explore specific strategies for integrating safety into every aspect of organizational performance, providing practical tools and insights for creating a culture where safety and performance go hand in hand. By embracing the safety-performance

THE NEW FOUNDATIONS OF HUMAN PERFORMANCE

workforce remains healthy, engaged, and capable of performing at high levels for years to come.

Companies that neglect safety may experience short-term gains in performance, but over time, the costs of accidents, turnover, legal fees, and reputational damage will erode their profitability and stability. On the other hand, organizations that invest in safety create a foundation for long-term success as they build a resilient workforce that can adapt to changes, innovate, and maintain high-performance levels.

Case Studies
Organizations That Exemplify the Safety-Performance Link
Case Study 1: Toyota's Commitment to Safety and Lean Performance

Toyota is a global automotive manufacturing leader known for emphasizing lean production and continuous improvement. At the heart of Toyota's success is its commitment to safety. Toyota has long recognized that safety and performance are inseparable and has integrated safety into every aspect of its operations.

At Toyota, safety is viewed as a critical component of quality. Employees are empowered to stop the production line if they identify a safety issue or quality concern, ensuring that problems are addressed immediately rather than allowing unsafe conditions to persist. This approach prevents accidents and enhances the overall quality of Toyota's products, leading to higher customer satisfaction and long-term success.

Toyota's focus on safety and performance has resulted in one of the world's most efficient and productive manufacturing systems, demonstrating that prioritizing safety does not hinder performance but drives it.

3. Safety Promotes Innovation and Continuous Improvement

A safe Workplace encourages a culture of continuous improvement, where employees feel empowered to speak up about potential hazards and suggest solutions. This culture of openness and collaboration fosters innovation, as workers are encouraged to think critically about their work processes and identify ways to improve efficiency, quality, and safety.

In contrast, an unsafe Workplace often stifles innovation. When workers are afraid to report hazards or suggest changes for fear of reprisal or blame, problems go unaddressed, and opportunities for improvement are missed. By promoting a safety culture, organizations create an environment where employees are encouraged to think creatively and are supported in implementing changes that enhance safety and performance.

4. Safety Improves Employee Retention and Attracts Top Talent

In industries where safety is a top concern—such as construction, healthcare, and manufacturing, employees increasingly seek organizations prioritizing their well-being. Companies with vital safety records are more likely to attract and retain top talent, as workers want to be part of organizations that value their safety and provide a supportive environment.

In addition to reducing productivity, high turnover rates brought on by safety concerns also raise the expense of recruiting and onboarding new staff. Conversely, when workers feel safe and secure, they are more inclined to remain with the company, which lowers turnover and produces a more skilled and knowledgeable staff.

5. Safety Contributes to Long-Term Sustainability

Sustainability is not only about environmental impact; it's also about creating organizations that can thrive over the long term. Prioritizing safety is a critical component of sustainability, as it ensures that the

THE NEW FOUNDATIONS OF HUMAN PERFORMANCE

The Safety-Performance Link: Why Safety Drives Performance
Safety and performance connect beyond preventing accidents or complying with regulations. A Workplace that prioritizes safety creates an environment where employees can perform at their best and the organization can operate more efficiently and effectively. Here are several vital reasons why safety is integral to performance:

1. Safety Reduces Downtime and Increases Efficiency
Workplace accidents lead to significant downtime as operations are halted to address the incident, investigate its cause, and implement corrective actions. Downtime is the enemy of performance. Every minute that production is halted due to a safety incident represents lost time, money, and resources.

When safety is prioritized, fewer accidents occur, meaning there is less need for unscheduled downtime. As a result, work processes flow more smoothly, deadlines are met, and productivity is maximized. Additionally, by proactively addressing potential hazards, organizations can prevent equipment damage and avoid costly repairs, reducing downtime and operational delays.

2. Safety Enhances Employee Focus and Engagement
Employees who feel safe and support are more focused and engaged. Workers can direct their energy and attention toward their tasks without concern for their physical safety, leading to higher performance levels.

In contrast, when safety is compromised, employees are more likely to be distracted by concerns about their well-being, resulting in mistakes, reduced productivity, and even more accidents. Safety provides a foundation of security that allows employees to perform at their highest potential, leading to better outcomes for both individuals and the organization.

lead to financial losses, reputational damage, and even criminal charges in severe cases.

4. Damage to Equipment and Property: Accidents often damage expensive machinery, tools, or the work site. Repairing or replacing damaged property can delay projects, increase costs, and reduce the team's productivity.

Indirect Costs of Safety Incidents
1. Lost Productivity: The entire workflow is disrupted when an employee is injured. The injured worker must take time off to recover, and colleagues may need to pick up the slack, often leading to delays, mistakes, and stress within the team. Depending on the severity of the incident, operations may have to halt altogether, causing significant disruptions to the business.

2. Reduced Employee Morale: A Workplace perceived as unsafe can decrease employee morale and engagement. Workers who feel unsafe are less likely to be motivated and productive. High-stress environments where employees are worried about their physical safety foster anxiety and burnout, further diminishing performance.

3. Turnover and Training Costs: When safety incidents occur frequently, employees may choose to leave the organization, leading to higher turnover rates. Recruitment, hiring, and training new employees come at a substantial cost in terms of time and resources. Moreover, inexperienced workers are often at greater risk of injury, creating a cycle of safety incidents.

4. Reputational Damage: In today's world, where transparency and corporate responsibility are increasingly valued, organizations known for unsafe working conditions risk losing their customers, partners, and investors. A single incident can tarnish a company's reputation, leading to long-term financial losses and difficulties attracting top talent.

THE NEW FOUNDATIONS OF HUMAN PERFORMANCE

On the other hand, performance was often measured solely by outputs: How much product was delivered? How many tasks were completed each time? What were the cost savings in labour or materials? In such environments, the relationship between safety and performance was, at best, ignored and, at worst, considered antagonistic.

However, this mindset has changed drastically over the last few decades. With advances in safety science, ergonomics, and human performance, organizations realized that an unsafe Workplace is not only morally irresponsible but also financially and operationally unsustainable. Safety incidents can have devastating effects on productivity, morale, and the overall performance of the workforce. Today, leading organizations understand that safety is not just compatible with performance, it is fundamental to achieving it.

The Cost of Unsafe Workplaces

The costs of unsafe workplaces are multifaceted. When safety is compromised, the consequences ripple throughout the organization, affecting not just the individuals involved but also the company's bottom line and long-term success.

Direct Costs of Safety Incidents

1. Medical Expenses: Workplace injuries, accidents, and illnesses often result in significant medical costs, including immediate emergency care, surgeries, rehabilitation, and long-term care. For companies that provide health benefits, these costs can stagger.

2. Workers' Compensation: In many countries, employers must provide workers' compensation to injured employees. The more accidents a company has, the higher its insurance premiums rise. This can lead to a significant increase in operational costs over time.

3. Legal Fees and Fines: Companies that do not comply with safety regulations face potential lawsuits, penalties, and fines from regulatory bodies. The legal ramifications of neglecting safety can

Part II

Modern Approaches to Workplace Safety

Chapter 5

The Safety-Performance Link

Why Safety Is Integral to Performance

In many organizations, safety and performance are often viewed as separate goals associated with compliance and risk management, while performance is linked to productivity, efficiency, and profitability. However, the reality is that safety and performance are deeply intertwined. The notion that one can be achieved at the expense of the other is flawed and can lead to disastrous consequences. In this chapter, we explore the integral connection between safety and performance, demonstrating why a culture of safety is not just a regulatory requirement but a critical driver of organizational success.

The Historical Divide Between Safety and Performance

Safety has often been seen as a burden, an additional cost, or a checklist item that slows production and reduces efficiency. This mentality, deeply rooted in many industries, comes from a time when the main goal was to get the job done as quickly and cheaply as possible, regardless of the risks involved. For many years, there was a tacit understanding in specific sectors—construction, manufacturing, and energy—that danger was simply part of the job. Workers were expected to take risks, and injuries were viewed as an unfortunate but inevitable byproduct of labour.

THE NEW FOUNDATIONS OF HUMAN PERFORMANCE

As we explore the facets of emotional intelligence in the Workplace, we will explore practical strategies for integrating these concepts into organizational practices, ensuring that emotional intelligence and Resilience become cornerstones of Workplace culture. Together, we can create environments where individuals thrive, adapt, and succeed in adversity, ultimately driving long-term success for employees and organizations.

2. Increased Productivity

Resilient individuals maintain focus and motivation, leading to increased productivity. They are less likely to be derailed by setbacks and more inclined to pursue their goals with determination.

3. Lower Rates of Burnout

Building Resilience reduces the risk of burnout among employees. Resilient individuals are better equipped to manage stress and maintain their well-being, leading to a healthier workforce.

4. Enhanced Organizational Adaptability

Resilient organizations are more adaptable to change. By fostering a culture of Resilience, organizations can navigate challenges and capitalize on opportunities in a rapidly changing environment.

5. Improved Overall Well-being

Fostering Resilience contributes to the overall wellbeing of employees. Individuals who can manage stress and adapt to challenges experience excellent mental and emotional health, leading to improved quality of life.

Conclusion: The Path to Long-Term Success

Emotional intelligence and Resilience are essential for long-term success in the Workplace in an unpredictable world. Organizations can create a supportive environment that nurtures growth and development by understanding the interplay between EI and Resilience.

Organizations can cultivate Resilience within their workforce by fostering a culture of support, promoting self-awareness, teaching stress management techniques, building problem-solving skills, and encouraging positive relationships. The long-term benefits of building Resilience are profound, impacting employee engagement, productivity, and overall well-being.

- **Facilitating Collaborative Problem-Solving:** Create opportunities for team-based problem-solving sessions. Collaborative efforts can lead to innovative solutions and foster Resilience within teams.
- **Providing Resources for Professional Development:** Offer training programs focusing on critical thinking and problem-solving skills. Equipping employees with these tools enhances their ability to navigate challenges effectively.

5. Promoting Positive Relationships and Teamwork

Building strong relationships among team members is essential for Resilience. Organizations can encourage positive relationships by:

- **Organizing Team-Building Activities:** Facilitate team-building exercises that promote trust, communication, and collaboration. Strong relationships can serve as a buffer against stress.

- **Encouraging Cross-Functional Collaboration:** Foster collaboration between departments to build organizational connections. Cross-functional teams can bring diverse perspectives and enhance problem-solving capabilities.

- **Recognizing Diversity and Inclusion:** Promote a culture of diversity and inclusion where all employees feel valued and respected. Inclusive environments foster positive relationships and contribute to Resilience.

The Long-Term Benefits of Building Resilience
1. Sustained Employee Engagement

Organizations that prioritize resilience experience higher levels of employee engagement. Resilient employees are more committed to their roles and contribute positively to the Workplace culture.

THE NEW FOUNDATIONS OF HUMAN PERFORMANCE

- **Implementing Training Programs:** Offer workshops on emotional intelligence and self-awareness. Training can equip employees with tools to recognize their emotions and understand their impact on behaviour.

- **Encouraging Journaling:** Promote journaling as a reflective practice. Employees can document their emotional responses to challenges, helping them gain insights into their feelings and triggers.

- **Facilitating Feedback Mechanisms:** Create opportunities for regular feedback where employees can reflect on their performance and emotional responses. Constructive feedback fosters self-awareness and personal growth.

3. Teaching Stress Management Techniques

Effective stress management is critical for Resilience. Organizations can provide resources and training on stress management techniques, including:

- **Mindfulness and Relaxation Techniques:** Introduce mindfulness practices like meditation or deep-breathing exercises. These techniques can help employees manage stress and enhance focus.

- **Time Management Training:** Offer training on time management strategies to help employees prioritize tasks and reduce overwhelming feelings.

- **Encouraging Work-Life Balance:** Promote a healthy work-life balance by encouraging employees to take breaks, use vacation time, and set boundaries between work and personal life.

4. Building Problem-Solving Skills

Resilience is closely tied to practical problem-solving skills. Organizations can foster these skills by:

- **Encouraging a Growth Mindset:** Promote the idea that challenges are opportunities for learning and growth. Encourage employees to view setbacks as valuable experiences rather than failures.

regulation enables them to approach problems rather than succumb to panic or frustration.

3. Motivation: Emotionally intelligent individuals are intrinsically motivated, allowing them to stay focused on their objectives despite setbacks. This motivation fuels Resilience and perseverance.

4. Empathy: Understanding the emotions of others fosters solid relationships and provides a support network during difficult times. Empathy also promotes collaboration and teamwork, which are essential for navigating challenges.

5. Social Skills: Strong social skills enable individuals to communicate effectively and build positive relationships. These connections can serve as a buffer against stress, enhancing Resilience.

Building Resilience Through Emotional Intelligence
Strategies for Cultivating Resilience in the Workplace
1. Fostering a Culture of Support
Creating a supportive work environment is fundamental to building Resilience. Organizations can foster a culture of support by:
- **Encouraging Open Communication:** Promote a culture where employees feel comfortable discussing their challenges and seeking help. Open dialogue can reduce feelings of isolation and foster a sense of community.
- **Providing Mentorship Programs:** Implement mentorship initiatives that connect less experienced employees with seasoned mentors. Mentors can offer guidance, support, and encouragement, helping mentees navigate challenges.
- **Recognizing Achievements:** Celebrate individual and team successes, no matter how small. Recognition reinforces a sense of accomplishment and encourages Resilience.

2. Promoting Self-Awareness and Self-Reflection
Encouraging self-awareness and self-reflection is essential for building Resilience. Organizations can support this by:

THE NEW FOUNDATIONS OF HUMAN PERFORMANCE

4. Optimism: Resilient employees maintain a positive outlook, viewing problems as opportunities for growth rather than insurmountable barriers.

The Importance of Resilience in the Workplace
1. Enhancing Performance: Resilient employees are better equipped to handle stress and pressure, improving job performance and productivity.

2. Reducing Turnover: Organizations that foster resilience experience lower employee turnover rates. Resilient individuals are likelier to stay devoted to their roles, even during challenging times.

3. Promoting Employee Well-being: Resilience contributes to mental and emotional well-being, decreasing the risk of burnout and promoting overall health.

4. Fostering Innovation: Resilient teams are more open to experimentation and learning from failure. This adaptability fosters a culture of innovation within the organization.

The Intersection of Emotional Intelligence and Resilience
How Emotional Intelligence Enhances Resilience
Emotional intelligence plays a vital role in building Resilience. Individuals with high EI possess the skills to navigate stress and adversity effectively. The critical components of emotional intelligence—self-awareness, self-regulation, motivation, empathy, and social skills—contribute to Resilience in several ways:

1. Self-awareness: Individuals who understand their emotions are better equipped to recognize when they feel overwhelmed or stressed. This awareness allows them to implement coping strategies proactively.

2. Self-Regulation: High EI individuals can manage their emotional responses, maintaining composure in the face of challenges. Self-

Building Resilience for Long-Term Success

In the ever-evolving landscape of modern work environments, Resilience has emerged as a crucial competency for individuals and organizations. Resilience, the ability to recover quickly from difficulties, is not merely a personal trait but a vital component of emotional intelligence (EI). Building Resilience becomes essential for long-term success as workplaces face unprecedented challenges—from economic fluctuations to technological disruptions. This chapter delves into the relationship between emotional intelligence and Resilience, exploring how organizations can cultivate both to foster a thriving workforce.

Understanding Resilience in the Workplace
What is Resilience?

Resilience is adapting to stress, adversity, and change while maintaining psychological well-being. It involves a merger of mental, emotional, and behavioural flexibility that allows individuals to bounce back from setbacks. Resilience is not static; it can be developed and strengthened over time through intentional practices and experiences.

In the Workplace, Resilience manifests in various ways, including:

1. Adaptability: Resilient employees can adjust to new situations, whether changing job roles, adopting new technologies, or navigating organizational changes.

2. Stress Management: Resilient individuals effectively manage stress, utilizing coping strategies that promote well-being and prevent burnout.

3. Problem-Solving: Resilience fosters a proactive approach to challenges, enabling individuals to identify solutions rather than dwelling on obstacles.

THE NEW FOUNDATIONS OF HUMAN PERFORMANCE

4. Increased Job Satisfaction

Employees who can manage their emotions effectively often experience greater job satisfaction. They feel more in control of their work, creating a sense of fulfilment and engagement.

5. A Culture of Support

Organizations prioritizing emotional intelligence and regulation foster a culture of support and well-being. This culture contributes to employee retention, satisfaction, and overall success.

Conclusion: Harnessing the Power of Emotional Intelligence

Managing emotions in high-pressure situations is essential for success in today's fast-paced and often unpredictable Workplace. Emotional intelligence helps navigate challenges, enhance decision-making, and foster positive relationships.

By investing in emotional intelligence development, organizations can cultivate a resilient, empathetic workforce capable of thriving in high-pressure environments. The strategies outlined in this chapter—self-awareness, stress reduction, self-regulation, empathy, and Resilience—provide a roadmap for individuals and organizations to enhance their emotional intelligence.

As we continue our journey through human performance, we will explore how emotional intelligence intertwines with cognitive performance and decision-making, further emphasizing its importance in creating a safe and effective Workplace culture.

- **Encouraging a Growth Mindset:** Foster growth thinking within the organization by promoting the idea that challenges are opportunities for learning and development. This mindset encourages individuals to approach high-pressure situations with optimism.
- **Providing Resources for Mental Health:** Ensure employees access mental health resources, including counselling and support programs. This support can help persons cope with stress and develop Resilience.
- **Celebrating Successes:** Recognize individual and team successes, even in high-pressure situations. Acknowledging achievements promotes a sense of accomplishment and reinforces Resilience.

The Benefits of Managing Emotions in High-Pressure Situations
Implementing effective emotional management strategies can yield numerous benefits for both employees and organizations:
1. Improved Performance
Employees who manage their emotions effectively are likely to perform at their best, even in challenging situations. They can make enlightened decisions and achieve better results by maintaining focus and clarity.

2. Enhanced Team Dynamics
Teams that practice emotional intelligence and manage their emotions collaboratively create a positive work environment. This leads to enhanced communication, increased trust, and stronger relationships among team members.

3. Reduced Conflict
Managing emotions can help diffuse tensions and prevent conflicts from escalating. Self-aware and empathetic employees are better equipped to navigate disagreements and find common ground.

3. Developing Self-Regulation Skills

Self-regulation is essential for managing emotions effectively. Here are some strategies to enhance self-regulation:

- **Identifying Triggers:** Encourage employees to identify their emotional triggers and develop procedures for managing their responses. This may involve creating a plan for how to respond to specific stressors.

- **Practicing Emotional Reappraisal:** Teach employees the skill of emotional reappraisal, which involves reframing negative thoughts to promote more constructive emotional responses. For example, instead of viewing a challenging project as overwhelming, one might see it as an opportunity for growth.

- **Implementing Coping Strategies:** Provide employees with a toolkit of coping strategies when faced with high-pressure situations. Techniques may include deep breathing, visualization, or positive affirmations.

4. Fostering Empathy and Social Skills

Cultivating empathy and social skills is crucial for navigating high-pressure situations. Organizations can promote these skills by:

- **Encouraging Active Listening:** Train employees in active listening techniques to foster better understanding and communication. Active listening encourages empathy and helps individuals respond thoughtfully to others' emotions.

- **Building Collaborative Teams:** Create opportunities for team-building activities that enhance collaboration and trust. Strong relationships can serve as a buffer during high-pressure situations.

- **Modeling Empathy in Leadership:** Leaders should model empathetic behaviour, demonstrating understanding and support for their team members. This sets a positive example and fosters a culture of empathy.

5. Developing Resilience

Resilience is the ability to recover from adversity. Building Resilience can help individuals manage emotions more effectively during high-pressure situations:

through practice and intention. Here are several effective strategies for managing emotions in high-pressure situations:

1. Cultivating Self-Awareness

Developing self-consciousness is the foundation of emotional intelligence. Here are some practical techniques:

- **Journaling:** Encourage employees to keep a journal where they reflect on their emotional responses to daily challenges. This practice can help individuals identify patterns and triggers, enhancing self-awareness.
- **Mindfulness Practices:** Implement mindfulness techniques like meditation or deep-breathing exercises. Mindfulness promotes present-moment awareness and allows individuals to observe their emotions without judgment.
- **Feedback Mechanisms:** Create a feedback culture where employees feel comfortable discussing their emotional experiences. Constructive feedback can enhance self-awareness and foster personal growth.

2. Implementing Stress-Reduction Techniques

Managing stress is crucial for maintaining emotional balance in high-pressure situations. Organizations can support stress reduction by:

-**Providing Training:** Offer training sessions focused on stress management techniques, including time management, prioritization, and relaxation exercises.
- **Encouraging Breaks:** Promote the importance of regular breaks during high-pressure periods. Short breaks can help employees recharge and regain focus.
- **Creating a Supportive Environment:** Foster a supportive Workplace culture that encourages open discussions about stress and mental health. Providing resources for mental well-being can significantly reduce stress levels.

impulsively rather than thoughtfully, leading to suboptimal decisions.

2. Effect on Team Dynamics: Stressful situations can strain relationships. Misunderstandings and conflicts may escalate, negatively impacting teamwork and collaboration.

3. Influence on Performance: Effectively managing emotions can significantly influence performance outcomes. Individuals who regulate their emotions are more likely to maintain focus and clarity, leading to better results.

The Role of Emotional Intelligence in Managing Pressure
Emotional intelligence serves as a buffer in high-pressure situations. By applying EI skills, individuals can navigate challenges more effectively, enhancing their performance and maintaining a positive Workplace atmosphere.

1. Self-Awareness and Self-Regulation: Recognizing one's emotional state is the first step in managing emotions. Self-aware individuals can identify when they feel overwhelmed and employ self-regulation strategies to regain control.

2. Empathy and Social Skills: Understanding colleagues' emotional states allows individuals to respond compassionately and constructively. Employing social skills can diffuse tensions and foster collaboration.

3. Motivation as a Driving Force: In high-pressure situations, intrinsic motivation can provide the necessary drive to push through challenges. Individuals who are passionate about their work are more likely to remain focused and resilient.

Strategies for Managing Emotions in High-Pressure Situations
While some individuals may naturally possess vital emotional intelligence, it is an expertise that can be cultivated and developed

5. Social Skills: Expertise in managing relationships and building systems, as well as finding common ground and building finding common ground and building rapport.

The Importance of Emotional Intelligence in the Workplace

Emotional intelligence is vital for individual and organizational success. Research has shown that high EI is linked to enhanced job performance, better leadership, and improved teamwork.

1. Enhancing Communication: Emotionally intelligent individuals communicate more effectively, reducing misunderstandings and fostering collaboration.

2. Improving Team Dynamics: Teams with high emotional intelligence demonstrate more robust collaboration and problem-solving capabilities. Empathy fosters trust, making it easier to address conflicts.

3. Supporting Leadership Effectiveness: Leaders with high emotional intelligence can influence and motivate their teams, creating a culture of engagement and accountability.

4. Boosting Employee Well-being: Employees with high EI are generally more resilient and better equipped to handle stress, improving mental health and job satisfaction.

Managing Emotions in High-Pressure Situations
The Nature of High-Pressure Situations

High-pressure situations can arise in various Workplace contexts, from tight deadlines to critical decision-making scenarios in high-stakes healthcare, emergency services, and corporate settings. These situations often elicit strong emotions, including stress, anxiety, frustration, and even fear.

1. Impact on Decision-Making: High-pressure environments can cloud judgment. When emotions run high, individuals may react

Managing Emotions in High-Pressure Situations

In the playable terrain of today's Workplace, where challenges and uncertainties are constant, the ability to manage emotions in high-pressure situations has emerged as a crucial skill. Emotional intelligence (EI) is a catchword and a competency that can significantly influence decision-making, teamwork, and overall

Workplace culture. This chapter explores the essence of emotional intelligence, mainly its role in managing emotions during stressful situations, and offers practical strategies for cultivating this invaluable skill within organizations.

Understanding Emotional Intelligence
What is Emotional Intelligence?

Emotional intelligence refers to the ability to recognize, understand, and manage one's own emotions as well as the emotions of others. Daniel Goleman, a prominent psychologist, identifies five key components of emotional intelligence:

1. Self-awareness: The ability to recognize and understand one's emotions, strengths, weaknesses, and values.

2. Self-Regulation: The capacity to control or redirect uncontrollable emotions and impulses and adjust to changing circumstances.

3. Motivation: A drive to achieve for the sake of achievement, including a passion for work and a propensity to pursue goals with energy and persistence.

4. Empathy is understanding other people's emotional makeup and treating them according to their emotional reactions.

3. Increased Productivity and Performance

Emotional regulation can enhance focus and decision-making and increase productivity and performance. Employees who manage their emotions are more likely to stay occupied, motivated, and focused on their tasks.

4. Stronger Leadership

Leaders with solid emotional regulation skills are better equipped to inspire and motivate their teams. They create a positive work philosophy that encourages employee development, engagement, and job satisfaction.

5. A Safer Work Environment

Emotional regulation is essential for ensuring safety in high-risk environments. Employees who can manage their emotions successfully are less likely to make impulsive decisions that could compromise safety protocols.

Conclusion: The Power of Emotional Regulation in the Workplace

Emotional intelligence, particularly the ability to regulate emotions, is critical to Workplace success. Individuals can enhance their focus, decision-making, and interpersonal relationships by developing emotional regulation skills.

Organizations prioritizing emotional regulation can create a supportive work environment fostering well-being, collaboration, and productivity. By investing in training, promoting open communication, and modelling emotional regulation at all levels, organizations can harness the power of emotional intelligence to drive success.

As we move forward in this book, we will continue to explore how emotional intelligence intersects with cognitive performance and decision-making, highlighting the importance of a holistic approach to human performance in the Workplace.

- **Mindfulness Practices:** Initiate mindfulness practices, such as meditation or breathing exercises, to help employees manage stress and cultivate emotional awareness.
- **Time Management Training:** Provide training on time management techniques to help employees reduce stress associated with overwhelming workloads. By managing their time effectively, workers can create space for emotional regulation.

5. Model Emotional Regulation at All Levels
Leaders play a significant role in shaping Workplace culture and influencing employee behaviour. Leaders can set a positive example for their groups by modelling emotional regulation. Leaders should:
-**Demonstrate Self-Regulation:** Exhibit self-regulation in their emotional responses. Leaders can inspire team confidence by staying calm and composed in challenging situations.
- **Encourage Vulnerability:** Leaders should encourage open discussions about emotions and vulnerability. By normalizing conversations about emotions, leaders create an environment where employees feel safe to express their feelings.

The Benefits of Emotional Regulation in the Workplace
Implementing emotional regulation strategies can yield numerous benefits for both employees and organizations.

1. Enhanced Employee Well-being
Emotional regulation promotes employee well-being by helping individuals manage stress, cope with challenges, and maintain a positive outlook. Employees who practice emotional regulation are less likely to experience burnout and are more resilient in adversity.

2. Improved Team Dynamics
Teams with members who practice emotional regulation are often more cohesive and collaborative. Emotional regulation fosters open communication and empathy, allowing team members to work together more effectively and resolve conflicts constructively.

- **Feedback Mechanisms**: Implement regular feedback sessions where workers can receive positive feedback from peers and supervisors. This feedback can enhance self-awareness and provide insights into how emotions impact interactions.

2. Provide Training and Development Opportunities

Training programs focused on emotional intelligence and regulation can equip employees with the expertise to manage their emotions effectively. Organizations should consider offering:

-**Workshops and Seminars:** Organize workshops on developing emotional intelligence and regulation skills. These sessions can include practical exercises and role-playing scenarios.

-**Coaching and Mentoring:** Provide access to coaching or mentoring programs where employees can receive personalized guidance on emotional regulation strategies.

3. Promote a Supportive Work Environment

Creating a supportive work environment is necessary for encouraging emotional regulation. Organizations can foster this environment by:

-**Encouraging Open Communication:** Foster open communication where workers feel comfortable expressing their emotions and concerns. This can help reduce feelings of separation and promote collaboration.

- **Providing Resources:** Offer resources for mental health and well-being, such as Employee Assistance Programs (EAPs) or access to counselling services. These resources can help employees manage their emotions effectively.

4. Implement Stress Management Techniques

Teaching employees stress management techniques can enhance their ability to regulate emotions in high-pressure situations. Consider implementing:

2. Enhancing Decision-Making: Emotions can significantly impact decision-making processes. High levels of emotional arousal may cloud judgment and lead to impulsive choices. By regulating emotions, individuals can approach decisions more rationally, considering all relevant factors.

3. Building Strong Relationships: Emotional regulation promotes healthier interpersonal relationships. When individuals can manage their emotions, they are more likely to respond empathetically to others, fostering trust and collaboration.

4. Improving Stress Management: Effective emotional regulation helps individuals cope more effectively. By recognizing and addressing emotions as they arise, workers can reduce the impact of stress on their well-being and performance.

5. Promoting Resilience: Individuals who practice emotional regulation are often more resilient in adversity. They can recover from setbacks, adapt to change, and maintain a positive outlook, contributing to Workplace morale.

Strategies for Developing Emotional Regulation Skills
While emotional regulation is a skill that some individuals may naturally possess, it can also be developed and strengthened over time. Organizations can implement various strategies to promote emotional regulation among employees.

1. Promote Self-Awareness
Developing self-awareness is the first step toward effective emotional regulation. Organizations can encourage self-awareness through:
- **Reflective Practices:** Encourage employees to practice reflective practices like journaling or mindfulness exercises. These activities can help individuals identify their emotional triggers and patterns.

2. Enhanced Collaboration: Teams with emotionally intelligent members are more likely to collaborate successfully. Empathy and social skills contribute to a positive team environment where members feel appreciated and supported.

3. Effective Conflict Resolution: Emotional intelligence enables individuals to navigate conflicts constructively. By recognizing the emotional dynamics at play, individuals can address issues calmly and seek resolutions that satisfy all parties involved.

4. Increased Job Satisfaction: Employees with high emotional intelligence often experience greater job satisfaction. They are more resilient in the face of challenges and better manage stress, leading to improved well-being and engagement.

5. Leadership Effectiveness: Leaders with high emotional intelligence can inspire and motivate their teams. They create a supportive environment that fosters open communication and encourages employee development.

The Role of Emotional Regulation
What is Emotional Regulation?
Emotional regulation is a subset of emotional intelligence that focuses on managing one's emotions effectively. It involves recognizing when emotions arise and using strategies to modify emotional responses healthily and constructively. Emotional regulation is essential for maintaining composure in high-stress situations, making rational decisions, and fostering positive relationships.

The Importance of Emotional Regulation in the Workplace
1. Maintaining Professionalism: Emotional regulation allows individuals to maintain professionalism in challenging situations. By managing their emotional responses, employees can communicate more effectively and avoid reactive behaviours that could lead to conflict.

identify how these emotions impact their behaviour and decision-making.

2. Self-regulation is the capacity to manage one's emotions healthily, control impulses, and adapt to changing circumstances. Self-regulation allows people to respond thoughtfully rather than reactively to emotional triggers.

3. Motivation: A drive to achieve personal and professional goals, often fueled by intrinsic motivation. People with high emotional intelligence are generally more motivated and optimistic, even when facing challenges.

4. Empathy is the capacity to recognize and share the feelings of others. Empathetic individuals can connect with their colleagues, demonstrate compassion, and respond appropriately to the emotions of others.

5. Social Skills: Building and maintaining healthy relationships, communicating effectively, and navigating social complexities. Solid social skills enable individuals to work collaboratively, resolve conflicts, and influence others positively.

The Significance of Emotional Intelligence in the Work Environment
Emotional intelligence plays a pivotal role in Workplace dynamics. Studies have shown that people with high emotional intelligence tend to be more effective leaders, better communicators, and more successful in their careers. Here are some primary reasons why emotional intelligence is essential in the Workplace:

1. Improved Communication: High emotional intelligence fosters better communication. Individuals who can recognize their own emotions and the emotions of others are better equipped to express their thoughts clearly and respond to others effectively.

Chapter 4

Emotional Intelligence in the Workplace

The Power of Emotional Regulation

In an era where technical skills and knowledge are often at the forefront of professional development, emotional intelligence (EI) is critical to Workplace success. Emotional intelligence encloses the ability to recognize, understand, and control one's own emotions and the emotions of others. Emotional regulation is at the heart of this concept, a fundamental skill that can significantly impact interpersonal relationships, decision-making, and overall Workplace effectiveness.

In this chapter, we will survey emotional intelligence and its intense matches in the Workplace, focusing on emotional regulation. We will delve into how emotional regulation can enhance individual and team performance, its role in leadership, and strategies for developing this essential skill. By understanding the power of emotional regulation, organizations can foster a culture that promotes well-being, collaboration, and success.

Understanding Emotional Intelligence
What is Emotional Intelligence?
Emotional intelligence, frequently shortened as EI or EQ (emotional quotient), is the ability to acknowledge, understand, and manage emotions—both one's own and those of others. Daniel Goleman, a pioneer in the field, identified five essential components of emotional intelligence:

1. Self-awareness: The ability to recognize and understand one's emotions, strengths, weaknesses, values, and motivations. Self-aware individuals are more in tune with their feelings and can

As we continue exploring cognitive performance and decision-making in this book, we will delve into the impact of stress on decision-making, further highlighting the importance of fostering cognitive skills for a thriving Workplace.

- **Promoting Work-Life Balance:** Inspiring workers to maintain a healthy work-life balance can reduce stress and fatigue. Flexible work arrangements, regular breaks, and promoting self-care practices can contribute to overall well-being.

4. Leverage Technology

Technology can play a significant role in enhancing focus and attention in high-risk environments. Organizations can utilize various tools to support employees:

- **Collaboration Tools:** Implementing collaboration tools can streamline communication and reduce the need for face-to-face interactions, minimizing distractions.
- **Attention-Enhancing Software:** Various software applications can help employees improve their focus and attention. For example, apps blocking distracting websites or tracking time spent on tasks can enhance productivity.
- **Wearable Technology:** Wearable devices that monitor stress levels and provide feedback can help employees manage their focus more effectively. These devices can alert individuals when their stress levels become too high, prompting them to take breaks or practice relaxation techniques.

Conclusion: Cultivating Focus and Attention for Safety and Efficiency

Improving focus and attention in high-risk environments is crucial for enhancing cognitive performance and ensuring Workplace safety. Understanding the mental mechanisms that underpin these skills and the factors that can hinder them is critical to developing effective strategies for improvement.

Organizations can create a Workplace that promotes focus and attention by optimizing the work environment, implementing training programs, fostering a supportive culture, and leveraging technology. They empower employees to make informed decisions, navigate challenges effectively, and contribute to a safer and more efficient work environment.

THE NEW FOUNDATIONS OF HUMAN PERFORMANCE

- **Declutter Workspaces:** Encourage employees to maintain organized workspaces. Reducing visual clutter can enhance focus and facilitate efficient task completion.
- **Create Designated Quiet Areas:** Providing quiet areas for employees to focus on complex tasks can help mitigate distractions and improve concentration.

2. Implement Training Programs

Training is crucial for improving cognitive performance in high-risk environments. Organizations should consider the following:

- **Focus and Attention Training:** Implement programs that teach employees techniques to enhance focus and attention. Techniques such as mindfulness meditation, concentration exercises, and cognitive games can be beneficial.
- **Stress Management Training:** Providing employees with tools to manage stress can improve their ability to focus. Stress management approaches, such as deep breathing exercises and time management skills, can help employees cope with high-pressure situations.
- **Simulation Training:** Using simulation training to replicate high-stress scenarios can prepare employees for real-life challenges. This type of training can enhance decision-making skills and improve focus under pressure.

3. Foster a Supportive Culture

Creating a supportive Workplace culture can enhance focus and attention among employees. Organizations can promote the art of safety by:

- **Encouraging Open Communication**: promote an environment where workers feel comfortable discussing challenges and seeking support. Open communication can help alleviate stress and improve focus.
- **Recognizing and Rewarding Focused Work:** Acknowledge and reward employees with solid focus and attention. Recognition can reinforce positive behaviours and motivate others to improve their cognitive performance.

2. Stress and Fatigue

Stress and fatigue can significantly impair cognitive performance. Stress hormones can inhibit the brain's ability to focus on high-pressure situations, while fatigue diminishes cognitive capacity.

Stress: High stress levels can lead to hyperarousal, where the brain is flooded with information but struggles to process it effectively. This can result in a narrowed focus that neglects essential details.

- **Fatigue:** Fatigue can severely impair attention and cognitive performance. Sleep deprivation reduces the brain's ability to concentrate, leading to lapses in judgment and decision-making.

3. Mental Health

Mental health matters, such as anxiety and depression, can affect focus and attention. Employees with mental health challenges may find it difficult to concentrate on tasks, increasing the likelihood of errors.

4. Lack of Training and Preparation

Inadequate training can leave employees ill-equipped to handle high-risk situations, impairing their ability to focus and make sound decisions. Proper training ensures that employees know protocols and can pay for critical tasks.

Strategies for Improving Focus and Attention

Organizations can implement various strategies to enhance focus and attention among employees in high-risk environments. These strategies can help mitigate distractions, reduce cognitive Load, and foster a culture of safety.

1. Optimize the Workplace

Creating a conducive Workplace is essential for improving focus and attention. Organizations can take several steps to optimize the workspace:

- **Minimize Noise:** Implement soundproofing measures or provide noise-cancelling headphones to reduce ambient noise. This can help employees concentrate better in noisy environments.

Extraneous Load refers to distractions or irrelevant information that can impede focus. For instance, loud noises or interruptions from colleagues can create an extraneous load.

- Germane Load: This Load contributes to learning and is essential for developing skills. Training programs that enhance relevant skills can increase germane Load while reducing intrinsic and extraneous loads.

Balancing cognitive Load is critical for improving focus and attention in high-risk environments. Organizations must strive to reduce extraneous loads while ensuring that intrinsic loads are manageable.

Factors Affecting Focus and Attention in High-Risk Environments
Several factors can hinder focus and attention in high-risk environments. Understanding these elements is critical to developing effective strategies for improvement.

1. Environmental Distractions
The physical surroundings play an important role in determining focus and attention. High-risk environments often have numerous distractions, including noise, visual clutter, and multiple stimuli.

Noise Pollution: Ambient noise in construction sites or factories can interfere with concentration. Workers may need help hearing critical verbal instructions or alarms, increasing the risk of accidents.

- Visual Clutter: Excessive visual stimuli can overwhelm cognitive processes in chaotic environments. For example, a cluttered workspace can divert attention from critical tasks.

The impact of distraction can be compounded in high-stress situations where the margin for error is slim. In these environments, maintaining focus is not just a matter of efficiency; it is a matter of safety.

Cognitive Mechanisms Underpinning Focus and Attention

Understanding the cognitive mechanisms that govern focus, and attention can help organizations develop effective strategies to enhance these skills in their employees.

1. The Brain's Attention Networks

The brain comprises several networks responsible for regulating attention. The two primary networks involved in attention are:

- **The Alerting Network:** This network maintains an alert state and prepares the brain to respond to stimuli. It plays a significant role in ensuring that individuals are ready to react quickly to environmental changes.

- **The Orienting Network:** This network allows individuals to focus on specific stimuli while ignoring others. It helps in directing cognitive resources to relevant information.

Both networks work in concerts to help individuals maintain focus and effectively process information. Disruptions of these networks can lead to difficulties in concentration and decision-making.

2. Cognitive Load Theory

Cognitive load theory posits that the brain has a limited capacity for processing information. When the mental Load exceeds this capacity, performance suffers. In high-risk environments, workers often face high cognitive loads due to the complexity of tasks and the need to make rapid decisions.

Intrinsic Load is the primary difficulty associated with a task. For example, operating complex machinery requires a high inherent load.

THE NEW FOUNDATIONS OF HUMAN PERFORMANCE

The Importance of Focus and Attention in High-Risk Environments

Focus and attention are essential cognitive skills that allow individuals to process information, make decisions, and execute tasks effectively. In high-risk environments, these skills are even more critical because the consequences of lapses in focus can be severe.

The Nature of Focus and Attention

Focus refers to directing cognitive resources toward a specific task or stimulus while filtering out distractions. Attention, conversely, encompasses various mental processes that determine how we process information, including selective attention, sustained attention, and divided attention.

1. Selective Attention refers to the capacity to concentrate on one task or stimulus while ignoring others. For example, a pilot must focus on the flight instruments while disregarding extraneous noise from the cabin.

2. Sustained Attention: This is the capacity to maintain focus over an extended period. For instance, a surgeon must maintain sustained attention during a lengthy procedure to avoid making mistakes.

3. Divided Attention: This involves the ability to process multiple sources of information simultaneously. An emergency room doctor must juggle various tasks, such as monitoring multiple patients while communicating with the nursing staff.

The Consequences of Distraction

Distractions can significantly impair cognitive performance in high-risk environments. When attention is divided or diverted, the likelihood of errors increases. Research has shown that even brief distractions can lead to severe mistakes. For example, a construction worker distracted by a conversation while operating machinery may overlook a safety hazard, resulting in an accident.

Conclusion: Navigating Decision-Making Under Stress

The impact of stress on decision-making is a critical aspect of cognitive performance that organizations must address to foster a safe and productive Workplace. Understanding how stress affects cognitive processes allows organizations to implement strategies that mitigate its adverse effects, ultimately enhancing employee well-being and performance.

By creating a supportive work environment, providing stress management training, and prioritizing employee well-being, organizations can empower their workforce to make informed and rational decisions, even under pressure. As we move forward in this book, we will explore the emotional factors that influence human performance, examining how emotional well-being intersects with cognitive processes and contributes to safety and efficiency in the Workplace.

Improving Focus and Attention in High-Risk Environments

Focusing and maintaining attention is paramount in high-risk environments such as construction sites, hospitals, and aviation. The stakes are incredibly high; errors can lead to catastrophic outcomes, including injury, loss of life, or significant financial repercussions. Therefore, understanding how to improve focus and attention in these settings is crucial for enhancing cognitive performance and ensuring Workplace safety.

This chapter will explore the importance of focus and attention in high-risk environments, the cognitive mechanisms underpinning these processes, the factors hindering them, and practical strategies to enhance focus and attention among employees. Organizations can create safer and more efficient workplaces by understanding and applying these principles.

THE NEW FOUNDATIONS OF HUMAN PERFORMANCE

3. Implement Flexible Work Arrangements

Flexibility in the work environment can significantly reduce stress levels and improve cognitive performance. Organizations can consider:

- **Flexible Scheduling:** Allow employees to pick their work hours or adopt flexible schedules that accommodate their needs. Flexibility can strengthen work-life balance and reduce stress.
- **Remote Work Options:** Providing remote work options can alleviate the stress of commuting and create a more comfortable work environment. Remote work can also empower employees to develop their ideal workspace.

The Role of Leadership in Stress Management

Leadership plays a crucial role in shaping Workplace culture and influencing employee well-being. Influential leaders can foster an environment that prioritizes mental health and supports employees in managing stress.

1. Lead by Example

Leaders who model healthy stress management behaviours can inspire their teams to adopt similar practices. Demonstrating a balanced approach to work, including setting boundaries and prioritizing self-care, encourages employees to do the same.

2. Support Employee Well-being

Investing in employee well-being can demonstrate commitment to mental health. Organizations can provide resources such as counselling services, wellness programs, and mental health days to support employees in managing stress effectively.

3. Foster a Culture of Learning

Encouraging a culture of continuous learning can empower employees to develop skills and knowledge that enhance their cognitive performance. Providing training and development opportunities helps employees feel valued and invested in their roles.

Approaches to Mitigate the Effects of Stress on Decision-Making

Recognizing the detrimental effects of stress on cognitive performance is the first place toward executing practical approaches to mitigate its impact. Organizations can adopt various methods to support employees and foster a culture of well-being.

1. Promote a Positive Workplace

Creating a positive work domain can help reduce stress levels and enhance cognitive performance. Key strategies include:

- **Encouraging Open Communication:** Promote an environment where workers feel comfortable expressing their concerns and discussing challenges. Open communication can alleviate stress and promote a sense of belonging.

- **Recognizing Achievements:** Celebrate employee achievements and milestones, no matter how small. Recognition boosts morale and reinforces a positive Workplace culture.

- **Fostering Inclusivity:** Promote inclusivity and diversity in the Workplace. An inclusive environment encourages collaboration and reduces stress associated with feeling marginalized or isolated.

2. Provide Stress Management Training

Training employees in stress management techniques can equip them with practical tools to manage stress. Some strategies to consider include:

- **Mindfulness and Relaxation Techniques:** Teach employees mindfulness practices, such as deep breathing exercises or meditation, to help them manage stress in the moment. These techniques can promote relaxation and enhance focus.

- **Time Management Skills:** Provide training on effective time management and prioritization techniques. Helping employees manage their time can reduce stress and improve decision-making efficiency.

THE NEW FOUNDATIONS OF HUMAN PERFORMANCE

- **Poor Judgment:** Stress can cloud judgment, causing individuals to make snap decisions without fully considering the consequences. The fear of failure may prompt workers to take shortcuts, potentially compromising safety protocols.

The Implications of Stress-Driven Decision-Making in the Workplace

The cognitive effects of stress have significant implications for Workplace safety and efficiency. When employees are under stress, the likelihood of errors increases, potentially leading to accidents or safety incidents. Understanding these implications is crucial for organizations that foster a safety and accountability culture.

1. Increased Risk of Accidents

Stressful decision-making can lead to catastrophic consequences in high-stakes environments like construction sites or manufacturing facilities. Research indicates that stressed workers are likelier to make mistakes, overlook safety protocols, or misjudge risks. For example, a worker under pressure to meet a deadline may need to wear proper safety gear or skip essential safety checks, increasing the likelihood of accidents.

2. Decreased Productivity

While some stress can enhance performance, excessive or chronic stress often decreases productivity. Stressed employees may need help to focus, become easily distracted, or take longer to complete tasks. This reduced efficiency can hinder team performance and impact overall organizational effectiveness.

3. Impaired Team Dynamics

Stress affects individual decision-making and can also impact team dynamics. High-stress levels within a team can lead to communication breakdowns, misunderstandings, and conflicts. Team members may become defensive or disengaged, further exacerbating stress levels and hindering collaboration.

- **Selective Attention:** Under stress, individuals may focus exclusively on the most pressing issues, ignoring peripheral information that could be critical for informed decision-making. For example, a manager under pressure may overlook essential data in a report while fixating on immediate concerns.

Distraction and Multitasking: Stress can also lead to difficulties in multitasking. Cognitive resources become strained when stressed, making it challenging to manage multiple tasks effectively. This can lead to mistakes, especially in environments where safety is paramount.

2. Memory and Information Recall
Memory is vital in decision-making, allowing people to draw on past episodes and knowledge. Stress can disrupt short-term and long-term memory, affecting the ability to recall relevant information when needed.

Impaired Working Memory: Stress can significantly affect the system that temporarily holds and manipulates information. This impairment can hinder the ability to keep track of relevant details while making decisions, leading to errors or incomplete analyses.
- **Inhibition of Long-Term Memory Retrieval:** Stress can also impair the retrieval of long-term memories. An individual may need help remembering essential safety protocols or past experiences relevant to the current situation, leading to poor decision-making.

3. Risk Assessment and Judgment
Stress can distort judgment and influence risk assessment, leading individuals to make hasty or ill-informed decisions. Under stress, people may overestimate threats and coping ability, resulting in overly cautious or reactive decision-making.
- **Risk Aversion**: High-stress levels can lead individuals to adopt a risk-averse mindset, causing them to shy away from innovative solutions in favour of safer, more conventional options. This can suppress creativity and retard progress in problem-solving.

- Heightening Alertness: The brain becomes more alert, focusing on the immediate task while filtering out distractions.
- Enhancing Energy Production: The body mobilizes energy resources, allowing for increased physical and mental performance. While this acute stress response can enhance performance in the short term, chronic stress can lead to negative consequences. Prolonged exposure to stress can result in cognitive impairments, emotional disturbances, and even physical health issues.

Acute vs. Chronic Stress

Acute Stress: This type of stress happens in response to immediate challenges and usually subsides once the challenge is resolved. For example, a tight deadline or an important presentation may cause temporary stress, enhancing focus and performance.

Chronic Stress: In contrast, chronic stress results from ongoing pressure and can be debilitating. It often stems from work-related issues, such as excessive workloads, interpersonal conflicts, or lack of support. Chronic stress can impair cognitive functions, leading to difficulties in decision-making and an increased risk of errors.

The Cognitive Effects of Stress on Decision-Making

Understanding how stress influences cognitive performance is critical for creating effective strategies to support employees in high-pressure situations. Research has shown that stress can affect various mental processes integral to decision-making.

1. Attention and Focus

Stress can significantly impact an individual's ability to concentrate. When stressed, the brain prioritizes immediate survival over complex thought processes, which can lead to narrowed attention. This phenomenon, known as "tunnel vision," can limit the ability to see the bigger picture, resulting in oversights or missed opportunities.

The Impact of Stress on Decision-Making

In today's fast-paced Workplace, the capacity to make effective decisions is crucial for success. However, decision-making is not merely a logical exercise; it is a complex cognitive process determined by numerous, one of the most significant being stress. When faced with pressure, the brain's functioning can change dramatically, affecting how individuals process information, assess risks, and arrive at conclusions. Understanding the impact of stress on decision-making is essential for developing a safe and productive work domain.

This chapter will explore the relationship between stress and cognitive performance, how stress affects the brain's decision-making processes, the implications for Workplace safety and efficiency, and strategies to mitigate its adverse effects. Through this understanding, organizations can better support their employees, ensuring that decisions made under stress are as informed and rational as possible.

The Nature of Stress: A Double-Edged Sword
Stress is often perceived as an opposing force to avoid or manage. However, stress is a natural response to challenges and can serve as a motivator, prompting individuals to rise to the occasion. The body reacts to stress through a complex interplay of physiological and psychological mechanisms, preparing the individual to respond to perceived threats commonly known as the "fight or flight" reaction.

The Stress Response
When an individual encounters a stressor, the body triggers the release of hormones, including adrenaline and cortisol. These hormones prepare the body for immediate steps by:
- **Increasing Heart Rate**: This ensures oxygen-rich blood flows quickly to vital organs and muscles, preparing for physical exertion.

THE NEW FOUNDATIONS OF HUMAN PERFORMANCE

3. Implementing Technology and Tools

Technology can play a significant role in upgrading cognitive performance. Utilizing tools and resources that support cognitive processes can improve efficiency and decision-making. Examples include:

- **Collaboration Tools:** Leveraging collaboration tools can streamline communication and information sharing among team members. These tools facilitate real-time collaboration and enhance productivity.

- **Decision Support Systems:** Implementing decision support systems can provide valuable data and insights to aid decision-making. These systems can analyze information and present options to help employees make informed choices.

Conclusion: The Cognitive Dimension of Human Performance

Cognitive performance and decision-making are integral components of human performance in the Workplace. Understanding how the brain influences safety, and efficiency enables organizations to implement strategies that enhance cognitive processes, reduce errors, and promote a safety culture.

By prioritizing cognitive performance, organizations can empower their workforce to make informed decisions, navigate challenges effectively, and subscribe to a safer and more productive work environment. As we move forward in this book, we will explore the emotional factors that influence human performance, examining how emotional well-being impacts safety and efficiency in the Workplace.

participants feel safe communicating their ideas and thoughts without fear of judgment. Strategies for building trust and psychological safety include:

- **Open Communication:** Encouraging open communication creates a domain where team members feel safe sharing their views and concerns. Active listening and validation of others' contributions are essential.
- **Recognizing Contributions:** Acknowledging and celebrating team members' contributions fosters a sense of belonging and reinforces the value of everyone's input.

Enhancing Cognitive Performance in the Workplace
Given the importance of cognitive performance, organizations must take proactive steps to enhance it. Here are several strategies that can improve mental performance and decision-making in the Workplace:

1. Training and Development
Investing in training and development schemes can help workers enhance their cognitive skills. These programs can focus on critical thinking, problem-solving, and decision-making. Organizations can empower employees to improve their mental performance by providing continuous learning opportunities.

2. Creating a Supportive Work Environment
A supportive work environment fosters cognitive performance by reducing stress and promoting well-being. Strategies to create a supportive environment include:

- **Promoting Work-Life Balance:** Encouraging workers to maintain a healthy work-life balance can lessen stress and improve cognitive performance. Flexible work arrangements and policies prioritizing employee well-being contribute to a supportive culture.
- **Providing Resources for Mental Health:** Offering resources for mental health, such as counselling services and stress management programs, can help employees cope with challenges and enhance their cognitive performance.

between mental processes and teamwork can enhance collaboration and productivity.

1. Communication and Information Sharing

Effective communication is crucial for team success. Cognitive performance impacts on how information is shared and understood among team members. Strategies to enhance communication include:

-**Establishing Clear Channels:** Clear communication channels can facilitate information sharing. Using cooperation tools and project management software can streamline communication.

- **Regular Team Meetings:** Regular team meetings allow members to discuss challenges, share insights, and reinforce shared goals. These meetings promote transparency and collective decision-making.

- **Feedback Loops:** Encouraging feedback within teams can enhance communication and cognitive performance. Constructive response helps people improve their performance and fosters a culture of continuous learning.

2. Leveraging Diverse Perspectives

Diversity of thought can enhance cognitive performance within teams. When team members bring different perspectives and experiences, it can lead to more experimental solutions and better decision-making. To leverage diversity, organizations can:

-**Foster Inclusive Environments:** Creating an inclusive Workplace culture that values diverse perspectives can enhance cognitive performance. This environment encourages open dialogue and collaboration.

- **Encourage Brainstorming Sessions:** Brainstorming sessions allow team members to share ideas freely. This practice encourages creativity and helps teams generate a broader range of solutions.

3. Building Trust and Psychological Safety

Psychological safety is essential for fostering effective teamwork. It enhances cognitive performance and collaboration when

2. Memory and Safety Protocols

Memory plays a vital role in ensuring workers remember and follow safety protocols. To enhance memory retention and application in the Workplace, organizations can employ strategies such as:

-**Clear Communication:** Clear, concise safety instructions can improve understanding and retention. Visual aids, such as posters and infographics, can reinforce key messages.

- **Regular Training:** Conducting regular safety training sessions helps reinforce knowledge and skills, ensuring that workers remain aware of safety protocols and procedures.

- **Peer Support:** Encouraging workers to support one another in remembering safety protocols can create a culture of safety and accountability. Team discussions and reminders can enhance memory retention.

3. Decision-Making in High-Stakes Situations

Effective decision-making can mean the difference between safety and disaster in high-stakes environments. Training workers to make informed decisions under pressure is essential. Strategies for improving decision-making include:

-**Scenario-Based Training:** Engaging workers in scenario-based training allows them to practice decision-making in realistic situations. This approach helps the growth of critical thinking skills and enhances confidence.

- **Encouraging Collaboration:** Encouraging teamwork and open communication can improve decision-making. When workers collaborate, they can collectively share insights, weigh options, and arrive at more informed decisions.

- **Stress Management Techniques:** Teaching stress management techniques, such as mindfulness or breathing exercises, can help workers maintain composure and clarity during high-pressure situations.

Cognitive Performance and Team Dynamics

Cognitive performance affects individuals, team dynamics, and overall organizational effectiveness. Understanding the interplay

evidence. Awareness of these influences can help people make more objective decisions.

- **Risk Assessment:** Effective decision-making requires the ability to assess risks accurately. Workers must consider potential hazards and weigh them against the benefits of their actions. Training in risk assessment can enhance decision-making skills.

- **Emotional Influence:** Emotions can heavily influence decision-making. Stress, anxiety, and fatigue can impair judgment and lead to hasty decisions. Creating a helpful work environment that reduces stress can foster better decision-making.

The Impact of Cognitive Performance on Safety
Cognitive performance is closely linked to Workplace safety. Understanding how mental processes influence safety can help organizations implement strategies to minimize risks and enhance workers' well-being.

1. The Role of Attention in Safety
Attention is critical for identifying hazards and making safe choices in the Workplace. Distracted or fatigued workers may miss crucial safety cues, increasing the risk of accidents. Strategies to enhance attention and focus include:

-**Minimizing Distractions:** Reducing environmental distractions, such as noise and clutter, can help workers concentrate on their tasks. Creating designated quiet areas or providing noise-cancelling headphones can enhance focus.

- **Training and Simulation:** Training that simulates real-life scenarios can help workers practice attention skills in a controlled environment. This point of view allows them to develop the ability to focus under pressure.

- **Regular Breaks:** Encouraging regular breaks can help prevent cognitive overload and fatigue, allowing workers to recharge and maintain attention throughout their shifts.

- **Cognitive Load**: The intellectual effort required to process information can affect attention. High cognitive Load may lead to fatigue and decreased focus, resulting in errors or accidents.
- **Environmental Factors**: Noise, lighting, and workspace layout can impact attention. A cluttered or distracting environment can make it difficult to concentrate on tasks.
- **Task Complexity**: More complex tasks require more excellent cognitive resources, potentially leading to decreased attention over time. Breaking tasks into achievable sections can help maintain focus.

2. Memory

Memory is crucial for learning and decision-making. It allows us to retain information, recall past experiences, and apply knowledge to new situations. Memory can be divided into different types:
- **Short-Term Memory:** This memory holds information temporarily for immediate use. It is essential for tasks that require quick recall, such as following instructions or remembering safety protocols.
- **Long-Term Memory:** Long-term memory stores information for extended periods, allowing us to draw on past experiences when making decisions. Strong long-term memory can enhance problem-solving and decision-making skills.

To improve memory in the Workplace, organizations can implement training programs, regular refreshers on safety protocols, and mnemonic devices to aid recall.

3. Decision-Making

Decision-making is a compound cognitive process that involves assessing options, weighing risks and benefits, and selecting a course of action. The quality of decision-making can significantly impact safety and efficiency in the Workplace. Key factors influencing decision-making include:

Cognitive Biases: Cognitive biases can lead to errors in judgment. For instance, confirmation bias may cause individuals to seek information supporting their beliefs while ignoring contradictory

1. The Prefrontal Cortex: This region is crucial for higher-order cognitive functions, including decision-making, problem-solving, and impulse control. It allows us to study options, consider consequences, and make informed choices.

2. The Amygdala: An essential component of emotional processing, the amygdala influences how people react to stress and danger. Its emotional impact may impact decision-making, especially under pressure.

3. The Hippocampus: The hippocampus is responsible for memory formation and retrieval and is essential for learning and retaining information. Memory influences how we approach tasks and make decisions based on past experiences.

4. The Parietal Lobe: This region is associated with spatial awareness and attention. It helps us navigate our environment, focus on relevant stimuli, and filter out distractions.
Understanding the functions of these brain regions can provide insight into how various factors, including stress, fatigue, and environmental conditions, influence cognitive performance.

Cognitive Processes in the Workplace
Cognitive performance encompasses several key processes affecting our thinking, learning, and decision-making. These processes are integral to daily Workplace tasks and understanding them can help us optimize performance.

1. Attention and Focus
Attention is the ability to concentrate on specific tasks while ignoring distractions. In a work environment filled with interruptions, maintaining focus can be challenging. Factors that influence attention include:

Chapter 3

Cognitive Performance and Decision-Making

How the Brain Influences Safety and Efficiency

In the intricate dance of human performance, cognitive processes play a crucial role, often overshadowed by the physical elements of work. While the muscles may lift heavy loads and the heart may pump vital blood, the brain orchestrates every action, reaction, and decision that shapes our ability to work efficiently and safely.

Cognitive performance—how we think, learn, and make decisions—can significantly influence our performance in the Workplace, impacting not only individual effectiveness but also team dynamics and overall organizational success.

This chapter will explore the fascinating world of cognitive performance and decision-making. We will examine how the brain processes information, the factors that influence cognitive performance, and the implications for safety and efficiency in the Workplace. By understanding the mental dimensions of human performance, we can implement strategies that enhance decision-making, reduce errors, and foster a culture of safety and productivity.

The Brain: An Overview of Cognitive Function

The brain, a highly complex organ responsible for every aspect of human thought and behaviour, is at the core of cognitive performance. The brain is divided into various regions associated with different mental functions. Key areas include:

THE NEW FOUNDATIONS OF HUMAN PERFORMANCE

5. Support for Active Lifestyles

Organizations can support active lifestyles by offering incentives for physical activity, such as gym memberships, wellness challenges, or participation in community fitness events. These initiatives can foster a culture of health and well-being among employees.

Conclusion: The Path to Enhanced Physical Capacity

Enhancing physical capacity is a multifaceted endeavour that requires individual effort and organizational support. By understanding the anatomy of physical performance and focusing on the critical components of strength, endurance, flexibility, and mobility, workers and employers can take proactive steps to improve physical capacity in the Workplace.

As we move forward in this book, we will explore additional dimensions of human performance, including the cognitive aspects of work, the importance of mental well-being, and the impact of behaviour on Workplace safety. By continuing to deepen our understanding of human performance, we can create a more productive, safe, and healthy work environment for all.

can lead to better outcomes, fewer errors, and improved job satisfaction.

Organizational Strategies for Enhancing Physical Capacity
While individuals can take steps to enhance their physical capacity, organizations also play a crucial role in fostering an environment that supports physical health. Here are several strategies organizations can implement:

1. Ergonomic Assessments
Conducting ergonomic assessments can help identify potential risks in the Workplace and suggest interventions to improve safety and comfort. Adjusting workstation heights, providing ergonomic tools, and ensuring proper lifting techniques can significantly enhance physical capacity.

2. On-Site Fitness Programs
Offering on-site fitness programs can encourage workers to engage in physical activity. These programs can include strength training classes, cardio workouts, and flexibility sessions tailored to the workforce's needs.

3. Education and Training
Education on the importance of physical health and strategies for enhancing physical capacity can empower workers to take charge of their fitness. Workshops, seminars, and practice sessions can cover topics such as proper lifting techniques, stretching routines, and the benefits of regular exercise.

4. Encouraging Breaks and Recovery
Encouraging workers to take regular breaks and prioritize recovery is essential for maintaining physical capacity. Providing designated break times and promoting a culture that values rest can help reduce fatigue and improve overall performance.

THE NEW FOUNDATIONS OF HUMAN PERFORMANCE

mobility. For example, training focuses on bending, squatting, and reaching can enhance the body's ability to perform daily tasks.
- **Mobility Drills:** Specific drills targeting joint mobility can help improve range of motion and coordination. Workouts such as leg swings, hip circles, and shoulder rolls can be beneficial.

The Relationship Between Physical Capacity and Workplace Safety

The connection between physical capacity and Workplace safety cannot be overstated. Workers with enhanced physical capacity are better furnished to control the physical demands of their jobs, reducing the risk of accidents and injuries. Here are several key points that illustrate this relationship:

1. Reduced Injury Risk

Inadequate physical capacity can lead to injuries, particularly in physically demanding jobs. Workers with low strength, endurance, or flexibility may be more susceptible to strains, sprains, and overuse injuries. By enhancing physical capacity, organizations can help reduce the likelihood of these injuries occurring.

2. Improved Performance

Physically capable workers can perform their tasks more efficiently, increasing productivity. For example, a worker who has undergone strength training may be able to lift heavier objects with less effort, allowing them to complete tasks more quickly and safely.

3. Greater Resilience

Enhanced physical capacity contributes to greater resilience, allowing workers to return from physical exertion more quickly. This resilience can help reduce fatigue and improve focus and decision-making on the job.

4. Enhanced Quality of Work

When workers are physically capable, they can better focus on the quality of their work rather than merely getting the job done. This

- **Interval Training:** Incorporating high-intensity activity intervals followed by rest periods can enhance aerobic and anaerobic endurance. This training method is effective for improving performance in physically demanding jobs.

Flexibility

Flexibility is coping with motion in a joint or group of joints. Improved flexibility can enhance overall physical capacity and reduce the risk of injuries. Strategies for enhancing flexibility include:

- **Stretching:** Regular stretching routines can improve flexibility by lengthening muscles and tendons. Both fixed stretching (holding a stretch for a period) and dynamic stretching (moving through a range of motion) are effective.

- **Yoga and Pilates:** These practices focus on flexibility, balance, and core strength. They can improve overall movement patterns and body awareness, which are crucial for physical tasks in the Workplace.

- **Foam Rolling:** Foam rolling is one of the self-myofascial release methods that may help reduce muscular tension and increase flexibility. This method might be beneficial for employees who handle repeated duties.

Mobility

Mobility has the capacity to move freely and easily through space. It involves coordinating muscles and joints, allowing for smooth and controlled movements. Enhancing mobility can improve performance and reduce the risk of injury. Strategies include:

- **Dynamic Warm-ups:** Performing dynamic movements before engaging in physical tasks can enhance mobility and prepare the body for work. This approach can improve joint function and reduce stiffness.

- **Functional Movement Training:** Incorporating exercises that mimic the movements required in the Workplace can improve

Components of Physical Capacity
Understanding the anatomy of physical capacity leads us to its core components: strength, endurance, flexibility, and mobility. Enhancing these components is critical to improving physical performance and Workplace safety.

Strength
Strength is the capacity of muscles to put in strength against resistance. It is a fundamental aspect of physical capacity and crucial for various Workplace tasks. There are several ways to enhance strength:

- **Resistance Training:** Incorporating weightlifting, resistance bands, and bodyweight workouts can help increase muscle mass and strength. Functional strength training, which mimics the movements performed in the Workplace, is particularly beneficial.

- **Progressive Overload**: Gradually increasing the resistance or intensity of exercises is essential for building strength. This principle allows muscles to adapt and grow stronger over time.

- **Balanced Training:** Focusing on all major muscle groups, including the core, upper body, and lower body, ensures balanced strength development and lessens the risk of injury.

Endurance
Endurance is the capacity to assist physical activity over an extended period. It encompasses both muscular endurance (the ability of a muscle to perform repeated contractions) and cardiovascular stamina (the capacity of the heart and lungs to supply oxygen during prolonged exercise). Enhancing endurance involves:

- **Aerobic Training:** Running, cycling, or swimming can improve cardiovascular endurance. Consistent aerobic training increases the heart's efficiency, allowing it to pump more blood and oxygen into working muscles.

- **Circuit Training:** Combining strength and aerobic exercises in a circuit format can improve muscular endurance. This method challenges the body and elevates the heart rate, promoting strength and stamina.

pairs: when one muscle contracts, the opposing muscle relaxes to allow movement. For instance, when you lift your arm, your biceps contract while your triceps relax.

2. Smooth Muscles: Smooth muscles are found in internal organs, and they are responsible for involuntary movements such as digestion and circulation. They are not directly involved in physical work but in overall bodily function.

3. Cardiac Muscle: The heart muscle pumps blood throughout the body. It works involuntarily like smooth muscles and is crucial for sustaining energy and endurance during physical activity.

Bones
Bones provide the framework for the body, supporting its structure and protecting vital organs. They serve as levers that muscles pull against to create movement. Strong bones are essential for physical capacity, as they help absorb the forces generated during movement. Weight-bearing activities like walking or lifting stimulate bone density and strength.

Joints
Joints are the link between bones that allow movement. Different types of joints offer varying degrees of flexibility and range of motion. For example, hinge joints (like the elbow) allow movement in one direction, while ball-and-socket joints (like the shoulder) enable a broader range of motion. Healthy joints are vital for maintaining mobility and preventing injuries.

The Nervous System
The nervous system is the body's control centre, coordinating movements and responses. It sends signals from the brain to the muscles, allowing us to perform complex movements. The nervous system's efficiency impact's reaction times, coordination, and overall physical performance.

Enhancing Physical Capacity for Work

The human body is a complex and dynamic system, finely tuned through millions of years of evolution to perform myriad tasks. From lifting and carrying to bending and reaching, our bodies have muscles, joints, and systems that allow us to engage in numerous physical pursuits. However, as our work environment has evolved, so too have the demands placed upon us. Today, optimizing physical capacity is not just a matter of natural ability; it's about understanding our bodies, training them effectively, and creating a work environment that enhances our potential.

In this section, we will explore the intricate relationship between human anatomy and physical capacity in the Workplace. We will examine the key components of physical capacity—strength, endurance, flexibility, and mobility—and discuss how these elements can be enhanced to improve performance and reduce injury. By understanding the science behind physical capacity and how to improve it, both workers and organizations can foster the arts of health, safety, and productivity.

The Anatomy of Physical Capacity

Before diving into ways to enhance physical capacity, it's vitally important to understand the anatomy involved in physical performance. The primary components contributing to physical capacity include muscles, bones, joints, and the nervous system. Together, they enable us to perform work efficiently and effectively.

Muscles

Muscles are the engine of physical performance. They generate force, allowing us to move our bodies and interact with our environment. There are three main types of muscles in the human body:

1. Skeletal Muscles: These are the muscles attached to bones, responsible for voluntary movements. Skeletal muscles work in

- **Encouraging Breaks:** Frequent, short breaks throughout the workday can help avert fatigue and improve overall performance. Organizations should encourage workers to step away from their tasks regularly, whether to stretch, walk, or simply relax.

- **Educating Workers on Recovery Strategies**: Many workers may need to be made aware of the importance of recovery or how to optimize their rest. Providing education on sleep hygiene, nutrition, stress management, and active recovery can help employees take control of their recovery process.

- **Adjusting Work Schedules:** In industries where shift work is shared, organizations should prioritize creating schedules that allow adequate rest between shifts. Rotating shifts to align with natural circadian rhythms (e.g., moving from day shifts to evening shifts rather than the reverse) can also help reduce fatigue.

Conclusion: Balancing Fatigue and Recovery for Optimal Performance

Understanding the role of fatigue and recovery is essential for optimizing human performance in the Workplace. While fatigue is a natural consequence of exertion, it is also a significant risk factor for accidents, errors, and long-term health issues. On the other hand, recovery is the antidote to fatigue, allowing workers to restore their energy, repair their bodies, and maintain their mental and emotional well-being.

Organizations can improve performance, enhance safety, reduce turnover, and foster a healthier, more engaged workforce by creating a workroom culture that values rest and recovery. In the next chapter, we will explore the cognitive aspects of human performance, looking at how mental focus, attention, and decision-making impact safety and success in the Workplace.

remain focused and alert. Workers in physically demanding jobs or hot territories should be encouraged to drink water hour after hour throughout the day to support performance and recovery.

4. Emotional Recovery: Managing Stress and Preventing Burnout

Emotional fatigue, often burnout, is a growing concern in many modern workplaces. Jobs that require high levels of emotional labour—such as customer service, healthcare, or social work—can lead to emotional exhaustion if workers are not given adequate time and resources to recover.

Emotional recovery involves activities that help reduce stress, build resilience, and restore balance. These might include devoting time to family and friends, engaging in hobbies, practicing mindfulness or meditation, or seeking assistance from a counsellor or therapist. Organizations that prioritize mental health and offer resources for emotional recovery—such as employee assistance programs (EAPs) or stress management workshops—are more likely to have an engaged, motivated, and resilient workforce.

Creating the Arts of Recovery in the Workplace

To truly support human performance, organizations must create a culture that values and facilitates recovery. This means going beyond the typical approach of "work harder, work longer" and recognizing that sustainable performance requires periods of rest and rejuvenation.

Some empirical steps organizations can take to foster a culture of recovery include:

- **Implementing Fatigue Management Programs:** These programs can help identify high-risk areas for fatigue, monitor worker alertness, and provide resources for rest and recovery. For example, some industries use wearable technology to track workers' sleep and fatigue levels, allowing for real-time adjustments to work schedules.

high-demand jobs or shift work, often must catch up to this target. Chronic sleep deprivation not only impairs performance but also escalates the risk of long-term health issues such as cardiovascular disease, diabetes, and depression.

In workplaces where long hours and shift work are ordinary, organizations must take proactive steps to encourage and facilitate adequate sleep for their employees. This might involve scheduling shifts to allow workers enough time to rest between shifts, providing rest areas for employees to take naps during breaks, or educating workers on the importance of sleep hygiene.

2. Active Recovery: More Than Just Rest
While sleep is essential, recovery is not just about lying down or taking a break. Active recovery involves low-intensity physical activities that help the body recover without causing additional strain. For example, stretching, light walking, or yoga can help increase blood flow, reduce muscle soreness, and speed up recovery after a physically demanding shift.

In mental fatigue, active recovery might involve engaging in activities that allow the brain to rest without shutting down entirely. For instance, taking short breaks throughout the workday to walk, engage in a creative task, or practice mindfulness can help prevent cognitive overload and improve focus.

3. Nutrition and Hydration: Fueling recovery
Just as the body needs energy to perform work, it also needs fuel to recover. Proper nutrition and hydration are crucial in replenishing the body's energy stores, repairing tissue, and restoring hormonal balance. After physical exertion, consuming foods rich in carbohydrates, protein, and healthy fats helps restore glycogen levels and promote muscle repair.

Hydration is equally important. Dehydration impairs physical performance and affects cognitive purpose, making it harder to

THE NEW FOUNDATIONS OF HUMAN PERFORMANCE

3. Hormonal Imbalance: Fatigue also affects the body's hormonal balance, particularly cortisol, the hormone associated with stress. Chronic fatigue or overwork can lead to elevated cortisol levels, suppressing the immune system, increasing blood pressure, and interfering with sleep. Over time, this creates a vicious cycle where fatigue leads to poor health outcomes, further exacerbating fatigue.

4. Circadian Rhythm Disruption: The human body operates on a roughly 24-hour circadian rhythm, which regulates sleep, wakefulness, and various physiological processes. When workers are required to perform tasks at odd hours—such as during night shifts or long overtime shifts, this rhythm is disrupted, making it harder for them to stay alert and perform optimally. Night shifts can lead to "shift work disorder," characterized by insomnia, excessive sleepiness, and impaired performance.

Recovery: The Essential Counterbalance to Fatigue

Suppose fatigue is the body's way of signaling the need for rest. In that case, recovery is when the body restores its energy reserves, repairs damage and prepares for the next round of activity. Recovery is not just about sleeping or taking breaks; it is a multifaceted process that involves physical, mental, and emotional restoration. In workplaces where performance and safety are paramount, understanding and facilitating proper recovery is essential.

1. The Role of Sleep in Recovery

Sleep is the cornerstone of recovery. During sleep, the body undergoes various therapeutic, critical restorative processes for physical and mental performance. Deep sleep, in particular, repairs muscle tissue, replenishes energy stores and strengthens the immune system. REM (rapid eye movement) sleep is when the brain combines memories, processes emotions, and clears out metabolic waste that accumulates during wakefulness.

For most adults, 7-9 hours of sleep per night is endorsed to ensure optimal recovery. However, many workers, particularly those in

The data backs this up: According to the National Safety Council (NSC), tired workers are more than three times as likely to be involved in a Workplace accident. Additionally, studies show that being awake for 17-19 hours produces disability equivalent to a blood alcohol level of 0.05% and being awake for more than 24 hours is like a 0.10% blood alcohol level—well above the legal driving limit.

The risks are even higher for industries that operate 24/7 or require shift work. Night shifts, long hours, and irregular schedules disrupt the body's natural circadian rhythms—the internal clock that regulates sleep and wake cycles, making it harder to stay alert and focused. Fatigue management is crucial to Workplace safety and human performance in such environments.

The Physiological Effects of Fatigue
To understand how fatigue affects performance, it's essential to explore the physiological mechanisms behind it. The human body is designed to operate in cycles, with periods of exertion followed by rest and recovery. When this balance is disrupted, either by extended periods of activity or inadequate recovery—fatigue sets in.

1. Energy Depletion: Physical fatigue occurs when the body's muscles run low on glycogen, the primary energy source for movement. As glycogen stores deplete, muscles become less efficient, leading to slower movements, reduced strength, and a greater risk of injury. This is why athletes, for example, "hit the wall" when they run out of energy during long endurance events.

2. Cognitive Decline: Mental fatigue results from prolonged cognitive effort, which consumes significant amounts of glucose in the brain. When the brain's energy reserves are depleted, cognitive functions such as attention, memory, and decision-making become impaired. This can lead to slower reaction times, declined precision, and increased errors.

2. Mental Fatigue: Cognitive tasks such as problem-solving, decision-making, and sustained attention require significant mental energy. Over time, the brain's ability to process information and make sound judgments diminishes, leading to mistakes and inefficiency.

3. Emotional Fatigue: High-stress environments or jobs that demand emotional labour—such as dealing with difficult clients or managing interpersonal conflicts—can lead to emotional exhaustion, characterized by a lack of motivation, irritability, and burnout.

The interplay between these types of fatigue can compound their effects. For instance, a physically exhausted worker may also experience slower cognitive processing, while someone dealing with emotional burnout might find it harder to stay focused and alert. Fatigue is not just about feeling worn out; it is a complex state that affects nearly every aspect of human performance.

Fatigue and Workplace Safety: The Hidden Dangers
Fatigue's impact on Workplace safety is well-documented and widespread. Fatigued employees are more likely to make mistakes, experience lapses in judgment, and suffer from slow-moving reaction times—all of which increase the risk of accidents. This is particularly true in environments where the margin for error is slim, such as construction sites, manufacturing floors, transportation industries, and healthcare settings.

Consider a factory worker who operates heavy machinery. If they are physically exhausted, their reaction time is slower, increasing the likelihood of accidents. A long-shift nurse may experience mental fatigue, leading to medication errors. A driver dealing with psychological and physical fatigue after hours on the road may fail to notice a hazard or react too slowly to avoid a crash. Fatigue is an invisible but potent risk factor that can lead to costly mistakes, injuries, and even fatalities.

The Role of Fatigue and Recovery in Performance

Fatigue is a universal human experience that touches every aspect of our lives, including the Workplace. Whether it's mental fatigue from long hours of cognitive effort, physical exhaustion from intense labour, or emotional burnout from dealing with stress, fatigue is an invisible force that undermines human performance.

In the modern Workplace, where demands on workers continue to rise, understanding the role of fatigue and recovery has become more critical. Organizations must account for how the human body and mind respond to stress, strain, and the need for rest to sustain performance, prevent accidents, and maintain long-term well-being.

This chapter will explore fatigue as an obstacle and a natural consequence of human effort. We will delve into its effects on physical, cognitive, and emotional performance and examine the science behind recovery. This essential process allows us to restore energy and maintain peak function. Whether your job involves physical labour, complex decision-making, or emotional interaction, fatigue is a factor that must be managed thoughtfully. Understanding how to balance work with rest is the key to enhancing human performance while safeguarding health and safety.

The Science of Fatigue: What It Is and Why It Matters

Fatigue can be defined as a state of lessened capacity for mental, physical, or emotional work resulting from sustained effort or lack of adequate rest. While many view fatigue as simply a need for sleep, it is a more complex phenomenon that impacts the entire body and mind. There are several types of fatigue, each affecting human performance in unique ways:

1. Physical Fatigue: This occurs when the body's muscles are overworked and depleted with energy, often resulting in reduced strength, slower reactions, and a diminished capacity for physical tasks.

Artificial intelligence and robotics advances also allow more sophisticated ergonomic solutions to be developed. For example, exoskeletons—wearable devices that support and enhance the body's movements—are used in industries like construction and manufacturing to reduce the physical strain on workers.

As these technologies continue to develop, the future of ergonomics will likely involve more personalized, real-time solutions that help workers perform their tasks safely and efficiently.

Conclusion: Building a Safer, More Productive Workplace Through Ergonomics

Understanding the human body is critical to creating safe, efficient, and productive workplaces. Ergonomics provides the framework for designing work environments that support the body's natural movements, reduce the risk of injury, and enhance performance.

By applying ergonomic principles—promoting neutral postures, minimizing repetitive motion, and reducing the need for excessive force—organizations can protect their workers from injury and improve their overall well-being. Whether in an office, factory, or construction site, ergonomics is essential for building a safer, healthier, and more productive Workplace.

As we continue to explore the science of human performance, it's clear that understanding the body's capabilities and limitations is fundamental to creating environments where workers can thrive. In the next chapter, we'll delve deeper into the cognitive aspects of human performance, exploring how the mind and body work together to shape our capacity to carry out tasks safely and effectively.

relieve the tension on the hands and wrists, preventing conditions like tendonitis and carpal tunnel syndrome.

2. Healthcare: Supporting Caregivers' Physical Demands
Healthcare workers, particularly nurses and aides, are often needed to lift and move patients, which can place significant strain on the back and shoulders. Ergonomics can help reduce this strain by promoting assistive devices, such as patient lifts and transfer belts, and encouraging proper body mechanics when lifting and moving patients.

Additionally, ergonomic improvements in the design of medical equipment and workstations can help reduce the risk of repetitive strain injuries for healthcare workers who spend long hours typing on computers or using medical instruments.

3. Manufacturing: Enhancing Efficiency and Reducing Strain
Workers often perform repetitive tasks in manufacturing, such as assembling products or operating machinery. Ergonomics can help lessen the risk of injury by designing workstations that promote neutral postures, reducing the need for repetitive motion, and minimizing the force required to perform tasks.
For example, conveyor belts can be adjusted to the appropriate height to reduce the need for workers to bend or reach. Similarly, ergonomic tools can reduce the strain on the hands and wrists, preventing repetitive strain injuries.

Ergonomics and Technology: The Future of Workplace Design
As technology continues to evolve, so too does the field of ergonomics. For example, the rise of wearable technology provides new opportunities to monitor and improve Workplace ergonomics in real-time. Wearable devices can track workers' movements, posture, and exertion levels, providing feedback that can help prevent injuries before they occur.

THE NEW FOUNDATIONS OF HUMAN PERFORMANCE

instead of their legs, they may develop chronic lower back pain. Over time, this pain can become debilitating, leading to missed workdays, reduced productivity, and, in acute cases, the lack of ability to continue working in the same role.

Poor ergonomics in office environments can lead to various musculoskeletal issues. For example, a worker who spends eight hours a day typing on a poorly designed keyboard may develop carpal tunnel syndrome, a painful condition that affects the wrist and hand. This condition impacts the worker's ability to perform their job and may also require costly medical treatment and time off work.

The financial and human costs of these injuries are significant. For employers, the costs include lost productivity, increased healthcare expenses, and higher compensation claims. For employees, the costs include physical pain, reduced quality of life, and the potential for long-term disability.

Applying Ergonomics Across Industries
While ergonomics is often associated with office environments, its principles are equally applicable across various industries. A focus on ergonomics can benefit every Workplace, from construction to healthcare, manufacturing to retail.

1. Construction: Minimizing the Risk of Injury
In the construction industry, workers are regularly exposed to physically challenging tasks, such as lifting heavy materials, operating machinery, and working in awkward postures. Ergonomics can help lessen the risk of injury by promoting proper lifting techniques, designing tools that reduce strain, and ensuring that workstations are set up to minimize awkward postures.

For example, adjustable scaffolding can help workers maintain a neutral posture while working at height, reducing the risk of back and neck strain. Similarly, power tools with ergonomic handles can

2. The Spine: The Body's Central Support System

The spine is the body's central support system for maintaining posture and balance. It comprises a series of bones (vertebrae) separated by discs that act as shock absorbers. When aligned correctly, the spine can support the body's weight with minimal strain.

However, poor posture or repetitive strain can lead to spinal misalignment, causing pain and increasing the risk of injury. Ergonomics helps protect the spine by promoting proper posture and reducing the need for repetitive bending or twisting. For example, using a height-adjustable desk allows workers to take turns between sitting and standing, reducing the strain on the lower back.

3. Nerves and Tendons: The Communication Pathways

Nerves and tendons are the communication pathways that pass on signals between the brain and the muscles. Nerves carry electrical signals that tell muscles to contract, while tendons connect muscles to bones, allowing for movement.

Injuries to nerves and tendons, such as carpal tunnel syndrome or tendonitis, are common in workplaces with repetitive motion or awkward postures. Ergonomics addresses this by designing tools and workstations that reduce the strain on nerves and tendons. For example, ergonomic keyboards and wrist supports can help prevent repetitive strain injuries associated with typing.

The Impact of Poor Ergonomics: Real-World Consequences

While the principles of ergonomics are easy to understand, the consequences of neglecting them are all too real. Poor ergonomics doesn't just lead to discomfort; it can result in serious, long-term wounds that affect workers' standard of life and ability to perform their jobs.

Consider the case of a warehouse worker who spends hours each day lifting heavy boxes. If workers consistently lift with their back

THE NEW FOUNDATIONS OF HUMAN PERFORMANCE

postures or repetitive reaching. It also promotes efficient movement, minimizing the time and energy spent moving between tasks.

For example, in a factory setting, workers should be able to access tools and materials without bending, twisting, or stretching. In an office, computers, phones, and other equipment should be positioned so workers can perform their tasks with minimal movement and strain.

Adjustability is critical here. Workstations should accommodate workers of different sizes and shapes, allowing for easy adjustments to chair height, desk height, and monitor position. This not only promotes comfort but also reduces the risk of injury.

The Science of Movement: How the Body Works

To fully appreciate the role of ergonomics in Workplace safety and performance, it's essential to understand the science of movement. The human body is an intricate system of muscles, bones, joints, and nerves that work together to produce motion. When we move efficiently, the body operates at its best. However, the risk of injury increases when movements are awkward, repetitive, or strained.

1. Muscles and Joints: The Engines of Movement

The muscles and joints are the primary drivers of movement in the body. Muscles contract and relax to produce motion, while joints act as the pivots that allow bones to move relative to one another. For example, when you lift your arm, the muscles in your shoulder and upper arm contract, and the joint in your shoulder acts as a pivot point.

Ergonomics focuses on minimizing the strain on muscles and joints by promoting natural movements and reducing the need for excessive force or awkward postures. For instance, lifting heavy objects with the legs rather than the back helps distribute the load more evenly across larger muscle groups, reducing the risk of injury.

arch over the keyboard, leading to imperfect posture and strain on the neck, shoulders, and lower spine. Over time, this can end in chronic pain and musculoskeletal issues.

Workstations that may be adjusted to suit each person's needs are necessary to promote neutral postures. Chairs should have feet level on the floor and knees at a 90-degree angle to accommodate the spine's natural curvature. To minimize the need for employees to bend forward or tense their necks, desks and monitors should be arranged so that workers can sit upright with their heads over their shoulders.

2. Force and Repetition:

Another critical aspect of ergonomics is managing the force required to perform a task. Excessive force, especially when combined with repetitive motion, can lead to overuse injuries. This is particularly true in industries like manufacturing or construction, where workers may need to lift heavy objects, operate machinery, or perform repetitive tasks like hammering or drilling.

Repetitive force can take a toll even in less physically demanding jobs, such as typing or using a computer mouse. The constant clicking of a mouse or tapping on a keyboard may seem harmless, but these small repetitive motions can lead to conditions like carpal tunnel syndrome over time.

Ergonomics addresses this by redesigning tasks and tools to reduce the required force. For instance, power tools can be designed with ergonomic handles that minimize the tension on the hands and wrists. In offices, ergonomic keyboards and mice can reduce the impact of repetitive motion on the fingers and wrists.

3. Workstation Design and Layout:

The design and layout of workstations play a critical role in ergonomics. A well-designed workstation ensures that all tools and equipment are within easy reach, reducing the need for awkward

well-being; they also significantly impact productivity, absenteeism, and healthcare costs.

Think about this: According to the Occupational Safety and Health Administration (OSHA), MSDs are one of the leading causes of lost workdays in the U.S., accounting for almost one-third of all worker injury and illness cases. The financial burden of these injuries is staggering, costing employers billions of dollars annually in direct and indirect costs. But beyond the numbers, the human toll is even more significant workers who suffer from these injuries experience pain, frustration, and, often, a diminished quality of life.

Ergonomics aims to prevent these injuries by designing work environments and systems that accommodate the human body's strengths and limitations. It's about creating a partnership between people and their workspace that promotes safety, comfort, and efficiency. In this chapter, we'll explore how the principles of ergonomics can be applied across various industries to enhance human performance and protect workers from injury.

The Fundamentals of Ergonomics: Fitting the Task to the Human

At its core, ergonomics optimizes the fit between people and their tasks. This involves understanding the physical capabilities and limitations of the human body and designing workspaces, tools, and functions that minimize strain and maximize comfort.

1. Posture and Alignment:

One critical principle of ergonomics is maintaining neutral postures. A neutral posture is one where the body is aligned and balanced, reducing stress on the muscles, joints, and spine. In contrast, awkward postures—such as bending, twisting, or reaching—place excessive strain on the body, increasing the risk of injury.

Take, for example, an office worker who spends hours typing at a desk. If the chair is too low or the desk is too high, the worker may

Chapter 2

Understanding the Human Body in Action

Ergonomics and the Science of Movement

When we think about human performance in the Workplace, one of the most critical elements that often comes to mind is how well people can move, adapt, and sustain their tasks without injury. The physical body is the machine through which work is performed, whether lifting, typing, standing for hours, or navigating complex machinery. But how can we ensure this "machine" is functioning at its peak, especially in environments where repetitive motion, awkward postures, and prolonged physical strain are part of the daily grind? Enter the science of ergonomics.

Ergonomics is the study of how people interact with their physical environment—specifically, how the design of tools, workspaces, and tasks can either support or hinder the human body's natural capacities. At its core, ergonomics seeks to fit the job to the employee rather than forcing the worker to adapt to a poorly designed system. This chapter delves into the world of ergonomics and the science of movement, exploring how understanding the human body in action can lead to safer, healthier, and more productive workplaces.

The Importance of Ergonomics in the Workplace

Before diving into ergonomics specifics, let's look back and consider why it matters. The human body is remarkably adaptable, but it also has its limits. In a work environment, especially where tasks are repetitive or physically demanding, pushing the body beyond what it can handle is easy. Over time, this leads to musculoskeletal disorders (MSDs) such as back pain, carpal tunnel syndrome, and tendonitis. These conditions don't just affect employees' health and

THE NEW FOUNDATIONS OF HUMAN PERFORMANCE

art where safety is not just a box to be examined but a deeply ingrained value.

Organizations can move beyond compliance and build a safe work environment by focusing on behaviour through leadership, peer dynamics, incentives, and accountability. In the chapters, we will explore more strategies and tools to foster this culture, ensuring that safety is a shared duty, and everyone is empowered to contribute to a safer, more effective Workplace.

2. Training and Continuous Education:

While many organizations provide safety training as part of onboarding, more is needed to create lasting behaviour change. Training must be ongoing, evolving as

New risks, technologies, and processes emerge. Moreover, practical training goes beyond imparting knowledge—it must actively engage workers and address the psychological and social factors that influence behaviour.

For example, role-playing scenarios, simulations, and hands-on exercises can help workers internalize safety procedures and understand the real-world consequences of their actions. Regular refresher courses can keep safety at the forefront of the mind, while targeted training can address specific contributing behaviours.

3. Creating a Culture of Accountability:

Lastly, fostering a culture of accountability is essential for long-term behavioural change. This doesn't mean adopting a punitive approach but emphasizing responsibility, learning, and continuous improvement. When workers know that safety is everyone's responsibility and will be held accountable for their and their peers' actions, they are more likely to engage in safe behaviours.

Accountability also means that leaders must be held to the same standards. If workers see their supervisors or managers engaging in unsafe practices without consequences, it undermines the entire safety effort. Leaders must lead by example, holding themselves and others to the highest safety standards.

Conclusion: Behavior as the Bedrock of Workplace Safety

Human behaviour is the cornerstone of Workplace safety. While systems, equipment, and protocols play a critical role, individuals' everyday choices, habits, and actions ultimately determine an organization's safety. Understanding the psychological, social, and organizational factors that shape behaviour is critical to creating the

THE NEW FOUNDATIONS OF HUMAN PERFORMANCE

Safety incentives must be structured to promote genuine, safe behaviour rather than just avoiding reporting incidents. If the focal point is solely attaining zero accidents, workers may be reluctant to report injuries or near-misses, leading to underreporting and a false sense of security.

Changing Behavior to Improve Safety: Practical Strategies
Understanding the role of behaviour in Workplace safety is one thing; changing behaviour to improve safety is another challenge. Here are several strategies that organizations can use to influence behaviour and create a safer working environment.

1. Behavioral-Based Safety Programs:
One of the most effective ways to change safety behaviour is through behavioural-based safety (BBS) programs. These programs focus on observing and analyzing behaviours that lead to accidents or near-misses and implementing strategies to encourage safer alternatives.
BBS programs typically involve:

- **Observation:** Regularly observe employees while they work, identifying both safe and unsafe behaviours.
- **Feedback:** Providing immediate feedback to workers about their actions, reinforcing safe behaviours, and correcting unsafe ones.
- **Involvement:** Encouraging workers to take an active role in safety, either through self-assessment or by participating in peer evaluations.
- **Tracking Progress:** Monitor changes in behaviour over time and adjust strategies as necessary.

By focusing on behaviour rather than just outcomes, BBS programs help organizations address the root causes of safety issues.

2. Peer Pressure and Group Dynamics:

In any Workplace, peer pressure is a powerful force that can influence behaviour for better or worse. People naturally look to their peers for cues on behaviour, especially in environments where safety rules may feel burdensome or unnecessary. If most of a team routinely ignores safety protocols, it becomes difficult for an individual to speak up or act differently.

This is particularly true for new employees or those in more junior positions. They may feel pressure to conform to the behaviours of more experienced workers, even if those behaviours are unsafe. Conversely, new employees learn to adopt safe practices when safety is part of the group norm.

Creating a positive safety culture means fostering an environment where peer pressure favours safety, not against it. One way to achieve this is by building a culture of positive reinforcement— celebrating safe behaviours and encouraging workers to look out for one another.

3. The Role of Incentives in Shaping Behavior:

In many workplaces, incentives are used to encourage productivity, but if not carefully designed, they can inadvertently encourage unsafe behaviour. For instance, if workers are rewarded solely based on how much they produce or how quickly they complete tasks, they may feel tempted to cut corners, skip safety checks, or take unnecessary risks to meet targets.

However, incentives can also be a powerful tool for encouraging safe behaviour. Some organizations offer rewards for meeting safety goals, such as achieving a certain number of accident-free days or recognizing employees who consistently follow safety protocols. When safety is part of the incentive structure, it sends a message that it is just as crucial as other performance metrics.

Social and Organizational Influences on Safety Behavior

Human behaviour is not just driven by individual psychology; it's also shaped by the social environment in which people operate. An organization's culture, norms, and expectations greatly influence safety behaviour in the Workplace.

1. The Role of Leadership: Setting the Tone for Safety

Leadership is perhaps the most potent driver of Workplace behaviour, including safety. When leaders prioritize safety and demonstrate that it is more important than speed, efficiency, or cost-saving, employees are more likely to follow suit. Conversely, if leaders emphasize productivity above all else or disregard unsafe behaviours, the workforce will get the message that safety isn't a priority.

Leaders influence safety behaviour in several ways:

- **Modeling Behavior:** Workers take cues from how their leaders act. If a manager consistently follows safety protocols, never takes shortcuts, and encourages others to do the same, it sends a strong message about the importance of safety. On the other hand, if leaders flout the rules, it undermines the entire safety culture.

- **Communication**: How leaders talk about safety matters. Workers are likely to adopt that mindset if safety is only mentioned in passing or framed as an obstacle to getting things done. But if safety is woven into every conversation, meeting, and objective, it becomes ingrained in the organizational fabric.

- **Accountability:** Leaders must hold themselves and others account for unsafe behaviour. This doesn't mean punishing every minor infraction but instead fostering a culture of responsibility. When workers know that safety lapses will be addressed promptly and fairly, they are more likely to adhere to protocols.

2. The Role of Stress and Pressure:

Another critical factor influencing safety-related behaviour is the stress or pressure workers experience. When people are pressured to meet deadlines, hit productivity targets, or deal with time-sensitive issues, they are more likely to take shortcuts, ignore safety procedures, or engage in risky behaviour.

Stress clouds judgment and can lead to poor decision-making. In high-pressure environments, workers may feel they need the luxury of stopping to ensure everything is done safely. This is particularly true in industries that value speed and efficiency highly, such as manufacturing, logistics, or construction.

Leaders and managers play a vitally important role in addressing this. If safety is consistently positioned as the highest priority—even above productivity—workers will be less inclined to take risks under pressure. On the other hand, if the message is that productivity trumps safety, unsafe behaviours will naturally follow.

3. Habitual Behavior and Routine:

Humans are creatures of habit, and much of our behaviour in the Workplace is driven by routine. Over time, workers develop habits—some of which are safe and others that may be less so. Once behaviour becomes habitual, it can be challenging to change, even if the individual knows it's unsafe.

For example, a machine operator may have developed a habit of bypassing a safety guard to speed up their workflow. This might save a few seconds on each task but significantly increases the risk of injury. The behaviour becomes ingrained because the operator has done this repeatedly without consequence.

Breaking these habits requires deliberate intervention. Training, reminders, and accountability are all essential tools for reprogramming unsafe behaviours into safe ones. Organizations must also create a culture where workers feel empowered to stop and correct unsafe habits in themselves and others.

THE NEW FOUNDATIONS OF HUMAN PERFORMANCE

These decisions, shaped by behavior, have severe implications for Workplace safety.

However, this is about more than simply individual decisions. Many variables influence Workplace behavior, including company culture, peer pressure, leadership, training, and rewards. We must explore these behavioral drivers to understand and influence Workplace safety.

The Psychology of Safety: Why People Take Risks

Psychology is at the heart of human behavior in the Workplace, the mental processes that influence how people perceive risks and make decisions. Understanding why people take risks, even knowing the potential consequences, is critical to creating a safer work environment.

1. Perception of Risk:

One of the primary reasons people take risks is their perception of the danger involved. The way we perceive risk is only sometimes rational. People often underestimate the likelihood of accidents, mainly when they have performed a task, usually without incident. This sense of familiarity breeds complacency. Workers may think, "I've done this a hundred times without getting hurt. I'll be fine this time, too."

Additionally, people are influenced by cognitive biases, such as **optimism bias** and the belief that bad things are more likely to happen to others than to themselves. This bias can lead workers to ignore safety protocols because they assume they won't be the ones to experience an accident.

Organizations need to combat this tendency by consistently reinforcing the real risks associated with unsafe behaviour and making safety a tangible, present concern rather than something abstract or distant.

The Role of Behavior in Workplace Safety

Safety in the Workplace is often viewed through the lens of compliance, procedures, and equipment. These are undeniably critical components of a safe working environment, but another layer plays a pivotal role: human behavior. Workplace safety isn't just about adhering to protocols or using the right tools; it's about the choices people make every day. How employees behave, interact, and respond to their environment and one another profoundly impacts the overall safety culture of an organization.

This chapter will explore how behavior influences Workplace safety, the psychological and social factors that shape behavior, and how organizations can harness these insights to create safer, more effective work environments. From how leaders set expectations to how individuals take responsibility for their actions, human behavior is central to any successful safety enterprise.

The Interplay Between Human Behavior and Safety

Workplace safety is not an isolated construct; it's deeply interwoven with human performance and behavior. While systems and equipment are designed to prevent accidents, the reality is that human behavior often determines whether these safeguards are adequate. Poor decision-making, complacency, or reckless behavior can undermine the best-designed safety systems.

At its essence, Workplace safety is a question of behavior: How do people act when performing tasks? How do they respond to hazards? And, perhaps most importantly, how do they balance productivity with safety?

For example, a construction worker might be aware of the need to wear a hard hat, but in the heat of the moment, under pressure to meet a deadline, they may decide to forego it. A forklift driver might know the importance of driving at a safe speed, but the desire to complete a task quickly might push them to take unnecessary risks.

THE NEW FOUNDATIONS OF HUMAN PERFORMANCE

Conversely, when workers are disengaged, motivation drops, leading to lower productivity, higher absenteeism, and a decline in the quality of work. Organizations that foster arrangement—through recognition, opportunities for growth, and a sense of purposes promote outstandingly better emotional performance across the board.

4. Stress and Resilience: The Emotional Impact on Performance
In high-pressure environments, stress is inevitable. However, managing stress and remaining emotionally resilient separates high performers. Emotional resilience is the capacity to recuperate from difficulties, stay focused under pressure, and maintain a practical outlook despite challenges.

Emotional performance can be supported by providing resources for stress management, such as mental health programs, mindfulness training, and promoting a work-life balance. Workers who are emotionally resilient not only perform better under stress but also contribute to a more stable and positive Workplace culture.

The Synergy of Physical, Cognitive, and Emotional Performance
Ultimately, human performance is about more than just optimizing physical, cognitive, or emotional factors in isolation. Actual peak performance comes from the collaboration of all three. For example, when an individual is physically fit, they can better handle cognitive challenges. When emotionally resilient, they can push through fatigue and maintain focus.

Organizations that understand and support this holistic view of human performance will see the most significant benefits in productivity, safety, and employee satisfaction. The following chapters will explore the strategies, tools, and practices that can enhance each dimension of human performance, setting the stage for sustained success in today's demanding work environments.

when workers are emotionally disengaged—whether due to burnout, stress, or dissatisfaction, performance suffers, and the risk of mistakes and accidents rises.

2. Emotional Intelligence: The Bedrock of Emotional Performance

Emotional intelligence (EQ) is the capacity to concede, understand, and manage our emotions and those of others. It is the key to emotional performance, as it allows individuals to steer the complexities of human interaction in the Workplace. High-EQ individuals are better at handling stressful situations, making peace, and fostering a positive work environment.

Emotional intelligence fosters trust, communication, and collaboration in a team setting. Emotionally intelligent teams can navigate conflict without it derailing performance, maintain motivation through challenges, and support each other in times of stress.

Organizations can enhance emotional performance by providing training in emotional intelligence, promoting open communication, and creating a culture where emotions are acknowledged and managed healthily.

3. Motivation and Engagement: The Emotional Drivers of Performance

Motivation is what turns intention into action. Motivated workers, especially those intrinsically motivated by a sense of purpose or passion for their work, are more productive, innovative, and committed. Emotional performance is closely tied to how engaged workers feel in their roles. When people feel connected to their work, their group, and the broader goals of the organization, their emotional performance—and, by extension, their overall performance—rises.

THE NEW FOUNDATIONS OF HUMAN PERFORMANCE

Training, experience, and mental models are crucial in enhancing decision-making under pressure. Imitations, real-time execution, and structured decision-making constructions allow individuals to build up their cognitive performance in high-stress situations.

However, it's about more than just making decisions quickly.
Forceful individuals balance speed with accuracy, use critical thinking skills to weigh options, anticipate outcomes, and make informed choices. Organizations can promote this by heartening the skill of learning and reaction, where people feel empowered to take a planned change and learn from their mistakes.

4. Learning and Adaptability: The Keys to Cognitive Resilience

In an ever-changing Workplace, cognitive performance is closely tied to the capacity to learn and adapt. The most fortunate individuals and teams can quickly absorb new information, integrate it into their work, and adjust to changing circumstances.

This continuous learning process is not just about acquiring new technical skills; it's about developing mental agility and the ability to last. Cognitive performance improves when individuals are encouraged to step out of their safety, try new approaches, and learn from successes and failures. Like the body, the brain grows more robust through challenge and adaptation.

Emotional Performance: The Often-Overlooked Factor
1. The Role of Emotions in Human Performance

While physical and cognitive presentation is often the focal point of Workplace optimization, emotional performance is just as pivotal—if not more so—for long-term success. Emotional performance involves managing emotions, maintaining motivating force, and cooperating effectively with others. Emotional resilience permits people to bounce back from difficulties, handle stress, and keep going when the going gets tough.

Emotions drive behaviour. When workers are emotionally engaged, they are more productive, creative, and committed. Conversely,

overload, and the increasing complexity of tasks, workers must process and respond to a staggering amount of information daily. Cognitive performance enables individuals to navigate these demands, prioritize tasks, and make sound decisions on time.

2. Focus and Attention: The Cornerstones of Cognitive Performance

One of the critical challenges to cognitive performance is maintaining focus in an environment full of distractions. Whether it's the constant ping of emails, the lure of social media, or the pressure to multitask, staying focused on the task is becoming increasingly difficult. Yet, focus is essential for high cognitive performance.

Studies have shown that multitasking, often desirable, can reduce cognitive performance by forcing the brain to switch between tasks rapidly. This "task-switching" increases the likelihood of errors and leads to mental fatigue faster than sustained focus on a single task. High-performing individuals and teams know how to create conditions for deep work—periods of uninterrupted focus—where the brain can fully engage with complex tasks.

Organizations recognize the importance of focusing and minimizing distractions in the Workplace—whether through better time management practices, open office layouts, or technology that reduces interruptions—see higher levels of cognitive performance across their teams.

3. Decision-Making Under Pressure: Cognitive Performance at Its Peak

Cognitive performance is most tested when individuals must make decisions under pressure. Whether a doctor making a life-saving decision in an emergency room or a CEO deciding a company's future during a financial crisis, thinking clearly under stress is a hallmark of high cognitive function.

THE NEW FOUNDATIONS OF HUMAN PERFORMANCE

Whether providing standing desks to reduce sitting time, creating tools that reduce the need for repetitive movements, or ensuring workers have the proper protective gear, ergonomics can dramatically improve safety and performance.

In a broader sense, ergonomics is about respecting the limits of the human body and creating an environment where people can perform their tasks with as little physical strain as possible. The result is fewer injuries, higher productivity, and greater job satisfaction.

4. Fitness and Health: The Foundation of Sustained Physical Performance

Finally, physical performance is heavily influenced by an individual's overall health and fitness. A physically fit workforce has greater endurance, resilience, and ability to recover from physical and mental strain. Encouraging physical fitness through wellness programs, gym memberships, or simple initiatives like walking meetings can profoundly affect individual and organizational performance.

Companies that invest in the physical well-being of their employees—whether through wellness programs, flexible schedules, or better break management—often see a return in the form of reduced absenteeism, lower healthcare costs, and a more engaged, productive workforce.

Cognitive Performance: The Power of Thought and Decision-Making

1. The Role of Cognitive Performance in Work

If physical performance is the engine of work, cognitive performance is the steering wheel. Cognitive performance encompasses the brain's ability to process information, make decisions, solve problems, and stay focused. The mental aspect of human performance allows us to adapt to complex environments, think critically, and respond to challenges.

In the modern Workplace, cognitive demands are higher than ever. With the rapid pace of technological change, the rise of information

But physical performance isn't just about raw power or endurance. It's about how efficiently the body performs over time. A well-conditioned, ergonomically supported worker can achieve far more than someone physically compromised by fatigue, injury, or poor posture. Even minor issues like a poorly designed workstation or inadequate breaks can significantly reduce physical performance and lead to long-term health issues.

2. Fatigue: The Silent Saboteur of Physical Performance
One of the most underestimated threats to physical performance is fatigue. In many industries, employees must perform repetitive or physically demanding tasks for extended periods, often without adequate rest or recovery. Over time, this leads to physical exhaustion, which reduces performance and increases the likelihood of errors and accidents.

Fatigue is not just an energy problem; it impacts coordination, reaction time, and decision-making. A tired body is a slow body, and a sluggish body can be dangerous, especially in environments where safety is critical. For example, in industries like aviation or healthcare, where a mistake can lead to catastrophic outcomes, fatigue is a significant factor that organizations must actively manage.

3. Ergonomics: Optimizing the Work Environment for Physical Performance
A fundamental principle of maximizing physical performance is ergonomics, the science of designing workspaces and tools to fit the human body. Poor ergonomics not only leads to discomfort but also contributes to chronic health problems like musculoskeletal disorders, carpal tunnel syndrome, and lower back pain. Over time, these conditions can significantly impair a person's ability to perform at their peak.

Proper ergonomics involves designing workstations, tools, and workflows that minimize physical strain and maximize comfort.

Physical, Cognitive, and Emotional Factors

The modern Workplace, no matter the industry, is a complex environment filled with demands, pressures, and opportunities that test the limits of human potential. Whether in a corporate office, a manufacturing plant, or a high-stakes surgical room, individuals' performance determines the operation's success—or failure—. But what is human performance, and how can it be understood to allow for improvement, optimization, and long-term success?

Human performance is the dynamic interaction between three key factors: physical, cognitive, and emotional. These dimensions don't operate in isolation but instead work together in a continuous feedback loop, influencing each other in ways that shape how we approach tasks, solve problems, and react to the environment around us.

Understanding and optimizing these factors is not just about improving a workforce's output, it's about creating conditions in which safety, well-being, and productivity align, allowing people and groups to perform at their peak sustainably. This chapter will explore these factors and examine how they form the foundation for human performance in today's Workplace.

Physical Performance: The Body as the Engine of Work
1. The Role of Physical Performance in the Workplace

Physical performance is often the most tangible aspect of human capability. It involves the body's ability to execute tasks effectively and efficiently, requiring endurance, strength, agility, or fine motor control. In physically demanding environments—such as construction, manufacturing, and healthcare—physical performance is the bedrock upon which all work is built. Even in more sedentary jobs, the physical ability to sit, type, or move comfortably without strain is vital for long-term productivity and health.

Resilience is the ability to bounce back from adversity, stay focused during challenges, and maintain a positive outlook despite setbacks.

Organizations can support emotional performance by offering stress management resources, such as mental health support, mindfulness programs, and stress resilience training. Resilient workers are better equipped to handle challenges and contribute to a more stable and positive Workplace culture.

The Synergy of Performance: Physical, Cognitive, and Emotional Alignment

While we've explored the individual components of human performance, it's essential to recognize that peak performance comes from the collaboration of all three domains—physical, cognitive, and emotional. These elements are deeply interconnected. For example, when we are physically tired, our mental performance suffers. Staying focused and making sound decisions becomes more challenging when emotionally stressed.

Organizations that are aware of this cooperative relationship and take steps to optimize all three domains will see the most significant gains in performance, productivity, and safety. This holistic approach to human performance is the cornerstone of success in today's Workplace.

In the following chapters, we will explore the practical strategies and tools to enhance each domain, ensuring your organization can support human performance in all its forms. This will improve safety and efficiency and unlock the whole perspective of your workforce, creating a territory where a successful outcome is built on a footing of sustainable, high-performance work.

This chapter lays the preliminary work for understanding the multifaceted nature of human performance, providing an engaging and comprehensive exploration of its core principles.

THE NEW FOUNDATIONS OF HUMAN PERFORMANCE

think and act, and it plays a crucial role in how we respond to challenges, collaborate with others, and maintain motivation.

1. Emotional Intelligence:

Emotional intelligence (EQ) is the ability to accept and manage one's emotions and understand and influence the feelings of others. High-EQ individuals are better equipped to handle stressful situations, maintain calm in adversity, and inspire confidence in those around them. They are also more effective communicators and collaborators, essential in any team-based environment.

Teams prioritizing emotional intelligence tend to perform better because they can navigate conflict, communicate openly, and support one another during challenging times. Leaders with high emotional intelligence can create environments where people feel valued and understood, which boosts morale and fosters higher performance.

2. Motivation and Engagement:

Motivation is the fuel that drives performance. Intrinsically motivated workers, those who find meaning and satisfaction in their work—tend to perform at a higher level than those who merely work for external rewards. Organizations can enhance emotional performance by creating environments where employees feel engaged, valued, and connected to the company's larger mission.

Recognition, opportunities for growth, and meaningful work are critical drivers of motivation when motivated workers are more likely to go above and beyond, taking pride in their work and contributing to a positive Workplace culture.

3. Resilience and Stress Management:

Stress is inevitable in today's fast-paced work environments. However, how we respond to stress—whether overwhelmed or resilient—depends mainly on our emotional performance.

be developed, and organizations that value deep work—periods of uninterrupted focus—tend to see higher-quality output.

Strategies such as time-blocking, reducing multitasking, and creating environments that minimize distractions can enhance cognitive performance. Many high-performing teams incorporate periods of focused work, followed by breaks, to ensure sustained cognitive engagement.

2. Decision-Making Under Pressure:

In high-stakes environments, cognitive performance is often tested when decisions must be made quickly, with incomplete information. This is where training, experience, and mental models come into play. People who are well-trained in their roles and have practised decision-making in simulated high-pressure scenarios tend to perform better under real-world stress.

Techniques such as mindfulness increase attention, decision-making, and stress resistance. Individuals who educate their brains to be present and calm under pressure may make more correct judgments and avoid cognitive overload, which leads to mistakes.

3. Learning and Adaptability:

The modern Workplace constantly evolves, and cognitive performance is deeply tied to our ability to learn and adapt to new circumstances. The most successful individuals and teams can quickly absorb new information, integrate it into their work, and adjust their strategies. Continuous learning is a hallmark of high cognitive performance, and organizations that foster a learning culture often find that their teams are more innovative and resilient in the face of change.

Emotional Performance: The Hidden Driver of Success

While physical and cognitive performance is more tangible, emotional performance is often the unseen force that drives success—or failure—in the Workplace. How we feel affects how we

THE NEW FOUNDATIONS OF HUMAN PERFORMANCE

2. Fatigue and Recovery:

Fatigue is one of the silent killers of physical performance. Over time, exhaustion wears down the body, leading to slower reaction times, increased errors, and a higher likelihood of injury. However, fatigue doesn't only affect physical tasks; it also spills over into cognitive and emotional performance.

The significance of relaxation and recovery cannot be overstated. Athletes understand this well as they build rest and recovery into their training regimes, allowing their bodies to repair and grow stronger. In the Workplace, this principle holds. Whether giving workers adequate breaks during long shifts or ensuring sufficient time off between shifts, promoting recovery is essential for maintaining long-term physical performance.

3. Physical Health and Fitness:

Beyond ergonomics and fatigue, physical health and fitness are crucial in human performance. Workers who maintain a baseline of physical fitness tend to have greater endurance, less fatigue, and a lower risk of injury. Encouraging employees to stay active, either through wellness programs or offering gym memberships, can have profound effects on both their physical and mental performance.

Cognitive Performance: The Power of Thought

Every action we take begins with a thought. Cognitive performance is at the heart of everything we do, whether it's a surgeon making a split-second decision during a critical operation or an executive navigating a complex business deal.

1. Focus and Attention:

Maintaining focus has become one of the most significant challenges to cognitive performance in today's world of constant distractions. With smartphones buzzing, emails flooding into boxes, and multiple tasks competing for attention, staying focused on the task at hand can seem impossible. However, focus is a skill that can

Physical Performance: The Engine for Productivity

Imagine a construction worker spending hours lifting, bending, and moving heavy equipment or a nurse in an emergency room standing and rushing for an entire shift. These individuals' physical demands are immense, yet their performance is not just about strength or stamina. It's about how their bodies move, the efficiency of their movements, and whether their environments support or hinder their tasks.

The key to physical performance is to recognize that the human body is an intricate machine. Like any machine, it requires proper maintenance, appropriate tools, and an environment that supports its function.

1. Ergonomics and Movement Efficiency:

One of the most significant factors influencing physical performance is ergonomics, the science of designing work environments and tasks to fit the worker's capabilities. Poor ergonomics lead to repetitive strain injuries, musculoskeletal disorders, and long-term health issues that can drastically reduce performance. Think about a poorly designed workstation where workers must constantly bend or stretch awkwardly. Over time, this leads to fatigue, discomfort, and injury, all undermining performance.

By contrast, an ergonomically optimized workspace allows workers to perform their tasks with less effort, reducing the risk of injury and enhancing productivity. Ergonomic interventions supporting physical performance include standing desks, adjustable chairs, and tools designed to minimize strain. In manufacturing environments, automation and tools that reduce the physical burden on workers are also critical.

THE NEW FOUNDATIONS OF HUMAN PERFORMANCE

flexibility, and coordination. Physical performance is more than just raw power; it is about optimally using the body to prevent injury and maximize productivity. Consider the importance of ergonomics in the Workplace—properly designed workspaces that reduce physical strain, improve comfort, and reduce the risk of long-term injuries, leading to sustained high performance.

2. Cognitive Performance:
While physical performance is essential, the brain orchestrates everything we do. Cognitive performance refers to how effectively we process information, make decisions, solve problems, and learn. It includes our ability to stay focused, process complex data, and react swiftly to changing conditions. Cognitive production can contrast success and failure in high-stakes environments like healthcare or aviation. Making quick, accurate decisions under pressure is a hallmark of high cognitive function.

3. Emotional Performance:
Often overlooked, emotional performance is as critical as physical and cognitive capabilities. It refers to our capacity to manage emotions, maintain motivation, and collaborate with others effectively. Emotional intelligence, our capacity to understand and manage our feelings and empathize with others—is pivotal in preserving resilience, fostering teamwork, and driving performance. Emotional performance determines how we respond to stress, whether we can recover from setbacks, and how we influence those around us.

Together, these three pillars create the foundation of human performance. However, optimizing these dimensions requires more than just individual effort. It requires understanding the environmental, organizational, and social factors influencing performance. Let's dive deeper into these components to see how they can be enhanced and aligned for more tremendous success.

Part I

The Foundations of Human Performance

Chapter 1

The Core Principles of Human Performance

The Building Blocks of Performance

Human production is the footing upon which all successful work is built. Whether you are working on a workstation, guiding a high-pressure sales force, or producing a complex forecast in a tech startup, the potential to perform at a high level directly impacts the outcome. However, performance is not simply the result of expertise or talent. It results from a dynamic interplay of multiple factors, which must be carefully understood and optimized to achieve sustainable success. In this chapter, we will tour the core principles of human performance—the building blocks that enable individuals and teams to thrive in any work environment.

The Anatomy of Human Performance

At its core, human performance can be broken down into three interrelated domains: physical, cognitive, and emotional. Each of these domains influences how we work, think, and respond to the demands placed upon us. Understanding these dimensions helps organizations and individuals unlock their full potential.

1. Physical Performance:

The physical domain is the most visible and prominent aspect of human performance. It involves the body's ability to carry out tasks efficiently and safely, encompassing strength, endurance,

THE NEW FOUNDATIONS OF HUMAN PERFORMANCE

can you create an environment where people are not just surviving work demands but thriving within them?

The answers to these questions lie ahead in the new foundations of human performance. Let's get started.

This introduction sets the stage for the book by emphasizing the central theme—safety as a driver of performance—and engaging the reader with real-world examples and a forward-looking perspective on human performance.

When discussing optimizing human performance, we're not just about improving productivity. We're discussing creating conditions where people can do their best work safely, sustainably, and consistently.

Modern human performance also recognizes the role of systems and environments. No matter how skilled or motivated an individual is, their performance is shaped by the systems they work within. Are the tools they use designed for efficiency and safety? Is their workload manageable? Are they receiving proper support from leadership? Is the Workplace culture one that encourages continuous improvement and open communication?

In the following chapters, we'll dive deep into these areas, offering practical insights and strategies for optimizing human performance in today's complex, fast-paced work environments. We'll look at the role of technology, from wearables that monitor fatigue to AI systems that enhance decision-making. We'll explore the impact of leadership on performance, examining how influential leaders foster a culture of safety and trust. And we'll provide tools for assessing and improving performance at every level of your organization.

A Roadmap for Safe, Effective Work

At its core, this book is a roadmap—a guide to navigating the complexities of modern work while keeping safety and human performance at the forefront. It's about breaking free from the outdated mindset that sees safety as a cost centre and performance as an isolated metric. Instead, it's about embracing a new vision of work where safety drives success, human potential is unleashed, and the Workplace becomes a place of innovation, collaboration, and achievement.

As we embark on this journey, I invite you to consider your Workplace. What are the hidden barriers to human performance? Where are the opportunities to enhance safety, not just as a protective measure but as a catalyst for better performance? How

The Shift Toward Safety-Driven Success

This book's core is that safety is not a barrier to performance; it is its foundation. For years, the conversation around safety and productivity has often been framed as a trade-off: either we focus on safety, which slows us down, or we push for maximum efficiency, which may compromise safety. But this is a false choice.

Consider the example of high-reliability organizations (HROs)industries like aviation, healthcare, and nuclear power, where the cost of failure is extraordinarily high. These industries have demonstrated that safety and performance are compatible and symbiotic. Pilots don't compromise on safety protocols to make faster flights, and surgeons don't skip safety checks to complete surgeries more quickly. The opposite is true: the highest performance levels are only possible because safety is prioritized.

In this book, we'll explore how the principles guiding HROs can be applied to various industries and workplaces. Whether running a small business or managing a large corporation, the lessons of safety-driven success are universal. They are investing in human performance—understanding the physical, cognitive, and emotional factors that influence can create a safer, more productive, innovative, and more successful Workplace.

Defining Modern Human Performance

So, what exactly is "human performance," and how do we define it in today's Workplace?
Human performance is the intersection of a person's physical abilities, cognitive capacity, and emotional state, all working together to achieve a goal. It's the complex choreography of mind and body, influenced by countless factors—fatigue, stress, environment, training, technology, and leadership, to name a few.

The Evolution of Workplace Safety and Performance

To truly appreciate the need for a modern update on human performance, we must step back and understand how we got here. The Industrial Revolution marked a focal point in human history—an era of remarkable innovation that changed how we worked forever. Machines took over tasks that once required immense physical labour, and productivity soared. But in the process, a new set of challenges emerged: the human cost of industrial progress.

For years, Workplace safety was an afterthought. Workers were expected to endure fatigue, hazardous conditions, and hours of repetitive tasks. Injuries, illnesses, and even deaths were considered inevitable consequences for the job. The human body was treated like a machine—expected to perform consistently without breakdown, regardless of its demands.

A shift began in the early 20th century. The rise in labour associations and the introduction of safety regulations reshaped how we thought about work. Workplace safety evolved from something that merely avoided catastrophes to something that aimed to protect workers from harm. But even then, the focus was primarily on physical safety—guardrails, helmets, safety protocols. Human performance was still largely neglected, especially regarding cognitive and emotional well-being.

Fast-forward to today, and we find ourselves amid another revolution driven by technology, automation, and a deeper understanding of human potential. We now know that human performance isn't just a physical issue. It's cognitive, emotional, and social. Most importantly, it's integral to both safety and productivity. The companies that thrive in this new era recognize the complex interplay between these factors and invest in fostering environments where their people can perform at their best.

The Hidden Cost of Overlooking Human Performance

Human beings are capable of incredible feats. From designing spacecraft that journey to the outer reaches of our solar system to performing complex surgeries with pinpoint precision, we have demonstrated time and again our ability to achieve what was once thought impossible. But there's a catch: we're not machines.

In the rush of daily tasks and deadlines, we often forget that humans operate within a delicate balance of physical, mental, and emotional performance. When that balance tips too far—when fatigue sets in, stress clouds judgment, or physical strain takes its toll—accidents happen. Productivity plummets, mistakes multiply, and safety is compromised. Yet, in most workplaces, we focus on technological solutions, procedural updates, and new systems to drive efficiency while paying scant attention to the very foundation of all work: human beings.

Why does this happen? Human performance is invisible until it isn't. We only consider the factors that keep us sharp, agile, and resilient once we encounter failure. When Monica nearly had her accident on the plant floor, the focus was on the error. However, the deeper issue was the conditions that led to that error, cognitive overload, and the design of her work environment.

This book, The New Foundations of Human Performance: Safety-Driven Success in Today's Workplace," is about bringing those invisible factors into the light. It's about understanding that human performance isn't just about avoiding mistakes; it's about actively creating environments where people can thrive, where safety and efficiency aren't competing goals but partners in success. It's about building a Workplace culture that sees human potential as the most critical asset and safety as the cornerstone of sustainable performance.

Introduction

Why Human Performance Matters in Today's Workplace

In the heart of a bustling manufacturing plant, where the sound of machinery hummed and workers moved with clockwork accuracy, one small moment she stood out as a turning point. Monica, a seasoned operator, had been on the floor for hours, concentrating on meeting her daily target. The recurrent tasks, the noise, and the weight of the requests had worn her down. As her shift was nearing its end, her mind momentarily drifted. Her hand, usually swift and steady, misjudged a small step in her routine. The safety precautions narrowly avoided a potentially fatal catastrophe caused by a tiny blunder. That day, they filed the incident as a close call—an example of "human error."

But was it indeed just a case of human error?
In another corner of the world, a young team of software engineers was working on a high-stakes project with tight deadlines. Over the past month, they'd sacrificed sleep, skipped meals, and pushed their cognitive limits to deliver on time. Once a haven of creativity, their office was filled with tension. The result? Lines of code with subtle, critical mistakes led to a system crash during a vital product demo, costing the company a significant client.

Monica and the engineers weren't just victims of bad luck or momentary lapses in judgment. These incidents weren't isolated; they were symptomatic of a much larger issue that permeates workplaces across industries, continents, and levels of expertise. This issue is human performance, a factor so often taken for granted that it only catches attention when something goes wrong.

Preparing for the Challenges of Tomorrow's Workplace *355*

The Road Ahead: Creating Safe, Efficient, and Sustainable Work Environments *360*

MEASURING HUMAN PERFORMANCE 303

Key Performance Indicators (KPIs) for Human Performance *303*

Introduction *303*

Tools and Techniques for Performance Measurement *309*

Introduction *309*

Using Data to Drive Safety and Efficiency *317*

Introduction *317*

CHAPTER 15 325

CONTINUOUS IMPROVEMENT: THE PATH TO
SUSTAINABLE SUCCESS 325

The Role of Feedback and Evaluation in Performance *325*

Introduction *325*

How to Create a Culture of Continuous Improvement *333*

Introduction *333*

Adapting to Changing Work Environments for Long-Term Success *341*

Introduction: The Power of Adaptation in a Rapidly Changing World *341*

CONCLUSION 349

THE FUTURE OF HUMAN PERFORMANCE AND SAFETY
.... 349

Emerging Trends in Workplace Safety and Performance *349*

TRAINING FOR PERFORMANCE...............................259

The Role of Continuous Learning in Developing Effective Training Programs
....259

The Role of Continuous Learning in Skills Development for Safety and Efficiency 266

Introduction..266

The Role of Continuous Learning in the Importance of Ongoing Learning and Adaptability...273

Introduction..273

PART IV: LEADERSHIP AND ORGANIZATIONAL SUCCESS
....281

CHAPTER 13 281

LEADERSHIP IN HUMAN PERFORMANCE AND SAFETY
....281

The Role of Leaders in Driving Performance 281

Introduction..281

Building Trust and Accountability in Teams 289

Introduction..289

Leading by Example—Integrating Safety into Leadership..............................296

Introduction..296

CHAPTER 14 303

THE NEW FOUNDATIONS OF HUMAN PERFORMANCE

OPTIMIZING HUMAN PERFORMANCE FOR SUCCESS . 195

CHAPTER 9 195

THE SCIENCE OF FATIGUE MANAGEMENT 195

Understanding Work-Rest Cycles 195

How Fatigue Impacts Safety and Performance 202

Strategies for Reducing Fatigue in the Workplace 208

CHAPTER 10 217

NUTRITION AND HYDRATION FOR PEAK PERFORMANCE
.... 217

Fueling the Body for Sustained Work 217

The Connection Between Diet and Workplace Efficiency 224

Hydration Strategies for Performance Optimization 230

CHAPTER 11 239

THE ROLE OF MENTAL HEALTH IN WORKPLACE
PERFORMANCE 239

Mental Health's Impact on Productivity and Safety 239

Recognizing and Addressing Mental Health Challenges 246

Promoting a Healthy Workplace Environment 252

CHAPTER 12 259

Case Studies of Safety-Driven Workplaces *119*

CHAPTER 6 ....*129*

HUMAN ERROR: UNDERSTANDING AND REDUCING MISTAKES *129*

Common Causes of Workplace Errors *129*

How to Design Systems That Minimize Human Error *135*

The Role of Leadership in Reducing Errors..................................... *142*

CHAPTER 7 ....*149*

SAFETY CULTURE: BUILDING A PERFORMANCE-ORIENTED ENVIRONMENT.......................................*149*

What Is a Safety Culture? *149*

The Role of Management in Shaping Culture *155*

Practical Steps to Foster a Safety-Driven Environment *162*

CHAPTER 8 ....*171*

SAFETY TECHNOLOGY AND HUMAN PERFORMANCE.*171*

How Modern Technology Is Improving Safety *171*

Wearables, AI, and Automation in the Workplace............................. *179*

The Future of Safety-Performance Integration................................. *186*

PART III..*195*

THE NEW FOUNDATIONS OF HUMAN PERFORMANCE

The Role of Fatigue and Recovery in Performance *47*

Enhancing Physical Capacity for Work *54*

CHAPTER 3 61

COGNITIVE PERFORMANCE AND DECISION-MAKING .. 61

How the Brain Influences Safety and Efficiency *61*

The Impact of Stress on Decision-Making *69*

Improving Focus and Attention in High-Risk Environments *75*

CHAPTER 4 83

EMOTIONAL INTELLIGENCE IN THE WORKPLACE 83

The Power of Emotional Regulation *83*

Managing Emotions in High-Pressure Situations *90*

Building Resilience for Long-Term Success *97*

PART II 105

MODERN APPROACHES TO WORKPLACE SAFETY 105

CHAPTER 5 105

THE SAFETY-PERFORMANCE LINK 105

Why Safety Is Integral to Performance *105*

The Cost of Ignoring Safety in Productivity *112*

Table of Contents

INTRODUCTION *10*

WHY HUMAN PERFORMANCE MATTERS IN TODAY'S WORKPLACE *10*

The Hidden Cost of Overlooking Human Performance *11*

The Evolution of Workplace Safety and Performance *12*

The Shift Toward Safety-Driven Success *13*

Defining Modern Human Performance *13*

PART I *17*

THE FOUNDATIONS OF HUMAN PERFORMANCE *17*

CHAPTER 1 .... *17*

THE CORE PRINCIPLES OF HUMAN PERFORMANCE *17*

The Building Blocks of Performance *17*

Physical, Cognitive, and Emotional Factors *24*

The Role of Behavior in Workplace Safety *31*

CHAPTER 2 .... *39*

UNDERSTANDING THE HUMAN BODY IN ACTION *39*

Ergonomics and the Science of Movement *39*

THE NEW FOUNDATIONS OF HUMAN PERFORMANCE

Copyright © 2024 by Cilla. All rights reserved.

No part of this book may be reproduced distributed or transmitted in any form without permission from the publisher.

Therefore, the content within can neither be stored electronically, transferred, nor kept in a database. Neither in Part nor full can the document be copied, scanned, faxed, or retained without approval from the publisher or creator.

I0445219

The New Foundations of Human Performance:

Safety-Driven Success in Today's Workplace

By

Cilla Langston